CALIGARI'S CABINET AND OTHER GRAND ILLUSIONS

A History of Film Design

The late Léon Barsacq worked closely with such famous directors as René Clair, Jean Renoir, and Marcel Carné, for whom he designed sets for *Les Enfants du paradis*, *Boule de suif*, and many others. Elliott Stein, who has worked as a screenwriter, actor, and subtitler, is presently a regular contributor to *Sight and Sound* and roving film correspondent for the London *Financial Times*.

Elliott Stein (screenwriter, actor, film critic) translates, revises, and expands the original text of the late Léon Barsacq, film designer for directors such as René Clair and Jean Renoir. A detailed history of film design is followed with several chapters dealing with technical matters. Barsacq sees film design history as a dialectic between the studio (Méliès created imaginative fantasies) and the street (Lumière filmed out-of-doors). Although Barsacq indicates that this dichotomy has its limitations, his preference for the artistic subtlety and sophistication possible only in the studio is explicit. Filming narratives entirely in natural settings is generally a result of economic limitation rather than aesthetic conviction, he suggests. This attitude leads him to speak condescendingly of certain important movements, most significantly the French New Wave. Nevertheless, this first comprehensive treatment of the subject is a valuable source for film scholars and filmmakers. The highly readable text contains 160 stills. A foreword by

CHOICE   JUNE '77
Performing Arts
Film

247

Continued

BARSACQ

CHOICE   JUNE '77
Performing Arts
Film

René Clair, an index, a selected bibliography, and various appendixes (including filmographies of art directors and production designers) are included.

CALIGARI'S CABINET AND OTHER GRAND ILLUSIONS

A History of Film Design

LÉON BARSACQ

Revised and edited by ELLIOTT STEIN

Foreword by RENÉ CLAIR

NEW YORK GRAPHIC SOCIETY • BOSTON

Library of Congress Cataloging in Publication Data

Barsacq, Léon, 1906–1969.
 Caligari's cabinet and other grand illusions.

 Bibliography: p. 251–253
 Includes index.
 1. Moving-pictures—Setting and scenery—History.
I. Title.
PN1995.9.S4B3413   1976   791.43′025′09   75-27222
ISBN 0-8212-0620-6

Le Décor de Film by Léon Barsacq
Copyright © 1970 by Éditions Seghers, Paris

The English translation, which contains revisions and expansions of the
original French text,
Copyright © 1976 by Little, Brown and Company

"Filmographies of Art Directors and Production Designers"
Copyright © 1976 by Elliott Stein

First English Language Edition

Designed by Betsy Beach

Translated by Michael Bullock
Revised and edited by Elliott Stein

New York Graphic Society books are published by Little, Brown and Company
Published simultaneously in Canada by Little, Brown and Company (Canada) Limited
Printed in the United States of America

Frontispiece: Monte Carlo, "art stucco" style, in Von Stroheim's *Foolish Wives* (a Universal
Super-Jewel, 1922). Sets by Richard Day and Erich von Stroheim. The program for the world
premiere contained a foreword by Carl Laemmle which boasted that "the settings alone cost
$421,000."

CONTENTS

Acknowledgments

Robin Bledsoe; Robert Boyle; Ben Carré; Carlos Clarens; Dale Hennesy; Wiard Ihnen; Leo Kerz; Tom Luddy of the Pacific Film Archives; Howard Mandelbaum; Poty Ribeiro de Oliveira; Michael Powell; Donald Richie; Bonnie Rothbart of the Margaret Herrick Library, Academy of Motion Picture Arts and Sciences; Susan Schneider; Jayé Schulman; Jeannette Silverstein; Helmut Young; the staff of the Department of Film, Museum of Modern Art: Mary Corliss, Steve Harvey, Larry Kardish, Adrienne Mancia, Emily Sieger, Charles Silver.

Photograph Credits

Photographs are from the Museum of Modern Art/Film Stills Archive with the exception of the following:
Léon Barsacq, *Le Décor de Film*: 4, 11, 27, 43, 74, 77, 79, 85, 89, 111, 133 right, 153 top, 184, 189
Cinemabilia, New York City: 117 bottom, 149, 181, 250 bottom
Morton Gottlieb: 254
Private Collections: 39, 62, 93, 113, 123 right, 124, 125, 146 top, 152, 174, 175, 176, 179, 185

FOREWORD

Scenery? In the theater, scenery is normal, since the stage is surrounded by walls that it would be better to hide behind some kind of decoration, such as a painted backdrop or black velvet curtain.

But in films, where, like fables, "the stage is the universe," why talk of scenery? The term is as inaccurate as the term "staging a film," when there is no stage. Film "scenery" is not decoration; it's generally a construction, a living room or a restaurant, for example, that tends to look the way the same living room or restaurant would look in reality. Now we need to know what we mean by "reality."

A photograph is not reality but a reproduction of reality that we take for real because of a convention we are so used to that we no longer recognize the deception involved. We refuse to throw away this piece of cardboard if it bears the features of someone we love, but to a dog, a photo of his owner is just a piece of cardboard.

From the very birth of moving pictures, a dialectic developed. The Lumière brothers, who came to films from photography, focused on aspects of reality (today their followers talk of cinéma-vérité). In turn, Méliès, who came to films from illusionism and the theater, was less interested in reproducing what he saw than in transforming it into what he imagined. A magician, he produced as if from a hat a surreal world that prefigured both the distortions of Caligari and the contemporary fantasies of science fiction. Between these two extremes lies the concept of "imitated" reality, the equivalent of sculpture as compared to a plaster cast.

In this area, the set designer, however realistic his sets, can impose a style. The height of art is reached when this style relates so closely to that of the work itself that the audience pays no special attention to it. So we could say with a minimum of paradox that in films, the most successful set is the least noticeable one.

Léon Barsacq enjoyed that kind of success, and yet, to a trained eye, whatever he designed revealed his touch. So, for the film The Gates of Paris, he built a whole series of streets and alleys whose reality, I think, few spectators would suspect. But when we tried to cut some shots of a real street into the shots of our fake streets, we had to give up the idea. The styles were too different. We might say that reality paled alongside its imitation. "You wouldn't recognize her," we sometimes say about a pretty woman surprised by a newsreel camera. Make up her face, light her properly, and you'll recognize her. The same is true for sets.

Here a master of the art tells the story of these great make-up artists of reality, the film set designers. This book written by Léon Barsacq in the last years of his life preserves the memory of works existing only as a few shadows on a fragile strip of film. What castles built for a few hours, what phantom towns, what still-new ruins! In Hollywood they used to take tours through those plywood and plaster cities, those imitation streets where the fake patina of paint was covered by the patina of time. A Romantic poet could have dreamed among those decrepit buildings that once imitated the past, later caricatured it, and today have disappeared. Fiction or reality? Méliès or Lumière? In our own memories, the real world where we thought we lived blends with the world of illusion.

RENÉ CLAIR
l'Académie Française

D. W. Griffith's Intolerance *(1916). Designed by Walter L. Hall; construction supervised by Frank Wortman.*

Introduction

The acting, plot, and photography of a film are obvious to an audience. These elements also form the basis of much film criticism. But it is often difficult to recognize the contributions made by the director and, even more so, by the composer and the set designer, because the atmosphere, the style of a film, is harder to analyze than the theme or the abilities of the actors. Nor can the function of a set designer be clear to a public readily admitting that films are always shot in real, existing buildings. This was true as early as Méliès and his trompe-l'oeil painted backdrops. This book attempts to illustrate the contribution of set design as a dramatic element, a character, and its decisive role in the creation of ambiance, or atmosphere.

The evolution of film sets has closely followed the evolution of film in general. Each school, from the primitives at the turn of the century, through the aesthetes of the twenties, to the neorealists, has had its own concept of set design. All these influences enriched the decorative realism inherited from Méliès's painted backdrops. And yet cinema is a young art! Everything moves quickly! The great periods and schools lasted an average of five years each. The evolution of set design most clearly reveals the theatrical, literary, pictorial, social, and economic influences that formed the basis for those cinematic schools. Unfortunately it is not always easy to rediscover the appearances, as varied as they were fleeting, of the sets that marked important stages in the history of film. Add to this purely material problem the lack of interest shown till recently in the technical side of filmmaking, and it is easy to see why no serious study of film sets has yet been published. In the hope of filling this gap, I have written the present work, in homage to all my predecessors who created and developed the art of film set design.

In stressing films that influenced the evolution of cinematic vision, this work does not intend to set up an honors list. Rather, it reflects the ideas and preoccupations of the author, who throughout adopts the viewpoint of a set designer. Hence the importance given to certain schools and directors, to the detriment of others whose contributions to film are not in question.

1

L'Eclipse de soleil en pleine lune/The Eclipse (1907), by Georges Méliès.

2

Film Perspective and
the Evolution of the Set

In a cinematic work the direction, as a determining element, is evident to the majority of viewers chiefly in spectaculars with lavish crowd scenes, sets, and costumes, or in musicals where the production numbers are subject to strict rules and display a dazzling richness. By the same token, sets attract the attention of the public only by their vast scale or intentionally decorative appearance.

There is a misunderstanding at work here, based on the transfer to film of concepts and terms taken from the theater. Since this confusion exists, let us try to compare scenery in the theater, closely allied to the whole production, with the film set, closely integrated with the action of the film.

People often speak of stage perspective. There is such a thing, just as there is a film perspective. It cannot be sufficiently stressed, however, that they are essentially very different. Stage perspective is the viewpoint of spectators seated in the theater, at a greater or lesser distance from the stage; hence the need to broaden certain effects. The actors have to play for both the front row of the orchestra and the upper balcony. Stage space is arranged to permit the entries, exits, and other movements of the characters. The scenery itself, whether built, painted, or even purely schematic, is accepted merely as a fiction. The proscenium arch and footlights separating the scenery from the audience are there to recall this fact. Even when the footlights have been done away with (theater in the round, open-air performances, and the like), the spectator has to play the game and gracefully accept the rules and conventions without which there can be no theatrical performance.

Over the last fifty years or so, the development of stage scenery has been determined by a truer understanding of stage perspective. Though still subject to all the fluctuations of literary or pictorial fashion, stage scenery has broken free from the grip of naturalism and seeks to suggest a place and an ambiance, rather than to provide the action with a precise frame. In fact, this role is the one traditionally assigned to scenery during the theater's great periods.

The film set, however—originally simply canvas painted to create an illusion—has developed in the opposite direction, toward a certain form of realism, toward authenticity. This development can be explained by the existence of a film perspective very different from that of the theater. It is no longer the spectator who follows the action taking place on the stage in front of him, but the camera, which penetrates the intimate world of the characters and accents this or that facial expression, this or that aspect of an object, setting, or landscape. The film set serves as a frame not only for the movements of the actors, but also for those of the camera, which passes through doors, accompanies an actor going upstairs, takes the place of the actor by leaning over the banisters in order to show the entrance hall in a high-angle shot, and so on.

The ability to isolate or enlarge a detail, the mobility, precision, even the indiscrimination of the camera eye, constitute cinema perspective. It demands a sobriety and an exactness of tone in both the acting and the purely visual aspects of the production.

On the day when real exteriors were introduced into film, the future of the film set was virtually decided. Rather than clash with the rest of the film, the set now had to succeed in re-creating a framework equivalent to reality. In so doing it was merely following the aesthetic and technical evolution of cinema in general. In order to form a clearer idea of this evolution, the following chapters consider the principal stages through which cinematic art has passed.

Left: Féerie du printemps, *by Méliès.*   Right: *The Méliès studio at Montreuil-sous-Bois.*

1 Painted Sets

The French Primitives 1895–1914

The Lumière brothers' first films (1895) were considered merely scientific curiosities, and the cinema had to confine itself to the realm of the newsreel before that word was even used. But astute proprietors of traveling shows quickly recognized the profit to be made from this new invention.

Charles Pathé and Léon Gaumont established the first two production houses in France, in order to turn out shorts intended for the fairground public. For some time Pathé and Gaumont were content to present newsreels or short documentaries such as *The Arrival of the Czar in Paris, A Cavalry Parade, A Caravan in the Botanic Gardens,* and the like. But they were to encounter a serious competitor in Georges Méliès.

In 1896, Méliès, who directed a small theater devoted to illusionism (the Théâtre Robert Houdin), shot a number of films that he had "imagined, produced, and acted" himself: *The Devil's Manor* (fantastic scenes), *The Last Cartridges* (historical scenes), *A Terrible Night* (comic scenes), and so on. Méliès was the real creator of the cinematic spectacle, for his very first films contain in embryo all the comic, magical, or dramatic films made since. While the inventor of the Cinématographe, Louis Lumière, only "caught nature in the act," Méliès invented the set.

After a hesitant period in Vincennes, the cinema set up house. The first studio, or *théâtre de prises de vues,* was built by Méliès on his property at Montreuil in 1897. It was a shed constructed entirely of glass, making it possible to shoot by daylight. Larger than a photographer's studio, this building contained a stage with a below-stage area and a rigging loft, just like a theater stage. Méliès installed an ingenious mechanism that enabled the characters to appear and disappear, to move through the air, and so on.

Compared to Méliès's theater, William Dickson's "Black Maria" studio, built in the United States in 1895 in order to make films using Thomas Edison's Kinetoscope method, was a primitive construction. It was nothing more than a plank shed with a corrugated iron roof, part of which opened up, making it possible to shoot by daylight. Dickson's only innovation was a circular rail enabling the shed to rotate in order to utilize sunlight throughout the day. In Méliès's studio the shooting was done with a stationary camera set up in a special recess at the far end of the theater, and the actors played facing the camera as though facing an audience. Cords or wooden laths connecting the foot of the camera with the edges of the set marked off a visual field out of which the actors could not step.

Méliès employed conjuring tricks, stage mechanisms, pyrotechnics, and chemistry, and he also discovered—by chance—all the cinematic tricks still used today: the freeze frame, substitution, the fade, superimposition, matting and counter-matting, and so on. He was also a brilliant pioneer in the field of set design.

Given the size of his motion-picture theater (61 by 23 feet), the speed with which films were shot, the subjects of his sketches, and the necessarily low monetary returns, the only possible solution was a painted set. He therefore used the scenery technique then current in the theater. This consisted of painting trompe-l'oeil perspectives that created an impression of relief and suggested depth. Unlike stage designers, Méliès avoided colors and contented himself with a scale of grays. According to him, "Color sets look terrible on film. Blue becomes white; reds, greens, and yellows become black, totally destroying the effect. So it is necessary to paint sets as if they were photography studio backgrounds."*

As a rule the set had three surfaces: a large canvas-covered frame flanked on either side by a smaller frame forming an obtuse angle with the main frame. Sometimes shooting was done in front of a simple backdrop. Sideboards, grandfather clocks, and pictures were painted on these surfaces. The floor was covered with a canvas painted to simulate parquet flooring, a carpet, or tiles.

Méliès's originality does not lie here. Others had employed the same methods. But he was the first and perhaps the only person to conceive and produce a cinematic work from start to finish. He was not only author, director, and actor, but also his own cameraman and designer. (He did work with assistants, however. In 1902, at the height of his success, he renovated his Montreuil studio and took on as set designer first H. Claudel, then Jacques Colas, and finally, when the latter joined Pathé, P. Lecointe.)

Méliès's sketches for his sets show that from the outset he attached far greater importance to the visual aspect of his work than to the story line. Everything was studied in detail: the general appearance of the setting, the mechanisms for special effects, the movements of the characters, the furniture, and the props. Today the construction of these sets may appear tinged with poetic naïveté. It was not so for the first filmgoers. Some news events that were reconstructed in the studio had a very powerful effect. The audience shrieked with fear as they watched *The Eruption of Mount Pelée. The Coronation of King Edward VII,* shot in the studio for convenience, fooled everyone, including Edward VII, who thought he recognized himself on the screen (the part was played by Méliès).

Despite the primitive means at his disposal, Méliès succeeded in giving spectators the impression of reality, even in his fantastic films. He was successful because at the start he discovered the laws governing film sets: an illusion of depth; a

* Georges Méliès, "Vues cinématographiques," in catalogue for the Exposition Commémorative du Centenaire de Georges Méliès (Paris: Cinémathèque Française, 1961), p. 58.

judicious choice of the elements composing the set; their detailed, realistic execution; and, finally, their effective presentation. Fantastic effects are still obtained simply by presenting apparently realistic elements in an unusual manner of selection, juxtaposition, or scale. (Later the surrealists employed these same means, both in painting and in films.) The audiences for the traveling theater were quite credulous; nevertheless, a critical spirit began to appear. This is how Méliès described the reception of his poster for *A Trip to the Moon* (1902),* which showed a huge moon being struck in the eye by a shell: "That same evening everything was ready; the crowd was beginning to arrive, the parades were going great guns, the public was crowding in front of the big moon, but the poster, while it made people laugh, was greeted with all kinds of wisecracks. 'It's a joke, it's trickery! Do they think we're idiots around here? Do you imagine they could have gone to the moon to photograph it? They're pulling our legs!' The audiences of that day imagined that it was impossible to photograph anything but real objects."†

Here, perhaps, is one of the fundamental requirements of the cinema: to give the impression of having photographed real objects. This is close to the statement by René Clair: "Most films tend to present an action exactly as it would have been if it had really taken place and had been photographed."‡

For realistic films, with sets for drawing rooms, rustic interiors, prisons, or castles, Méliès was forced to conform to the stereotyped view of stage scenery in his day, but in films of pure fantasy he gave free rein to his imagination. The laboratory in *Four Hundred Pranks of the Devil* is conceived in baroque terms: the ribs of the steel dome, the alchemist's ovens, the giant retorts, are entirely made up of curves, concentric circles, volutes, spirals, and conchoids. Everything combines to produce a feeling of the fantastic, of dreams. In the same film the devil's coach, drawn by a skeleton horse, is built of strange shapes emphasized by comet tails, revolving suns, and sparkling stars.

It is easy to understand the surrealists' infatuation with some of Méliès's films. In *Twenty Thousand Leagues under the Sea* the nymphs, from the corps de ballet of the Châtelet Theater, are nonchalantly stretched out in enormous shells; mermaids with long fish tails seem to float underwater; and as a background, across which swim sea monsters with shells and tentacles, there is a mysterious cave, and right in the middle of it a surprising spiral staircase. In *The Conquest of the Pole*, Méliès plays on the contrast between the Giant of the Eternal Ice, a kind of wild Santa Claus whose enormous cardboard head and rapacious hands move by means of wires and pulleys, and a petrified geometric landscape of ice prisms.

The subjects of many of Méliès's films—*A Trip to the Moon, New York–Paris by Car*, and so on—led to his being dubbed the Jules Verne of films, but that severely delimits this brilliant pioneer by recalling from the enormous repertoire of the Star Film Company (about 450 films) only those with fantastic themes. Reconstructing current events was an important branch of his activity. These reconstructions were

* As a rule, film dates given correspond to the year of release of a film in its country of origin.

† Maurice Bessy and Lo Duca, *Georges Méliès, mage*, pp. 89-90.

‡ René Clair, *Reflections on the Cinema*, p. 93.

executed with a serious care astonishing for the period, utilizing photographic documents and sketches of sites. Thus, before shooting *The Coronation of Edward VII,* Méliès went to London, visited Westminster Abbey, brought back sketches, and then arranged for the assistance of a clergyman and an authentic chamberlain during the shooting. *L'Affaire Dreyfus* was re-created with the same "constant care for realism," as Star Film publicity said.

But what Méliès's work radiates above all, characterizing his art, is poetry. As we examine the hand-tinted pictures in some of his films—*Féerie du printemps, Midsummer Night's Dream, The Kingdom of the Fairies*—we are struck by the similarity between these moving pictures and paintings by Douanier Rousseau. They share the same candor and the same skill in composition, the same bold colors that miraculously harmonize, and the same seriousness in the characters, who always avoid being ridiculous despite their strange garb.

Méliès described himself in touching terms: "I was born an artist in my soul, very dexterous with my hands, skillful in most things, inventive, and an actor by nature. I worked with both brain and hands."* In fact Méliès, who was the first to consider cinema as an art, was not only an inventor, director, designer, and actor, but also an entrepreneur. He put his brother Gaston at the head of his New York branch, sold his films throughout the entire world, and in 1909 presided over the International Congress of the Cinema, during which a standard size film was adopted. Unfortunately, he ran his business like an artisan, refusing to enter into partnership or to become a limited company. Finally the large film companies, supported by the banks, plagiarized his films and ruined him. His work was largely destroyed or scattered, and he finished his days in a charitable institution at Orly. He died of cancer at the age of seventy-seven, on January 21, 1938.

In 1897, noting the success of Méliès's films, the Pathé and Gaumont companies began to extend their production to "composed" films, both comic and dramatic. During the first few years, these productions openly plagiarized those of Méliès but failed to achieve the same perfection. Nevertheless, Charles Pathé and Léon Gaumont must be credited with building new motion-picture theaters and forming permanent film crews, which were the starting point for later developments. In these crews the sole representative of the new technique was the cameraman. A few ambitious, more or less competent photographers quickly brought themselves up-to-date and learned to turn the camera crank to the rhythm of popular military marches of the day. The rest of the staff came from the theater or the café: young actors, stage managers who improvised as directors, and the stage designers and scene painters (who brought with them a few stagehands).

The designers and painters were organized in specialized studios, many of which worked for the Opéra, the Opéra Comique, the Comédie Française, and private theaters in Paris. The studios (which still used the scenographic methods of the eighteenth-century architect Giovanni Servandoni) designed theater scenery skillfully painted in trompe-l'oeil perspective. From these studios came virtually all the artists who designed sets for French films of the next twenty years.

* Bessy and Lo Duca, p. 15.

Hugues Laurent, the doyen of film architects, recorded in his memoirs the way in which film crews were formed at the Pathé, Gaumont, and Eclair companies. The basis for hiring was always studio friendships. The first to work on several films for Pathé in 1897 was Maurice Fabrège of the Butel and Valton studio; soon he called in to assist him students from the same studio: Vasseur, Colas, and Gaston Dumesnil.

The first Théâtre Pathé was built in the Rue du Bois at Vincennes in 1901. This little theater was replaced at the end of 1904 by a larger one measuring 73 by 40 feet. A team of designers and scene painters worked there, including Vasseur, Colas, Dumesnil, and Henri Ménessier. When the latter left to do his military service, he designated Hugues Laurent to replace him. Laurent later wrote: "G. Dumesnil and H. Ménessier were both skillful painters with a very special style. If they were asked to paint the port of Dunkirk or Marseilles or a square in Algiers or the Bay of Along or the entrance to New York Harbor, once they had the documentary material in their hands, a backdrop measuring twenty by thirteen feet was placed on the ground, and four hours later the backdrop was in position on the stage. During filming it was impossible not to believe one was in the intended location."*

The scenery was painted flat, like stage scenery. The canvas was tacked to the floor, and after applying a coat of glue size and whiting, the designer drew the design in charcoal. For complicated architectural sets a small sketch was made and squared for enlargement. Since the size paint was used hot, a scale of grays running from black to white was prepared in advance in small flameproof buckets. The scene painter worked standing, walking on the canvas (in rope-soled shoes or socks) and using very long-handled brushes; straight lines were drawn with the aid of a long flat ruler, similarly attached to a handle. To judge the whole, in order to accentuate effects if needed or to remove unnecessary details, the artist had to mount a ladder. The completed canvases were attached either to wooden frames to form the flats, or else, for backdrops, to vertical poles so they could be rolled up.

The designer–painters were responsible for certain special effects, above all moving scenery such as a rising sun or moon, undulating waves, trains or cars in motion, collapsing walls, scaffolding (in chase scenes), and so on. The majority of these special effects were achieved very simply with trapdoors, invisible wires, and counterweights, as in the theater; but very soon, following Méliès's example, the technique of shooting with reduced-scale models was perfected.

The director of production at the Pathé studio was Ferdinand Zecca, a former café singer. His first successes were realistic films—*The Story of a Crime* (1901) and *The Victims of Alcoholism* (1902)—then, in an entirely different style, *The Passion of Our Lord Jesus Christ* (1902–05). All these films were shot against painted scenery, treated with a great sense of effect. According to Laurent, "Zecca, who also produced 'trick films,' was always on the watch for what came out of the Méliès studio. He often discussed the latest special effects with his designers, and after those conversations, which aroused intense interest in everyone, Zecca's stimulated imagination always gave birth to a new film."

Several directors at the Pathé studio were trained by Zecca. Among the most

* Hugues Laurent, *Bulletin de l'A.F.I.T.E.C.*, no. 16 (1957).

important were Lucien Nonguet, who made *The Rebellion of the Battleship Potemkin* (1905), among other newsreels shot in the studio; André Heuze, a specialist in comic films based on the chase (*La Course aux sergents de ville* and others); and Louis Gasnier, who made the first Max Linder films and, in the United States, several episodes of *The Exploits of Elaine* and later *Reefer Madness*.

"The 'newsreels' were reproductions of the most striking events of the past week," recalled Laurent. "If, by chance, it had been possible to get a few shots on the spot, they were inserted during editing between those taken in the studio, but this was very rare. During peak seasons the scarcity of cameras made it impossible, and at best it could be done only when the events took place in Paris or its environs. The speed of production demanded by M. Pathé made it impossible to wait for material shot too far from the capital. The time available was shortened still further if, for example, M. Pathé had heard that a rival company was working on the same scene. It was essential to be first on the screen with sensational shots."*

Great "newsreels" of the time were *The Russo-Japanese War*, *The Chicago Theater Fire*, and *The Attempt on the Life of the St. Petersburg Chief of Police*.† "For *The Russo-Japanese War*," Laurent wrote, "we used the Vincennes military training ground with the addition of constructed elements (armored turrets and big cardboard guns to represent the Port Arthur forts). The battle of Mukden was shot among the ruins of old shanties in Montreuil, with Chinese signs and a few pieces of Asiatic scenery. Genuine reporting was not without risk. At the scene of the mining disaster at Courrières, Pathé's cameramen were greeted with stones by the miners and their families, who were not willing for a film to be made under such circumstances for the entertainment of an audience at a movie theater in the evening."

There was no sharp separation between directors and designers at Pathé. The administration frequently asked the designer to direct a scenario that had been his idea to begin with. This was most likely to happen where special effects were involved, for in this kind of film the creation of the sets demanded greater inventiveness and skill than the actual direction.

"In 1903," Dusmenil recalled, "Pathé had two cameramen, Ventzel and Legrand. The latter was in charge of training new arrivals Fourell, the godson of Mme. Pathé, and Caillau, a tapestry-maker by trade and son-in-law of the president of the company. Legrand was paid 55 francs a week, which rose to 60 when he left on a world tour at the end of 1905. The designers, much better paid, began at 90 francs a week (a week at this time was 60 hours and payment was made every Saturday in gold). Directors received the same salary. Scenarios (comic scenes, trick scenes) were bought by the Pathé company for the generous sum of 100 francs."‡ The Pathé company was originally run as a family business, but in the space of six years (1903–09) Charles

---

* The filmmakers were inspired above all by the colored pictures in the *Petit Journal Illustré*.

† In 1904, in addition to newsreels, Lorant Heilbronn, a Pathé designer-painter (pupil of Georges-Antoine Rochegrosse and cousin of Mme. Pathé) produced the first "cine-novels." The scenarios were barely two pages long, but for the production of the films, Heilbronn supplied small sketches which he painted himself in black-and-white wash.

‡ Gaston Dusmenil, *Bulletin de l'A.F.I.T.E.C.*, no. 16 (1957).

A Pathé set before . . .

. . . and during shooting.

11

Pathé's enterprising spirit transformed the craftsman's cinema into a great industry, of which Vincennes became the world capital.

After 1906, Pathé's great rival was no longer Méliès but Gaumont. Until 1905 Louis Gaumont had shot his films in a small garden in the Ruelle des Sonneries in Belleville, under a sort of veranda backing onto a brick wall. Small backdrops measuring about thirteen by ten feet were set up against this wall. Painted in sepia and usually representing a public square or a conservatory, they were made by Charmois, from the Moisson studio. This was the first "stage" set up by Gaumont. In 1905, Gaumont, lagging behind Pathé, built a large studio in Paris and employed Henri Ménessier to direct the design department. When production was stepped up, Ménessier took on Robert Jules Garnier (later to become Feuillade's designer) and Jean Perrier, who would play an important part in the development of the film set. Other painter–designers, all from the Boilly studio, were hired later.

The Gaumont company, supported by the powerful Bank of Switzerland and France, was run with strict economy. "Go ahead, and make sure it doesn't cost too much," Gaumont enjoined his collaborators. In 1907 Alice Guy, who had been in charge of production up to then, left for the United States to present the Chronophone (the first talkie, in which the film was synchronized with a phonograph roll). Her place as managing director was taken by Louis Feuillade. His role would be decisive in setting a section of French cinema on the path to poetic realism, especially with *Fantômas* (1913–14) in five episodes, then with *The Vampires* (1915) and *Judex* (1917) in twelve episodes.

The scenarios were often conventional, the overacting still reminiscent of pantomime, but Feuillade knew how to express the fantastic aspects of reality through his choice of scenery, creation of atmosphere, beauty of photography, and composition of the shots. Garnier's interiors, with their rococo paneling and heavy drapes, played their part in the mystery, but what moves us today is above all the unprecedented beauty of the exteriors. Feuillade discovered the photogenic quality and poetry of the suburbs and outskirts of Paris. The most improbable adventures take place against such real backgrounds as the elevated railway, the Paris quays, the subways, the funicular railways, the reservoirs, or just an empty lot or a street of ordinary houses. The director had merely to introduce into these gray-tinted landscapes a character in a black overcoat or tights for the spectator to feel a thrill of excitement and fear. Feuillade had a marvelous instinct for scenery, discerning the unsuspected tragic quality of a villa with closed shutters, a park railing, or a pebbly beach in the countryside around Nice. The miraculous in the everyday, recognized by Feuillade, is as unfamiliar as the miraculous totally re-created in the fantastic sets of Méliès.

As manager of the Gaumont studios, Feuillade contributed to the formation of a team of excellent directors, most of whom continued their careers after the war (Henri Fescourt, Léon Poirier, Abel Gance, and Jacques Feyder). Two of the earliest were Jean Durand, whose absurd comic films dominated silent films in France, and Emile Cohl, a former newspaper cartoonist who invented animated drawing and animated films in general. Two painter–designers would also make their marks after the war: Robert

Garnier, who after working with Feuillade joined Louis Delluc and much later Jacques Becker, and Jean Perrier, afterward the designer for Raymond Bernard.

In 1906 the Eclair company, in turn, built a stage on the estate of the Comte de Lacépède at Epinay-sur-Seine. At first the scenery was supervised by G. Personne, then by Colas, and then, in 1911, by Dumesnil and Laurent, all formerly designers at the Pathé studios. In 1908 the company took on as artistic director Victorin Jasset, a pupil of sculptor Jules Dalou. Jasset was a fan painter, costume designer, and producer of pantomimes at the Hippodrome before he started work at Eclair. His *Nick Carter* series, shot in nine episodes (1908–12), made him famous. Following the adventures of *Zigomar*, he produced realistic dramas such as *In the Land of Shadows*, and *The Earth*. He was perhaps the most artistic of the pre-1914 French directors: together with, and occasionally ahead of, Feuillade, he imposed a poetic style on reality, a method that became a constant feature of the best French films.

Up to 1908, production at both Pathé and Gaumont was confined mainly to comic films, trick films, or "slices of life," and aesthetic considerations played little part in the development of scenarios or the choice of actors. The founders of the new Art Film company, the Laffite brothers, had a very different outlook. They sought ideas from established playwrights and members of the Academy, and recruited actors from the Comédie Française. They also turned to the Théâtre Français for their scenery designer, Emile Bertin. Paradoxically, it was Bertin—a professional stage designer who had painted very conventional canvases for the Art Film company's first success, *The Assassination of the Duc de Guise* (1908)—who a few years later was one of the first to steer the French film toward constructed scenery.

Dazzled by the success of the Art Film company, Pathé, Gaumont, and Eclair jumped on the bandwagon, and between 1908 and 1914, the whole literary and theatrical repertoire was used in film production. The well-known titles and the famous actors attracted to the cinema new and more discriminating audiences, aesthetically more sophisticated than those at the old fairground shows. Unfortunately, however, the policy of the Art Film company, well intentioned though it was, had a devastating effect on French cinema by perpetuating its subservience to the theater. The company's influence was also felt in Italy, Great Britain, Russia, and even (to a lesser degree) the United States.

If aesthetically the cinema of this period often followed the wrong path, by contrast, technical progress was constant. From 1908 to 1914 methods of direction were perfected and filmmakers moved toward a concept of scenery that was far broader and very different from that in the theater. Art Film had already built a Seville square, measuring eighty-two feet from front to back, as a setting for *Carmen*. In another case, for *The Castle of Fear*, the scenery was extended by a model devised to create the illusion of continuous space. Following the example of André Antoine, whose Théâtre Libre propounded a new naturalism, experiments were made in realism. Special lighting (arc lamps, batteries of tubes, or mercury vapor lamps) compensated for any lack of sunshine. Increasingly, exterior shots were incorporated in films shot in the studio, which forced designers to strive more strenuously for authenticity.

13

In 1911, the publicity for a "realistic drama on the life of miners" stated: "The Eclair company brought from Charleroi a crew of miners who built a whole series of galleries on the Epinay estate, in exact conformity with the layout of a real mine. Efforts were made to keep as close as possible to reality." Furniture and objects played an increasingly important role. Just as it was no longer enough to paint a sideboard on a backdrop, so it became difficult to tolerate a door painted on canvas that shook whenever it was touched. Once the principle of the plywood door had been accepted, it was only a short step to replacing the molding painted in trompe-l'oeil by wooden molding, and so on.

Imperceptibly but steadily, painted scenery turned into constructed scenery. The first film set constructed entirely of plywood frames appeared in France in 1914: the drawing room in *L'Aiglon*. This set, designed and built by Emile Bertin, was decorated with ornaments and moldings of staff (a mixture of hemp fiber and plaster of Paris). The use of plywood, hardboard, and staff introduced new specialists into the film business: carpenters, sculptors, experts in staff work, house painters, and the like. This development, incidentally, did not necessarily please the large companies, which considered that it added unnecessarily to the expense.

But World War I halted the progress of French cinema, the world's foremost in both the quality and quantity of its films, and encouraged the development of the Italian, Swedish, and particularly American cinema, which took over first place in the international film market.

2 Constructed Sets

Italy 1910–1915

The first man to venture deliberately into three-dimensional scenery was Enrico Guazzoni, a painter and stage designer, who grew up in the Italian pictorial tradition. He used the first gigantic sets specially constructed for film. Instead of filming on location, using classical landscapes and the remains of antiquity as his predecessors had done, Guazzoni shot almost all of his films—*Brutus* (1910), *Agrippina* (1910), *The Maccabees* (1911), *Quo Vadis?* (1912)—in constructed sets.

The constructed set reached its highest point almost immediately in *Cabiria* by Giovanni Pastrone (known as Piero Fosco). *Cabiria* (1913) is a landmark in the history of film scenery: it not only influenced Griffith's *Intolerance*, but may be considered the prototype of the great spectacular, the more or less free reconstruction of history. In it are crystallized the faults and the virtues of a genre that draws crowds even today. The scale of these constructed sets, supported by a timber framework and covered with staff, the nobility and sobriety of a three-dimensional composition more reminiscent of great painting than of the theater, was without precedent in the history of cinema.

In contrast to the much more sober Roman sets of Guazzoni's designs, the film architects sought to stress the fabulous and exotic aspects of the opulence of Carthage. In the set for the palace, gold elephants, larger than life and carrying on their backs huge barbaric capitals, support the roof. The highly realistic frescoes, mosaics, and marble floors underline the oriental richness of the decor, which seems to have been inspired by a Hindu temple. The perspective is accentuated by a succession of columns and statues or by openings, bays, and doors, creating an impression of depth. The stairs and landings provide different levels for staging the scenes. For the first time, rules governing constructed scenery were developed to replace the methods of trompe-l'oeil painted decor.

The Italian designers did not flinch from any problem: the Temple of Moloch was 130 feet high; during the siege of Carthage, battle scenes alternated with fires that blazed in the scenery. They portrayed the eruption of Etna and the destruction of the Roman fleet by Archimedes' burning mirrors. This scene was shot with the aid of

Telefono nel Medioevo/Medieval Telephone *(1907) with Lydia de Roberti and Ernesto Vaser.*

reduced-scale models, and the vessels burned rather quickly because no one had yet thought of shooting such scenes in slow motion.

Three-dimensional constructed scenery influenced not just the staging, but also the photography. The cameraman Segundo de Chomon, originally from Pathé, used electric light to get back-lighting effects. He was also the first to mount a camera on wheels. The sumptuous (almost too sumptuous) costumes, the well-regulated movements of the crowd, excellent photography, and actors who were famous at the time (among them the astonishing Bartolomeo Pagano in the role of Maciste), made this film a triumph.

16

Cabiria (1914). Directed by Giovanni Pastrone.

Shortly after *Cabiria*, the historic genre ran out of steam. Periodically another film would be made of *The Last Days of Pompeii, Theodora,* or *The Destruction of Carthage,* but there was a progressive disappearance of true values, and academicism set in. The production of "society dramas" was hampered by the flowery literary style of D'Annunzio, then almost all pervasive in Italy. The abuses of the stars, whose demands and caprices weakened the competing companies, Italy's entry into World War I, and the appearance on the market of American films, which were more varied and supported by an unequaled commercial organization, ruined Italian production, which died as abruptly as it had been born.

17

Teodora (1919), starring Rita Jolivet. Produced by Arturo Ambrosio; directed by Leopoldo Carlucci.

In the final analysis, the Italian cinema from 1912 to 1915 is most notable for its contributions to scene design. The Italians had come a long way from the stammering beginnings of the Art Film company and the first French attempts at constructed scenery; they were a good ten years ahead of the other European set designers. Apart from the excessive exuberance of decoration, accompanied by a certain spareness of style, the sets might have been designed for contemporary super-productions.

The enormous lead gained by the Italians can be explained only by the contribution from architects, who replaced stage designers and scene painters, and by the large-scale use of decorative sculpture and staff techniques, both specialties of the talented Italian craftsmen.

The United States 1915–1920

American cinema, which was the true beneficiary of the upheaval of World War I, had begun to make itself felt as an original force in 1915, the year that D. W. Griffith made *Birth of a Nation*. After the triumph of this film, the first to deal with a political problem, Griffith, Thomas Ince, and Mack Sennett, the three true creators of the American cinema, formed a group called Triangle.

Phallic splendor in a chariot race from Messalina *(1923). Directed by Enrico Guazzoni, the Italian Griffith who made a lavish* Quo Vadis? *in 1912 B.C.—Before* Cabiria.

In 1916, thanks to the credit he had gained through the success of *Birth of a Nation*, Griffith embarked upon the most immense and ambitious work the cinema had ever seen, *Intolerance*. Vast material resources were enrolled in the service of a noble idea. The film tells four parallel stories: *The Judean Story* (*The Nazarene*), *The Babylonian Story* (*The Fall of Babylon*), *The Medieval Story* (*The St. Bartholomew's Day Massacre*), and *The Modern Story* (*The Mother and the Law*).

The key set in *Intolerance*, the Babylonian palace—with 165-foot high towers, ramparts along which the chariots sped, and 4,000 extras in Belshazzar's Feast—surpassed the very best that Italians had done in this genre. To film the crowd scenes the cameraman, Billy Bitzer, was perched with his camera in the gondola of a captive balloon. On other lots, sets were built to represent Jerusalem in the time of Christ and a corner of Paris in the Middle Ages. The sets for *Intolerance* were markedly influenced by *Cabiria*. Frank "Huck" Wortman was construction supervisor; the designer was Walter L. Hall. Technically, the sets attain almost complete perfection, accompanied by a sort of decorative delirium. The precincts of the Babylonian palace, with its ramparts and towers, has grandeur in its simplicity; the colossal inner court is a huge set piece—a monstrous but marvelous assemblage of bulbous columns surmounted by rearing elephants. However, the set for the Paris of the St. Bartholomew's Day Massacre derives from the aesthetic of the Art Film company and

19

Intolerance. *Designed by Walter L. Hall; construction supervised by Frank Wortman.*

recalls the errors of the flat theatrical style in that company's *Assassination of the Duc de Guise.*

It is the modern part of *Intolerance* that moves us the most—the episode of the strike, in particular, is treated in a powerful, realistic manner. This would henceforth be one of the constant factors in American cinema: realistic sets and costumes for everything connected with the history and daily life of the United States, imagination and freedom of inspiration (neither of them always happy) as soon as the subject was a foreign country, or European or ancient history.

The film cost a fortune, but when it was presented to the public in 1916 it proved a failure. There was not even enough money to demolish the mind-boggling sets of wood and staff, and the remains of Babylon stood for years at the corner of Sunset and Hollywood Boulevards. Nonetheless, *Intolerance* greatly influenced subsequent developments in film. In visual and technical areas it became the Bible of filmmakers; even its dramatic structure, which bewildered the public, had a seminal effect.

Griffith's associate at Triangle, Thomas Ince (a former actor), had become a director in 1910. Using the folklore of pioneer life, he drew his themes from the Far West and breathed an epic spirit into the western. Westerns take place almost entirely out of doors; nature plays the principal role, and no doubt this is why westerns were the first films to integrate built sets with the landscape. First there was the western small town, with frame houses, wooden balconies and posts, and hitching rails. There were the local bank, the sheriff's office, and the entrance to the honky-tonk. And finally there was the saloon, with its immense bar—the favorite spot for epic gunfights.

From their inception, but especially in the films of Ince, western sets attained a hitherto unknown authenticity. Yet these small towns of the Far West were built on Hollywood lots, where they were preserved for many years and adapted to the needs of various films. The interiors were constructed in the studio, with a care and attention to realism astonishing for the period. There was no discordance between the interior shots and the countryside as seen from galloping horses.

The third member of Triangle, Mack Sennett, created the burlesque film, another characteristic genre of American cinema. Sennett, first an actor and then Griffith's assistant, made the first Keystone Comedy in 1912, drawing his inspiration from the French school of comedy. He soon evolved a style peculiarly his own, based on a torrent of stunts and the accumulation of specifically cinematic devices (notably slow, fast, and reverse motion). Filming was done in the open with a team of acrobats and stunt men, elaborating within a concise framework the craziest, most improbable scenes. Cars and streetcars became entangled, motorcycles were driven along telegraph wires, houses flew away hooked onto balloons. For his chase scenes Sennett created a mob of policemen with drooping moustaches, the Keystone Cops. Soon he replaced the Cops with the Bathing Beauties, a bevy of pretty girls in extravagant bathing costumes who appeared in the most unlikely settings.

The sets in American burlesque films played the part of extras. Beneath a realistic, even humdrum appearance, they were really adapted strictly to the needs of the scenario. Construction of the sets, as well as every design detail, was worked out with mathematical precision; every step, every gesture counted. If there was a gate in the set, it was going to be slammed in someone's face; a staircase had to be designed so that someone could be sent sprawling down it; a sash window was made to catch somebody's fingers or beard. The chandeliers served as swings; custard pies spread on the floor made it as slippery as a skating rink; trapdoors and manhole covers opened at just the right moments; the giant vase in which the fugitive hid was not placed at random.

In the Keystone films the sets were used only for interiors or as links between scenes shot outdoors. In contrast, Charlie Chaplin's street scenes were filmed against constructed scenery. The sets were treated like the background of a humorous sketch:

everything was subordinate to the character, and only those elements appeared distinctly that contributed to the comic effect (such as the gas lamp that bends to asphyxiate the thug in *Easy Street*). The rest of the scenery was sketched in perfunctorily, barely indicated. It was a bias of Chaplin's: he seemed hostile to any pursuit of three-dimensional effects in the backgrounds of his films, preferring to leave them looking intentionally artificial. But the elements that played a role were carefully thought out and meticulously executed, such as the trench and the shelter in *Shoulder Arms* or the cabin swaying on the edge of the precipice in *The Gold Rush* (with sets by Charles D. Hall).

Left: Irene Castle in the Pathé–International serial Patria *(1917). The wildly jingoistic plot concerns a Mexican–Japanese conspiracy to conquer the United States and was probably inspired by the fears of the producer, William Randolph Hearst, that Villa's activities were a threat to his landholdings in Mexico. President Wilson wrote to Hearst, requesting that the film not be shown in theaters, as it would undoubtedly stir up international ill will—it was not withdrawn.*

Right: A Woman of Paris *(United Artists, 1923). Written and directed by Charles Chaplin. Art director: Arthur Stibolt. Jean (Carl Miller) kills himself at the fountain in the cabaret lobby.*

3 Toward a Film Aesthetic

Sweden and Germany 1917–1922

Early Swedish films were made with limited budgets and shot almost entirely out of doors; but Victor Seastrom and Mauritz Stiller, taking their themes from Swedish legends, attained a lyricism and charm hitherto unknown on the screen. For the first time the cinema penetrated a domain reserved till then for officially recognized art forms. The poetic transposition of life, which owed its charm entirely to the original resources of the "seventh art," was the true revelation of Swedish cinema.

In Seastrom's *The Outlaw and His Wife* (1917), there is no longer any break in style between the farm interiors, built in the studio by Axel Esbensen, and the mountain landscapes. Nothing is left to chance; the set, lighting, and landscape bring out the character of the scenes and reveal the psychology of the drama. In *The Phantom Carriage* (1920), Seastrom perfected the old device of superimposition for the fantastic scenes, while shooting the realistic sequences in hovels whose grating authenticity was due to designers Axel Esbensen and Alexander Bakö. Esbensen appears again, this time as the costume designer, in Stiller's *Sir Arne's Treasure* (1919), adapted from a story by Selma Lagerlöf. The remarkable sets by Harry Dahlström and Bakö—the farm, the prison with its circular dungeon—and the natural scenery become active elements in the film. Visually *Sir Arne's Treasure*, with its funeral procession describing arabesques on the ice, would inspire Fritz Lang's *The Niebelungen Saga* and Eisenstein's *Ivan the Terrible*.

All these films, though profoundly Swedish in spirit, influenced directors in many countries. Furthermore, they won for the cinema a new audience, until then reluctant to accept this form of expression. In the early twenties, however, American producers attempted to bring the best Swedish directors and actors to Hollywood. This exodus signed the death warrant of the Svenska company, and Swedish cinema stagnated for some fifteen years.

In 1917, under the aegis of Field Marshal Erich von Ludendorff, German magnates founded the powerful film company UFA (Universum Film Aktiengesellschaft). Composed of a cartel of the principal film producers, UFA built at

Sir Arne's Treasure (1919). Directed by Mauritz Stiller. Designed by Harry Dahlström and Alexander Bakö.

Potsdam–Badelsberg near Berlin the largest studios in Europe, magnificently equipped and including a vast lot for exterior sets. Still under the spell of the huge, complex sets constructed in Italy, the administrators of UFA directed its production toward historic films, known as costume films, but for some reason drew its stories from foreign history.

UFA's great director during this period was Ernst Lubitsch, a pupil of Max Reinhardt, the producer who had revolutionized German theater. Lubitsch introduced an intimate note into his historical reconstructions, attempting to explain historic events through sexuality and the secrets of the bedchamber. Despite the commercial success of his works and his undeniable wit and intelligence, connoisseurs were not deceived by Lubitsch. "A style consisting of gorgeous spectacles devoid of soul but overflowing with crowd scenes, decoration, and reconstructions," wrote the film theorist Riciotto Canudo of several films by Lubitsch, including *Madame Dubarry*, and he added: "It is the history of France and elsewhere, illustrated by the perverse and sexual pencil of the Germans."*

If these films possess a certain interest, it is due to the crowd movements, the often sumptuous costumes, and the sets. Lubitsch's designers were Karl Machus, whose designs for *Gypsy Blood* (1918), *The Oyster Princess* (1918), and *Madame Dubarry* (*Passion*, 1919), are stylish; and Ernst Stern, designer for *The Loves of Pharaoh* (1922) and for Reinhardt's Deutsches Theater. Both men were strongly affected by Italian films, especially *Cabiria*. This influence is particularly evident in set

* Quoted in René Jeanne, "L'Evolution du cinématographe," in *Le Cinéma des origines à nos jours*, p. 232.

construction. The main structures were erected outdoors on wooden frames and were built with great care, making extensive use of staff. Their artistic conception, however, differs: whereas the Italians saw their structures as more or less faithful archaeological reconstructions, Ernst Stern, following the example of Reinhardt's great spectacles, juggled with historical details in order to produce a visual style.

Take as an example *The Loves of Pharaoh*. The sketch for the Egyptian street set clearly shows the designer's intention to alternate filled and empty areas, the heaviness of the house fronts (barely pierced by openings) and the lightness of the loggias, the verticals of the walls, and the diagonals of the stairs and buttresses. What mattered to Stern was the interplay between volumes and light; so-called decoration is banished, and all the richness is reserved for the costumes. Nothing is left to chance; even the fork of the streets is deliberate because it allows the movements of the crowd to be channeled and varied. Every element contributes to the visual effect, but without the superfluity of *Cabiria* or the delirious character of *Intolerance*.

During the same years that all these UFA films were produced—between 1919 and 1923—a new direction in German cinema, expressionism, was arising in complete opposition to the commercial style of historical films. Predominantly German, expressionism was a musical, literary, architectural, and above all pictorial movement. "We must detach ourselves from nature, say the Expressionists, and strive to isolate an object's 'most expressive expression. . . .' The Expressionist does not see, he has 'visions.'"*Expressionist theories were applied to the theater, to posters, to window dressing. Only the cinema continued to depend on the realist heritage of its founders of the early 1900s, until 1919 when a few German filmmakers applied expressionist precepts to Robert Wiene's astounding *The Cabinet of Dr. Caligari*.

Lotte Eisner cites a manuscript by Hermann Warm, one of *Caligari's* designers, on the inception of the film:

The producer was . . . Rudolf Meinert. So it was Meinert . . . who, following the practice current in those days—when the sets were given more importance than everything else—gave the script of Caligari *to the designer Warm. The latter studied it with two friends employed at the studios as painters, Walter Röhrig and Walter Reimann. "We spent a whole day and part of the night reading through this very curious script," writes Warm. "We realized that a subject like this needed something out of the ordinary in the way of sets. Reimann, whose painting in those days had Expressionist tendencies, suggested doing the sets Expressionistically. We immediately set to work roughing up designs in that style."*

Next day Wiene gave his agreement. Rudolf Meinert was more cautious and asked for a day to think about it. Then he told them, "Do these sets as eccentrically as you can!" †

The sets of *Caligari* are painted, but they are a long way from the painted scenery used at the beginning of the century. Everything has been subordinated to visual effect, to create a nightmare atmosphere, to arouse anxiety and terror. There are no

* Lotte H. Eisner, *The Haunted Screen*, pp. 11, 10.
† Ibid., p. 19.

25

26

Three films directed by Ernst Lubitsch. Opposite, top: Madame Dubarry/Passion (1919), designed by Karl Machus and Kurt Richter. Opposite, bottom: Sumurun/One Arabian Night (1920), designed by Richter. Above: Sketch by Ernst Stern for Das Weib des Pharao/The Loves of Pharaoh (1921), designed by Stern and Richter.

verticals or horizontals, perspectives have been wilfully distorted, and the tortuous alleyways force a path between the twisted housefronts leaning toward each other. The doors and windows dancing a jig, deformed streetlamps, a dungeon whose angles outline a monstrous cage with a prisoner crouching in the center, the point of a roof emerging from a forest of strange chimneys—there are so many elements from which the designers of *Caligari* succeeded in distilling the "most expressive expression." The background demanded stylized costumes, makeup, and acting. Werner Krauss (Dr. Caligari) and Conrad Veidt (Cesare, the sleepwalker) manage to integrate themselves into the setting, the former by his jerky, broken gestures and hopping walk, the latter by the slowness of his movements and his gliding somnambulist's gait.

Although *Caligari* did not produce a true school, it did exercise a strong influence on German films. Many directors later displayed the same taste for stylized sets, contrasts of light and shadow (lighting effects were often reinforced by the painting), and jerky, mechanical movements by the main characters.

Abroad the film enjoyed great success as a curiosity. Despite the boycott of German films in Allied countries, *Caligari* was secretly shown in Paris. Louis Delluc launched a campaign against the cinema managers' ban, and it was soon lifted. In a review of *Caligari* in *Le Théâtre* for December 1922, René Clair wrote:

In face of the realist dogma that, with a few exceptions, has seemed to us unassailable, Caligari comes and affirms that the only interesting truth is the subjective. There should have been some mitigating circumstances. We should have liked to believe that this doctor with the pointed hat was mad. But Destiny immediately proved to us that such madness is very reasonable. Which caused some scandal.

27

Das Cabinet des Dr. Caligari (1920). Directed by Robert Wiene. Designed by Hermann Warm, Walter Reimann, Walter Röhrig. The criminal (Rudolph Klein-Rogge) has been jailed for the murders actually committed by Cesare.

Opposite, top: Das Cabinet des Dr. Caligari. Cesare (Conrad Veidt), the somnambulist, murdering Alan (Hans Heinz von Twardowski).

Opposite, bottom: The Night of the Hunter (United Artists, 1955), with Shelley Winters and Robert Mitchum. Directed by Charles Laughton. Art director: Hilyard Brown.

28

29

We must resign ourselves to the inevitable. The cerebral cinema has been created. We have to admit that reshaped nature is at least as expressive as "natural" nature. The sets, the lighting, the acting, even the artificially impassive faces of the actors, form a whole of which intelligence is pleased to know itself the master. This absolute power of the brain is in fact a danger threatening films of this type.

We fear that the feeling of humanity has no place in them. Such films astonish; we wish, for their success, that they succeeded better in moving.*

After the failure of *Genuine*, his second expressionist film, Wiene took on a young Russian designer, Andrei Andrejew, for *Raskolnikoff*. For this film, based on Dostoyevsky's *Crime and Punishment*, Andrejew created a hallucinatory atmosphere. This time the sets were not painted but constructed in three dimensions; nevertheless, we can again see the designer's constant care to avoid horizontals and verticals in

* Clair, *Reflections on the Cinema*, p. 23.

Raskolnikoff (1923). Directed by Robert Wiene. Designed by Andrei Andrejew.

favor of diagonals. Andrejew's development of this motif endows the key element of the film's decor, the staircase, with an extraordinary spellbinding power.

A striving for a stifling or fantastic atmosphere that is often morbid and always strange characterizes all the films linked more or less directly to the expressionist school. Lighting played an increasingly important role in emphasizing the elements calculated to create this visual obsession: faces, symbolic objects, lines of the set.

Paul Wegener, who had been an actor in Reinhardt's company from 1906 to 1920, adapted for the films the lighting techniques employed at the Deutsches Theater. In *The Golem* (1920), he made use of visible light sources—the glow of the hearth, the lantern, the oil lamp, torches—to bring significant characters out of the shadows and to model their faces in the manner of Rembrandt. But Wegener, who unlike other expressionists did not strive for violent lighting effects, denied having sought to make *The Golem* into an expressionist work. If the film looks expressionist this is due primarily to the sets by the architect Hans Poelzig.

However, the *Golem* sets are far removed from the *Caligari* designs. The houses with their stiff, very tall, very narrow gables recall authentic medieval buildings; the design is a barely abstract interpretation of an unsanitary and overpopulated ghetto. In addition, and this is another constant in expressionist films, a formal correlation exists between the sets and the costumes. Here the high gables parallel the Jews' pointed hats.

If we were to summarize in one word the working methods of the expressionist directors, that word would be premeditation. Even in exteriors, nothing is left to chance; thus in Murnau's *Nosferatu* (1922), every aspect of nature, every house front, every view of the castle (all seen at a certain angle), is calculated to evoke anguish and terror. For years, Germany's Hoffmannesque taste for terror, its deep romanticism, imposed upon expressionist filmmakers nightmare visions: haunted castles, vampires, sleepwalkers, madmen—and for good measure, images of coffins, skeletons, rats, and owls. In the field of set design, this obsession with the horrible is translated into a preoccupation with dark, twisting stairways, vaulted corridors, mirrors, flames, and shadows cast by the characters. Doors open on their own, and window curtains are ruffled by a breath from the beyond.

We find the fantastic and a preoccupation with death in Fritz Lang's film *Destiny* (1921). Lang was the German filmmaker most strongly influenced by Reinhardt, but like Wegener he evolved from this background a very personal vision. The sets in *Destiny* were designed by Robert Herlth, Walter Röhrig, and Warm. Lang, himself an architect and painter, enhanced them admirably by the play of light. A satanic atmosphere rules the laboratory of the little apothecary, giving it the appearance of an alchemist's den; the luminous molding of a Gothic doorway seems to spring up toward the sky, in contrast to the dark walls. As a result of the lighting effects employed in *Destiny*, it became general practice to light sets from below in order to emphasize architecture and bring out relief surfaces. This method of lighting became one of the characteristics of German film.

Lang's *Nibelungen Saga,* consisting of *Siegfried* (1924) and *Kriemhild's Revenge* (1924), was shot entirely in landscapes re-created in the studio or on the adjoining lot. "[Rudolph] Kurtz, for his part, declared that for a film to become a work of art nature had to be stylized. . . . Only when a director builds his own landscape can he give it a soul and make it play an active role in the plot."* The sets for *The Nibelungen Saga* were designed by Otto Hunte, Erich Kettelhut, and Karl Vollbrecht. Oddly enough, German designers often worked in small teams. In this case, Hunte made the initial sketches, which were elaborated on by Kettelhut, and Vollbrecht was responsible mainly for construction. Lang himself made the sketches for some of the sets.

The painter in Lang sought to bring to life the famous canvases of Arnold Böcklin through these artificial landscapes. Nothing is left to chance; everything—the balanced volumes, the linear arabesques, the lighting effects, the softness or violent contrast of blacks and whites—is calculated. Every shot is composed like an easel painting, hence a certain coldness; but the forest, the pond, and the steppes re-created in the studio are undeniable successes.

Lang, who had previously made *Dr. Mabuse* (1922), a detective film with expressionist sets, was also responsible for one of the most interesting films from the viewpoint of design, *Metropolis* (1926). The evocation of the underground city presented the designers (the trio of Hunte, Kettelhut, and Vollbrecht) with the problem of immense constructions. Lang and his designers made use of a trick shot—the *Spiegeltechnik*—which had been invented by Eugen Schüfftan in 1923 and which later

* Eisner, p. 152.

Der Müde Tod/Destiny (1921). Directed by Fritz Lang. Designed by Robert Herlth, Röhrig, and Warm. The Chinese Tale was designed by Herlth.

became known as the Schüfftan process. This miniatures-reflected-in-mirrors technique was used for the first time in *Metropolis* and converted the models into what appears as a giant fantasy city.

The sets were resolutely modern, whether they represented buildings with their geometric volumes, the machine room, or the laboratory. Although the grandiloquent, often puerile scenario, and in particular the acting, may seem outmoded today, the sets are surprisingly contemporary. This derives on one hand from the inventive genius and visual sense of the designers, and on the other from the very careful, realistic construction. The director's office, highly simplified, contains prophetic elements such as the small screen that allows the boss to see his interlocutor at a distance: it is a television set before the fact. The machine room and the vaulted tunnels have a note of authenticity rare for the period; furthermore, Lang handles the lighting admirably. The iron bands encircling the Robot during the experiment in the laboratory, the flashes given off by the machines in action, the brief illuminations by the searchlights that bring to life the industrial architecture, the huge beehives of factories with hundreds of lit windows, create a mobility and vitality that counterbalance the possibly over-systematized, over-stylized motions of the crowds, which never move except in columns, never form groups except in geometric shapes.

Paul Richter as Siegfried (1924). Directed by Lang. Designed by Otto Hunte, Karl Vollbrecht, and Erich Kettelhut.

Metropolis (1926). Directed by Lang. Designed by Hunte, Vollbrecht, and Kettelhut. Above: Brigitte Helm as the bogus Maria, as she appears in the Pleasure House. Opposite: Brigitte Helm, as the true Maria hanging from the cathedral bell, in a shot missing from prints circulating in the United States.

For his *Waxworks* (1924), Paul Leni, an expressionist painter and filmmaker, chose a fairground environment, which always lends itself well to mysteries. He adopted the formula of three episodes taking place at different periods and in different countries. A skillful designer, he used for the first two episodes architectural shapes harmonizing with the physical appearance and costumes of the characters, as Wegener had done in *The Golem*. By contrast, in the Russian episode he strove for something other than a decorative expressionism: the architecture determines the behavior and attitudes of the characters by preventing them from moving about normally. The low ceilings, arches, low doorways, and straight, narrow staircase force bodies to bend, to double up, to move jerkily, and to make abrupt gestures. This pattern noticeably influenced Eisenstein's *Ivan the Terrible*.

Lupu Pick created a new trend in German cinema, the *Kammerspielfilm* (a name borrowed from the Kammerspiel, the small theater that Max Reinhardt had opened next to his large theater to stage more intimate plays). After *Shattered* (1921), Pick made *New Year's Eve* (1923), based on a scenario by Karl Mayer. He conceived the film as a psychological work, with few characters and action confined to a limited setting: a kitchen, a dining room, a cabaret; the street is already the outside world, indifferent to the drama. The very clear theme of the film allowed the elimination of titles, the bane of the silent screen.

Mayer, the most famous scenarist of the German cinema, became the theoretician of the *Kammerspielfilm*. From his scenario, Murnau made the masterpiece of the new school: *The Last Laugh* (1924), with Emil Jannings in the main role. The sets by Robert Herlth and Walter Röhrig have realistic tendencies: there are no longer expressionist distortions, deformed shapes, or violent searchlight illuminations. The sets are reduced to the essential, sometimes to a ceiling and a mirror. In his initial sketches Herlth, influenced by Murnau, began by roughing in characters as they were positioned in a particular scene; then the volume of the set seemed to create itself. Thus interiors became simpler and simpler, barer and barer.

Despite this simplification, all the tricks of set design and camera movements were utilized, and sometimes invented, for this film. Scale models on top of actual buildings made it possible to give a vertiginous height to the facade of the Grand

Der Letzte Mann/The Last Laugh. *(1924). Directed by F. W. Murnau. Sets by Herlth and Röhrig.*

Hotel. The illusionistic perspectives of the streets, with houses and cars diminishing in size from foreground to background, had been used before in German films, but never with such success. The camera became extremely mobile: it was attached directly to the cameraman's body, or else camera and cameraman stood on a fireman's ladder or in a hoist, in order to follow a character's movements.

In *Variety*, filmed in 1925 by Ewald André Dupont, the director made clever use of the last vestiges of expressionism, such as the view from above into the courtyard of a prison, where the circle formed by the prisoners seems to be rotating as though at the bottom of a well. Dupont and the designer, Oscar Werndorff, drew their inspiration for this scene from van Gogh's painting *The Prisoners,* which van Gogh himself had modeled on a drawing by Gustave Doré.

The expressionist period in German cinema, lasting about seven years, was particularly rich in experiments of every kind, especially in the field of set design and camera work (lighting, framing, camera movements). Never before had design exercised so much influence on cinematic vision: for the first time, films created atmosphere. During this period, film design came of age. As Marcel Lapierre wrote, "Expressionism . . . taught a lasting lesson. It proved the value, often disputed, of systematic set design. When the pros and cons had been totted up and the entirely gratuitous distortions set aside, the advantages that design could place at the service of reality itself became clear."* The sets became elements as active as the characters. What the Swedes had achieved with nature, the Germans created in the studio.

Expressionism, in spite of its exaggerations, even its faults, has had and will

* Marcel Lapierre, *Les Cents Visages du cinéma,* p. 456.

Alraune (1928). Directed by Henrik Galeen. Designed by Reimann and Max Heilbronner. Mia Pankan(?) has just learned from Paul Wegener of the truly extraordinary insemination which awaits her.

continue to have a great influence on film set designs. As soon as one ventures into the domain of the fantastic, the strange, the unusual, he invariably finds himself caught up in the wake of the great age of German cinema.

France 1918–1926

During World War I, film production in France was practically paralyzed; most producers, technicians, and actors had been mobilized. The French cinema, having lost nearly all its foreign outlets and facing at home the competition of vastly superior American films, had only one chance of survival: to produce works of great value. Unfortunately, the major companies hesitated to take the risk; consequently, the financial resources available to French filmmakers were minimal. That French cinema ultimately advanced was due to the ingenuity of its directors and technicians.

As for set design, a rather timid start was made in producing true constructions of timber and staff. Painted canvas was still in use and disappeared only gradually. Not until about 1926 were sets regularly constructed with plywood frames; until then, and even later, directors were content to draw upon the studio's stock. This famous studio "repertoire" consisted of varied and heterogeneous interiors accumulated during the years: dining and drawing rooms, kitchens, prisons, winter gardens painted on pliable canvas-covered frames, souvenirs of a heroic epoch. But as soon as the

37

camera began to move about inside the set, the three-sided set had to be abandoned and replaced by something closer to reality. However, only for certain films made by very exacting directors were sets specially designed for the scenario; normally it was considered sufficient to use stock sets adapted more or less to each film. Filming was always done in studios built of glass, in daylight reinforced with artificial lighting. In 1922 a few teams of American filmmakers (among them Pearl White's team, which included the designer Henri Ménessier) came to Paris and rented French studios. Because the Americans wanted to work entirely by artificial light, as they did at home, the studio glass was painted over in black, and henceforth the French, too, had to work with artificial light.

If film scenery continued to progress technically, the same cannot be said of its aesthetic evolution. Directors stuck to the old, tried-and-true formulas: dining rooms were necessarily Renaissance, bedrooms Louis XV, and offices Empire. Similarly, period films remained faithful to the outworn aesthetic of the theatrical scene painters, themselves victims of a hundred years of routine. Classical antiquity, the Middle Ages, and the Renaissance were seen through the eyes of a season-ticket holder at the Opéra.

In 1922, however, changes began to take place. The technical evolution of film scenery no longer required the architect–designer to use trompe-l'oeil painting, so newcomers flocked to the profession: interior decorators, young architects, stage designers who had started in the modern theater—the Ballets Russes, the Vieux Colombier, the Atelier, and others. With this infusion of new blood, film scenery began to free itself from the conventions of *fin de siècle* theater.

Around the same time, a team of Russian emigré filmmakers formed under the aegis of Josef Yermoliev. The group soon became the Albatros company, directed by Alexander Kamenka. Free from the heavy administrative apparatus of big firms like Pathé, Gaumont, and Aubert, Kamenka's company, housed in the former Pathé studios at Montreuil, produced a series of films that combined a search for novelty with artistic quality. The actor Ivan Mosjoukine, the directors Alexander Wolkoff and Victor Tourjansky, the technicians, and especially the Russian designers—first Ivan Lochakov, then Boris Bilinsky—brought to French cinema a certain taste for display, for spectaculars, which had been unknown to it. Because of their fullness and visual richness Lochakov's sets played a large part in the success of *Kean* (1923), *The Burning Brazier* (1923), *Secrets of the Orient* (1928), and *Michael Strogoff* (1926). *Casanova* (1927) and *Monte Cristo* (1929) had magnificent sets by Bilinsky, who also designed the costumes and posters.

Lochakov's and Bilinsky's styles were different from those of the Paris designers, because of the influences to which they had been exposed first in Russia and then in Germany. In pre-Revolutionary Russia, cinema followed the teachings of Stanislavsky, whose theories and productions made Russian theater preeminent. Thus Russian designers, including Lochakov and Bilinsky, conceived film decor in fairly realistic terms; but one must not overlook the contribution of a group of painters, illustrators, and designers, working together on the journal *Mir Iskutva* (*World of Art*), who would revolutionize stage scenery, especially ballet scenery. Under the patronage of Diaghilev and his ballet company, these designers sought inspiration in Russian folk art, Persian

38

Geheimnisse des Orients/Secrets of the Orient (1928). Directed by Alexander Wolkoff. Sets by A. Lochakov and W. Meinhardt.

miniatures, and the works of the great Italian and French designers of seventeenth- and eighteenth-century operas.

Instead of being craftsmen, like the painters and designers who had invented and perfected film scenery in France, Lochakov and Bilinsky were creators open to all artistic currents. In their work in the Berlin studios, they had learned the new techniques of constructed scenery, staff, scale models, and so on. In the palace set for Henri Fescourt's *Monte Cristo*, Bilinsky re-created a vision of the palace as it might have been conceived by Italian opera designers of the eighteenth century, by Bibiena or Piranesi, with a monumental stairway, colonnades, arcades, and balconies; but it was a constructed set, at least up to a certain height: the upper part consisted of a scale model and the base was painted in trompe-l'oeil. In Wolkoff's *Secrets of the Orient*, Lochakov made use of the same scale-model procedure, this time to produce a delirious visual effect: the onion-shaped domes of the minarets, the twisted and pointed horseshoe arch, the spiral towers flanking it are all related to the decor of the Ballets Russes as interpreted by German expressionism. Given the type of film produced by Albatros, Lochakov and Bilinsky directed their efforts toward the spectacular aspect of scenery, toward an overall effect rather than atmosphere or the search for exact detail.

In any case, the painted canvas and the plywood frame timidly clad with moldings were through. For major sets, designers used wooden frames, to which were applied sheets of staff, with or without ornament. The reduced-scale model was perfected, thanks to Minine and Wilcke, model makers and experts in special effects. In general, through their exacting demands and their achievements, the Russian designers contributed to raising the status of film designers to one of close collaboration with directors.

Parallel with the success of the more or less high-budget commercial films, a movement toward revival developed and became a dominant factor during the years 1921–26. Louis Delluc, a journalist and playwright, headed the group. Abel Gance, Marcel L'Herbier, Germaine Dulac, and Jean Epstein gathered around him, bringing with them a new generation of designers. This group, which was later called impressionist to distinguish it from German expressionism, was the first French avant-garde to do battle with the commercial cinema. Delluc was not content to print at the top of his magazine *Cinéa*, "Let French cinema be cinema, let French cinema be French." He also entered the arena himself. *Fièvre*, which he made in 1921, takes place in a Marseilles brothel. For the first time in France, a film strove for atmosphere, in its choice of characters from the lowest strata of Marseilles society, in the lighting, and in the realistic sets designed by Robert Jules Garnier. These sets successfully express the closed world within which the action occurs; and in its concern to combine this unity of place with unity of time, *Fièvre* can be compared to the first works of the German *Kammerspielfilm*.

Louis Delluc died prematurely in 1924 at the age of thirty-three, but his influence on the aesthetics of film and therefore on film set design was considerable, especially through his critical essays.

Abel Gance, called by Léon Moussinac "the Victor Hugo of the screen," was a romantic at heart, but he was passionately interested in technical research; he was also the first filmmaker to construct an exterior set on location. For example, in *The Wheel* (1924), the house of the railway engineer Sisif was built next to the siding at the Nice railway station. (Jean Renoir later adopted this technique, which he used frequently, for *La Bête humaine*, building the apartment of the engineer on a platform overlooking the tracks of a railway station.)

To make *Napoléon* (1927), Gance assembled an impressive technical team: six assistants, of whom two were established directors; six of the best cameramen around; and, as set designer, Alexandre Benois, one of Diaghilev's leading designers. This was Benois's first experience in film, but as a ballet and stage designer, an illustrator, and an art historian (formerly a curator at the Hermitage Museum in Leningrad), he possessed vast artistic knowledge and undeniable gifts as an artist. His sketches for *Napoléon*, inspired by original period documents, are both full of life and scrupulously authentic. It was the first time that the sets for a period film had been treated with such seriousness. The sets for this enormous film were executed by Schildknecht (known as Schild), a Russian set designer who made the best possible use of the existing techniques of studio construction.

The film teems with symbols and superimpositions, and perhaps Gance tended to overwork a new technique: a portable camera equipped with a clockwork mechanism, making it independent of the cameraman (the camera was still hand operated). Nevertheless, the most interesting feature of the film is its visual, artistic aspect. Perhaps some of the sets are rather too theatrically majestic, but the evocation of the Club des Cordeliers and the Convention have genuine grandeur, and there are beautiful shots of the Italian campaign and the siege of Toulon.

Returning to Grimoin-Samson's idea, the "Cinérama" that had been the attraction of the 1900 Paris World's Fair, Gance worked out with the aid of André Debrie, a mechanic, a system of projection onto a triple screen. The process involved using three synchronized cameras for a screen three times normal size. Three different pictures—which might themselves be formed of several superimposed images—made up a triptych. (If, instead, the shots had been taken with three cameras that were superimposed but had divergent optical axes, projection would have produced a single "panoramic" view.) The projection of *Napoléon* on a triple screen at the Marivaux theater was an enormous success. A more advanced form of this same process can be seen in American Cinerama or Soviet Kinopanorama.

After adapting Balzac (*The Red Inn*), Jean Epstein made his best film, *Coeur Fidèle* (*The Faithful Heart*), in 1923. Shot on location in Marseilles, it was a sensation with its fairground treated in high-speed montage. Epstein, a philosopher and brilliant essayist, wrote of it, "The countryside and the fairground are immense collective characters that must live, move, grow, shrink, age. There are no props in the cinema. Every object is a gnome full of genius and malice."

Following *La Belle Nivernaise* (1923), a film that takes place almost entirely on barges and canals, Epstein allowed himself to be seduced by German expressionism, making in the studio *Mauprat* (1926) and *The Fall of the House of Usher* (1927), both with sets by Pierre Kéfer. Kéfer's sets are atmospheric, a phenomenon rare in French cinema at that time, and worthy of further consideration. In his sketch for *Mauprat*, he indicated a lighting effect that is the central motif of the scenery; two converging pencils of light concentrate attention on a strange canopy bed. Unlike the German designers, he used neither curves nor diagonals, treating everything in the set vertically—the posts of the bed drawn out like the uprights of a guillotine, the luminous slits of the windows, the giant figures in the frescoes. In some ways, however, Kéfer's approach was close to the methods of the German expressionists: systematic distortion of proportions, designs, and light sources that created a visual center of interest at the exact spot where the action occurred.

The post-war era, throughout the world and especially in France, favored an extraordinary ferment of ideas, theories, and schools in painting, architecture, literature, and the theater. These advanced movements later gave rise to avant-garde cinema, but before that, Marcel L'Herbier tried to apply to films the discoveries of

41

A Robert Mallet-Stevens set for L'Inhumaine/The New Enchantment *(1923). Directed by Marcel L'Herbier. Art directors: Claude Autant-Lara, Alberto Cavalcanti, and Mallet-Stevens.*

modern painting and architecture. It is easy, today, to reproach him for "decorative aestheticism," but the experiment had to be attempted, and L'Herbier made the attempt with great courage.

Despite its commercial failure, L'Herbier's most important work was *L'Inhumaine* (*The New Enchantment*, 1923). He wanted the cinema to participate in the aesthetic experiments of the years 1920–26: for the first time in France, the sets of a film would be resolutely modern. In addition to Claude Autant-Lara and Alberto Cavalcanti, who had already worked with him, L'Herbier obtained the services of the cubist painter Fernand Léger and Robert Mallet-Stevens, a progressive young architect.

One of L'Herbier's first collaborators, Claude Autant-Lara, had created for *Don Juan et Faust* (1922) sets and costumes in a very free style. Their simplified, strong,

Raymond Bernard (who directed the film), at left, and Jean Perrrier (who designed it) with models for the sets of Les Misérables *(1934).*

modernized lines were extremely daring for the period. In *L'Inhumaine,* Autant-Lara filled the winter garden with stylized plants whose artificial, larger-than-life flowers and leaves have the simplified shapes and stiffness that fit the style of the film. The bedroom by Cavalcanti is as abstract as a stage set could be: the diminishing sizes of the three parallelepipeds, the diagonal lines of the steps, the zigzags traced by the light from the lighting boxes, the vertical stripes of the white painted cables, and the patches of light that make the characters stand out from the darkened set, all create an avant-garde atmosphere very typical of *L'Inhumaine.* That part of the film designed by Fernand Léger is very similar to his paintings, yet it is a three-dimensional set. He accentuates depth by a succession of planes of different tones decorated with the geometric shapes so dear to him: triangles, disks, semicircles, giant holes. This set springs from the same aesthetic as Léger's film *Ballet mécanique* (1924).

In *L'Inhumaine* Robert Mallet-Stevens introduced the first manifestations of contemporary architecture to the screen. Inspired by the principles that guided him in his real-life buildings—neither the industrial modernism of *Metropolis* nor the decorative modernism of Cavalcanti's or Autant-Lara's experiments—his sets were composed of simple, geometric volumes, combinations of plain surfaces and window openings. All decoration was eliminated and replaced by the unconcealed skeletons of reinforced concrete structures—jambs, beams, overhanging tiles; he emphasized the whiteness of the walls by surrounding the openings with dark frames. Adding to the film's deliberate modernity, Darius Milhaud wrote the score. The result was predictable: the movie house owners uttered cries of horror and didn't want "that stuff" in their theaters. But despite its weaknesses, *L'Inhumaine* considerably influenced the development of film design in France.

43

Enrique Rivero in Le Sang d'un Poète/Blood of a Poet (made 1930, first public showing 1932). Written and directed by Jean Cocteau. Sets by Jean d'Eaubonne.

In 1925, before abandoning his formal experiments for more commercial works such as *Money,* L'Herbier adapted for Albatros a novel by Pirandello, *The Late Matthew Pascal.* Cavalcanti's "synthetic" set designs strive for dominant lines—curves, diagonals, concentric circles—reminiscent of parallel experiments by German designers but showing greater feeling. Cavalcanti's assistants for this film were Lazare Meerson, who would later revolutionize film set design, and Erik Aaes, a Dane who would create sets for Jean Renoir and Cavalcanti when the latter became a director. Aaes was later to design *Day of Wrath,* directed by Carl Dreyer.

Despite his absorption in architecture, Mallet-Stevens remained passionately interested in the cinema. In 1924 he designed the sets for *The Miracle of the Wolves,* "a chronicle of the times of Louis XI," one of Raymond Bernard's best films. The admirably arranged battle scenes were shot outside the ramparts of Carcassonne. For the interiors, Mallet-Stevens eliminated all unnecessary details: splendid, shiny floors and high fireplaces are the only visually rich areas. This kind of stylization was in keeping with the age portrayed. The visual qualities, the breadth and the movement of *The Miracle of the Wolves* made it one of the great successes of the silent cinema: it had the privilege of being the first film presented at the Paris Opéra.

Mallet-Stevens also worked for Raymond Bernard on *The Chess Player* in 1926. During the preparation for it, he met Jean Perrier, one of the first designers for Gaumont, who would also work on the film. Pondering the problems of film set design with the curiosity of a neophyte, Mallet-Stevens had discovered the empirical approach of the professional designers. He began to study camera angles, which varied

Cocteau at work on Blood of a Poet.

according to the focus of the lens employed. Intrigued by these studies, Perrier took them up as well and developed a rational concept of film set design as a function of the position of the camera and the lenses. The graphic method that he worked out enabled him to determine which plan and dimensions of a set would produce the image desired and drawn by the designer. By the same token, starting from a pre-established plan, it became possible to draw the set the way it would appear on the screen if the camera were placed in a given position and equipped with a given lens.

Thus, with great ingenuity, Perrier resolved all set design problems posed by the exigencies of a scenario. The movements of the camera and of the actors were determined in advance, and the director's work became that much easier. From 1926 on, Perrier worked on all of Bernard's films: *The Chess Player*, with its vast exterior sets such as the courtyard of the Winter Palace at St. Petersburg; *Tarakanova* (1929), with its sober and powerful reconstructions of eighteenth-century Russia and the port of Ragusa; then the sound films *The Wooden Crosses* (1932), *Les Misérables* (1934), and others.

Because of his abilities as an illustrator, Perrier had a particularly highly developed sense for the framing of the film image. He studied his construction plans on the basis of his "page settings," which, with the greatest economy of means, showed the most spectacular aspects of the set. To create the impression of a review of troops outside the Winter Palace, for example, all he had to do was focus the camera from above upon a balcony and have a column of troops pass along a paved sidewalk before house fronts built up to the second story. He constructed only what was essential, but he paid close attention to realistic execution. He defended new techniques and more faithful observation of true, evocative details in advance of Meerson, though perhaps with less passion.

A campaign for "pure cinema" was mounted by Germaine Dulac, an experimental filmmaker. Pure cinema rejected neither sensibility nor drama, but it tried to attain them through purely visual elements. The program was broad enough to include films conceived in many different ways. Between 1923 and 1926, Autant-Lara, Léger, Cavalcanti (all designers for L'Herbier), Man Ray, René Clair (with *Entr'acte*), Jean Renoir, Henri Chomette, and Jean Grémillon were the most typical representatives of this second avant-garde force. All the films produced by this movement had one element in common: they were shot out of doors and with very limited resources, in an inevitable reaction against the excesses of aestheticism, the dullness of the scenarios, and the tyranny of producers.

The surrealist films, especially those by Luis Buñuel, stand slightly to one side of this avant-garde. No longer pure cinema as understood by its founders, the films attempted to place the means of cinematic expression at the service of surrealist theories.

The surrealist movement grew from a split in Dada. The dissident group was led by André Breton, who in 1924 published the first surrealist manifesto, in which he gave directions for "forcing the doors of the unconscious." The first films of the new school were a short by Germaine Dulac, *The Seashell and the Clergyman* (1928), from a scenario by Antonin Artaud, and *The Starfish* (1928) by Man Ray, film director as well as painter and photographer. Luis Buñuel made the first medium-length surrealist film, *Un Chien andalou* (1928), based on a scenario by Salvador Dali. Buñuel's second film, *L'Age d'or*, made in 1930, used numerous symbols and fables.

The sets of Buñuel's films look realistic, even commonplace. The atmosphere is created by unusual, unexpected elements in the sets and by the entirely unpredictable behavior of the characters. In *Un Chien andalou* (sets by Schildknecht), an impassive man drags across the room two grand pianos laden with slaughtered donkeys. In *L'Age d'or*, a tip-cart drawn by a Percheron appears in the middle of a drawing room where a society reception is taking place, and later a cow sprawls on a Louis XV bed. (Screwball incidents along these lines had been used in 1912 in Jean Durand's *Onésime* series, but for purely comic purposes.) Certainly, an apparent realism of sets, characters, and objects was much more effective in creating the atmosphere of an absurd dream or a nightmare than the precious aestheticism of the strange *Blood of a Poet*, directed by Jean Cocteau in 1930 with sets by Jean d'Eaubonne.

The avant-garde movement was a research laboratory whose discoveries enriched French film; surrealism, in particular, has had a lasting effect on cinema. Furthermore, since the experimental films had little chance of being shown on the normal circuit, they led to the establishment of specialized theaters and film clubs, which exercised a great influence on the cinematic education of an increasingly larger audience.

4 Natural Scenery

Russia 1914–1930

As in France and Germany, the art of film scenery in Russia was influenced by the theater, but it was a theater inclined toward realism. The great designer Victor Simov, who worked at Stanislavsky's Moscow Art Theater from 1908 to 1932, was one of the first set designers for Russian cinema. The Moscow Art Theater was also the starting point for Vladimir Egorov, who made his cinematic debut in 1915 with the sets for Meyerhold's *The Portrait of Dorian Gray,* and for Yevgeni Bauer, painter, designer, and (from 1913 to 1917) stage and film director. Bauer's productions were mainly society melodramas, but he was one of the first to take an interest in film aesthetics and set design. He was the first Russian designer to use three-dimensional, studio-built sets. Sergei Kozlovsky, trained as a painter, designed his first sets in 1913 for Guriev's *A Hunting Drama,* and was later the designer for Pudovkin's silent films. C. Sabinsky developed the technique of collapsible folding scenery.

But Russian films for the years preceding World War I never rose above the level of honest mediocrity; the revelation of Russian cinema did not occur until after the 1917 Revolution. At that time, Russia was still a world leader in avant-garde art, and it was within these movements of futurism, constructivism, and others that the new direction of the Soviet cinema was first elaborated. One group of young filmmakers, including Grigori Kozintsev, Sergei Yutkevich (both professional painters and designers), Leonid Trauberg, and Sergei Gerasimov, named themselves The Factory of the Eccentric Actor (F.E.K.S., 1921) and preached the use of violent scenic effects, citing the "entries of clowns" in circus and fairground parades. In 1924 the group produced a joyous futurist sketch entitled *The Adventures of Oktyabrina.*

Dziga Vertov directed the work of news cameramen during the civil war, and then from 1922 to 1924, the Kinopravda weekly newsreels, in which he successfully used montage to give emotional and aesthetic meaning to commonplace images. He was also a theorist: his manifestos written in the futurist style—*We, He and I, Kinoki,* and *Kino-Glaz (Cinema Eye)*—proclaimed that the cinema must reject plot, actors, costumes, scenery, the studio, and artificial lighting—in a word, fiction. In his view, the art of film lay almost entirely in editing. Throughout the period of the silent screen, these theories had considerable influence on Soviet directors, leading them for the most part to reject the studio and the set. The theory demanding that "life be taken unawares" proved more difficult to put into practice. Vertov's cameramen tried discreetly to film scenes of everyday life, but no doubt through a lack of equipment specially adapted for this purpose, the results, except for the footage that was of standard newsreel type, were disappointing. Vertov's most important films—*Stride, Soviet!* (1926), *A Sixth of the World* (1926), and *Three Songs of Lenin* (1934)—made use of "objective documents" such as newsreels.

Vertov initiated a cinematic genre that later bore fruit in Frank Capra's World War II American propaganda series *Why We Fight* (1942–45), and in such compilation films as *Paris 1900* by Nicole Vedrès (1947). All montage films making use of newsreels descend from Vertov's theories.

The direction taken by the great Soviet filmmakers may be explained partly by the importance they attached to editing and the influence of the documentary, partly by the scant resources available to the studios after years of civil war and the economic blockade. Although during the era of the silent screen, many interesting films were shot in studios, Soviet cinema of the period was characterized chiefly by the perfection of its exterior shots. For the first time, images of an unaccustomed breadth linked formal beauty with generosity of emotion, a lyricism that gave an epic sense to the films of Eisenstein, Pudovkin, and Dovzhenko.

These three directors amplified the idea of the set, in keeping with the historical events which their films relate. They did not use anonymous or simply photogenic backgrounds: they chose landscapes, streets, palaces, and factories with an evident concern for making them participate closely in the rhythm of the film. Sergei Maximovich Eisenstein, who began as a stage designer (a fact which helps explain his visual gifts), possessed a staggering sense of film image. Although the major shots of faces, the movements of crowds, and the arabesques of parades form part of his narratives, the settings themselves, with their architectural details, almost always have an allegorical value. Note the "jumping lions," row upon row of the Odessa steps in *Battleship Potemkin* (1925), with sets by Vasili Rakhals,* the gigantic feet of the marble colossi in *October* (*Ten Days That Shook the World*, 1928), with sets by Vasili Kovrigin, and the terrifying details of the Aztec temples in *Que Viva Mexico!* (1931). The constructed sets for his sound films, *Alexander Nevsky* (1938) and *Ivan the Terrible* (1944, 1958), were also treated in a symbolic manner.

Eisenstein's contemporary, Vsevolod Pudovkin, served his apprenticeship in Lev Kuleshov's Experimental Laboratory, where he became a scenario writer, actor, and then designer and assistant to the director. In 1926, after two documentaries, he made one of his finest films, *Mother*. For him the central character was not the "people," but two individuals, a man and a woman who reflected the aspirations of a milieu and an era. His choice of actors and the setting within which the action takes place reveals an

* During the silent era, Eisenstein avoided studio sets, but he did have to reconstruct the bulk of the *Twelve Apostles*, the twin sister of the *Potemkin* that had been demolished years ago. There were no gun turrets, no bridges, no masts left. On the deck of the real ship the designer Rakhals had these superstructures rebuilt in wood to restore the exact silhouette of the *Potemkin* according to drawings preserved in the Admiralty.

Top: *Eisenstein's* October/Ten Days That Shook the World *(1928). Designer: Vasili Kovrigin.*

Bottom: *Merian C. Cooper taking the measurements for King Kong's mitt—to make a good fit for Fay Wray.* King Kong *(RKO, 1933) was directed by Cooper and Ernest Schoedsack. Art directors: Carroll Clark and Al Herman. But Willis O'Brien, special effects genius (model animation and glass paintings), was responsible for the look of most of the film. The gigantic hand which clutches Miss Wray was designed and constructed by Marcel Delgado.*

infallible instinct for the evocation of this time and place. The working-class districts, the bridge, the prison in *Mother*, the stock exchange in *The End of St. Petersburg* (1927), designed by Sergei Kozlovsky, and the extraordinary fur fair in *Storm over Asia* (1928) become dramatic elements inseparable from the narrative. The interiors for all of Pudovkin's films were shot in the studio. In order not to break the epic rhythm of the works, his designer, Kozlovsky, conceived sets of stark restraint, almost bare, with just a few pieces of furniture necessary to the action.

A certain similarity of style links Alexander Dovzhenko with Eisenstein and Pudovkin: the same breadth and beauty of the images, the same lyricism, and the same emotion. Dovzhenko, born in the Ukraine, had been a schoolmaster, caricaturist, and painter. Starting in cinema as a scenario writer, he made his debut as a director in 1926. *Arsenal* (1929), designed by Isaac Shpinel, made him famous, but his masterpiece was *Earth* (1930), with sets by Vasili Krichevsky. This highly sensuous film, rich in painterly images, is set in the Ukraine, but the setting is neither symbolic nor merely descriptive: rarely have men been so intimately linked with the earth, the landscape. The Ukraine was to become the central theme of Dovzhenko's films, and throughout his life he remained attached to the image of his native land, in the serenity and plenitude of peace or in the horrors of war.

The great Soviet silent films treated the themes of the struggles and the first victories of the Revolution; hence the dynamism, violence, and at the same time lyricism that distinguishes the style of the Russian filmmakers from that of Griffith, for example, to whom technically they owe a great deal. Their works are as far removed from stylization as they are from purely objective realism, from photographic verism. Although Eisenstein, Pudovkin, and Dovzhenko, to name only the great trio, employed real—one might say anonymous—elements, they carried concern for the composition of images, dramatic sense, and rhythm even further than the expressionists. This was also the first time in the history of film that the state placed such vast resources at the disposal of directors: the army, the navy, extras by the hundreds, public monuments, and so on. For *Ten Days That Shook the World*, Eisenstein had the Winter Palace at his disposal for several months. Soviet designers had to reckon with this new breadth of images, this powerful rhythm, just as sound arrived. The directors had come a long way from films based on a simple montage of newsreel shots following Vertov's theories.

5 The Triumph of Realism

Hollywood after 1920

After 1920, the success of the American cinema, which flooded the international film market, was based on the commercialism and superficiality of the star system. New creative life was brought to Hollywood by a few comic actors of genius—but above all by the influx of great European directors. This contribution, which began with the French and the Swedish, became decisive with the influx of German and Viennese directors such as Ernst Lubitsch, Friedrich Murnau, and Fritz Lang, who all contributed to breaching the wall of puritanism that bowdlerized Hollywood production.

With Erich von Stroheim the American cinema got its first taste of sophisticated eroticism and a view of the world that is simultaneously brutal, cynical, and full of pathos. Like Chaplin, Stroheim was not only a great actor but also an author whose personality, ideas, and audacity were exceptional. He also designed sets and costumes for his films. Given his demand for realism, his influence on the development of set design in the United States from 1920 to 1928 is incontestable.

For the first two films he directed, *Blind Husbands* (1918) and *The Devil's Passkey* (1919), Stroheim also wrote the scenarios and designed the settings. In *Foolish Wives* (1921), besides being the scenarist, director, and designer, he also played the film's abject hero. However, since the scenario required the building of enormous sets, reconstructing the Casino of Monte Carlo together with the surrounding palaces and mansions, Stroheim collaborated with designer Richard Day (see frontispiece).

Foolish Wives was the first million-dollar picture (or at least Carl Laemmle, head of Universal, said it was). Laemmle hesitated for a long time, but he decided to finance it when R. H. Cochrane, vice-president of Universal, hit upon the idea of utilizing the cost of production for publicity purposes. For more than a year during production, a huge billboard in New York showed the cost of the film so far. Each week firemen with a long ladder came to alter the figures under the title of the film and Stroheim's name, in which the S was replaced by a dollar sign.* These unusual publicity methods began a tradition that has continued down to our own day.

* *Erich von Stroheim*, ed. F. Buache (Paris: Seghers, 1972), pp. 33–34.

Section of one of a series of illustrated publicity cards distributed in theaters as a preview of The Hunchback of Notre Dame, *starring Lon Chaney (Universal, 1923).*

After the success of *Foolish Wives*, Stroheim made *Merry-Go-Round* (1923), then adapted for the screen Frank Norris's novel *McTeague*, which became *Greed* (1924). Having decided to film it on location, Stroheim found in San Francisco a burnt-out house, abandoned for thirty years. The whole interior was rebuilt and designed for the installation of arc lights, but the ceilings were preserved. Similarly, he rented a coal mine and set up an entire underground studio. Then he filmed in a real San Francisco dentist's office.* Finally, the whole crew was transported for a month to sinister Death Valley, where the exteriors were shot. *Greed* is filled with almost unendurable violence. As Stroheim summed up his concept of cinema, "I became involved with films because, as a lover of the arts, I found there the greatest means of artistic expression. The theater possesses only limited means; it is incomplete and often factitious. The cinema is free from all limitation and there you can show life as it is: filth! I wished and I still wish to show real life, with its degradation, baseness, violence, sensuality, and a singular contrast in the midst of this filth, purity."†

After this ferociously realistic film, Stroheim made *The Wedding March* (1928), in which he played the lead once again. Again assisted by Day, he designed the costumes and baroque sets for a decadent Vienna, this time expressing a transmuted realism. He exercised a great influence on the development of set design in the United States, enriching the realistic trend that was already present in embryo. But in 1928 production was halted on *Queen Kelly* after Stroheim had shot only ten of the

* Jean Tedesco and Pierre Henri, *Cinéa-Ciné pour tous* (Sept. 1, 1926).
† Erich von Stroheim, *Ciné-Club* (April 1949).

Opposite: *Douglas Fairbanks in* The Black Pirate *(1926). Art director: Carl Oscar Borg, assisted by Edward Langley and Jack Holden.*

Bottom: *Eisenstein's* Strike *(1925). Designer: Vasili Rakhals.*

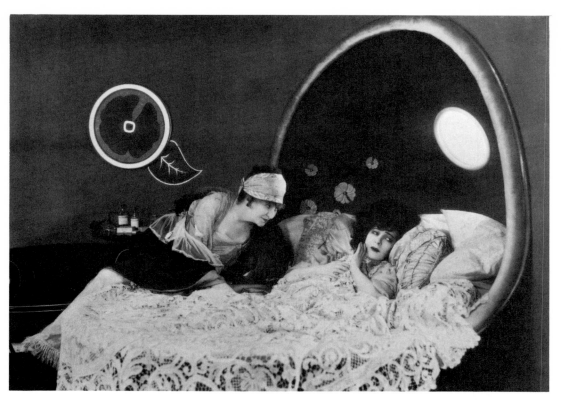

Alla Nazimova as, top, Camille (1921) and, bottom, Salome (1922). Sets designed by Natacha Rambova.

54

Top: *A set still from* Enchantment *(1921). Sets by Joseph Urban. A Cosmopolitan (Hearst) production, released by Paramount, starring Marion Davies. The earliest known use of a modern setting in an American film.*

Bottom: *The first of the three versions of* The Great Gatsby *(Paramount, 1926), with Lois Wilson (Daisy) and Warner Baxter (Gatsby). Directed by Herbert Brenon.*

Left: *Unidentified damned extra in Dante's Inferno (Fox, 1924). Directed by Henry Otto. The film bears no art director's credit, but the Inferno sequence is based on the Doré illustrations.*

Right: *Ramon Novarro up to his knees in a Paris sewer designed by Ben Carré, in The Red Lily (MGM, 1924). Onlookers are cameraman Vincent Milner and the perturbed director with megaphone, Fred Niblo. The lily sought by Novarro is Enid Bennett (offscreen), in real life Mrs. Niblo.*

projected twenty reels. The film was produced by Joseph P. Kennedy, father of the future president, for his friend and favorite movie star, Gloria Swanson. Stroheim was fired in mid-production; the alleged reason, which convinced no one, was the advent of sound. The film could have been synchronized. The real reason was that Kennedy had been advised by friends that as an eminent Catholic he would do well to shelve this film about a runaway nun. Miss Swanson later saw to it that the footage shot by Stroheim was jumbled together and released with a new ending which Stroheim had no hand in filming.

As directors became dethroned, the era of producers and businessmen began. Because the industrial methods introduced by the big Hollywood studios were incompatible with aesthetic experiment, American designers, unlike their European counterparts, showed little influence from the theater or painting. Film decor began to evolve mainly in the direction of a rather impersonal technical perfection.

As a result of the specialized division of labor imposed by Hollywood studios, designers often assumed responsibility for more and more of a film. A supervising art director such as Cedric Gibbons at MGM might finally control nearly all the visual aspects, while the director remained in complete charge of the actors. The American

The enormous castle, perhaps the largest set ever constructed in Hollywood, designed by the American movie industry's first veritable art director, Wilfred Buckland, for Douglas Fairbanks's Robin Hood (Fairbanks/United Artists, 1922). Directed by Allan Dwan.

cinema's first real art director joined the industry in 1914 when the great theatrical designer, Wilfred Buckland, was signed by Famous Players–Lasky. Buckland's masterpiece is the enormous castle designed for Douglas Fairbanks in *Robin Hood* (1922). Subsequently, the importance assumed by set design and the prestige enjoyed by art directors must be attributed to the efforts and abilities of three men: Cedric Gibbons, Richard Day, and Hans Dreier.

Despite the extreme degree of mass production current in Hollywood, Cedric Gibbons succeeded in imposing his personal style on the sets for most of the films produced by MGM, where he was supervising art director for over thirty years. Finesse and impeccable execution, added to an imagination not without humor, created a certain similarity between the styles of Gibbons and the French designer Lazare Meerson. Both men were able to invent and to create entirely from imagination sets which nevertheless retained a perfectly authentic look.

Gibbons was with MGM from the formation of the studio in 1924 until his retirement in 1956. He designed the huge, complicated sets for Fred Niblo's *Ben Hur* (1925). For Ernst Lubitsch's *Merry Widow* (1934), Gibbons employed stylized, witty sets perfectly in harmony with the *boulevardier* spirit of the director. Although in

57

Five sets by Gibbons (MGM). "In the days of Cedric Gibbons, if Cedric Gibbons did a picture, it looked like the last picture Cedric Gibbons did. It didn't have its own meaning."—Richard Sylbert

Opposite, top: Our Blushing Brides (1930), directed by Harry Beaumont. "Up this ladder is a little treehouse where I go to be alone." Robert Montgomery, trying to seduce poor-but-pure Joan Crawford, who sells undies in his dad's department store. Up they go, into an art deco treehouse roughly twelve times the size of the Rainbow Room. Opposite, left: Joan Crawford doing a few steps in an art deco setting in Our Modern Maidens (1929), directed by Jack Conway. Opposite, right: Set still from Dynamite (1929), directed by Cecil B. De Mille; co-designed by Mitchell Leisen. Top: Set still for the lobby of Grand Hotel (1932), directed by Edmund Goulding. This is where Garbo wanted to be alone. Bottom: Set still for Born to Dance (1935), directed by Roy del Ruth.

59

Clarence Brown's *Anna Karenina* (1935) the sparkle of the chandeliers, the shimmer of the fabrics, and the gleam of the floors are somewhat exaggeratedly luxurious, Gibbons's sets for Sam Wood's *A Night at the Opera* (1935), designed in collaboration with Ben Carré, are completely effective. This Marx Brothers film takes place in the auditorium and backstage of an opera house. The sets, reproducing the grandeur and richness of the opera, look perfectly real, but everything is an ingenious fake: the curtains, flats, and stage lights soar off into the flies, collapse, and are ripped to shreds, the machinery of the theater with its below-stage and its winch system takes part in the chase sequence—and the effect is irresistible. *San Francisco* (1936) includes amazing earthquake scenes. The falling houses and the yawning chasms in the road that open up before our eyes are strikingly realistic; collaborating with Arnold Gillespie and James Basevi, experts in special effects, Gibbons adapted his style to the spirit of the film.

Richard Day worked with Erich von Stroheim on most of his films. Art director for Samuel Goldwyn during most of the thirties, he later worked for Twentieth Century–Fox and Warner Brothers. Day was perhaps the most eclectic Hollywood

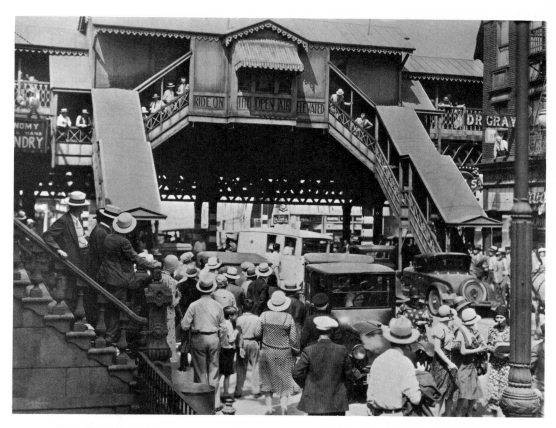

This page and opposite: *Three films designed by Richard Day; all produced by Samuel Goldwyn for United Artists release. Top: Street Scene (1931), directed by King Vidor. Bottom: Arrowsmith (1931), directed by John Ford. To maintain the illusion, a shot using painted perspective is generally very brief and without camera motion.* **Opposite:** *Dodsworth (1936). Directed by William Wyler.*

designer. Influenced heavily by Stroheim, he was one of the fiercest defenders of realism in the cinema. Except for George Marshall's *The Goldwyn Follies* (1938), a film marked by great scenic invention, Day used what might be called a documentary style for most of his films, including Raoul Walsh's *The Bowery* (1933), William Wyler's *Dodsworth* (1936), King Vidor's *Stella Dallas* (1937), Wyler's *Dead End* (1937), John Ford's *How Green Was My Valley* (1941) and *Tobacco Road* (1941), Anatole Litvak's *This Above All* (1942), and others. His best sets, in which he combines imagination, feeling, and realism, are his later ones: Elia Kazan's *A Streetcar Named Desire* (1951) and *On the Waterfront* (1954), where the sets look like extensions of the real locations.

Hans Dreier, art director at Paramount for thirty years, began his career as assistant designer at the German UFA studios in 1919; four years later he arrived in Hollywood. Although he could turn out sets in the standard Hollywood style, he was a truly inventive designer who added to them a fantasy, a mysterious, disquieting atmosphere rare among American designers of the period. He was also a top-notch organizer who produced an immense body of work by surrounding himself with the best co-workers.

After Ernst Lubitsch's *The Patriot* (1928), he worked on a masterpiece of atmosphere, Josef von Sternberg's *The Docks of New York* (1928), noticeably

Sketch by Hans Dreier for Raoul Walsh's East of Suez *(Paramount, 1925).*

influenced by the *Kammerspielfilm*. Similarly, a Germanic disquiet is evident in his remarkable sets for Mamoulian's *Dr. Jekyll and Mr. Hyde* (1931), especially in the café scene. By chance, his next film was a prototype of the "American comedy," Lubitsch's scintillating *Trouble in Paradise* (1932). The evocations of Venice, with the gondolier furthering the romance while collecting the morning trashcans along the Rialto (a set built in the studio), and the baroque theater with its vast and complicated corridors, are perfectly adapted to light comedy. The designs for Sternberg's *The Scarlet Empress* (1934) are also reminiscent of the baroque. This is a strange world not far removed from surrealism, peopled with Byzantine statues and paintings, which one enters through enormous doorways and takes by assault, riding upstairs on horseback. In collaboration with John Meehan, Dreier signed his name to an extraordinary evocation of the Hollywood of 1925, *Sunset Boulevard* (1950) by Billy Wilder, a film of savage humor about the life of a great ex-star. The sophisticated interiors of a luxurious old-fashioned villa on Sunset Boulevard are intentionally in atrocious taste, and the scenes on the film set are painted with a brush dipped in vitriol.

Left: *Marlene Dietrich as* The Scarlet Empress *(Paramount, 1934). Directed by Josef von Sternberg. Art director: Dreier—but the look of the film was dictated by Sternberg, who had the sets decorated with dozens of statues by Peter Ballbush and icons by Richard Kollorsz.*

Right: *Dreier, Paramount's supervising art director, shows Charlotte Henry (Alice) and director Norman Zenos McLeod a miniature house to be used in* Alice in Wonderland *(1933). Designed by William Cameron Menzies and Robert Odell.*

Ill at ease reconstructing biblical times or old Europe (which for many American filmmakers and filmgoers was resolutely medieval), American designers achieved near-perfection when it came to showing life in the United States in all its aspects. Another type of film enjoyed a renewed vogue, following the international success of John Ford's *Stagecoach* (1939): the western. The landscapes of the Far West vary little, and the plots obey the rules of the genre, like the sets, which attained a kind of perfection at the very beginning of the western. Wiard B. Ihnen's sets for *Stagecoach*, James Basevi's designs for Ford's *My Darling Clementine* (1946), *Fort Apache* (1948), and *She Wore a Yellow Ribbon* (1949), and Rudolph Sternad's for *High Noon* (1952) by Fred Zinnemann are typical examples.

Ford's *The Informer* (1935) took place in his native Ireland. For scenes in Dublin, Van Nest Polglase, one of the great Hollywood art directors, created sets steeped in darkness and mist. They skillfully drew attention to the only elements visible in this haze, drowned in shadow broken here and there by rays of light from the streetlamps. The following year Polglase designed Alfred Santell's *Winterset,* and later worked on

Left: Jerry Thompson, the reporter (William Alland, hatted), to Raymond, the butler (Paul Stewart): "And that's what you know about Rosebud?" Citizen Kane, produced, directed, co-scripted by Orson Welles (RKO, 1941). Art director: Perry Ferguson; supervising art director: Van Nest Polglase; set decorator: Darrell Silvera. Right: Kane (Welles, off-still) to Susan (Dorothy Comingore): "What are you doing?" Susan: "Jigsaw puzzles . . . makes a whole lot more sense than collecting statues. A person could go nuts in this dump. . . . Nobody to talk to, nobody to have any fun with. I want to go to New York. I wanta have fun. Please, Charlie . . . please."

Tim Holt, as George Amberson Minafer, on his way to get his "come-uppance" in The Magnificent Ambersons *(1942), directed and written by Welles. Art director: Mark-Lee Kirk; set decorator: Al Fields. It remains a great but mutilated film—43 minutes were cut by RKO.*

Orson Welles's *Citizen Kane* (1941) in collaboration with Perry Ferguson. The monumental rooms transformed by the collector Kane into a vast furniture warehouse, the newspaper city room, the opera house, and the halls used for election meetings are memorable. Gregg Toland's constant use of great depth of focus, low angle shots in ceilinged rooms, and the studied chiaroscuro lighting already reveal the influence of expressionism on Welles's style. This influence is just as evident in *The Magnificent Ambersons* (1942), and it strengthened as time passed.

The fine turn-of-the-century sets for *The Magnificent Ambersons* were designed by Mark-Lee Kirk. The great house, which we see first in all its splendor, then abandoned and dilapidated, becomes part of the drama, expressing the personality of the Ambersons. The photography was carefully planned for effect: the night scenes inside the house, even during the ball, are barely lit by gas lamps; a very fine staircase appears in either high angle or low angle shots. A carefully studied street set is seen only as a reflection in a shop window during a long traveling shot, the reflected images suggesting the beauty and richness of the town, the movement of the vehicles, and the animation of the street. This is great art.

The opulent interiors of the monied class appear again in William Wyler's *The Little Foxes* (1941). Stephen Goosson's sets and Gregg Toland's cinematography contribute to make this study of a greedy Southern family a magnificent work. Similarly *The Heiress* (1949), which Wyler made some years later, benefited from

Harry Horner's well-conceived sets, which harmonize perfectly with the characters' habits and way of life.

The monotonous, dreary existence of the middle class and the genteel poverty in big cities are dealt with by a new generation of American directors, who come from avant-garde theater, documentaries, and television. Their films are shot mainly out of doors, which makes the quality of their sets all the more evident: they re-create with an implacable realism interiors of unsuspected banality and ugliness unrelieved by the picturesque. Walter Holscher for Laszlo Benedek's *The Wild One* (1953), Malcolm Bert for Nicholas Ray's *Rebel Without a Cause* (1955), and Lyle Wheeler and Mark-Lee Kirk for Joshua Logan's *Bus Stop* (1956) displayed great talent in reconstructing all that is dreariest and most commonplace in American life.

Bottom: In Old Chicago *(20th Century–Fox, 1938). Directed by Henry King. Art directors: Rudolph Sternad and William Darling; special effects director (fire scenes): Bruce Humberstone.*

Opposite: *A sketch* (above) *for the wedding scene* (below) *in William Wyler's* Wuthering Heights. *Produced by Samuel Goldwyn (United Artists release, 1939). Art director: James Basevi. Merle Oberon as Cathy.*

Above: Victor Jory as Oberon in A Midsummer Night's Dream (Warner Bros., 1935). Directed by Max Reinhardt and William Dieterle. Art director: Grot; costumes by Max Ree.

Opposite:

Top: *Amazon waiting room from Ein Sommernachtstraum/A Midsummer Night's Dream (1925). Directed by Hans Neumann. Sets and costumes designed by Ernö Metzner.*

Left: *John Barrymore as Svengali (Warner Bros., 1931). Directed by Archie Mayo. Art director Anton Grot was nominated for an Oscar for this film.*

Right: *"Ah, but what is the sound of the organ compared to the music of Big Bertha." Alexander Kirkland to Leila Hyams in Surrender (Fox, 1931). Directed by William K. Howard. This little-known but fascinating World War I drama takes place in a prisoner-of-war camp designed by Grot.*

69

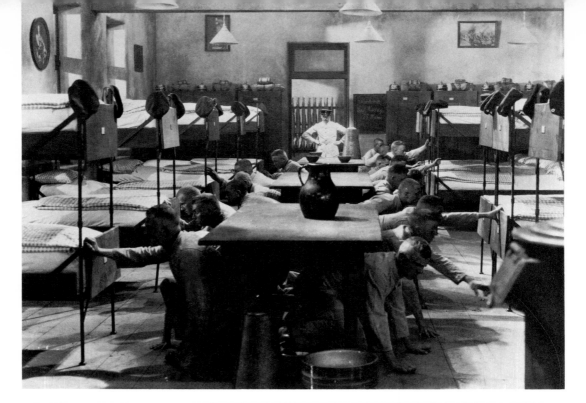

Top: All Quiet on the Western Front (Universal, 1930). Directed by Lewis Milestone. Art directors: William R. Schmidt and Charles D. Hall.

Bottom: James Whale's Show Boat (Universal, 1936) contained a production number by dance director LeRoy Prinz which traced the evolution of American dancing from African folk rhythms to jazz. It was apparently cut from release prints, and all that remains of it may be this still. The set by Charles D. Hall is reminiscent of his vast nightclub set for Paul Fejos's Broadway (1929).

Top: *Nils Asther, Barbara Stanwyck, Toshia Mori in Frank Capra's* The Bitter Tea of General Yen *(Columbia, 1933).*

Bottom: *Fred Astaire and Lucille Bremer in the "Limehouse Blues" number from Minnelli's* Ziegfeld Follies *(MGM, 1946). "We did the dream sequence with chinoiserie costumes designed by Irene Sharaff. The art department, in looking over her sketches, noticed the 18th-century chinoiserie artifacts which Irene had drawn in the background. Her suggestion was so right that it was adopted; thus Irene wound up doing the sets as well."—Minnelli,* I Remember It Well.

Above: Stan Laurel and Oliver Hardy in Brats (produced by Hal Roach for distribution through MGM, 1930). Directed by James Parrott. No art director credit available. Jean Harlow is in photo above fireplace. Oversize furniture to diminish actors was also used in The Incredible Shrinking Man, The Devil Doll, and Dr. Cyclops.

Opposite, top: Babes in Toyland (produced by Hal Roach for distribution through MGM, 1934), also starring Laurel and Hardy. Directed by Gus Meins and Carl Rogers. No art director credit available. Florence Roberts as the Widow Peep and Charlotte Henry as her daughter Little Bo.

Opposite, bottom: Twiggy and Christopher Gable in "A Room in Bloomsbury" in Ken Russell's The Boy Friend (MGM, 1971). Sets designed by Tony Walton. Art director: Simon Holland; set dresser: Ian Whittaker. "He [Russell] doesn't know anything about acting. . . . He spends hours on the background detail, on the sets and costumes, on how it's going to look, and you just get on with it."—Glenda Jackson, New York Times Magazine, Jan. 19, 1975.

73

It would be incorrect to attribute the new direction taken by French films solely to the advent of sound. The tendency toward some kind of realism, more or less transformed according to the character of the director, had been marked from 1926 on. Various influences merely accentuated the trend: the documentary, which took a new turn with the works of the avant-garde; Soviet films; and certain American films that attained a rare degree of violence with the works of Stroheim (*Greed*) and Sternberg (*Underworld*). The development was quite normal, conforming to a cycle common to all the arts: bursts of growth are followed by a return to greater simplicity of expression, and periods of cerebral stylization are followed by a return to realism and nature. Inevitably, set design had to follow this trend or become an element alien to the film. Where fantasy, ostentation, and a certain sense of composition had formerly been enough, other qualities and methods were now necessary.

During this transitional period Jean Renoir, son of the painter Auguste Renoir, abandoned avant-garde experiments to make *Nana* (1926) in the naturalistic style of Zola's novel. The influence of the impressionist painters (Manet, Monet, Renoir), who had left their mark on Zola's era, is evident in the photographic style, the sets, and particularly the remarkable costumes of Claude Autant-Lara (who subsequently abandoned set design for direction). Jean Grémillon made *Maldone* (1927) with modern

Scene using a glass shot from Jean Renoir's Nana (1926). Sets designed by Claude Autant-Lara. Everything above the stairs (except the central door) is not constructed set but an illusion created by the use of a painting on a sheet of glass, placed in front of the camera, which matches the real set. In a sense a glass shot is the opposite of a process shot, where the rear projection screen is behind the actors. The first known glass shot in a film was in Missions of California, made by Norman O. Dawn in 1907.

 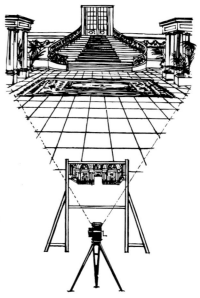

sets, strikingly sober for the period, by André Barsacq (a designer at the Atelier theater), who also designed the interiors for *Gardiens de Phare* (1929). Barsacq replaced Meerson as set designer for L'Herbier's *Money* (1928), before devoting himself primarily to the theater.

Carl Dreyer, a Danish director, made a masterpiece in France: *The Passion of Joan of Arc* (1928), a film in which emotions are expressed almost solely by faces photographed in magnified close-up. Fine sets by the expressionist designer Hermann Warm and Jean Hugo, a theatrical designer and scene painter, were constructed on an exterior lot in a suburb of Paris. The very stylized sets provided cameraman Rudolf Maté with white walls against which the characters and instruments of torture stood out. The influence of both *Kammerspielfilm* and Soviet cinema are evident.

But it was primarily Lazare Meerson who transformed French film design. Meerson began at the Albatross studios as a scene painter, then as assistant designer; but his stature was not evident until after his work with Jacques Feyder in *Gribiche* (1925) and René Clair in *La Proie du vent* (1926). It was no coincidence that Feyder and Clair, directors who had always fought the streak of aestheticism in French films, called in Meerson. The quality of his sets was constant; without attracting undue attention, they harmonized perfectly with the action, the atmosphere, and the very different styles of the two directors.

Jacques Feyder began as an actor in films by Méliès and Feuillade; in 1915 he became a director at Gaumont. He made his name with *L'Atlantide* (1921), when he took the unprecedented step of transporting the whole film crew to the Sahara, where he shot the exteriors, while painter Manuel Orazzi built the interior sets in a suburb of Algiers. The special effects in his next film, *Crainquebille* (1922), won critical acclaim, but the film is significant chiefly for its images of the people's Paris, images that move toward the poetic realism of the future French school of cinema. Feyder designed his own sets for *Crainquebille*.

Like Feyder's, René Clair's work stood slightly apart from the dominant trend in contemporary French production. Around 1922–23 he joined the avant-garde directors associated with L'Herbier and Epstein, but abstract or pure cinema did not interest him: he was the more or less conscious heir of the "primitives" of French cinema, from Lumière and Méliès to Feuillade and Linder. In 1924, he made *The Ghost of the Moulin Rouge*. Neither a horror film nor a fantastic film, it portrayed a facetious ghost whose humor foreshadowed Clair's *The Ghost Goes West*. The sets were by Robert Gys, one of several young designers who began film careers at this period. He also designed the sets for *The Imaginary Voyage* (1925), a film of pure enchantment that takes place in a dream parody of a fairy story.

Meerson became Clair's designer in 1926, for *La Proie du vent*. Although well made, the film was not a great success, because the theme did not suit the director. In 1927, Clair agreed to adapt for the screen, on behalf of the Albatros company, *An Italian Straw Hat;* it was his masterpiece of the silent screen. Transposed to the *fin-de-siècle*, Labiche's comedy became a precise, farcical ballet. Ironically but gently, it pokes fun at the petty bourgeoisie of the Belle Epoque, a theme common to several of Clair's films. The interiors were conceived by Meerson as a caricature of early Pathé

Annabella and René Lefèvre in René Clair's Le Million *(1931). Designed by Lazare Meerson.*

sets. The curtains, porcelain vases filled with plants, Oriental screens, and antiquated furniture are a perfect foil for the characters with their intentionally magnified features. By contrast the street, treated with a realism ahead of its time, possesses a poetic simplicity that foreshadows the great scenery of *Under the Roofs of Paris*.

After *Gribiche*, Meerson created for Feyder the sets for *Carmen* (1926). Constructed after numerous sketches made in Spain, they have an entirely new authenticity in the same style as the exteriors shot on location, like the fine bull fight. But Feyder was constantly changing genres, and Meerson next worked on his satirical *The New Gentlemen* (1929), for which he reconstructed in his own manner the Chamber of Deputies, a dancing class at the Opéra, and other scenes. This satire on parliamentary government provoked severe censorship, so Feyder accepted MGM's offer and left for Hollywood, to return four years later.

With the arrival of the talkies, Tobis–Klang–Film, the German holders of the only European sound system in competition with the American systems (Western Electric and RCA), moved into the old studios at Epinay-sur-Seine built by a German named Menchen in 1913. There Tobis produced the great films of Clair and Feyder, and there Meerson created the set for *Under the Roofs of Paris* (1930), a film that spread throughout the world the image of a good-natured people's Paris. It was a large set, at once realistic and poetic, representing a corner of an old district of Paris, with a vista of roofs, a belltower, small shops, and street singers.

In 1931, Clair made *Le Million*, adapted from a light comedy similar to *An Italian Straw Hat*, and, like the latter, it turned into a chase ballet: this time the hunt was for a winning lottery ticket left in an old jacket. There were some realistic sets like the opera house, some that were barely sketched in behind gauze hangings, and some comic evocations like the police station and the junk shop. Following its enormous success, Clair made *A Nous la liberté* (1931), which dealt satirically with the regimentation of workers in factories. Very astutely, Meerson set up the studio courtyard to look like an

76

ultra-modern factory floor. Unlike *Metropolis*, this was a prison factory, as spotless as factories in Switzerland—hence all the more sinister. For *Quatorze Juillet* (1932), once again the setting was Paris with its bistros, musicians' platforms, and lanterns in the popular dance halls. In 1934, Clair left Tobis to make *The Last Millionaire* at Pathé–Nathan, with its crazy baroque sets (parodying the pretentious style of a Balkan town casino) designed by Lucien Aguettand.

After Feyder returned from Hollywood, Meerson worked on the designs for his *Le grand Jeu* (1934) and *Pension Mimosas* (1935), one of Feyder's best films. The sets, depicting a family boardinghouse in Monte Carlo, are exemplary in their evocative power, simplicity, and subtlety of means employed. The coffee room, for instance, is suggested by its reflection in a mirror, seen from a telephone booth.

Earlier, Meerson had produced the sets for *Carnival in Flanders*, transforming the studio courtyard into a Flemish town traversed by a canal (built in cement). He traveled to Flanders and took notes that served to give a feeling of authenticity to the exterior and interior architecture of the houses, the furniture, and the accessories. To give the set greater depth, he used scale models for the long shots of roofs, gables, clocktowers, silhouetted houses. The farther from the camera these elements were, the more their scale was reduced, in order to create an illusion of a set extending indefinitely. Thanks to the sets, the film reflects both Flemish opulence and truculence.

A sketch by Meerson for Jacques Feyder's La Kermesse héroïque/Carnival in Flanders (1935).
Associate art directors: Alexandre Trauner and Georges Wakhévitch.

Such effectiveness and evocative power are characteristic of Meerson's sets, for the young designer brought to his work sure taste, great inventiveness, and a highly developed technique.

It is always interesting to examine the point of departure for a design—the first sketch or first rough draft. Meerson had the vision of a painter, an impressionist painter, one might say: his small sketches were painted very freely, in a range of soft, subtle colors, indicating merely volumes, principal lines, and atmosphere. From there he developed his sets little by little, with the aid of his assistants. Even during set construction he did not hesitate to modify certain proportions or details, making sketches on scraps of paper or cigarette packs while the work progressed. To Meerson set design was a continual act of creation that did not end until the shooting began: hence, no doubt, the sense of quivering life, the aerial quality of his designs, which seem never to be fixed, but to pulse with the same rhythm as their films.

Meerson studied set placement very carefully. The camera never focused on a blank wall, for whatever its position, he always arranged for something to be happening in the background of the set—a procedure which offered additional resources to the director. His meticulous execution and finely observed detail provided an absolutely new standard of authenticity and truth. The word "authenticity" is more applicable than "realism," for poetry is never absent from his sets. What is fresh is the search for accurate, telling detail, which he pursued across Paris, Spain, Algeria, or Flanders, camera at hand, and which he sought from the wealth of documentary material and books with which he surrounded himself.

All the procedures that had been routine among producers, technicians, and studio staff for thirty years were challenged by Meerson with a vehemence that became proverbial. He was the first to use, on a large scale, materials such as iron, glass, cement, and oil paint, a practice which seemed at the time truly revolutionary, if not scandalous. Exacting, even finicky, sparing neither his efforts nor his health, he died at the age of thirty-eight in London, after designing Clair's *Break the News* and Feyder's *Knight Without Armor*. His pervasive influence helped establish the new direction taken by set design in French cinema: his elders, his contemporaries, and a whole new generation of designers profited from his experience.

Despite their dissimilar temperaments and training, Jean Perrier and Lazare Meerson were working in the same direction. The outcome of the symbolist trend personified by Andrei Andrejew would be quite different. Andrejew, of Russian origin, worked in Germany until 1932. There he designed very personal, atmospheric sets for such films as Wiene's *Raskolnikoff*, Feyder's *Thérèse Raquin* (1928), Pabst's *Pandora's Box* (1928), and above all, the latter's *Threepenny Opera* (1931). For this film he turned for inspiration to Gustave Doré's London illustrations, and succeeded in creating an ambiance both fantastic and realistic. *Threepenny Opera* contains unforgettable images: the docks with their bricks glistening with damp, the port suggested by a forest of masts, and the smoky tavern with a staircase that spirals around enormous barrels of beer. The staircase leads to the entrance of the brothel, whose drawing room, with its heavy drapes and its circular divan surmounted by a winged cupid, is a masterpiece of simplicity and effectiveness.

Set sketch model by Jacques Krauss for Julien Duvivier's Pépé le Moko *(1937).*

This relative simplicity is one of the hallmarks of Andrejew's sets. He seeks the characteristic motif, the sign that will symbolize a given place, and stresses this motif by giving it unusual volume while treating the rest of the set very simply. In *Thérèse Raquin*, shot in Berlin, the dirty windows covering the passage turned it into a kind of unhealthy greenhouse whose obsessive presence symbolizes the petty bourgeois home. The Empress of Austria's study in Litvak's *Mayerling* (1936) consists of a desk, a tapestry serving as background, an imposing column suggesting the power of the Empire, and over the entrance door the characteristic detail: an enormous cartouche representing the two-headed Austrian eagle.

Andrejew moved to Paris in 1932 but divided his time among French, British, Czech, and Italian studios. His designs began to reflect tendencies already noted in Lochakov: a striving for a grandiose framework and a concentration of all effort on a general effect, the set as a totality. One may speculate whether this was due to the influence of German directors, to his Russian background, or to his own temperament. He pushed the grandiose to the point of the colossal, the cyclopean, and he progressively reduced his sets to a few essential elements which recur, barely altered, from one film to another.

Andrejew's sketches are very revealing of his style. They are treated in broad areas of charcoal or ink, shaded zones throwing the highlights into prominence. The essential elements are enlarged disproportionately, like the chimney stacks in *Threepenny Opera* or the colossal caryatids by the staircase in Ozep's sound version of *Tarakanova* (1938). Everything excessive and arbitrary in his style is clearly visible in this film, which is crushed by its sets: the columns, doorways, and staircases are so

Marcel Carné's Quai des brumes/Port of Shadows *(1938). Designed by Trauner.*

large the characters appear Lilliputian. In their reviews the critics denounced the preponderant role that designers' work seemed to be enjoying in films, and thereafter Andrejew toned down his sets slightly. Nevertheless, the symbolism remained; unlike Meerson, he rejected documentary references as a hindrance to creative freedom and to the expression of his personality, which was unquestionably very strong. This explains his influence on other designers, including Serge Pimenoff, Ferdinand Bellan (formerly his assistant), Roger Furse, and John Bryan.

Tobis was the first great production center to develop after the advent of sound, but others soon followed. In 1929, Bernard Nathan purchased and reorganized the Cinéroman Studios and then the Pathé company. Under the name of Pathé–Nathan, this would become the most important center of production in France. The circuit of Pathé theaters, distribution agencies, film labs, and supporting mercantile bank made it a veritable trust, in imitation of the great American companies.

Many of the films produced by Pathé–Nathan were designed by Lucien Aguettand, who began as a stage designer. Among his best designs were those for Julien Duvivier's *Poil de carotte* (1932), with its very realistic rustic interiors, and René Clair's *The Last Millionaire* (1934). For Litvak's war film *L'Equipage* (1935), Aguettand returned to realism, then gave in to his imagination and a kind of decorative exuberance for Maurice Tourneur's *Koenigsmark* (1935).

Architect Guy de Gastyne specialized in grand sets with flair and a rather official-looking richness. Royal reception rooms, with gleaming floors and gilded ceilings (shot from scale models), crystal chandeliers, and pompous furniture serve as a setting for Marc de Gastyne's *La Châtelaine du Liban* (1926), Tourneur's *Katia* (1936), and *The Imperial Tragedy* (1938) and *Entente Cordiale* (1939), two commercial films by Marcel L'Herbier. He also designed the sets for two very successful small-scale films dealing with private worlds: Christian-Jaque's *The Assassination of Santa Claus* (1941) and (with Christian Bérard) *Les Parents terribles* (1948) by Jean Cocteau.

80

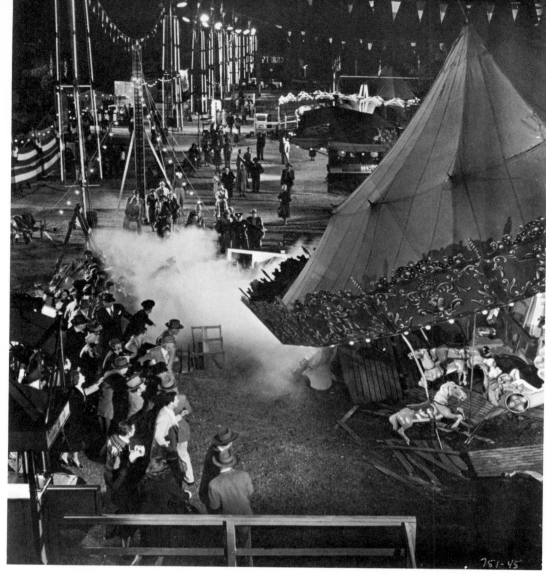

Alfred Hitchcock's Strangers on a Train *(Warner Bros., 1951). Art director: Ted Haworth; set decorator: George James Hopkins. "The big difficulty with that scene was that the screen had to be angled differently for each shot. We had to move the projector every time the angle changed because many of the shots of the merry-go-round were low camera setups. We spent a lot of time setting the screen in line with the camera lens. Anyway, for the carrousel breakdown we used a miniature blown up on a big screen and we put live people in front of the screen."—Hitchcock, in François Truffaut,* Hitchcock.

Jacques Krauss, trained as a painter, became Julien Duvivier's regular designer at Pathé–Nathan, notably on *La Bandera* (1935), *They Were Five* (1936), and *Pépé le Moko* (1937). These three films are perhaps the best by Duvivier, who, through the brutal realism of his style, was one of the main promoters of the renaissance of French cinema from 1934 to 1940. The sets for *Pépé le Moko*, representing the Casbah of Algiers, have an evocative power not possessed by exteriors shot on location. The governing idea of the film—the Casbah as a lair, a labyrinth, an impregnable fortress—is far better expressed by the sets, which do indeed give the impression of a closed world within a maze of precipitous alleyways and blank walls, than by a documentary view of the real Casbah, which disperses interest by its inherent picturesqueness. During the war, Krauss designed sets portraying the plush-lined ambiance of Claude Autant-Lara's *Mariage de chiffon* (1942) and *Douce* (1943). Without attempting to impose his personal style, he produced sets of great sensibility, perfectly adapted to the subjects of the films and powerfully evocative.

Two-man teams began to form. While Meerson was working with Clair and Feyder, his assistant Alexandre Trauner began a fruitful collaboration with Marcel Carné. The interior and exterior sets for *Bizarre, Bizarre* (1937), *Port of Shadows* (1938), and especially *Hôtel du Nord* (1938) and *Le Jour se lève* (1939) played a major part in the success of these films, whose poetical realism typified this period in French cinema and influenced many foreign filmmakers, especially the Italian neorealists.

Trauner's approach has points in common with Meerson's. Both men began by assembling complete documentation on the places to be depicted; Trauner, however, retained only those elements that affected him by their unusual aspects, thereby coming close to the surrealists. With this selection, aided by his own recollections, he composed very personal sets. He made use of trick perspectives and distortions in order to increase depth. His characteristic habit of setting parts of the scene in a "V" allowed him to show two divergent perspectives in the same image, giving the director an opportunity to move the characters in two directions. His sketches indicate only the essential, giving free play to the imagination, but despite the sets' very free interpretation of the real place or the documentary material which served as a point of departure, their careful execution down to the least detail gives them a realistic, authentic appearance. This transposition, this sublimation of reality, characterizes Trauner's best sets.

Jean Renoir was rather eclectic in his choice of designers, working with Erik Aaes, Autant-Lara, Gabriel Scognamillo, Hugues Laurent, Jean Castanier, Robert Gys, Georges Wakhévitch, and Léon Barsacq. In 1936, Renoir teamed up with Eugène Lourié, who began his career in the theater but turned to film in 1934 and quickly came to be considered one of the best French designers. His first designs were for Pierre Chenal's *Crime and Punishment* (1935), whose dramatic atmosphere owes much to the sets, and Marc Allegret's *Under Western Eyes* (1936). Then he joined Renoir for *The Lower Depths* (1936), which was only partly successful, because Renoir did not fully transpose Gorky's novel. The director mixed actors full of Parisian banter with others, real or supposed Russians, with white flowing beards; and the action, set in an undefined country, did not suit Renoir's realistic temperament. Lourié's sets, however, though neither Russian nor French, are nonetheless convincing, for they portray the miserable confines within which the film's heroes are struggling: since poverty is international, it was enough for Lourié to depict reality.

La Grande Illusion (1937), Renoir's masterpiece, and *La Bête humaine* (1938), freely adapted from Zola, are the works from this era of poetic realism that have remained freshest. The "real" characters, speaking a "real" language and having "real" feelings, owe nothing to fashionable populism or to the artifices of up-to-date filmmakers. Whether they depict the airmen's mess, POW camps, the office of the governor of the fortress, or the modest interiors of the engine driver's lodgings and the railroad workers' ball, Lourié's sets indicate only the essential. Reality has been captured so precisely that the whole film gives the impression of being shot on

82

Les Enfants du paradis (1945). Directed by Marcel Carné. Designed by Alexandre Trauner, Léon Barsacq, and Raymond Gabutti. Top: Sketch by Trauner. Bottom: The boulevard.

location: yet how simple the sets appear, how well they act as supernumeraries compared with the heaviness of the "natural" sets so often used today.

After the fine sets representing the interior of the château in *The Rules of the Game* (1939), Lourié joined Renoir in the United States during the war. This was the beginning of an American career perhaps unique among French designers, but the name of Eugène Lourié will remain forever linked with that of Jean Renoir.

Renoir was an improviser; too much preparation impeded him. Some of his best ideas came to him on the set: in *La Marseillaise* (1938), Léon Barsacq could never get his opinion of a set until the camera was in position. He was an anti-aesthete. (During the filming of *Paris Does Strange Things*, he exclaimed, for the edification of those present: "Good taste is shit! In France we're dying of good taste!") He fought the artistically blurred image, demanding lenses that gave a clearcut picture. He was also one of the first directors to place constructed sets (the shop front in *Boudu Saved from Drowning*, walls with a window in *La Marseillaise* and *La Bête humaine*) in front of real landscapes, using the animation of real streets, railroads, and other outdoor locations.

Jean Vigo, who was the hope of French cinema at the beginning of the talkies, made only two films after his social documentary *A propos de Nice* (1930). They were both masterpieces. *Zéro de conduite* (1933), which had its source in his childhood memories, was banned by the censor for twelve years (no doubt for fear that the revolt of boys in a boarding school would be catching). *L'Atalante* (1934), a film about the life of sailors, is a lyric account of sexual passion. Francis Jourdain designed the remarkable barge interior (Michel Simon's "den"), more surrealist than naturalistic. The locks, the canals, the dance halls on the banks of the Seine, the sidings and vacant lots in the industrial suburbs (landscapes that have since been worked to death) serve as a framework for a simple drama; they go beyond everyday reality to attain lyricism. This great director died at the age of twenty-nine, of blood poisoning.

At the beginning of his career, Jean Grémillon had difficulty reconciling his profound aspirations with the tastes of producers. He made his best films between 1940 and 1950: *Remorques* (*Stormy Waters*, 1941), with sets by Alexandre Trauner, including a remarkable wedding ball in a dance hall; and *Lumière d'été* (1943), a film with a strange atmosphere of contrasts. The exteriors shot at the enormous construction site of a dam are contrasted with the cozy sets of a strange mountain inn and the interiors of a château inhabited by a madman, all designed by Max Douy and Léon Barsacq in collaboration with Trauner. Some years later, Barsacq re-created a disturbing atmosphere for *Pattes blanches* (1948), set in a fishermen's bar and a Breton château of ascetic bareness.

Some important films were shot during the Occupation, despite difficulties of all kinds. *Les Visiteurs du soir* (*The Devil's Envoys*, 1942), by Marcel Carné, was a dramatic fairy tale set in the Middle Ages. The new, white castle caused some surprise, in spite of the logic that inspired its designers, Wakhévitch and Trauner.

After the success of this film, Jean Delannoy and Jean Cocteau made *The Eternal Return* (1943). The myth of Tristan and Isolde, transposed to an unspecified country, gained an enormous audience during the Occupation. Wakhévitch's rich and spacious

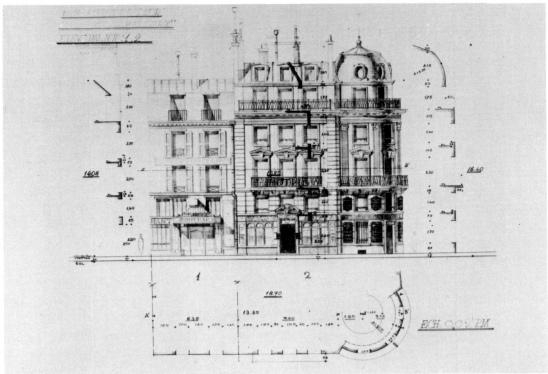

Top: *Set sketch model by Barsacq for Jean Renoir's* La Marseillaise *(1938).*

Bottom: *Set plan by Barsacq for René Clair's* Le Silence est d'or/Man-About-Town *(1947).*

sets played a large part in the film's visual success. Robert Bresson made his first full-length film, *Les Anges du péché* (1943), in which dramatic tension is accompanied by very spare images. The monastically simple sets are by René Renoux. Trauner worked with Barsacq on the sets for *Les Enfants du paradis* (1945), the most elaborate and masterful film produced by the team of Marcel Carné and Jacques Prévert. The film

85

deals with the Boulevard du Crime and its theaters, minor trades, and good-natured crowds; Debureau, Frédéric Lemaître, the snobs, and the cutthroats bring to life the images inspired by Daumier. A veritable treatise on style, the film is also the masterpiece of the stylistic trend that typifies the films of the Occupation.*

The Liberation was followed by the formation of new teams. Alexandre Trauner joined forces with Carné again, constructing for *The Doors of Night* (1946) sets that revealed the poetic urban gloom of proletarian Paris—the elevated Métro station of Barbès–Rochechouart, the Saint-Martin Canal, and so on. He also designed the very poetic sets for Carné's *Juliette or the Key of Dreams* (1950), an unsuccessful fantasy film.

From 1950 Trauner worked with American directors, usually in France. In Morocco and Italy he created broad, sweeping sets for Orson Welles's *Othello* (1952), followed by designs in an almost documentary style for Jules Dassin's *Du Rififi chez les hommes* (1954). He worked with Billy Wilder in Paris on *Love in the Afternoon* (1957), then in Hollywood on *The Apartment* (1960) and *Irma la Douce* (1963), with its amusing evocation of the Paris market district. He worked for Howard Hawks on *Land of the Pharaohs* (1955) in Egypt, and with Fred Zinnemann on *The Nun's Story* (1959) in Rome and the Congo. Back in Paris, Anatole Litvak chose Trauner for the sets of *Aimez-vous Brahms?* (1961) and *The Night of the Generals* (1967); lastly there was *La Puce à l'oreille* (1967), made for an American company by Jacques Charron with very successful Gay Nineties sets.

Eugène Lourié left for the United States in 1940 and joined Renoir, Duvivier, Clair, and others in Hollywood. There he remained to embark on a new career. He resumed his collaboration with Renoir, designing sets for *This Land Is Mine* (1943), *The Southerner* (1945), and *The Diary of a Chambermaid* (1946); he also worked with Duvivier on *The Imposter* (1944). All these films were made during the war. *The Southerner*, a realistic story of poor whites in the South, is the only one which escaped the Hollywood influence that sugar-coated the rest supposed to take place in France.

After the war Lourié worked with Robert Siodmak, Zoltan Korda, and Litvak, then accompanied Renoir to India to make *The River* (1951), a film in very fine color shot mostly out of doors. In 1952 he worked on Charlie Chaplin's *Limelight*, designing half-realistic, half-suggested sets very much in the Chaplinesque style. Turning to direction, he made (in eight days, with a modest budget) *The Beast from 20,000 Fathoms* (1953), a film whose financial success earned him the sobriquet "specialist in science fiction films based on prehistoric animals." He also directed *The Giant Behemoth* (1958) and, in London, *Gorgo* (1960). After a few television films, he returned to set design and worked on Sam Fuller's *Shock Corridor* (1963) and *The Naked Kiss* (1964). For *The Crack in the World* (1965) and *The Battle of the Bulge* (1965) he designed the sets and was responsible for the special effects—volcanic eruptions, storms, and battles.

During the war, Léon Barsacq worked with Carné, Jacques de Baroncelli, and Grémillon. In 1945 he did sets for Christian-Jaque's *Boule de suif* (1945) and Georges Lampin's *The Idiot* (1946), two period films, then those for Roger Leenhardt's *Les*

* Georges Sadoul, *Le Cinéma français (1890–1962)*, p. 95.

Martine Carol in Lola Montès *(1955). Directed by Max Ophüls. Designers: Jean d'Eaubonne and Willi Schatz.*

Dernières Vacances, a modern film ten years ahead of the New Wave. In 1947 he began a ten-year partnership with René Clair, starting with *Le Silence est d'or* (1947). This film evokes, with a hint of melancholy, the heroic days of the cinema and the Paris of the Belle Epoque.

The exteriors as well as interiors of all Clair's films were shot almost entirely in large sets built on the studio lot: *La Beauté du diable* (1949), an interpretation of *Faust; Belles de nuit* (1952, GB: *Night Beauties,* US: *Beauties of the Night*), a sort of philosophical story, a large part of which takes place in a dream, with "suggested" sets; and his first color film, *Summer Maneuvers* (1955). In his period films, Barsacq sought to sketch in the essential lines of a style, and his big exterior sets became a condensation or summary of reality without degenerating into gratuitous stylization. For him, the main aim of a set was to create the right atmosphere. His sketches, which are generally small, look like illustrations but still indicate the main lines of the set and the light effects calculated to create the desired ambiance. This search for the atmosphere peculiar to each film guided his conception of the sets for Giuseppe De Santis's *Rome Eleven O'Clock* (1952), Henri-Georges Clouzot's *Diabolique* (1955), Duvivier's *Pot Bouille* (1957), Louis Daquin's *Bel Ami* (1954), and Robert Hossein's *I Killed Rasputin* (1967).

Max Douy built sets of a very highly developed realism for Clouzot's *Quai des orfèvres* (*Jenny Lamour,* 1947) and *Manon* (1948). Then he teamed up with Autant-Lara. Some fifteen films, including *Le Diable au corps* (*Devil in the Flesh,* 1947), are the fruit of this long and close collaboration. The sets are precisely adapted to the style of the films: realism for *Le Diable au corps,* stylization for *The Red and the*

Black (1954), and decorative expressionism for *Marguerite de la nuit* (1955). Douy was also the designer for Renoir's *French Cancan* (1954) and Dassin's *Phaedra* (1961). The layout of his sets was a function of the way characters would move in them; the most precise instructions in the shooting script were followed to the letter during filming, thus saving a good deal of money.

The style of Douy's designs is stark realism, free from unnecessary detail; though he makes wide use of existing decorative elements—paneling, fireplaces, ornamented doors—he integrates these into his interiors and bestows on them a personal stamp.

Paul Bertrand, who had been Trauner's assistant, worked with Marc Allegret and Louis Daquin. He created sets of an almost literal realism that nevertheless possess great charm, as in René Clément's *Forbidden Games* (1952) and particularly *Gervaise* (1956), with its *fin-de-siècle* district in Paris, and *Plein Soleil* (1959), shot in Italy. Not without reason, he gave primary importance to the execution of his designs, to their "aging" and the patina of surfaces subject to the action of time.

Trauner, Barsacq, Douy, and Bertrand—despite their different styles—all continued the tradition of Lazare Meerson. The work of Jean d'Eaubonne is more sensitive to decorative arabesque. His designs for Max Ophüls—*La Ronde* (1950), *Le Plaisir* (1951), *Madame de* (1953), and *Lola Montès* (1955)—reveal an expressionist influence in very beautiful baroque images. D'Eaubonne also worked with Jacques Becker on *Casque d'or* (1952) and *Touchez pas au grisbi* (1953).

The affinities between directors and designers, which lay behind the formation of teams, were generally fruitful. Jacques Colombier teamed up with André Cayatte to create the sets for *Justice est faite* (1950) and *We Are All Murderers* (1952), which are authentic documents on the weakness of the French penal system. Robert Gys designed the sets for almost all of Christian-Jaque's films, including *Fanfan la Tulipe* (1952) and *Si tous les gars du monde* (1955). His spontaneous style owes much to improvisation.

The new generation of designers includes Maurice Colasson (formerly assistant to Wakhévitch), creator of atmospheric sets for Soldati's *Eugenia Grandet* (1946), and Yves Allegret's *Dédée* (1948) and *Une Si Jolie Petite Plage* (1949), with their black despairing realism.

Robert Clavel, formerly an assistant to Barsacq and Trauner, began his design career with Marcel Achard's *The Waltz of Paris* (1949), a film of great richness, and subsequently designed sets for some fifty films, including Daquin's *Master after God* (1950) and Duvivier's *The Man in the Raincoat* (1957). All these films show an accuracy of detail and restraint of design. With Buñuel's *Belle de Jour* (1967), he had an opportunity to design sets for a more ambitious work.

Jean André, who was Max Douy's assistant for a long time, designed the sets for Renoir's *Paris Does Strange Things* (1956). Roger Vadim's *And God Created Woman* (1956) began a fruitful collaboration that continued with *Sait-on jamais?* (1957), *Blood and Roses* (1960), *Nutty, Naughty Chateau* (1963), and finally *The Game Is Over* (1966). André also designed sets for Clouzot's *The Truth* (1960) and Rene Clément's *Les Félins* (GB: *The Love Cage*, US: *The House of Joy*, 1964). He succeeded in creating a series of very pleasant modern interiors by contrasting refined furniture and objects with the intentionally coarse surfaces of his sets. A very gifted painter and draftsman,

L'Année dernière à Marienbad/Last Year at Marienbad *(1961). Directed by Alain Resnais. Sets designed by Jacques Saulnier.*

André now seems to have abandoned the psychological truth of a set in favor of the subtle play of colors and combinations of volumes.

Jacques Saulnier and Bernard Evein, who both studied at the Institut des Hautes Etudes Cinématographiques (I.D.H.E.C.), worked together for two years on set designs for New Wave directors, including Louis Malle's *The Lovers* (1958), Claude Chabrol's *The Cousins* (1959), and Philippe de Broca's *The Games of Love* (1959). Then they parted. Saulnier, a designer of great talent, created sets based on his close observation of reality. In Alain Resnais's *Last Year at Marienbad* (1961), which takes place in a baroque palace, his sets are perfectly integrated with the real interiors shot on location. Saulnier constructed his best sets for Resnais's *Muriel* (1963), Clive Donner's *What's New, Pussycat?* (1965), and Malle's *The Thief* (1966).

In all his films the sets look very close to real interiors, but his methods are far from a servile imitation of reality. Saulnier frequently uses somber colors, which some cameramen had been reluctant to photograph because of lighting difficulties. His rooms, ingeniously adjusted in relation to one another, are of normal dimensions, but he always manages to give them an airiness by using openings and passages.

Bernard Evein, more of a painter than an architect, has a feeling for spectacle and poetry. His sets for Malle's *Zazie dans le Métro* (1960) and *Private Life* (1962), Agnes Varda's *Cléo from 5 to 7* (1961), and Jacques Demy's *Lola* (1961), *The Umbrellas of*

89

Cherbourg (1964) and *The Young Ladies of Rochefort* (1966), are closer to abstraction than reality. The poetical quality of his sets for Serge Bourguignon's *Sundays and Cybele* (1962), and the entrancing bright colors he used for Malle's *Viva Maria* (1965), which was especially well suited to his imaginative temperament, are definite successes.

Great Britain after 1930

British cinema is one of the earliest—Birt Acres filmed the Oxford and Cambridge Boat Race, the Derby, and the opening of the Kiel Canal in 1895 (the latter is said to be the very first newsreel of an important event). In 1904, the Will Barker Company produced its version of *Hamlet*, all of which was shot in one day, except for Ophelia's drowning scene. This extraordinary rapidity of production was possible because the sets for this *Hamlet*—there were more than twenty—were built one inside the other, like an onion skin. When one scene was shot, the set was torn down and shooting went on quickly inside the next layer.

Although British cinema showed early promise during and after World War I, the expansion of American cinema proved fatal to it. Not until the advent of sound and contributions by foreign filmmakers did British productions of quality appear. The first typically British film, *Cavalcade*, was shot in 1932 in Hollywood. According to Alistair Cooke, this film turned British film production "in the direction of 'fake antiques.'" Others would say that it gave it a sense of greatness.*

Alexander Korda, a Hungarian by birth, began the "series" with *The Private Life of Henry VIII* (1933). The remarkable sets for this film are the work of Vincent Korda, Alexander's brother and a former painter who began his film career as a set designer in Paris in *Marius* (1931). The immense success of *Henry VIII* inspired other films in the same vein: *Catherine the Great* (1934), *The Private Life of Don Juan* (1934), *Rembrandt* (1936), and so on.

Vincent Korda was involved in the making of all these films. Well known for his generosity, he helped a great many young men find their way as designers by taking them on as assistants. Highly cultured, gifted with imagination and a sense of humor, he succeeded in imprinting his style on the vast undertakings of his brother Alexander, who increasingly called in foreign directors. His sets for *Things to Come* (1936) directed by William Cameron Menzies, and for *The Ghost Goes West* by René Clair sparkle with malice. Michael Powell's *Thief of Bagdad* (1940), Ernst Lubitsch's *To Be or Not to Be* (1942) and Zoltan Korda's *The Jungle Book* (1942) are just a few examples of Korda's work. His position can be compared to that of only three or four great American designers, artistic directors for the major studios. With an admirable knowledge of the craft and a feeling for cinematic effect, he touched on all styles, welcoming all those qualities that might contribute to the success of his department. He saw big, he saw beautiful, and he constructed with prodigality, often introducing

* Lapierre, p. 566.

90

last-minute changes into his sets, to the despair of those working with him. His sets move from realism to stylization, according to the subject, but they are always effective.

A typically British film, *Pygmalion* (1938) directed by Anthony Asquith, enjoyed great success. The sets by Laurence Irving, one of the first designers in British cinema, portray well the comfort and finish of English domestic interiors. In the United States Irving worked with Menzies on *The Taming of the Shrew* (1929); he then returned to England where, confronted by the apathy and ignorance pervading British film studios, he preferred to devote himself to stage design. But he returned to the cinema in 1937, and worked on numerous films, especially those based on Shaw's plays. After the war he was employed by Arthur Rank to design the sets for C. F. Frank's rich-textured *Uncle Silas* (1947). Irving was one of the first British designers to conceive the sketches for his sets in terms of the characters as described in the scenario.

Alfred Hitchcock made *The Thirty-Nine Steps* (1935) in realistic sets perfectly adapted to the style of the film by Oscar Werndorff. The Master of Suspense had entered the British film industry more than a decade earlier in several capacities, including that of art director. *Woman to Woman* (1923), *The White Shadow* (1923), *The Passionate Adventure* (1924), *The Blackguard* (1925), and *The Prude's Fall* (1925) were all directed by Graham Cutts—and all were designed by a slim young man named Alfred Hitchcock.

The end of World War II saw the prodigious rise of a new magnate in the film industry, Arthur Rank, nicknamed King Arthur. With money from the flour trade, Rank monopolized sixty percent of the movie houses and half the studios in Britain. Founded in 1946, the Rank Organization competed with Hollywood for control of the film market. Rank-controlled companies had earlier made two ambitious films, Gabriel Pascal's *Caesar and Cleopatra* and Laurence Olivier's *Henry V* (1944), one of the most interesting post-war films. In order to illustrate this work while preserving its intentionally artificial appearance, designer Paul Sheriff, assisted by Carmen Dillon, employed false perspectives and the brilliant colors of the *Très riches heures du Duc de Berry*. It was a successful experiment in the use of procedures normally reserved for stage design: a background of painted canvas representing stylized landscapes, furniture and scenery constructed in false perspective, and so on. The exteriors were also treated to obtain the equivalent of landscapes as depicted by medieval illuminators.

David Lean's *Brief Encounter* (1945) was one of the most engaging British films of this period. The sets by L. P. Williams so authentically translate the ambiance of English middle-class life that some viewers believed the film had been shot in natural settings. In *Dead of Night* (1945), a film made up of separate sketches directed by Alberto Cavalcanti, Charles Crichton, Robert Hamer, and Basil Dearden, the feeling of terror radiating from the work as a whole is a tribute to Michael Relph's sets. Relph is a designer with a rich imagination and more importantly, a sense of effect. The collections of strange pieces of furniture and properties, as well as the set for the Italian room reflected in a ghostly mirror, are really haunting. Relph was also Cavalcanti's designer for *Champagne Charlie* (1944) and *Nicholas Nickleby* (1947).

Woman to Woman (1923). Directed by Graham Cutts. The art director was a young man named Alfred Hitchcock, who designed sets for four other Cutts films. On this film the art director married the script girl (she was also the editor), Alma Reville—Mrs. Hitchcock for many years now.

Apart from the documentary movement represented by the Scottish critic and essayist John Grierson and Alberto Cavalcanti, British cinema had no avant-garde or purely aesthetic movement. Without well-established national traditions in the area of film design, English designers were strongly influenced by foreign, notably German, work. Andrei Andrejew, for one, acquired disciples while working on several films in London; he designed the sets for Basil Dean's *Whom the Gods Love*, a film set in the eighteenth century—this and the nineteenth century were his favorite periods. He designed several of the best films made in Paris during the German occupation, such as Clouzot's *Le Corbeau (The Raven*, 1943); and after the war he returned to London, called by Korda to do the sets for Duvivier's *Anna Karenina*.

Andrejew's sketches were often "fair copied" by his long-time collaborator and assistant Ferdinand Bellan, who came to London with him in 1937. Hired by a British company, Bellan remained in England, where he had a distinguished career as a designer. A draftsman, painter, and designer gifted with extraordinary skill and a phenomenal visual memory, he made sketches for sets, furniture, and costumes, as well as frescoes, tapestries, and pictures, which he painted at an incredible speed, scarcely glancing at the reference, which his brain had registered instantaneously. He had started at UFA, where he worked for Lubitsch on *Anne Boleyn, Passion,* and other films. Influenced by Andrejew's style, he transmitted it to certain British designers.

" 'Why! This is a section of the Strand!' exclaimed Miriam Jordan, whose home is in London, when taken to the London 'set' for 'Cavalcade' [1933] on the Fox Films lot. In the background is a typical London building and at the left is an exact replica of a small London park. Natives of the British Empire and world travelers are amazed at the fidelity with which William Darling, art director of Fox Films studios, reproduced London street scenes. Even the lamp posts are authentic."—caption on original photo release.

In Carol Reed's *Odd Man Out* (1947), the sets by Roger Furse and Ralph Brinton are close to the fantastic world of E. T. A. Hoffmann and give a strange and romantic vision of an Irish town during the Troubles. The two designers complement one another. Furse, the more imaginative, was initially a stage designer, especially for the Old Vic where he was associated with excellent productions of Shakespeare. Brinton, trained as an architect, introduces into the sets a realistic note that corrects what may be called the scenic element in Furse's designs.

Furse later designed the sets for Olivier's *Hamlet* (1948), for which the director abandoned the brilliant colors of his *Henry V* in favor of an etched effect. The sets by Furse and his assistant Carmen Dillon are very bare, even geometrical. The mists of Elsinore and the very studied lighting are somewhat reminiscent of some of Lang's expressionist films. In *Richard III* (1956), also directed by Olivier, Furse carried the tendencies of his *Hamlet* designs a step further, giving his sets an intentionally theatrical flavor.

Another gifted designer strongly influenced by Andrejew was John Bryan. Like most British designers, he started in the theater, where he met Laurence Irving who influenced his film career. After the war, he was entrusted with the sets for *Caesar and Cleopatra* (1945), under the direction of Oliver Messel, a former costume and set designer for revues and ballets. Messel's typically British background, with no training in architecture or illustration, helps explain the specific character of British film designs: they are interesting formal experiments but often lack authenticity or veracity, which can detract from the atmosphere. This is evident in the rather impersonal sets for *Caesar and Cleopatra*, which Messel created in an elegant, slender Pompeiian style.

In designing the sets for David Lean's *Great Expectations* (1946) and *Oliver Twist* (1948), Bryan was inspired less by English illustrators of Dickens than by Gustave Doré's *London*. Bryan's drawings were full of life; his way of distributing and accentuating light and shade and his exaggerated perspectives manifested his disdain for convention. Bryan died in 1969, but the films preserve the atmosphere of his sketches, thanks to close collaboration with the director and the director of photography, Guy Green. This experiment was most important for British cinema.

The German designer Alfred Junge did more for the reputation of British set design than any Englishman. He began his career in his native land, and in 1932 moved to London, where he worked on Victor Saville's *The Iron Duke* (1935); King Vidor's *The Citadel* (1938); Sam Wood's *Goodbye, Mr. Chips* (1939); Hitchcock's *Young and Innocent* (1937); and several films co-directed by Michael Powell and Emeric Pressburger, among them *A Matter of Life and Death* (US: *Stairway to Heaven*, 1946), and *Black Narcissus* (1947). A skillful draftsman gifted with a rich

Two films co-produced, -directed, and -written by Michael Powell and Emeric Pressburger. Production designer for both: Alfred Junge. Bottom: David Niven, Kim Hunter, and Raymond Massey in A Matter of Life and Death/Stairway to Heaven *(1946). Opposite: Sabu and Jean Simmons in* Black Narcissus *(1947), a superb job of art direction in Technicolor.*

imagination—his power of creation and suggestion is exceptional—Junge succeeds with great economy of means, using a few admirably chosen details to create widely varied environments. In *A Matter of Life and Death* a great part of the action takes place beyond the grave; *The Iron Duke* is a period film about the Duke of Wellington; and the exotic exteriors of *Black Narcissus*, all created in the studio, are incredibly realistic.

Hein Heckroth, also German, had been a designer for the Kurt Jooss ballet company and one of the defenders of the movement, led by Gordon Craig and Adolphe Appia, against realism in the theater. He began his career in British cinema by designing the costumes for *Caesar and Cleopatra, A Matter of Life and Death,* and *Black Narcissus.* Michael Powell then commissioned him to design the sets and costumes for the color ballet film, *The Red Shoes* (1948), for which he produced advanced designs that were revolutionary at the time. He designed the sets for several other Powell and Pressburger films, including *The Elusive Pimpernel* (1950), *The Tales of Hoffmann* (1951), and *Oh, Rosalinda!!* (1955). Heckroth, who died in 1970, was always experimenting, trying out different styles, and fighting conventional realism.

Edward Carrick, the son of Gordon Craig, began as a skillful designer of sets and costumes for the theater.He worked on many films for Dean and Douglas Fairbanks, Jr., and produced very clever sets for Frank Launder's *Captain Boycott* (1947) and Terence Young's *The Red Beret* (1953). Britain owes to Carrick the establishment in 1938 of the A. A. T. Film School (the country's first school devoted to the art of film). He has written several books on film design.

Powell and Pressburger's The Red Shoes, *with Moira Shearer (1948). Production designer: Hein Heckroth. High kitsch on points—the film that shooed a whole generation of young women to ballet class.*

Carmen Dillon, who had assisted Sheriff and Furse, enjoyed great success with her sets for Asquith's *The Importance of Being Earnest* (1952) and later for Joseph Losey's *Accident* (1967) and *The Go-Between* (1971). Her designs for George Cukor's *Love Among the Ruins* (1975), with Laurence Olivier and Katherine Hepburn, rank among the very best ever created for a television production.

In the 1950's British cinema achieved a deserved success with films based on British humor. Though they shared in the general gaiety of the films, the sets were resolutely realistic. A new generation of designers, whose training was cinematic rather than theatrical, now worked in the London studios. Roy Oxley designed Henry Cornelius's *Passport to Pimlico* (1949), producing sets in a documentary style suited to this satire. William Kellner introduced into his English interiors comical details that add to the macabre humor of Robert Hamer's *Kind Hearts and Coronets* (1949), a masterpiece of the genre. Finally, Jim Morahan, one of the most gifted of the younger English designers, teamed up with Alexander Mackendrick on *Whisky Galore* (US: *Tight Little Island*, 1949), *The Man in the White Suit* (1951), and the side-splitting *The Ladykillers* (1955), passing with elegance from a documentary style to an almost abstract bareness.

But this vein was soon exhausted, and the collapse of the Rank Organization along with the catastrophic drop in attendance at movie houses forced young English

96

filmmakers to look for a new style. After experimenting with Free Cinema they turned against the current, adapting the successes of cinéma-vérité to films in a strange, personal style. *A Taste of Honey* (1961) and *The Loneliness of the Long Distance Runner* (1962) were shot by Tony Richardson in natural settings; for Richardson's *Tom Jones* (1963), Ralph Brinton designed rich, carefree, and attractively colored sets. Clive Donner made *What's New, Pussycat?* (1965) in France, with fine, highly effective sets by Saulnier.

David Lean shared in the prestige of British films of the day with such international successes as *The Bridge on the River Kwai* (1957), *Lawrence of Arabia* (1962), whose many Oscars included one for John Box's sets, and *Dr. Zhivago* (1965), shot largely in Spain among reconstructions of pre- and post-Revolutionary Russian streets and interiors. John Box admirably fulfilled the task demanded of him in *Dr. Zhivago*: the interiors, joined directly to the exteriors, give to their scenes a breadth and verisimilitude rarely attained in this type of reconstruction. A plentiful supply of references supports the designer's talent, and though basically a colorist, he catches the atmosphere of an expensive apartment just as successfully as that of a cattle truck used to transport a crowd of wretched, starving people. The set for the main street is less convincing, because of its color and a certain dryness in the treatment.

Some talented foreign directors worked in England during the sixties. If the beautiful palace interiors by John Box and Terry Marsh for Zinnemann's *A Man for All Seasons* (1966) are sometimes a little solemn, Antonioni's *Blow-Up* (1966) sparkles like a symphony of colors in the "arranged" natural settings by Assheton Gorton.

The USSR after Sound

With the arrival of the talkies, Soviet films took a new direction, perhaps to make them more accessible to the masses and to the many cultural groups in the USSR. Purely formal experimentation was abandoned in favor of realism, a greater concern for psychological truth, and simplicity of plot. Important parts were entrusted to great actors, and filmmakers made more and more use of studio resources, but nature—location shooting in the countryside—remained a constant theme in Soviet cinema. Above all, with the advent of sound, Russian technicians really learned to make use of constructed sets and artificial lighting. And once films were made with substantial constructed sets, Soviet designers were able to contribute to their success.

In his very first films, Pudovkin used sets by Sergei Kozlovsky, one of the first Soviet designers. Kozlovsky began working in films in 1913 as designer, actor, and even director, as the need arose. He made a significant contribution to Protazanov's *Aelita* (1924), which showed a Soviet landing on Mars, with unusual constructivist sets. He then worked on Pudovkin's *Mother* (1926), *The End of St. Petersburg* (1927), and *Storm over Asia* (1928), all using very simple sets. He also designed the interiors and arranged the exteriors of *Outskirts* (1933), a film of rare tenderness and charm by

Above: Aelita (1924). Directed by Yakov Protazanov; based on Alexei Tolstoy's novel. Sets designed by Sergei Kozlovsky, Isaac Rabinovich, and Victor Simov. Costumes: Alexandra Exter (1882–1949). Opposite: Martian Beautiful People in Aelita. The film was a great success in the Soviet Union; many babies born there in 1924 were named Aelita.

Boris Barnett that takes place in a small provincial town before the Revolution. His sets for other films that are little known outside the Soviet Union are simple and incisively drawn. Kozlovsky transmitted to films the tradition of Russian fin-de-siècle painting, an anecdotal genre in a charmingly realistic style.

Another early film designer was Vladimir Egorov. While still at the Moscow Art Theater, he attracted critical attention with his scenery for Maeterlinck's Bluebird. He began working for the cinema in 1915; and in one of his first films, Meyerhold's The Portrait of Dorian Gray, his conception of set design is already evident: everything is organized around one characteristic element, one disproportionately enlarged detail which becomes the center of the composition and the center of the action.

In 1920 Egorov abandoned the theater and devoted himself entirely to film design, working notably with Protazanov and Pudovkin. A skilled illustrator, he used the expressionist aesthetic to create the atmosphere of his period films. In Pudovkin's *Admiral Nakhimov* (1947), he combined a striving for historical truth with continual visual inventiveness. Sets like the naval shipyard or Nakhimov's death chamber admirably express the film's theme, and the reconstructions of big sailing ships and the naval battle filmed with scale models are in no way inferior to the best American productions in the genre. *Admiral Nakhimov* advanced markedly from Egorov's earlier films, Petrov's *Kutuzov* (1944) and Pudovkin's *Suvorov* (1941). In these films the symbolism of the exaggeratedly enlarged details is over-insistent: for example, Napoleon before the countless domes of the Church of the Twelve Apostles in *Kutuzov;* or the throne room of Paul I in *Suvorov* with the drapery of the throne, in the center of the set, bearing a huge cross of the Knights of Malta.

Yevgeni Enei, who began working in the cinema in 1923, is one of the best Soviet designers of that generation. He worked with directors Kozintsev and Leonid Trauberg and cameraman Moskvin. His sets for *The Overcoat* (1926), adapted from Gogol's novella by Grigori Kozintsev and Trauberg, emphasize the drama of the story. For the same directors' *The New Babylon* (1929), about the struggles of Paris workers, he drew inspiration from the impressionist painters. The team's best films are *The Youth of Maxim* (1935) and *The Return of Maxim* (1937), whose typically Russian sets are astonishingly realistic. In 1957 Kozintsev shot the exteriors of *Don Quixote* in the desert regions of the Crimea; Enei's sets have the beauty of the backgrounds in paintings by Zurbarán and Velásquez. For *Hamlet* (1964), also directed by Kozintsev, Enei successfully conveyed the sinister atmosphere of the prison state.

The designer for Petrov's *The Storm* (1934), Zarkhi and Heifitz's *Baltic Deputy* (1937), and Ermler's *The Great Citizen* (1937) was Nikolai Suvorov. Suvorov uses his talent to bring out the meaning, the expression of an era—the signs of the past—by relatively simple means. He is also primarily an illustrator, gifted with a great sense of ellipsis. The breadth and simplicity of his designs and his sense of proportion make him one of the best set designers in Soviet cinema.

Isaac Shpinel, a gifted painter, used his talent in the remarkable sets for *The Great Warrier Skanderberg* (1954), a color film directed by Yutkevich. Before that he designed *Alexander Nevsky* (1938) for Eisenstein, and influenced by this director he imparted a symbolic value to his sets. This tendency was further accentuated in *Ivan the Terrible, Part 1* (1944), becoming a kind of expressionism of great visual beauty.

Alexander Utkin is more of a decorator than an illustrator. His designs are far more elaborate, because instead of seeking out the typical detail he relies upon the accumulation of decorative elements to evoke a given place. He is a perfect technician, and his sets for Alexandrov's *Glinka* (1952) show what can be achieved in a color film by close collaboration among director, designer, and cameraman. The exteriors, re-created by Utkin from models and touched-up negatives of real landscapes, seem "painted" by the cameraman, Edward Tisse.

The next generation, trained at the State Institute of Cinematography in Moscow, further demonstrated the innate taste of Russian designers for illustration, to the point of seeming to sacrifice experimentation with sets in order to emphasize merely story values. This approach may be compared to the American system, in which illustrators are employed to draw all the images of the film, frame after frame, take after take (often in the style of a cartoon strip). In fact, Soviet designers seem to have been instructed to work out the visual style of the film, for their sketches indicate camera angles and movements and any unusual centering of the frame, as well as the movements of crowds, the outlines of actors, and the main lines of the landscape. Possibly these practices may be explained by a greater degree of specialization, for it must not be forgotten that many of the previous generation of directors had been trained as painters or designers, which is perhaps no longer so.

Mikhail Bogdanov and Gennady Myasnikov, the designers of the first great Soviet color film, Alexander Ptushko's *Stone Flower* (1946), refined their palette when they came to work for Alexander Dovzhenko on *Michurin* (1948) and with Sergei Vasiliev on *The Heroes of Shipka* (1955). Alexis Parkhomenko, with his sets for Yuli Raizman's *The Cavalier with the Golden Star* (1951), and Volin and Savostin with those for Josif Heifitz's *The Big Family* (1954), reconstructed with honesty real interiors in a humble milieu, giving the films documentary value concerning life in the USSR.

Between 1944 and 1950, the Soviet Union produced a series of films about the war. These reconstructed documentaries included vast crowd scenes: Donskoi's *The Rainbow* (1944), Petrov's *Battle of Stalingrad* (1949), and Chiaoureli's *Fall of Berlin* (1949), with its extraordinary reconstruction of the Reichstag in flames, taken by storm. The enormous set was constructed in the ruins of the Soviet sector of Berlin by Vladimir Kaplunovsky and Parkhomenko.

In the next decade a new trend emerged: war films about characters whose feelings were more true to life and less systematically heroic. *The Cranes Are Flying* (1957), by the veteran Mikhail Kalatazov, enjoyed well-deserved success throughout the world. Its designer, Y. Svidetelyev, made over a hundred sketch illustrations, "research drawings" as he called them, adding, "In drawing a landscape, in planning an expressive interior, I always try to find the outstanding details, the characteristic 'signs' of the period." The same striving for atmosphere, for the distinctive sign, guided Boris Nemechyok in his sketches for Grigori Chukhrai's *Ballad of a Soldier* (1959) and Ippolyt Novoderezhkin in Sergei Bondarchuk's *Destiny of a Man* (1959).

Adaptations of novels and plays reappeared, including Sergei Yutkevich's *Othello* (1955), with sets by Valery Dorrer, and Ivan Pyriev's *The Idiot* (1958), filmed with Wolkoff's very expressive sets in rich but muted colors. Two films adapted from stories by Chekhov—Samson Samsonov's *The Gadfly* (1955) and Heifitz's *The Lady with the Little Dog* (1960)—belong to a more intimist genre. The sets and costumes for these films are masterpieces of taste, sensitivity, and creativity. Those for *The Gadfly* are by L. Chibisov, and those for *The Lady with the Little Dog* by B. Manevich and I. Kaplan.

Numerous Soviet designers possess real talent for illustration—Semion Uchakov, Abram Freidin, Alexandroskaya, and others. The title of artist—painter—scenographer* used in the USSR suits them much better than architect—designer. The same phenomenon of specialization occurred in the USSR as in the United States: set designers (or artist—painter—scenographers) are essentially concerned with working out a film's visual style, illustrating a scenario; their sketches are studied by the Office of Architect—Constructors, whose members are responsible for drawing the plans and supervising the set construction.

* Costume designers and makeup artists have similar titles: artist—painter for costumes and artist—painter for makeup.

6 Post-War Trends

Italy and the Influence of Neorealism

The neorealist movement—the term was first used in 1943 by writer and theorist Umberto Barbaro—is a realistic trend that sprang from the opposition of many young Italian filmmakers to Fascist propaganda films on the one hand, and to the romantic, bourgeois, formalist cinema of the years 1940–44, on the other. The most gifted representatives of these genres, who reappeared a few years later as neorealist directors, were pejoratively referred to as calligraphers—a term by which Italian Marxist critics meant the ultimate sin: formalism.

Gastone Medin was the favorite designer of the calligraphers. A skilled technician with imagination and a certain "scenic" sense, he attempted to lend credibility to sets within which conventional stories took place. He did not always succeed. In order to create a precious, elegant background, he made excessive use of alabaster colonnettes and candelabra, fake marble, drapes, and festoons, thoroughly in keeping with the spirit of these films—"drawing brilliant arabesques in the void." After Mario Camerini's *Men Are Such Rascals* (1932), a pleasant comedy that enjoyed some success, he designed the sets for *A Romantic Adventure* (1940), a charming trifle also directed by Camerini, then those for *Little Old-fashioned World* (1941) by Mario Soldati, a brilliant writer and scenarist who was making his first appearance as a director with the help of Alberto Lattuada. This time the sobriety of the sets and the simplicity and truthfulness of the landscape corresponded to a certain humanity in the characters.

Renato Castellani adapted *Un Colpo di Pistola* (1941) from Pushkin. Medin's sets for this cold, pretentious film are no more than stereotypes of aristocratic Russian interiors, of which he has merely captured the surface appearance without expressing the spirit. In 1943, Castellani made *Zazà*, a French comedy of the Belle Epoque. In order not to disappoint the director, who wanted to make a film full of frou-frou, Medin overloaded his sets with nineties lace curtains, fringes, and arabesques.

The first film considered neorealist in both spirit and form was Luchino Visconti's *Ossessione* (1942). Visconti, a former stage designer, entered the cinema as assistant to

Top: *Arabesques of decor and directorial style, a high point in the "calligraphic" period of Italian cinema, in* Un Colpo di Pistola/A Pistol Shot *(1941), adapted from Pushkin. Directed by Renato Castellani. Art directors: Gastone Medin and Nicolà Benois.*

Bottom: *Roger Pigaut and Madeleine Robinson in* Douce *(1943), one of the finest films made in France during the Occupation. Directed by Claude Autant-Lara. Sets designed by Jacques Krauss.*

Clara Calamai faced with some very neorealistic dirty dishes in Luchino Visconti's first and best film, Ossessione *(1942).*

Jean Renoir. Influenced by French poetic realism and the American *film noir*, he seems to have taken his story from James Cain's novel *The Postman Always Rings Twice*, changing the locale from southern California to northern Italy.

If the spirit of revolt against government-sponsored cinema and official criticism existed from 1942 on, it was the post-war era that let loose a veritable revolution in Italian cinema. The reasons were chiefly material—studios abandoned or serving as camps for displaced persons, the complete disorganization of the film industry, and the dispersal of production teams—but the desire of young filmmakers to show Italy in transition was an almost equal determinant. The new school that the critics named "neorealist" availed itself of the only means at hand. Enthusiastic film crews, shrinking from no difficulty, produced films shot almost entirely out of doors or in real interiors, at very low cost. The great difficulties in production often resulted in technical flaws; but these films surprised audiences by their freshness, violence, and freedom of treatment.

Roberto Rossellini's *Open City* (1945) and *Paisa* (1946) and Vittorio De Sica's *Sciuscia* (1946) were the first films to bring the young Italian cinema to the notice of the public. Most of the scenes were shot in the ruins of Naples or Florence, in the streets of Rome, or in convents or barracks. Almost nothing was filmed in the studio, and the camera style approached that of newsreels. For reasons of economy these films were shot without sound. Sounds and words were added later (synchronized), often by professional actors who specialized in dubbing. The use of amateur actors in most of the parts became an added asset: the unknown faces conferred upon the first neorealist works an authenticity comparable to that of the Soviet cinema in its early days.

Aldo Vergano's *Il Sole Sorge Ancora* (*Outcry*, 1946) is a document about the social structure of occupied Italy. The sets for the interior of the castle, the main scene of the story, are by Fausto Galli; they have the same realistic tone as the exteriors of the Lombard countryside. Luigi Zampa's *To Live in Peace* (1946) is an example of comedy born of war. These films, like the first works of Rossellini and De Sica, retrace the incidents of the Resistance and the Liberation. Alberto Lattuada's *The Bandit* (1946) is a political melodrama, like his *The Mill on the Po* (1948). This direction henceforth dominated neorealism, beginning with Giuseppe De Santis's *Tragic Hunt* (1947), whose peasant interiors were very convincing sets by Carlo Egidi. Two major successes of the new school were made in 1948, De Santis's *Bitter Rice* and Visconti's *La Terra Trema*. Visconti made his film in a village of Sicilian fishermen, and subtle visual effects give this work a very special, poetical tone. That same year, De Sica gave Italian cinema a new masterpiece based on a theme by Cesare Zavattini, the scenarist for most of the great neorealist films: *The Bicycle Thief*. All these films from 1946 to 1948, with a few exceptions, were shot on natural locations, and did not use studio sets. However, for *Germany Year Zero* (1948), a large part of which was filmed in the ruins of Berlin, Rossellini used realistic studio sets.

The films of the young Italian school met with success in every country except Italy, where audiences hungered for spectacular films removed from everyday life. A certain nostalgia for comic films, for *bel canto*, and even for period films with huge casts was clearly observable. Audiences preferred Giuseppe Scotese's *Apocalypse* (1946) and Soldati's *Eugenia Grandet* (1946), which were shot in constructed sets. Operas filmed by the veteran Carmine Gallone, who began working in the cinema in 1913, also flourished in the forties. The designer for *La Traviata*, *Il Trovatore*, *Tosca*, and *La Bohème* was once again the prolific Medin. His sets are always quite abstract, and not until his collaboration with De Sica on *The Gold of Naples* (1954) and *The Roof* (1956), films in a realistic mode, does he create the proper atmosphere.

Older designers—Medin, Guido Fiorini, and Virgilio Marchi, the most gifted of the three—profited from the neorealists' experimentation with natural settings. Their later work was more carefully executed and marked by greater precision. A trained architect and a man of great artistic culture, Fiorini was involved with the early work of Le Corbusier and then with the Italian surrealists. His start in films in 1934 led to work with Augusto Genina on *The Gondola of Chimeras* (1936) and *The White Squadron* (1936), and with Gallone on *Giuseppe Verdi* (1938) and *Manon Lescaut* (1940). The style of the Italian films of this period did not permit him to do any original work; it was not until after the Liberation, with Lattuada's *Giovanni Episcopo's Crime* (1947) and *Miracle in Milan* (1950), a film of excruciating humor by De Sica, that Fiorini had an opportunity to use surrealism to evoke the outskirts of Milan and the climactic flight on witches' broomsticks.

Virgilio Marchi, who started out as a stage designer, specialized from the outset in period films such as *The Two Sergeants* (1936) by Enrico Guazzoni, and *An Adventure of Salvator Rosa* (1939), a swashbuckler by Alessandro Blasetti with richly brilliant sets. Marchi revealed an unbridled imagination in designing fabulous Byzantine-baroque sets for Blasetti's masterpiece, *The Iron Crown* (1940). Some critics considered the film oneiric, others regarded it as a practical joke, but it was a huge popular success. With the advent of neorealism Marchi changed his style. A more intense observation of reality and a rejection of all references to theatrical conventions gave his sets an entirely new quality. His films of the great neorealist era were preceded by his work for *A Pilot Returns* (1942; from Rossellini's so-called Fascist period) and Blasetti's *Four Steps in the Clouds* (1942), set in humble surroundings. He created remarkable sets full of life and accurate detail for Augusto Genina's *Sky over the Marsh* (1949), but some of his finest work went into the designs for the family hotel in De Sica's *Umberto D* (1952). He also designed the sets for Duvivier's *Don Camillo* (1951) and *Europa '51* (1952).

A new generation of film designers, most of them trained as architects, entered the profession, but their work in films of the fifties still lacked the lightness and flexibility of sets constructed in the studio. On the one hand, cameramen and directors, inured to the difficulties of working with real interiors, were satisfied with what they had; on the other hand, the young architects tended to treat film sets as real, permanent constructions. Lack of experience, the absence of specialists in set design and construction, and low wages forced designers to consider their work finished as soon as they had delivered their plans to the studio and chosen the main pieces of furniture. Subsequent technical progress in both direction and set design was the result of exposure to foreign film crews, especially from France and America, who were working in the Rome studios.

A strange opera film, Carlo Menotti's *The Medium* (1951), was shot in spell-binding sets by Georges Wakhévitch, representing the interior of a medium's house. The first period of neorealism closed with two dramatic works: *Umberto D*, possibly De Sica's finest film; and De Santis's *Rome Eleven O'Clock* (1952), with sets by Léon Barsacq, which told the story of an event that really happened three years earlier, when a staircase collapsed under the weight of two hundred women who had come to apply for a single secretarial post.

Indeed, quite a few early neorealist scenarios, especially those by Cesare Zavattini, were based on investigation of the survivors of some accident, the inhabitants of a particular region or district, or a social group. Two markedly individualistic personalities arrived on the scene when Michelangelo Antonioni and Federico Fellini finished their apprenticeships and started making their own films. Antonioni's *Cronaca di un Amore* (1950), designed by Piero Filippone, and Fellini's *I Vitelloni* (1953), with sets by Mario Chiari in an almost documentary style, led Italian cinema toward a realism more subtle and more receptive to literary influences, to psychological study, and to personal memories.

Ettorio Giannini's *Carosello Napoletano* (1954), a film full of high spirits, benefited from a stunning series of wittily stylized sets by Chiari, one of the best Italian costume and set designers, who also designed beautiful sets and costumes, with a sober but rich palette, for *The Golden Coach* (1952), the first film made by Renoir on his return to Europe. Chiari also collaborated with Mario Garbuglia to design *War and Peace* (1956), filmed in Italy by King Vidor.

Between 1938 and 1950, Ottavio Scotti, the designer for numerous period films, worked with such directors as Guido Brignone and Mastrocinque, men whose style was slick and impersonal. His meeting with Visconti gave him an opportunity to design sets for one of the finest period films, *Senso* (1954), a masterpiece of refinement and a kind of cinematic opera. Parts were shot inside the stunning Teatro La Fenice in Venice and in several Palladian villas.

Gianni Polidori (who had been Chiari's assistant on *The Golden Coach*), after designing the sets for Visconti's *Bellissima* (1952), was commissioned to design Lattuada's *The Overcoat* (1952), a film based on Gogol's short story transposed to contemporary northern Italy. His sets were simple and incisive, a style that perfectly suited Antonioni's films: *The Vanquished* (1953); *La Signora senza Camelie* (1953), which demystifies film stars; and *Le Amiche* (*The Girl Friends*, 1955), based on a story by Cesare Pavese.

In *La Dolce Vita* (1960) designer Piero Gherardi followed Fellini's intentions and allowed himself to be seduced by the baroque and even by a certain expressionism visible in his treatment of the sets and his emphasis on certain symbols. The same expressionist influence is evident in Visconti's *White Nights* (1957). Based on a tale by Dostoyevsky, the film is set in an indeterminate world: the characters are not placed in any geographical location; there is only a phantom town with bridges and canals, this nowhere land submerged in darkness and mist.

The sets of Chiari and Garbuglia are quite stylized, almost theatrical, which inevitably happens when a designer wants to avoid realism. In designing for René Clément's *The Sea Wall* (*This Angry Age*, 1957), Garbuglia, one of the most gifted men of the younger generation, created sets precisely fixed in time and space. A war film treated as a tragicomedy, *The Great War* (1959) by Mario Monicelli (director of *I Soliti Ignoti*, 1958), allowed Garbuglia to demonstrate that a realistic framework can underline, in counterpoint, the comedy of a situation. The sumptuousness of Visconti's *The Leopard* (1963), shot in a Sicilian palace arranged and furnished by Garbuglia with an acute feeling for color harmonies, led some critics to classify this film as the work of an aesthete.

In *General della Rovere* (1959), Rossellini made one of his best films and gave De Sica, as an actor, a chance to create an unforgettable character. The sets were by Piero Zuffi, who succeeded in making completely realistic interiors appear dramatic. Carlo Egidi teamed up with Pietro Germi for the neorealist films *Il Ferroviere* (*The Railway Man*, 1956) and *The Man of Straw* (1958). Germi is an underrated director. He tackled satirical comedy with *Divorce Italian Style* (1961) and *Seduced and Abandoned* (1963), recalling the black humor of some British films and transposing it to Sicily. Egidi's designs are marvels of creativity, authenticity, and wit.

In a bare, cerebral, uncompromising style, Antonioni made *Il Grido* (1957), a tragic picture of contemporary Italy, and then *L'Avventura* (1960), one of his best films, in which poignantly desolate exteriors contrast with Piero Poletto's highly photogenic baroque interiors. Poletto also designed *The Red Desert* (1964), Antonioni's first film in color. The geometric sets and the exquisite, almost unnatural colors accentuate the

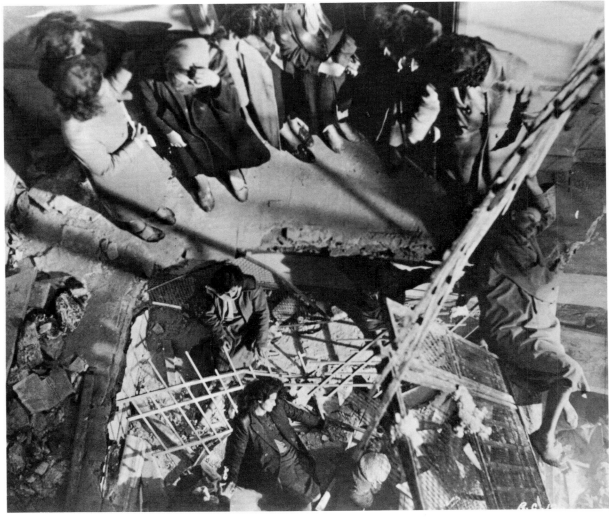

108

abstract quality of Antonioni's work. A large part of the film takes place out of doors, but all has been repainted—houses, trees, earth, grass, all of nature has been re-created by the director and his designer. Poletto's superb taste is best to be savored in his extraordinary designs for Francesco Rosi's *C'Era una Volta* (*More Than a Miracle,* 1967)—by all odds among the most ravishing films ever made south of the Alps.

For *Blow-Up* (1966), shot in London, Antonioni used many natural settings, but only after they had been completely transformed, repainted, and refurnished by English designer Assheton Gorton. Nothing was left but the skeleton of these real

Opposite, top: Teodora, l'Imperatrice di Bisanzio/Theodora, Slave Empress (1954), *starring Gianna Maria Canale; directed by Riccardo Freda; designed by Antonio Valente. Opposite, bottom: Roma, Ore 11/Rome, 11 O'Clock (1952); directed by Giuseppe de Santis; designed by Léon Barsacq.*

Bottom: Mark Frechette (left) in Antonioni's Zabriskie Point (MGM, 1970); production *designer: Dean Tavoularis. A press agent's blurb on Frechette read: "He's 20 and he hates!" After starring in Francesco Rosi's excellent war film,* Uomini Contro, *Frechette was convicted of armed robbery; in 1975 he was found dead, under strange circumstances, in the recreation area of the Walpole State Prison, Massachusetts.*

locations and the possibility of showing the movement of life as if through windows. Again, the choice of colors and a strange atmosphere give Antonioni's film a special style, a kind of realistic abstraction.

In his first American film, the much-maligned but intermittently brilliant *Zabriskie Point* (1970), Antonioni employed production designer Dean Tavoularis, whose later work on *The Godfather, Parts 1 and 2* (1972, 1974) has been justly acclaimed.* For his latest film, *The Passenger* (1975), Antonioni renewed his collaboration with Poletto. The result is a simplistic existential-political fable, served up in incredibly complex "takes," filled with audacious and elaborate manipulation of people within an ever-pulsating frame surface, often of uncommon visual luxuriance—Gaudí's delirious architecture in Barcelona takes over from the characters for an entire reel. In sum, it is the richest hollow film of recent memory.

Ermano Olmi combined a rare gift of observation with freshness of approach and direct tone to produce *Il Posto* (*The Sound of Trumpets*, 1961). One section of the sets, showing the premises of a vast office, was shot on location; other interiors were constructed in the studio by Ettore Lombardo. Visconti, Antonioni, Olmi, and other

* This paragraph is by Elliott Stein.

David Hemmings in Blow-Up (MGM, 1966). Directed by Michelangelo Antonioni. Designed by Assheton Gorton.

Italian directors continued to shoot part of their films in real locations, and part in studio sets so realistic that it is impossible to distinguish them from the actual interiors.

Neorealism made a considerable contribution to Italian cinema by freeing it from the embellishments of its pre-war days. Yet for some time now, certain directors have shown a distinct leaning toward baroque sets and even an element of expressionism. In placing his film 8½ (1963) midway between dream and reality, Fellini received considerable assistance from the sets and costumes by Gherardi. All the interiors and exteriors were shot in constructed sets. The spa, built in a modern district of Rome on a military parade ground, grew from Gherardi's somewhat faded childhood memories of an Italian spa in which he had spent a summer with his parents. Fellini intermingled memories of his own childhood and youth, and the results achieved precisely what the two men were after: to retain only the strangest and most distorted elements of a spa, as they might be imprinted on a child's memory. The same procedure was employed to conjure up a railroad station in the studio. This is not a reconstruction of a real station, but a simplified, childish or dreamlike vision retaining

Left: Federico Fellini's 8½ (Avco Embassy, 1963). Art director: Piero Gherardi. Right: Fellini Satyricon (United Artists, 1969). Sets and costumes: Danilo Donati (sketches by Fellini); architect for sets: Luigi Scaccianoce.

Fellini Roma (United Artists, 1972). Production designer: Danilo Donati.

only the shock elements: locomotive, platform, white walls, steam. Gherardi's costumes for 8½ are also midway between reality and fiction.

In *Juliet of the Spirits* (1965), it is impossible to identify Gherardi's exact contribution, but without question it was basic to the film. Fellini and his designer stimulate and supplement one another, outdoing one another during long discussions. They share a taste for the baroque and for the delirium of dreams. Their vision is a crucible in which all contributions are fused: expressionism, surrealism, even orientalism (both of them adore Japanese films and oriental costumes).

The interior of Juliet's home, constructed in the studio, is part art nouveau and part art deco, producing a jumbled mélange of architectural lines. Juliet's set is all white, symbolizing purity; her friend's set is red, yellow, and violet, symbolizing all the pleasure haunts of the world. To Gherardi, "a costume is a 'state of mind'; [Gherardi] has it made long before filming begins, but remakes it on the set at the last moment with scissors and pins. Improvisation is also important to Fellini. After talking a lot about the sets, he prefers not to see them until the morning that shooting is to start, in order to be forced to change something because you have to expect some last minute trouble with the set. . . . That can be stimulating." * It is difficult to go farther into fiction than Fellini did in this film, and he has been taken to task for having allowed himself to be swamped by formalism to the predominance of colors, costumes, sets, and photography over content.

Neorealism soon branched out in various directions: toward photographic verism, a kind of documentary style like that of Francesco Rosi (*Salvatore Giuliano,* 1961; *Le*

* From writings by Gherardi collected by Christian Dubuisson.

112

Geheimnisse des Orients/Secrets of the Orient (1928), starring Nikolai Kolin. Directed by
Alexander Wolkoff. Sets by A. Lochakov and W. Meinhardt; costumes by Boris Bilinsky. One of
the greatest "Prunk" films ever produced by UFA. As in the other still from the movie (p. 39),
the fantastic architecture at the top is a "hanging miniature" placed between the camera and
the actors: it has been scrupulously constructed to match the real set and appear many times
larger than it really is. "The symmetry reminds us of the primitive games and buildings of
children. But quantity and quality have been enhanced to gigantic proportions. . . . This
consummate enhancing of ingenuousness is the most cunning to be imagined."—A.
Kraszna-Krausz, "Secrets of the Orient—A Fairy Tale Film," Close Up 3 (Dec. 1928).

Left: *Joseph Mankiewicz's* Cleopatra *(Elizabeth Taylor) with her son by Caesar, Caesarion (Loris Loddi), borne into the Roman forum (20th Century–Fox, 1963). Production designer: John De Cuir; art directors: Jack Martin Smith, Hilyard Brown, Herman Blumenthal, Elven Webb, Maurice Pelling, and Boris Juraga.*

Right: *Claudette Colbert was Cecil B. De Mille's* Cleopatra *(Paramount, 1934). Art directors: Hans Dreier and Roland Anderson, assisted by Ralph Jester. "A year to make! Gigantic sets that cover 400,000 square feet! A love boat 500 feet long!"*

Mani sulla Città, 1963), and toward psychological and aesthetic experiments. These different tendencies presently dominate Italian cinema. But there is also a more commercial trend favored by a wider public: period and mythological films and westerns. In fact, the success of Blasetti's *Fabiola* (1948) during the heyday of neorealism shows that the Italian tradition of the period film satisfies the tastes of a vast audience. Color, the wide screen, and extravagant production have also helped Italian producers to make period films that compete successfully with television.

Americans set the first example by filming in Rome Mervyn Le Roy's *Quo Vadis?* (1951) and, later, William Wyler's *Ben Hur* (1959). These two films required huge sets, which were created in a pseudo-Roman style by Hugh Hunt from designs by Edward Carfagno and William Horning. Joseph Mankiewicz's *Cleopatra* (1963), one of the most expensive films ever made, had to face all sorts of complications. The exceptionally large sets by John De Cuir and Hilyard Brown were built in London, then dismantled and rebuilt at Cinecittà. The main scenes of *The Fall of the Roman Empire* (1964) were also shot in Rome, in much more sensitive sets by the team of Veniero Colasanti and John Moore.

Ottavio Scotti was commissioned to build sets for many of these pseudo-historical films: *The Mongols* (1961), *Arrivano i Titani* (1962), *Son of Spartacus* (1962), and so on. Generally produced with relatively modest resources and carrying over the

114

same sets and costumes, barely altered, from one production to the next, these "peplums" are often saved from grandiloquence and absurdity by a good-natured light-heartedness that sometimes amounts to humor.

Much more unexpected is the wave of Italian "spaghetti westerns," another form of spectacular, to which a great number of the young are attracted. The environment of the Rome studios has been transformed by a strange menagerie of fake cowboys, Indians, and barroom singers who seem somewhat out of place against this background which has seen so many togas and peplums pass. Often made by Italian directors and actors disguised with American-sounding names, spaghetti westerns have invaded European screens, and now compete with American westerns on their home ground.

Italian neorealism influenced a great many young filmmakers in various countries. Even more than the formal aspects, the search for topical themes and contemporary social issues surfaced in the best works of the younger directors. American, British, and French films did not escape this influence (Free Cinema, *cinéma vérité*, New

Left: *Marlene Dietrich, about to take off her gorilla head and sing "Hot Voodoo" in Josef von Sternberg's* Blonde Venus *(Paramount, 1932). Art director: Wiard Ihnen.*

Right: *Lana Turner as Samarra, high priestess to Baal, in* The Prodigal *(MGM, 1955). "Adapted from the Bible by Joe Breen, Jr." Directed by Richard Thorpe. Art directors: Cedric Gibbons and Randall Duell; set decorator: Edwin B. Willis. Duell, for many years at MGM, today directs an architectural firm specialized in amusement parks.*

Wave, and so on); but the effect of neorealism was felt most visibly in countries that did not have, or no longer had, strong national traditions, such as the Central European countries, Spain, Greece, and India. Subjects varied according to the culture and social structure of each country; but the generosity of spirit, a certain intellectual probity, and the spontaneous expression remained the same.

As in the early days of Italian neorealism, most of these films were shot out of doors or in real settings. Studio sets generally represented only interiors of modest dimensions that could be realized with restricted budgets. This applied particularly to topical films, for as soon as these same directors achieved some notoriety and switched to historical subjects or more ambitious films, they also turned to constructed sets of considerable size.

In Poland well-known designers like Roman Mann (Jerzy Kawalerowicz's *Mother Joan of the Angels,* 1961), Anatol Radzinowicz (Andrzey Wajda's *Ashes,* 1965), and Jerzy Skrzepinski (Kawalerowicz's *Pharaoh,* 1965) designed vast sets, ingenious in conception and extremely carefully built.

In Spain Enrique Alarcon (Juan Antonio Bardem's designer), Francisco Canet, who designed strange sets for Buñuel's *Viridiana* (1961), and special effects expert Emilio da Ruis followed Siegfried Burman and Schildknecht.

In Romania Liviu Ciulei, a stage and film designer who became a theater manager and a director for both stage and film, made *The Danube Waves* (1960) and *The Forest of the Hanged* (1965). Among the best-known designers are Paul Bortnovshi, who works chiefly for the stage; Marcel Bogos, who designed Henri Colpi's *Codine* (1964); Ion Oroveanu, who designed Colpi's *Mona, the Star Without a Name* (1966); and Giulio Tinco, who designed *The Forest of the Hanged* (1965).

The Enrichment of National Traditions: Sweden and Japan

Swedish cinema was influenced little by neorealism. Its best-known representative, Ingmar Bergman, is the heir of Seastrom and Stiller, directors in Sweden's golden age.

The word "summer" constantly recurs in the titles of Bergman's early films—*Sommarlek* (Summer Interlude, 1951), *Smiles of a Summer Night* (1955)—and the exteriors shot during the brief Scandinavian summer are largely responsible for the pagan charm and slightly acid eroticism of these works. Before making his masterpiece, *Wild Strawberries* (1957), Bergman made *The Naked Night* (1953), a spellbinding film that is in some ways reminiscent of German expressionist films. The strange atmosphere, heavy with sensuality, is due largely to Bibi Lindstrom's sets, which conjure up a bizarre, cruel world. Swedish designers such as Lindstrom, Gittan Gustafson (*Wild Strawberries*), Nils Svenwall (*Sommarlek*), and P. A. Lundgren (*The Seventh Seal, Smiles of a Summer Night*) are generally adept at creating just the right atmosphere. Their sets are conceived without grandiloquence and built with taste, restraint, and an attention to detail that surpasses the best American examples.

Top: Fröken Julie/Miss Julie (1950). Ulf Palme and Anita Björk in Alf Sjöberg's (direction and screenplay) masterful version of the Strindberg play. Designed by Bibi Lindstrom.

Bottom: Jungfrukällan/The Virgin Spring (1960). Max von Sydow (center) in Ingmar Bergman's tale of rape and murder. Art director: P. A. Lundgren.

Japan is another country that was only partially touched by neorealism. Movie studios have been producing films in Tokyo since 1908, but it was not until 1950 that Japanese films were shown with any regularity in the West. At first, modern subjects were filmed in Tokyo and screen versions of classical plays mainly in Kyoto. Up to the present, Japanese production has followed these two separate trends: Samurai films and films on contemporary themes.

It was Akira Kurosawa who gained recognition for post-war Japanese cinema in Europe and the United States with *Rashomon* (1950), a sober, moving film of great visual beauty whose photography is in the style of sixteenth-century Japanese grisaille landscape paintings. *Rashomon's* art director was So Matsuyama, who also designed Kurosawa's *Stray Dog* (1949), *The Idiot* (1951), and *Ikiru* (1952). *Gate of Hell* (1953), directed by the former *onnagata* (female impersonator) Teinosuke Kinugasa, created a sensation in the West because of its extraordinary color photography. Kisaku Itoh's sets made ingenious use of classical Japanese architecture, with its moveable and transparent elements that seem to have been made expressly for filming. The colors, inspired by Japanese prints, possess an unusual subtlety and freshness.

Preparations for the death of Macbeth (General Washizu, played by Toshiro Mifune) in Akira Kurosawa's Kumonosu-jo/The Throne of Blood/Cobweb Castle *(1957). Art directors: Yoshiro Muraki and Kohei Ezaki.*

118

Mizoguchi, one of the world's greatest directors, made some one hundred films. Those that have been released in the West include *The Life of Oharu* (1952), *Ugetsu* (1953), and *New Tales of the Taira Clan* (1955), all linked to Samurai legends. Hiroshi Mizutani created poetic sets of great delicacy in the pure tradition of Japanese painting. Contemporary subjects are treated with brutal realism but at the same time with a dignity and discretion in the acting and a very special rhythm that are a heritage of the Kabuki theater. In addition to *Oharu*, Mizutani also designed other great films for Mizoguchi: *The Story of the Last Chrysanthemums* (1939), *The Loyal 47 Ronin of the Genroku Era* (1942), and *A Story from Chikamatsu* (1954).

The New Wave and *Cinéma-Vérité*

In the United States, France, Great Britain, and Italy, a feeling of dissatisfaction, a search for novelty, and a more or less conscious desire to shock underlay disorganized experiments that were almost always sincere and frequently interesting. These movements took names like New Wave, *cinéma-vérité*, and Free Cinema, and their promoters were film critics, documentary makers, or television directors.

Although some of these films recall the first manifestations of neorealism, the subjects are different. Their theme is contemporary anguish, especially in the young. The illustration of the theme is not without faults: the sequence of scenes, photography, cutting, and acting often give an impression of improvisation or makeshift filming. Nonetheless, the doubtful conditions under which these films are made can sometimes be an advantage, if the director succeeds in communicating his enthusiasm, a fresh approach, and his personal vision.

It is instructive to observe the working methods of a New Wave director. His first film is almost always shot in nature and on location. If this film remains unnoticed by critics, he shoots the next one under the same conditions; but if it is a success, he makes his next film in a studio, with constructed sets. This fact tends to prove that natural settings are not a stylistic or aesthetic necessity, but a last resort, a way to cut down on studio costs or to avoid an immediate expenditure of capital.

It must not be imagined, however, that it is easy to transform a barn into a nightclub, or a haberdashery shop into a notary's office, as has been done for some films. And so the New Wave experiment has made its contribution to the evolution of the set. Shooting in real locations has accustomed young cameramen to lighting difficulties unknown in the studio. The increased sensitivity of film and new lighting techniques (less polished and employing lighter, less cumbersome equipment) make it possible to design sets closer in size to reality. Sets with ceilings, for instance, are no longer considered technical feats.

Set still for Donald O'Connor's solo number in Singin' in the Rain (MGM, 1952). Produced by Arthur Freed; directed by Gene Kelly and Stanley Donen. Art director: Randall Duell; set decorators: Edwin B. Willis and Jacques Mapes.

TECHNIQUE

The Role and Conception
of Set Design

From the time of the very first motion pictures at the end of the nineteenth century, the cinema has followed two paths: filming out of doors—as Louis Lumière did for *The Arrival of a Train at La Ciotat Station*—and filming in studios—like Méliès, whose work foreshadowed all future fairytale and dramatic films.

Sometimes there was a mixture of genres: newsreels were faked in constructed sets, and dramas and comedies were shot out of doors. And some years later, exteriors and scenes shot in the studio were combined in the same film. In fact, the combination of the two methods became the dominant trend, with one or the other approach more apparent, according to the director and the subject of the film.

But from time to time schools or movements came into being that, in the name of aesthetic, ideological, social, or economic principles, usually avoided filming out of doors in favor of the studio and of stylized acting by professional actors (German expressionism, French aestheticism); while other schools rejected the studio for nature, real interiors, and amateur actors (the first Soviet films, early neorealism in Italy, and to some extent the New Wave in France). A pendulum movement regularly brings the cinema back to one of the two poles—naturalism or abstraction—but as Georges Sadoul has rightly said, "The dichotomy between the studio and the street, the antithesis between Lumière and Méliès, are false oppositions when one attempts to find in them the solution to the problem of realism and art. Films completely outside time have been shot out of doors; completely realistic films have been shot in the studio."*

A film without exteriors, with neither sky nor sun nor vegetation, finally produces a feeling of suffocation (which can be counteracted by building some of the sets on outside lots). On the other hand, there are only two kinds of film for which natural locations are inescapable: documentaries and newsreels, either genuine or reconstructed. In documentaries the setting is very often the actual subject of the film, for a documentary aims to show a particular aspect of nature or a product of human genius, whether a mountain landscape, cathedral, fishing port, factory, or palace. The

* Georges Sadoul, "Les Sources et les thèmes dans l'oeuvre de Marcel Carné," *Ciné-Club* (December 1949).

121

genre owes a great deal of its attraction to the absolute authenticity of all elements in the film. Nevertheless, the selection and presentation of these elements reflect the director's ideas, so that even the most commonplace documentary is an enhancement of reality. The documentary filmmaker selects those features that seem best suited to convey an impression he has experienced or his personal conception of the subject. A designer has to proceed in the same manner to re-create in the studio a given location.

Now consider the use of natural settings in films depicting great social upheavals such as war or revolution. Whether the films are shot during the actual events or are reconstructed, it is absolutely essential to give them the unembellished, spontaneous appearance of a newsreel. Because the documentary aspect of events must not be neglected, the ideal, in the case of a reconstruction, is to shoot the film on the very site where the events took place. This is possible only if the events are sufficiently recent for the background to have remained unchanged. If that is not the case, the film enters the significantly different domain of the period film.

But reality "caught in the act"—the spontaneous, authentic appearance of certain images which are enough to move us in a film dealing with real events—is no longer a determining element when a film portrays a conflict of emotions or a series of situations (which is the foundation of all dramatic, comic, or poetic works). In making such films, to dispense with the studio and hence with the sets is to impoverish the means of cinematic expression.

Taken in its broadest sense, the film set is a discreet but ever-present character, the director's most faithful accomplice. It is simply a question of finding for each film the setting best calculated to situate the action geographically, socially, and dramatically. Certainly the effect of a love scene played by the same characters speaking the same words will vary according to whether it takes place in a gondola in Venice, on the sofa of a living room in a small town, or next to a kitchen sink.

Now, from a strictly dramatic point of view, only the choice of setting is important. Whether it is real or a studio re-creation does nothing to change the story. But from a technical standpoint, which determines a film's visual style, the results may be quite different if the designer utilizes the resources of the studio or if instead he submits to the restrictions of a natural location.

There are two main arguments in favor of real interiors: the absolute authenticity of the setting, and the possibility of using existing structures at little cost. For the first point, it must be said that the lesson of neorealist films (and even those of the New Wave) has benefited many scenario writers, directors, cameramen, and designers who had tended to confine themselves to comfortable academic formulas. As for the legitimate desire to use very rich or extensive interiors, unfortunately this has proven possible only for rather short scenes. Every dramatic or comic scene demanding a certain precision of execution faces such technical difficulties (lighting, composition of the shot, acoustics, etc.) that the advantages of the real setting are outweighed. Consequently, a transposition becomes inescapable in order to obtain on the screen the equivalent of reality as seen by the human eye, which is so much more mobile than the camera. This transposition is possible only by using a set that re-creates the essentials of a given place. This set is conceived in terms of the shooting script, which foresees, as exactly as possible, all the movements of the actors and the camera.

It is not so much logic as the requirements of the production that should guide the designer in drawing up his plans. These needs should determine the location of doors, windows, fireplaces, furniture, and so on. Very often the normal architecture of a room may be modified or dislocated. In order to introduce into the screen frame the greatest possible number of elements characteristic of a given location, it may be necessary to lower the ceiling, bring columns closer together, change the angle of a wall, or even lengthen a room, to create perspective effects by adding in length what has been taken away in height or width. The main angles and movements of the camera must also be studied. This makes it possible to foresee which parts of the set serve no purpose, because they will not be seen, and which must be moveable so that the camera can pull back. The plan of a set that satisfies all these requirements, as well as those of the lighting, ends up looking rather surprising, bearing little resemblance to an architect's plan.

Once the general plan has been established, the next problem is to make sure the appearance of the set suits not only the situations but also the spirit of the film. This is the most interesting part of a designer's work. Unlike the director and the director of photography, who work with concrete elements (the set, the actors, and objects) the

Left: *Olivia de Havilland in* The Heiress *(Paramount, 1949). Produced and directed by William Wyler. Production designer: Harry Horner; art director: John Meehan; set decorator: Emile Kuri.*

Right: *Shangri-La in Frank Capra's* Lost Horizon *(Columbia, 1937). Art director: Stephen Goosson.*

123

designer has at his disposal only the words in the scenario, which he has to express visually. He is the first to create the images of the future film. His work may be compared with that of the scenarist and the composer, who have to translate ideas into words and sounds.

It must never be forgotten that sets enter a film as background, while actors occupy the foreground. The spectator has no time to analyze his sensations; therefore such settings must be characterized without any equivocation. In order to obtain the effect of reality, it is necessary to bring out the essential characteristic of a set—whether it is luxurious or sordid, overfurnished or bare, fragile or heavy—by exaggerating the dominant features and suppressing useless detail. In every case, this comes down to selecting the typical elements and arranging them so that they form part of the composition of the visual images, indicate the setting of the action, and often express the atmosphere of a place.

Film design is sometimes reproached for a lack of originality or for anonymity. But more often criticism has been directed toward its artificiality, its pasteboard quality. Admittedly, a film designer cannot always express his personality, especially if he is designing a courtroom or a dentist's office. On the other hand, he can avoid errors of conception or execution that may give a set the pasteboard look absolutely incompatible with the evolution of cinematic aesthetics and technique.

Sketch by Ernst Fegté for Lubitsch's Design for Living *(Paramount, 1933).*

A bit of New York, as designed on the Fox back lot by Max Parker, for The Power and the Glory *(1933). Directed by William K. Howard.*

With a few rare exceptions, the actors in a film move in clearly defined locations. The designer must at all costs avoid stereotypes and seek the particular; he must eschew the facilely picturesque to choose a framework with character. It is a question not only of observation and documentation, but also of imagination. One look is sufficient to see that the roofs of Paris have a characteristic appearance found nowhere else. The shops and sidewalks change from town to town; a country inn has nothing in common with a fashionable bar; as for hospital wards or prison visiting rooms, they are as varied as Regency drawing rooms and Gothic fireplaces. But it is not a matter of servilely copying a given place: in that case, a film may just as well be shot on location. The problem is to replace reality by another truth—the truth of art, which is more persuasive and does not clash with the general style of the film. To quote what Louis Delluc wrote of Thomas Ince, the pioneer western director, which applies not only to all the great directors, but also to the ideal designer: "The case of this director is extraordinary: He looks and then he imagines, following what he has seen, what he might have seen. . . . Starting from an inner poetic or human impulse, to fulfill it he relies on details that are precise, everyday, living, and, in their totality, intense because they are very ordinary."

A set must take into account one other factor: the psychology and behavior of those intended to inhabit it. If it is successful, the set will replace with its mere appearance a whole page of description in a novel and verbal explanations that would be boring on film. Robert Mallet-Stevens, who was one of the first to study seriously the role of the set in a film, wrote, "A film set, in order to be a good set, must act. Whether realistic or expressionist, modern or ancient, it must play its part. The set must present the character before he has even appeared. It must indicate his social position, his tastes, his habits, his life style, his personality. The sets must be intimately linked with the action."*

Twenty years later, André Bazin wrote about a film by Marcel Carné, *Le Jour se lève* (sets by Trauner), and said, "We see how the set plays as great a part as the acting in justifying situations, explaining characters, and giving credibility to the action."

Having examined the set in terms of the action of the film, the atmosphere to be created, and the psychology of the characters, we are led to consider the set in relation to the style of the film. The same interior or exterior must be treated differently according to whether the film is a drama, thriller, comedy, musical, or so on. Naturally lighting plays a major part in the manner of presenting a set, as does color (light colors are suited to comedy, and dark, contrasting colors to drama); but beyond this, sets may be, by their very essence, gay and even comical or else sad or terrifying. A musical comedy has to avoid being too realistic; stylization of the sets is almost a necessity. The thriller, however, does well with an almost documentary style. The designer's inventiveness and sensibility, his personal gifts, allow him to adapt to the style that the director intends to give the film.

As a general rule, airy sets with many windows or other openings give an impression of gaiety, and thick walls, narrow windows, and low ceilings create a heavy atmosphere. The designer must know how to gauge the correct amount of decoration: an accumulation of details, whether of ornaments or objects, provokes a feeling of discomfort. On the other hand, simplicity can be a sign of nobility. The designer can play with height and depth, large or small scale, matte surfaces or gleaming floors, gold, and mirrors, with a range of dull colors or violently contrasting tones. Each combination arouses different feelings that are difficult for the spectator to analyze but of which he is nevertheless aware.

Perhaps no one has better expressed the evocative power of the set than Louis Aragon, in a text dating from 1918. "To endow with a poetic value that which did not possess it before, to restrict at will the area of objective fact in order to intensify expression, these are two properties that contribute to making the film set an adequate framework for modern beauty." †

* Mallet-Stevens, *L'Art cinématographique.*

† Louis Aragon, *Le Film* (Sept. 1918).

126

7 Researching the Set

It is relatively easy to obtain necessary sources for the different environments to be depicted, if a film takes place in one's own country and time. As soon as the action takes place abroad, difficulties begin.

A curious convention impels filmmakers to conceive settings for life abroad in a rather realistic manner. Signs and inscriptions are written in the language of the country concerned; costumes and hairstyles are inspired by what is known of the populace; but all these "foreigners" usually express themselves in English, French, Russian, or Italian, depending on the country which makes the film. Nonetheless, whenever possible a study trip is highly desirable for the designer, who must otherwise content himself with photographic references, drawings, paintings, and the like. In either case, the designer must distrust his first impulse, which pushes him to choose the most picturesque or exotic elements, instead of searching out the country's truly dominant characteristic, which always lends itself to simple treatment.

A typical example of what should at all costs be avoided comes to us from the United States. American directors and designers, so accurate where their own country is concerned, have for several decades imposed upon their audiences a rather simplistic vision of Old Europe (out of carelessness rather than lack of references). The totally false archetypes have become so deeply implanted in the minds of audiences that American filmmakers have continued to create spurious folklore, in order not to bewilder their public (though far less so since the end of the war, no doubt due to the influence of newsreels, documentaries, and television). Even Jean Renoir's *The Diary of a Chambermaid*, made in Hollywood during the war, does not entirely escape reproach. Eugène Lourié (who was also responsible for the sets of *La Grande Illusion*, *La Bête humaine*, and *The Rules of the Game*) strove to make the atmosphere as authentic as possible. Numerous sources served as a basis for the sets and costumes, and yet they do not ring true. Perhaps it was a question of different furnishings, human types, language, or attitudes; but in my opinion it was mostly the Hollywood ambiance that acted insidiously, falsifying details.

I remember seeing reduced models of Roman statues, made in the United States, arriving in the Rome studios for the American version of *Quo Vadis?* (1951). The statues looked more like the work of Arno Brecker (the favorite sculptor of Adolf Hitler and Jean Cocteau—his bronze bust of Cocteau adorns the tomb of the director of *Blood of a Poet* at Milly-la-Forêt) than like the Augustuses and Caesars with which Roman museums overflow. Yet these Hollywood models were enlarged to cyclopean dimensions in Rome. The same phenomenon explains the peasants with goatees and velvet berets and the thatched cottages that are supposed to represent rural France. Italian designers took as their model the Paris of Joan of Arc in order to portray scenes from the Revolution of 1848 in *Les Misérables.* I am not quite sure that we have never made the same mistakes in France.

While designing in Vienna and Berlin the sets for films supposed to take place in France (Daquin's *Bel Ami* and *La Rabouilleuse*), I became aware of the difficulties inherent in this kind of enterprise. The smallest details posed problems: the styles of furniture were different from French styles of the same period, and objects that are common enough in France were unavailable: double beds, coffee tables with marble tops, pews (which had to be made). The floors were different, not to mention the door handles, fireplaces, and the French way of making beds, which the property men had to learn; the carpenters fitted out the Paris garret with a double window such as they were accustomed to make in their own country. It was never more than a matter of details, but an accumulation of repeated minor errors is enough to falsify completely the spirit of a set, which explains how hard it is to express satisfyingly the ambiance of a country that is not one's own.

Period Films

If the majority of films deal with contemporary life, nineteenth- and early twentieth-century novels continue to be adapted regularly for the screen. It is interesting to note that the novels that periodically inspire filmmakers (novels by Eugène Sue, Balzac, Stendhal, Hugo, Zola, Maupassant, Dickens, Tolstoy, Dostoyevsky, and Chekhov) belong with few exceptions to a period when male dress already prefigured what it is today: that is, one century of history from 1815 to 1915. (Fashion, created by great couturiers and frequently returning to shapes inspired by the past, has rendered the public less sensitive to the metamorphoses of women's clothes.) The spectator, neither distracted nor disoriented by a hero in wig, tights, doublet, or toga, quickly forgets the minor differences in the outward appearance of the setting and costumes. This brings the characters and their emotions closer to him, to his sensibility, with the added charm of a previous era.

If the attraction of well-known titles or well-written stories partially explains the infatuation of filmmakers with certain novels, the visual richness of period films (for example, nostalgia for the Gay Nineties, for a disappearing way of life) inspired original works. Note, among many others, Carné's *Les Enfants du paradis,* Clair's *Le*

Silence est d'or and *Les Grandes Manoeuvres (Summer Maneuvers)*, Renoir's *French Cancan* and *Paris Does Strange Things*, Ophüls's *Lola Montès*, Welles's *The Magnificent Ambersons*, Huston's *Moulin Rouge*, Visconti's *Senso*, and Cukor's *My Fair Lady*.

In all these period films the appearance of the characters and settings has been idealized, for photographic documents, which have existed since 1840, reveal that reality was not that attractive! Costumes and sets have to be brightened, simplified, almost modernized; their spirit has to be emphasized by freeing them from excess fringes, pompons, and flounces. This dusting off can be facilitated by studying the paintings and drawings of the nineteenth century. Daumier, Gavarni, Toulouse-Lautrec, Degas, Manet, Renoir, Guys, and Doré have left a record of their age that is an interpretation, a re-creation of reality, but is, in the last analysis, more convincing than photography.

In the twenties, Robert Mallet-Stevens, presenting a collection of photographs of modern film design, wrote at the end of his introduction: "These few sets were produced at the cost of numerous material difficulties, but the directors had the will to succeed. They had the great honor of presenting sets with new designs and that complemented the action developed in their films. They dared. Let us congratulate and thank them. Thanks to them the cinema will evolve in the right direction; they enable us to glimpse the day when the ridiculous films shown to us now will leave the screen forever."*

Leafing through this album reveals, unfortunately, that despite their good intentions, the modernistic designers produced sets that, with rare exceptions, have aged as much as, if not more than, the "ridiculous" films treated with such contempt by Mallet-Stevens. They can teach us modesty and something else of importance: the only sets in this collection that still seem to have some value, even today, are the abstract constructions reduced to a few lines and simple volumes. The moment art deco appears, everything seems false and outmoded. [Since these lines were written, the art deco style is no longer out of fashion. Women's dress from the twenties (cropped hair, low waists, short skirts, and cloche hats) as well as jewelry, knicknacks, and fabric designs have enjoyed an unexpected vogue, confirmed by the several major art deco exhibitions in France and the United States.]

For Vadim's *La Curée (The Game Is Over, 1966)*, Jean André used art deco styles for certain sets and succeeded in creating a warmly colored ambiance that was also strange and rather disquieting. The next development—sparked by the film *Bonnie and Clyde* (1966)—was a return to favor of the thirties style that, in general, is nothing but an extension of art deco.

The case of art nouveau is different. It is generally used to decorate films set in the nineties, but I came to realize that it must not be overdone. Art nouveau is an irresistible blossoming of organic forms that end up looking like evil, monstrous mandragoras. There is nothing old-fashioned about an art nouveau interior. It can be designed seriously and built skillfully, yet leave an uneasy impression, like certain Far Eastern works. In René Clair's films *Le Silence est d'or* and *Les Grandes Manoeuvres*,

* Robert Mallet-Stevens, *Le Décor moderne au cinéma*, p. 6.

129

both set between 1905 and 1910, I made use of only a few items of art nouveau furniture. A shop front and a café with the lines unique to this style were sufficient to suggest the period. For the rest, the attractive atmosphere of these films is due to the much more anonymous turn-of-the-century decor and furnishing. On the other hand, I am convinced that very successful horror films could be shot in purely art nouveau sets.

Historical Films

This category does not include swashbucklers such as *The Three Musketeers*. These are primarily adventure films whose heroes are all more or less related to the characters created by Douglas Fairbanks. Psychological or historical subtleties can only be detrimental to this kind of spectacle, which is more suited to luxurious and brilliant sets that alternate pleasantly with rides across the countryside.

The farther we move away from the nineteenth century, the more difficult it becomes to fake the peculiarities of each epoch. Architecture, fashions, and life styles, influenced by economic and social conditions, produced behavior, speech patterns, and even emotions that are far removed from our own habits and mentality. Historical films, whether they deal with the seventeenth century, the Renaissance, the Middle Ages, or antiquity, tend to accent great religious or political events and the particular ambiance that characterizes the period, rather than conflicts of feeling. By drawing his inspiration from "eyewitness" sources such as paintings, engravings, miniatures, tapestries, or bas-reliefs, the designer will find, in addition to purely material details, an indication of the general spirit in which the film should be treated.

It is not a matter of faithfully reproducing a series of works of art of the day, but rather of extracting from them information about the manner in which contemporaries depicted the setting of their day-to-day life, festivals, battles, and ceremonies. With great foresight, Mallet-Stevens spoke of the historical film as it ought to be made, and, in 1929, seemed to foresee Laurence Olivier's *Henry V* of 1944.

Whether it is a question of costumes, utensils, furniture, landscapes, or architecture, we see these images with the eyes of the artists of the time. A fifteenth-century forest interpreted in a miniature, a forest painted by Watteau, a forest of the time of Louis Philippe [1773–1850] portrayed in a lithograph, a contemporary forest reproduced by photography are totally different from one another. . . . The spectator must find on the screen the vision of the past to which he is accustomed.

The landscape of a film conjuring up scenes from the thirteenth century must be in false perspective, with really unusual objects, as we see them depicted in the canvases of the primitives. . . . Tartuffe acted in a Cubist set would be as ridiculous as Joan of Arc filmed hearing voices in the present-day countryside of Lorraine. One would have the feeling that at any moment a bus would turn off the road and that her eyes raised to heaven are following the flight of an airplane. *

In fact, for Carl Dreyer's *The Passion of Joan of Arc* the sets for a historical film were treated in an almost abstract manner. Hermann Warm and Jean Hugo, drawing

* Mallet-Stevens, *L'Art cinématographique.*

130

Henry V (1944). Directed by Laurence Olivier. Art director: Paul Sheriff, assisted by Carmen Dillon.

their inspiration from medieval painting, constructed a huge set representing the marketplace at Rouen, a street, the tribunal, and the prison, on a lot near Montrouge. The extremely simple volumes in the set, the use of scale models for the silhouette of the town, the bell turrets, the gables, the exclusive use of white slightly tinged with pink (for photographic reasons), make of it a kind of neutral background against which objects and faces stand out. Hoping to convey only the profoundly human significance of Joan's trial and death, Dreyer concentrated above all on the faces, shot in extreme close-up. This attempt at synthesis leaves the spectator almost unaware of the presence of the set.

In Olivier's *Henry V*, designer Paul Sheriff employed false perspectives for the interiors and the furniture, as they appear in fifteenth-century miniatures. The elements of the sets are reduced in scale, so that the characters clearly dominate, in accordance with the principles of the paintings of the French primitives. The landscapes were shot out of doors, but re-created, modified by the addition of scale models (outlines of castles, clumps of trees), by the avoidance of natural colors, and by the presence of stylized elements such as costumes and tents.

For *Carnival in Flanders*, Jacques Feyder and Lazare Meerson took as their point of departure Flemish and Dutch paintings of the sixteenth and seventeenth centuries—paintings that are both robust and rich in intimate themes, everyday gestures. There is nothing declamatory or heroic about the Flemish painters, and the film closely follows its models. Feyder pushed virtuosity so far that he composed

131

tableaux in the style of the period—which does somewhat hold up the action. In the interior sets everything combines to create an impression of cleanliness, opulence, and also intimacy. The rooms with their tile floors and gleaming furniture look as though they really were lived in. The exterior sets are an undeniable triumph. In a limited space, Meerson succeeded in building a kind of synthesis of a Flemish town with its canal, belfry, city gates, middle-class houses with stepped gables, and shops overflowing with food and lengths of cloth. It is a reflection of Bruges, but Bruges interpreted by the camera lens.

Flanders again served as a film background in *Les Aventures de Till l'Espiègle* (*Till Eulenspiegel*, 1956), directed by Gérard Philipe, and it was to Brueghel that I turned for inspiration in designing the exteriors. The Flemish villages and the castle

Alexander Nevsky (1938). Directed by Sergei Eisenstein, co-directed by Dmitri Vasiliev. Designers: Isaac Shpinel and Nicolas Soloviov. The sets were executed from plans made by Eisenstein, who also did preliminary sketches for the costumes, weapons, and ornaments.

Eisenstein's Ivan Grozny/Ivan the Terrible (Part 1, 1944; Part 2, 1958). Art director: Isaac Shpinel, who worked from designs by Eisenstein. Right: One of the director's sketches.

built on the studio lot in Nice, the winter landscapes filmed in Sweden, the battle scenes shot near Berlin, and finally a few shots of Flanders with its canals were the locations used. The typical elements of Flemish architecture, some silhouettes of models (church clock towers, mills), and the lines of willow trees introduced into the landscapes link all these apparently disparate exteriors and give the film its Brueghelesque look. For the village set I tried to preserve Brueghel's style in the houses, church, and belfry, but I used photographs for the architectural details.

These three films proceed from almost identical conceptions of the historical film. A quite different set of ideas governed Eisenstein in making his two historical films, *Alexander Nevsky* and *Ivan the Terrible*. In both cases, he rejected the idea of representing a historical hero in the shape of an accessible being and preferred to operate on the plane of tragedy. This conception gave rise not only to the visual style of the films but also to the musical background and the acting. The director's mind was increasingly haunted by grandeur and the monumental. In according symbolic value to the various locations in which the action takes place, Eisenstein was deliberately returning to the scenery of theatrical tragedy.

In preparing for *Alexander Nevsky* (the prince of Novgorod) he hesitated over a style for the film. Then one day, studying the ancient architecture of Novgorod and struck by the perfection of the Church of the Holy Savior of Neredits, he thought, "People who could erect a building like this in a few months were no icons or miniatures, high reliefs or engravings! They were people like you and I!" And he

133

repeated the painter Surikov's words: "I believed stones, not books."* The paradoxical result of all these reflections was that on a formal plane Eisenstein finally arrived at an expressionist style quite close to that of Nicholas Roerich, the Russian stage designer.

To shoot the film's climax, the battle on the ice of Lake Peipus, Eisenstein abandoned the idea of waiting for winter and decided to film at high summer in order to gain nearly a year (World War II was imminent). "The artificial winter was a success, complete and indisputable. No one saw the difference. The reason we succeeded was because we did not try to imitate winter. We told no 'lies' and did not try to fool the public with glass icicles and 'prop' details of the Russian winter, which cannot be copied faithfully. What we took was the most important aspect of winter—its proportions of light and sound, the whiteness of the ground and the darkness of the sky. We took the winter formula, so we had no need to lie, for the formula corresponded to the truth."†

"We took the winter formula." This is not far from the "most expressive expression" of the German cinema in the 1920s.

* Sergei Eisenstein, *Notes of a Film Director*, pp. 39, 37.

† Ibid., pp. 41-42.

Helen of Troy *(Warner Bros., 1956). Directed by Robert Wise, second unit director Yakima Canutt. Art direction: Edward Carrere, assisted by Ken Adam.*

Eisenstein went even further with *Ivan the Terrible*, about which he said, "All our efforts were directed toward communicating to the audience a sense of the grandiose power of the Russian state. That is why the rooms are huge, the ceilings high, the brocades, furs, and jewels sparkle and gleam, and why the powerful choruses of the ancient liturgical chants ring out with solemnity." The sketches and studies which Eisenstein, a former designer, made for *Ivan the Terrible* are even more significant. In contrast to the monumental grandeur of the sets in which the czar appears, the conspirators slip through low doorways, compelled by the vaulted ceilings and narrow stairs to crouch and contort themselves. It is all reminiscent of the expressionism of the Russian episode in Paul Leni's *Waxworks*.

Films dealing with antiquity, whether Roman, Greek, Egyptian, or biblical, must be considered from a different viewpoint. These are merely pretexts for crowd scenes, for larger-than-life sets, for spectaculars reminiscent of *Cabiria* and the great age of Italian cinema. Little progress has been made since then. Factual references are numerous enough (bas-reliefs, a few frescoes, vases), but the public is used to seeing the monuments of antiquity in ruins, covered with the patina of time, and brand-new Roman or biblical temples look false, no matter how skillful the reconstruction. Perhaps sets for the Old Testament should be inspired by the landscape, architecture, and costumes of the poorest regions of North Africa and Asia Minor. The director Michael Cacoyannis tried an interesting experiment in his *Electra* (1962), shot in the Greek countryside and by the walls of Mycenae, the birthplace of the Atreides. The film fully expresses a Greece that is passionate, arid, and abjectly poor, as it may have been in antiquity.

Musicals

The musical is one type of film that obeys its own laws. By combining the resources of the musical theater with all the potential of the cinema, Hollywood, invincible in this domain, has produced some remarkable films. The prototype for this genre was Lloyd Bacon and Busby Berkeley's famous *42nd Street* (1933), followed by the *Gold Diggers* series. Robert Z. Leonard filmed *The Great Ziegfeld* (1936) in effective sets of dazzling lavishness designed by Cedric Gibbons. All these films, made up of various sketches, like vaudeville, are characterized by admirably choreographed dances, chorus routines of machine-life precision, and enormous sets inspired by Broadway musicals. These sets are carefully designed to permit elaborate crane and tracking shots, great mobility of the scenery, and rapid lighting changes. The repeated use of high-angle shots explains the care given to the floor coverings, which were often glass or ice and later plastic. There may be a multiplicity of luminous stairways and glass fountains, or else repetition *ad infinitum* of a luxurious motif: a hundred white pianos with charming lady pianists or dozens of elaborate, frilly beds in which scantily dressed young women all wake at the same time. The "West Point Cadets," sword in hand, drill like

Top Hat (RKO, 1935). Fred Astaire and Ginger Rogers in the B.W.S. of Venice in the "Cheek to Cheek" number. Directed by Mark Sandrich. Art directors (nominated for an Academy Award): Carroll Clark and Van Nest Polglase. The designs for this and other Astaire–Rogers films at RKO originated with Allan Abbott. "Venice is itself a stage set, and Polglase's designers needed little prompting to get into the right spirit. The Big White Set normally occupied the largest share of the physical costs of production. For Venice the studio decided to shoot the works. Two adjoining sound stages were flung open, a winding canal was built across both of them, and this was spanned by two staircase bridges at one end and a flat bridge at the other."—Arlene Croce, The Fred Astaire and Ginger Rogers Book.

tin soldiers, or Eleanor Powell dances under a tunnel formed by the trumpets of an orchestra made up of fifty black sailors, or the Busby Berkeley girls' bodies form all kinds of moving geometrical figures, even human flowers when seen from above in high-angle shots.

Musicals had been repeating themselves and were becoming mere routine formula, when Vincente Minnelli came to Hollywood and brought new life to the genre. Minnelli had worked on sets and costumes for the Paramount Theater in New York and for Earl Carroll's Vanities. He became art director at Radio City Music Hall and had to get a new show together there nearly every week for several years. He then directed and designed a series of Broadway musicals. MGM producer Arthur Freed

The all-color, all-sound *Gold Diggers of Broadway* (Warner Bros., 1929), with Ann Pennington, Winnie Lightner, and Nick Lucas. Directed by Roy del Ruth. Art directors: Max Parker and Lewis Geib. Songs by Al Dubin and Joe Burke: "Painting the Clouds with Sunshine," "Tiptoe through the Tulips," "In a Kitchenette," "The Poison Kiss of That Spaniard," and more. A lost film—no prints of it seem to be available anywhere.

convinced him to come to Hollywood; and in his first year or so at MGM, Minnelli worked in all the departments and wrote and shot numbers for various films directed by others. His first solo directorial effort was the all-black musical *Cabin in the Sky* (1943). The sets were by Cedric Gibbons and Leonid Vasian. This was followed by *I Dood It* (1943), designed by Jack Martin Smith and Merrill Pye, and *Meet Me in St. Louis* (1944), designed by Smith and Lemuel Ayers. Minnelli attached great importance to the sets and costumes, giving them a personal touch. He always worked very closely with art directors, and has stated, "I was lucky in having men of the caliber of Preston Ames and Jack Martin Smith to help me with the designs."* In musical comedy he found the possibility of expressing dreams, first by means of dance, then through sets and color.

* Charles Higham and Joel Greenberg, *Celluloid Muse: Hollywood Directors Speak* (Chicago: Regnery, 1969), p. 175.

137

To Minnelli, musical comedy is a "spectacle within a spectacle." As a framework for his musicals he often uses a cabaret, a music hall, or a ballet, and the show takes place partly on stage, partly backstage, and features the actors, the dancers, the painters. There is no longer any barrier between art and life; the fantastic bursts in upon the reality of the sets. For dream sequences Minnelli often turns to surrealism or abstract art.

An American in Paris (1951) had music by Gershwin, sets by Preston Ames, and costumes by Irene Sharaff. Minnelli was no longer content to turn to the great painters just for inspiration; several of the sketches are danced in front of vast canvases actually painted in the manner of Toulouse-Lautrec or Dufy. Those backgrounds painted with areas of flat color, with no attempt at relief, made it possible to use the bright colors that are one of the features of the film.

From this period on, Minnelli's universe became increasingly baroque and sophisticated. Bright colors splatter constantly changing decors. His designers followed his evolution toward dandyism. Songs replaced dialogue, the story became no more than a pretext, dream became delirium, and nature itself, re-created in the studio with unreal colors and a festival atmosphere, became an illustration of the marvelous.

Stanley Donen and Gene Kelly, dancers and choreographers, made films that shared in the triumph of American musical comedy between 1950 and 1955. Their sets retain a more or less realistic appearance; the enchantment is created by the intrusion of dance and music into the barely stylized framework. The spectator has the impression that everyday objects have lost their weight and that movement is dissolving reality. Color merely adds to the pleasure of the senses, the object of every musical comedy. Not so aesthetically inclined as Minnelli, more direct in their approach, Donen and Kelly made their first film, *On the Town* (1949), with help from the providential Arthur Freed, a former lyricist. The best of the Donen–Kelly films is *Singin' in the Rain* (1952). *It's Always Fair Weather* (1955) was the last made by the team; before this, Donen made a film of unbridled verve, *Seven Brides for Seven Brothers* (1954), and a charming, subtle, even sophisticated film with Audrey Hepburn and Astaire, *Funny Face* (1957), music by Gershwin. Alfred Junge did the sets for Gene Kelly's ballet film *Invitation to the Dance* (1956); the genre then seemed eclipsed for a while. Otto Preminger's remarkable *Carmen Jones* (1954) was followed by his *Porgy and Bess* (1959), which has great musical and choreographic qualities, but in which the contribution of the film medium is not very evident. The sets seem dull and heavy, all the more noticeably after the fireworks of Minnelli's films.

But *West Side Story* (1961), by Robert Wise and Jerome Robbins, was incredibly successful. The film is sung, above all danced in choreography inspired by athletics and fighting. This time the work is enriched by cinematic techniques. The sets by Boris Leven are of rare quality. Contrary to the laws of the genre, interiors and exteriors are treated with vigor. No mannerism is employed to depict a street in a New York slum, a basketball court, the front of a tenement, or the underside of a bridge, but each of these sets has been subjected to a sifting process. Leven preserved only the essential elements to frame the arabesques of the dance. Even the colors of the sets

Shirley Jones and Bambi Lynn in the "Out of My Dreams" ballet in Oklahoma! (Magna, 1955). Produced by Arthur Hornblow, Jr.; directed by Fred Zinnemann. Production designer: Oliver Smith; art director: Joseph C. Wright; set decorator: Keogh Gleason. The first film shot in the Todd-AO process—brainchild of Mike Todd, who asked the American Optical Co. to give him "something that will come out of one hole" to rival Cinerama. "Movie makers, captivated by the rural realism of the film, will wonder how Arthur Hornblow will be able to swing into the mood of epic symbolism necessary to the big ballet. His breathtakingly beautiful accomplishment of this difficult transition is assisted by some of the finest technical help the screen has ever seen. Oliver Smith's production design achieves unity by using backdrops showing infinite fields of wheat beneath lowering prairie skies and Joseph Wright's art direction keeps this constantly present by creating skeleton sets that prevent any shift in locale from doing violence to the overall mood. Keogh Gleason's set decorations, selecting precisely the right prop for each second of the ballet, sets a standard for members of his craft to shoot at."—The Hollywood Reporter, Oct. 11, 1955. All of the location shooting for Oklahoma! was done in Arizona.

have been chosen to emphasize the characters, either by their neutral tones or by their contrast with the costumes. These sets are almost stylized, yet they blend well with the helicopter shots of a real New York neighborhood.

The sets for George Cukor's *My Fair Lady* (1964) by Gene Allen and the costumes by Cecil Beaton are the most striking features of this famous film. Beaton, the British stage and screen designer and photographer of London society, showed wit, freedom, and talent in designing the costumes, especially those for the women. The interiors were conceived with taste and built with great care for detail, preserving a touch of elegance in their realism. However, the large set of Covent Garden does not escape artificiality: it reeks of the studio. It is a pity that the designer did not create a more abstract evocation, like the Ascot stands, for example, which perfectly fulfill their role as a frame for the brilliant costumes.

In France, Jacques Demy attempted two interesting experiments in musical comedy: *The Umbrellas of Cherbourg* (1964) and *The Young Ladies of Rochefort* (1966). In *The Umbrellas of Cherbourg*, dancing plays no part. To music by Michel Legrand, the actors exchange intentionally commonplace sung dialogue. The conventional story borders on melodrama, but the film's freshness and experiments with color were a pleasant surprise. There are few sets, but the exteriors—walls, fences, façades, and even the ground—were repainted according to the instructions of the designer, Bernard Evein, and the results are ravishing.

As for classical or modern ballet, there have been few successes. Many famous ballets and dancers have been filmed in the Soviet Union; unfortunately, most of the films are little more than documentaries, since the directors have been content to film the ballets in their stage settings. There have been some attempts to "aerate" the action—ballets begun on stage and then continued in three-dimensional sets constructed in a studio (*The Fountain of Bakhtshisarai*), or even outdoors, on a real lake with a flight of animated cartoon swans (*Swan Lake*)—but with disappointing results.

In France, too, some ballets have been filmed in the studio, again against sets like stage sets. This type of film may have some documentary value. But like the musical, the ballet film needs to be entirely re-created for the camera, because theatrical scenery, whether it is painted or made up of abstract elements, loses all its character as soon as it is forcibly adapted to the needs of the cinema. The camera cannot be content to follow the show from a seat in the orchestra. It has to penetrate into the interior of the set to capture an attitude, an expression, a gesture of the dancer, a detail, or else the overall effect, shot from any angle. And each time the set must play its part, must be present with its volumes, its lines, its colors. The filmed ballet is a difficult genre, and there is only one complete success, *The Red Shoes*.

Unlike the ballet film, the musical gained a new lease on life. One remarkable example is Carol Reed's *Oliver* (1968). Many of the vast, striking sets by John Box representing various districts of London, are based on Doré's engravings. The necessary interpretation of reality, using simplified forms and carefully chosen colors, makes these sets a framework perfectly adapted to the production numbers.

Fantastic Films

Ever since Méliès, fantastic films have been made in all periods and all countries. These works may be classified in two categories. First are those which start from a fantastic situation. They are generally adventure films involving special effects or science fiction: *The Thief of Bagdad, The Adventures of Baron Münchhausen, Gulliver's Travels* (themes already dealt with by Méliès), *The Invisible Man* (adapted from H. G. Wells), *King Kong*, etc.; or science fiction films: *La Fin du monde* (Gance), *Things to Come* (Menzies), *Flash Gordon, Forbidden Planet*, and *The Time Travelers*. Second are films based on a fantastic atmosphere. They include the various Faust, Golem, and vampire films, and films dealing with the next world: *Liliom* (Lang), *A Matter of Life and Death* (Powell and Pressburger), fairy-tale or dream films such as *Beauty and the Beast* (Cocteau), *Dead of Night* (Cavalcanti, Hamer, Crichton, Dearden), *Belles de nuit* (Clair), and *Orphée* (Cocteau).

140

The technical devices employed in films coming under the heading of fantastic situations are numerous, including slow motion or fast motion, freeze frame, and masking. All these procedures, although perfected later, date from Méliès. They have been supplemented by the Dunning process, back projection, traveling matte, small-scale models, animated drawings, and so on. The success of these films depends largely on the care given to special effects. In the United States, as in the Soviet Union, there are special departments with their own staff, equipment, and even studio space to deal with the planning and shooting of special effects scenes.

Now consider the films that attempt to create a fantastic atmosphere through subject, set, lighting, music, acting, and color. Interestingly, these films are aesthetically more difficult to make than those in the preceding category. Like it or not, cinema is an art that expresses itself with elements that are real or appear so. What creates fantastic effects is the unusual presentation of these elements and not systematic distortion or stylization of reality. The forms created, with purely aesthetic aims, by German expressionism or French aestheticism during the years 1920–25 are absolutely incompatible with current vision. However, an expressionist state of mind and some of the procedures resulting from it appear in various contemporary cinematic styles; examples are Bergman's *The Naked Night*, Fellini's *La Strada* and *La Dolce Vita*, Franju's *Eyes Without a Face*, Welles's *Macbeth*, and most of his other films, especially *The Trial* with sets by Jean Mandaroux.

Oddly enough, today baroque or even rococo architecture and interiors are frequently called into play to evoke the strange or unusual, unlike the expressionist predilection for the Middle Ages. This evocative power of the baroque appears in Vadim's *Blood and Roses*, Resnais's *Last Year at Marienbad*, and Antonioni's *L'Avventura*. René Clair had already used baroque interiors as a background for his film *La Beauté du diable*, a version of the Faust story set in the romantic era with designs by Léon Barsacq. In 1948 I worked with Raymond Bernard on preparations for another *Faust*, no less romantic, which was never filmed. Leafing through Goethe's work, illustrated without much conviction by Delacroix, it occurred to me to base the sets on typically romantic fantasies like the drawings of Victor Hugo and the engravings of Célestin Nanteuil.

For Cocteau's *Beauty and the Beast*, Christian Bérard created a fairy-tale atmosphere similar to that of his ballet scenery: black drapes, candelabra with sparkling lights, living arms emerging from the walls to form brackets, beautiful costumes, and a superb mask for the Beast. Details inspired by Vermeer were used for Beauty's home. Cocteau filmed *Orphée* in the ruins of the Ecole de Saint-Cyr, with interiors by d'Eaubonne; but he was inspired by his first film, *Blood of a Poet* (1930), with its precious aestheticism, and the result was a magic tinged with the surrealism of the late twenties.

In a film, it is difficult to differentiate between dream and reality. In *A Matter of Life and Death* (sets by Junge), Powell and Pressburger used color for the real scenes, and black and white for the scenes taking place in heaven. For Clair's *Belles de nuit*, wholly in black and white, no such solution was possible. After several experiments we finally gave an unreal look to the dream sequences by the almost total absence of

141

relief in the sets. The white walls, a few almost invisible lines, the grayish-white floor that hardly seemed solid, were made even hazier by gauze. The characters looked as if they were moving in sets that had been "erased." Sets with contrasting values and normal props made the real-life sequences stand out. *Dead of Night* utilizes the whole arsenal of dream films: premonitions, hearses, mirrors reflecting strange scenes, a ventriloquist. The impressive stories owe much to the strange atmosphere created by Michael Relph's heavily charged but apparently realistic sets.

Douglas Fairbanks in The Thief of Bagdad *(United Artists, 1924). Directed by Raoul Walsh. Designed by William Cameron Menzies, assisted by Anton Grot and Park French; costumes by Mitchell Leisen. "The opulence of the German superproductions coming to America in the early twenties made an impression on Douglas Fairbanks, the showman. He spent the then-unheard-of sum of two million dollars on this fairy-tale fantasy, outdoing Robin Hood in the splendor of the sets and scope of the production. He purchased American rights to Fritz Lang's Der Müde Tod (Destiny), holding up its release while he copied many of its special effects. Following the tradition of the German studio-built production, a team of craftsmen worked under William Cameron Menzies to create a world of unreality: trees were painted; objects and architecture were designed all out of human proportion; and a highly-polished black floor was devised to reflect buildings, which had been painted darker at the top to make them seem to float. Like Nazimova's Salome made two years earlier, the style of decoration was Art Nouveau, with a lavish use of scroll-work."—Eileen Bowser, Museum of Modern Art Film Notes, 1969.*

The Beloved Rogue (*United Artists, 1927*), starring John Barrymore as François Villon. *Directed by Alan Crosland. Art director: Menzies. "Visually, it's a stunner, with some of the most impressive sets, decor, costuming and photographic composition that the silent screen ever created. Looking just at stills from the film, one is struck by its rather formal eloquence, and reminded particularly of Fritz Lang's Siegfried. Certainly it has a tremendous amount of Gothic/Germanic feeling to it. Yet its deliberate and occasionally self-conscious artistry never gets in the way of its being first and foremost an entertainment. More of an eye-popper than even Menzies's Thief of Bagdad, The Beloved Rogue is a major re-discovery."—William K. Everson, notes for a screening of the film at the New School, N.Y., April 10, 1970.*

Ernest Thesiger, Colin Clive, and above them, five rings down from the top, Dwight Frye, in the great creation sequence of James Whale's The Bride of Frankenstein (Universal, 1935). Art director: Charles D. Hall. The electrical props by Kenneth Strickfaden were brought out of storage nearly 40 years later to be reused in Mel Brooks's Young Frankenstein.

Top: In Just Imagine (Fox, 1930), El Brendel, who had been killed by lightning in 1930, is revived by scientists in the New York of 1980, where he proves a great curiosity. This sci-fi musical was directed by David Butler. Art director: Stephen Goosson. The mechanical effects director, Ralph Hammeras, created several extraordinary miniature sets representing a futuristic New York, which were inspired by Lang's Metropolis.

Bottom: "Bird's eye view of one of the huge sets constructed at Universal City for The Bride of Frankenstein, Karloff's latest starring vehicle."—caption on original photo release.

Top: Son of Frankenstein (Universal, 1939). Art directors: Richard Riedel and Jack Otterson. "Castle Frankenstein is the showplace of the neighborhood! Such a paradise of low, brow-bursting beams! Such endless miles of corridors, rendered fascinating by skiddy turns, pneumonic draughts and sudden breakneck stairways!"—Crisler, New York Times, Jan. 30, 1939.

Bottom: Stanley Kubrick's Dr. Strangelove (Columbia, 1964), designed by Ken Adam.

Opposite: Things to Come (Korda–UA, 1936). Two Americans, director–designer William Cameron Menzies and effects expert Ned Mann, joined forces with Hungarian art director Vincent Korda and French cameraman Georges Périnal—the result was an extraordinary British science fiction film. The composite shot (top) was apparently achieved by means of a hanging foreground miniature combined with real people.

146

Above: Ken Russell's Tommy (Columbia, 1975). St. Marilyn's shrine—a scene shot in a deconsecrated church in Portsmouth, England, decorated by John Clark. Art director: J. Clark; set designer: Paul Dufficey.

Opposite, top: Betty Field and Robert Cummings in Flesh and Fantasy (Universal, 1943). Produced by Charles Boyer and Julien Duvivier; directed by Duvivier. Unit art directors: Richard Riedel and Robert Boyle; supervising art director: John Goodman; set decorations: R. A. Gausman, E. R. Robinson. For many years Gausman was head of Universal's property department.

Opposite, below: A religious festival known as "The Game of the Cross" in Cristo Proibito/Strange Deception (1951). Script, direction, and music by novelist Curzio Malaparte. Art directors: Orfeo Tamburi and Leonida Maroulis.

149

Top: The Adventures of Tom Sawyer (Selznick–UA, 1938). Art director: Lyle Wheeler. The menacing anthropomorphic trees are similar to those in the graveyard scene of Great Expectations (1946). The design of both scenes derives from Disney's Flowers and Trees (1932), which had been influenced by Arthur Rackham's book illustrations.

Bottom: Bedlam (RKO, 1946). Art directors: Walter Keller, Albert D'Agostino. The standing set of the church built for The Bells of St. Mary's was reused as part of the madhouse.

150

Top: *Paola Borboni in Le Sorelle Materassi (1942). Directed by Ferdinando Maria Poggioli.*

Bottom: Veteran actress Julia Dean in the role of veteran actress Julia Farren in The Curse of the Cat People (RKO, 1944). Produced by Val Lewton; directed by Robert Wise and Gunther von Fritsch. Art directors: Walter E. Keller and Albert D'Agostino; set decorators: Darrell Silvera, William Stevens. "The studio had requested another Cat People; Lewton cleverly evaded their instructions and gave them what may well be the most poetically conceived movie about the world of the child ever attempted in Hollywood."—Siegel, Val Lewton: The Reality of Terror. See also David Reisman, The Lonely Crowd.

Another type of fantasy film, the science fiction genre, will certainly continue to enjoy wide popularity. Roger Vadim's sex and sci-fi opus *Barbarella* was based on a comic-strip book; its designers were inspired by the book's creator, Jean-Claude Forest. Certain sequences in the James Bond films, especially in *You Only Live Twice,* also fit in this cinematic category. British designer Ken Adam seems to have been one of the first to isolate the laws governing pseudo-scientific sets. As the designer of *Dr. Strangelove* and most of the Bond films, he worked out spectacular effects: cars with clever devices for attack and defense, women transformed into gold statues, fake planes and helicopters, a fake mountain lake whose shimmering surface rolls back to reveal an enormous hangar housing an interplanetary rocket. His evocation of the Pentagon was not without humor. All his sets are extremely modern: cobweb-like stairways, sliding or revolving doors, wide windows, illuminated screens and spheres, retractable walls and floors. The furniture, machinery, and other props are made of molded plastic or metal; everything gleams, sparkles, moves; the floors are real mirrors, the colors bright and pleasant. Then there are explosions, floods, disasters of all sorts, all masterfully handled by the special effects team.

One of the best science fiction films made up to the present is Stanley Kubrick's *2001: A Space Odyssey* (1968). The special effects and the tricky sets executed

Boris Karloff conducts a Bauhaus black mass (note overturned double cross) in the Balkans in The Black Cat *(Universal, 1934). Directed by Edgar G. Ulmer. Art director: Charles D. Hall and (uncredited) Ulmer. Karloff plays Hjalmar Poelzig, an Austrian architect and engineer. Although Ulmer chose the name as some sort of homage to Hans Poelzig, the German art director and industrial engineer with whom he had been acquainted in Weimar Germany (where Ulmer himself had worked as a designer with Reinhardt, Lang, and Murnau), the character is loosely based on Aleister Crowley. See Myron Meisel in* Kings of the Bs, *and the chapter on* The Black Cat *in* Cinema of the Fantastic.

Top: *Stanley Kubrick's 2001: A Space Odyssey (MGM, 1968). Production designers: Tony Masters, Harry Lange, Ernie Archer; art director: John Hoesli. Thirty-five designers and draftsmen worked on the film's futuristic sets.*

Bottom: *Solaris (1972). Directed by Andrei Tarkovsky; based on the novel by Stanislas Lemm. Art director: Mikhail Nikolayevich Romadin (born 1940). Although officially regarded as the Soviet answer to 2001, Solaris was criticized at home as being "too arcane and whimsical for the average audience to understand"* (New York Times, *April 12, 1975).*

according to designs by Tony Masters, Harry Lange, and Ernie Archer, were all carried out with great care, considerable resources, and excellent taste. A wide variety of special effects were brought into play, some purely mechanical, but also huge-scale models (the model for the spaceship *Discovery* was 54 feet long), and others based on matte work or combination shots filmed with the aid of prisms or mirrors.

153

8 The Use of Color

The first color films were the hand-tinted frames used in Méliès's *A Trip to the Moon* (1902) and *20,000 Leagues Under the Sea* (1907). These films were colored frame by frame by women factory workers, each of whom brushed on a separate color. This procedure demanded a great deal of time and care, but aesthetically it posed no problems: the artist selected the colors to be used and the films had the naive freshness of "tuppenny colored" picture sheets. The method was used for some time. Naturally the number of colored copies was limited, because the process was expensive. Soon coloring by stencil was introduced: stencils were cut for each color, and the color was stippled onto the film positive. In 1905, Mery perfected the method by inventing a coloring machine with rollers steeped in color. This was the technique used to produce the short comedies or documentaries of the Pathé–Color series. From 1903 on, film was sometimes toned or tinted: blue for night, red for fire or battles.

Charles Urban, an American pioneer in color film research, worked in England, where he developed a process named Kinemacolor. With the English photographer George Albert Smith, Urban founded the Natural Colour Kinematograph Company in 1908. Kinemacolor was a great success when first publicly demonstrated in 1908; it became the first two-color process used theatrically, with the 1911 premiere of *Round the World in Two Hours* at London's Scala Theatre. Urban's *The Durbar at Delhi* (1911), a report on the crowning of George V as Emperor of India, an even greater success, was the first well-known color film. In 1912 a trichromatic or three-color process was developed in France by Gaumont and called Chronochrome. After World War I, Gaumont Chronochrome was brought back to use in footage shot of the victory parade of July 14, 1919.

Dr. Herbert Kalmus developed the Technicolor process in the United States, and to exploit it, founded the Technicolor Motion Picture Corporation with his associates Comstock and Westcott in 1915. *The Toll of the Sea*, the first film made by the Technicolor subtractive method, was made in 1921. The demand for the film was enormous, and the company's labs were small: it was not until 1923 that sufficient prints of the picture were in general release. By the time of the two-color Technicolor feature *The Black Pirate* (1926), which was a huge success, the process had been greatly improved. Other systems (Keller-Dorian, Berthon, Dufacolor, Gasparcolor) were developed but failed to compete with Technicolor, which succeeded in capturing the world market in twenty years. By then it was a trichromatic process. Walt Disney used the three-color Technicolor printing method for his Silly Symphony, *Flowers and Trees* (1932). *Becky Sharp* (1935), directed by Rouben Mamoulian, was the first Hollywood feature picture to use the new Technicolor three-strip camera.

The same year saw the emergence of the sensational new Kodachrome process, which made it possible to photograph in color on monopack film (three layers of emulsion superimposed on one base). This represented an enormous advance over Technicolor, which involved the running of three rolls of film simultaneously and necessitated a monstrously cumbersome camera. On the other hand, printing copies in Technicolor is a simple process of transferring the pictures from a primary film to a gelatined base by impregnation. This process is similar to the offset method used in reproducing in color works of art. Soon an agreement was reached between Technicolor and the Kodak Company that made possible filming on Monopack Kodak (Kodachrome and later Eastmancolor) and printing by Technicolor methods. David O. Selznick's superproduction *Gone with the Wind* finally appeared in 1939. It contains some remarkable scenes of battles and fires, first-rate acting, and fine sets by Lyle Wheeler that make intelligent use of the antebellum style—but the color is still at a primitive, "natural" stage.

In Germany, the I. G. Farben company developed Afgacolor for Joseph Goebbels. The first widely released film shot in the Agfacolor monopack process was Veit Harlan's *Die Goldene Stadt* (*The Golden City*, 1943), with location backgrounds shot in Prague. Emphasis was placed upon the motley costumes of gypsies (the director declared enthusiastically, "The film must be built of materials that allow reality to be brought to the screen. One of these is color."). Goebbels decided in the early forties that the twenty-fifth anniversary of UFA in 1943 should be celebrated with the release of the greatest superspectacle ever produced by the company. The sets alone took five months to prepare. German technicians carefully studied Korda's *The Thief of Bagdad* and many Disney pictures. After two years of work, *Münchhausen* (directed by Josef von Baky) was released in 1943. The color was not bad, the special effects quite interesting.

The great directors hesitated for a long time to make films in color, less from principles—as had been the case with sound—than from a certain timidity regarding the new process, a lack of points of reference. Erich von Stroheim said pertinently of color,

Life is not black and white. If the weather is melancholy we are in a bad mood and everything is black. But if the sun is shining we are joyful and then everything is in color. This, put simply, is my conception of color in the cinema. This is what I did in The Wedding March *(the Corpus Christi procession in St. Stephen's Church, Vienna, 1927). In 1919 for* The Devil's Passkey *I had the flames of the candles in a candelabrum painted by hand in six prints. I had filmed the heroine's face through the candles. The effect was marvelous.*

In Greed the leitmotiv is gold. I had everything that was in gold painted in on six prints of the film—from the gleaming brass knobs on the bedposts to the birdcage found in the desert.

Even at this early stage, therefore, I recognized the value of color. The cinema of tomorrow cannot fail to be in color and three dimensions, for life is in color and three dimensions. *

Everyone seems to have agreed on what they ought not do, but it seems to have been difficult to lay down laws on what should be done with color in the cinema—and already there was talk of three dimensions! "Just wait," said the humorists. "They're going to invent the theater!"

In *Histoire du cinéma* by M. Bardèche and R. Brasillach, published in 1948, the authors declared, "It is possible to imagine a cinema in color. The absurdity would be to understand by that 'in natural color.' What does not interest us is precisely natural colors, and in any case what does that phrase mean? What does interest us is to imagine a film as far removed from nature as Brueghel, Rembrandt, or Renoir can be. We must hope for the advent of a Delacroix of the screen, a Cézanne of the screen, a Modigliani or an El Greco of the screen, each with his personal distortion, his favorite color, his individual tones."

If at first glance this statement seems praiseworthy, nevertheless it contains the most fatal error and the one most widespread among people of taste, an error of judgment that has paralyzed many filmmakers by giving them an artist complex. However little anyone knows about films and painting, it is obvious that to compare a film with an easel painting is absurd. Since the actors, sets, and furniture possess volume with some parts lit up and others in shadow, all flat areas of pure color, so familiar to painters, must be ruled out. It is pointless to talk about a Cézanne, a Brueghel, or a Delacroix of the screen: painting is static and film is above all a dramatic progression.

The question of color was analyzed with the greatest clarity by Sergei Eisenstein, a remarkable achievement considering that *Notes of a Film Director* was written in 1948. In it he said, "The red of the flag pierced *Potemkin* like a fanfare but here its effect was due not so much to the color itself as to its meaning. So when we approach the problem of color in film we must think first of all of the meaning associated with a given color." The red flag had been colored by hand on the prints, like the gold in *Greed.* Later, in the section on "Color Film," Eisenstein wrote:

Hence, the first condition for the use of color in a film is that it must be, first and foremost, a dramatic factor.

In this respect color is like music.

Music in films is good when it is necessary.

Color, too, is good when it is necessary. . . .

* Von Stroheim, *Ciné-Club* (April 1949).

The argument that in a color film color is present on the screen all the time whereas music is introduced only when it is necessary, does not change the matter. Because we do not call a film a musical in which at one moment we see an accordion-player and at another hear a ditty sung, while the rest is taken up by dialogue.

A film is a musical if the absence of music is regarded as a pause or caesura (it may last a whole reel, but it must be as precise as the rhythmically calculated measures of silence on the sound track). *

It is exactly the same with color. "It disappears from sight as soon as the situation does not compel it to intervene as a dramatic element." The chapter ends with the following sentences: "I think that from the point of view of method the best thing would be to show such a principle in action on a concrete example. So I shall give a short description of how the color sequence was constructed in *Ivan the Terrible*" † (left unfinished by Eisenstein; the last lines were written on February 10, 1948, the eve of his death). He is referring to the final scene of Part 2, a fantastic black and red ballet by Ivan's bodyguards.

Olivier's *Henry V*, shot in Technicolor in British studios, was perhaps the first film conceived in terms of color. This is no longer coloring; color plays a dramatic role, to use Eisenstein's idea. By 1946, in Powell and Pressburger's *A Matter of Life and Death*, color had become absolutely necessary to the construction of the film. An interesting experiment was made in 1948 in *The Red Shoes*, also by Powell and Pressburger. Hein Heckroth, the designer of the sets and costumes, made a hundred sketches in color representing the various phases of the ballet. These sketches were filmed in Technicolor and projected onto the screen like an animated cartoon. In this way the filmmakers could carefully construct the choreography of the ballet and make editing decisions in advance in terms of color.

In the Soviet Union an improved version of Agfacolor appeared under the name Sovcolor. The first documentary film in color was Yutkevich's *Greetings, Moscow!* (1946). That same year *The Stone Flower*, in color, was premiered—a fairy-tale film made by Ptushko, a former designer. This is a Siberian legend full of special effects, scale models—and colors. In 1948, Dovzhenko made *Michurin* (*Life in Bloom*), the first Russian film in which music and color are blended successfully.

No color films were shot in France before 1951. Since Technicolor was too expensive, Gevacolor, a Belgian process derived from Agfacolor, was used. The first major color film was Christian-Jaque's *Bluebeard*, with sets by Georges Wakhévich. More color films followed in 1952: Robert Vernay's *Andalusia*, Richard Pottier's *Imperial Violets* with sets by Léon Barsacq; and then in 1953, Raymond Bernard's *La Dame aux camélias*, also designed by Barsacq. In 1952, Technicolor appeared on the French market in Christian-Jaque's *Lucrèce Borgia*, with sets by Robert Gys; and in 1953 French filmmakers began to use the most recent process, Eastmancolor (Kodak), which was much easier to use than Technicolor. Jean Renoir made *The Golden Coach* in Rome with sets by Mario Chiari that are most attractive in their restrained color.

* Eisenstein, pp. 117, 121, 123.

† Ibid., p. 128.

The only French process used commercially was Rouxcolor, but problems in projection, which required extreme care, made it a financially shaky venture. In three years, the heroic period of color film in France was over. After some initial experiments, producers, directors, and cameramen became sufficiently experienced to tackle color film with complete confidence.

Every time a new technique appears in films, its arrival is accompanied by the training of a body of specialists whose task is to apply the new technique with blind devotion. Thus at the beginning of the talkies, the sound engineers trained by the Americans acquired considerable importance. Every time the sets were changed, the sound engineer in charge would appear with an air of consternation, clap his hands, cock his head, listen to an imaginary echo, and declare bluntly that it was impossible to film in that set. The windows would have to be eliminated, the walls placed at an angle and covered with absorbent material. Generally these demands had to be met, at least in part. Otherwise the expert "would not answer for the consequences."

A similar phenomenon—the appearance of the color consultant—occurred with the introduction of Technicolor. (The other processes, fortunately, did not have time to train specialists.) The American Technicolor company had a branch in London with its own cameras, technicians, and labs. European producers got their supplies from London. In Hollywood, Nathalie Kalmus established dominion over all Technicolor productions in her job as color consultant; in London, her colleagues had to apply the "right methods." The color consultants intervened at every stage of production, from the shooting script to the final cut, and were entitled to inspect the colors, materials, makeup, lighting, and sequence of sets and scenes. The most obvious result was to make most Technicolor films uniform and banal, until Eastmancolor ousted its predecessor as the leading color process.

The superiority of Eastmancolor over other monopack processes lay chiefly in its greater sensitivity. It demanded less light and distant objects appeared more clearly; however, colors stood out too violently, especially the blues. Since then, these problems have almost disappeared, but at first blue was strenuously avoided. It was never enough, however. A set painted gray came out as bright blue. In order to obtain a tolerable gray, beige had to be used. I still remember an apparently innocuous blue bottle which the props man had casually placed on the café counter in *Le Grand Jeu*. When the film was shown, the only thing to be seen was the bottle: it was the star and everyone waited for something to happen to it, but nothing did. It was content to outshine the actors.

In Clair's *Les Grandes Manoeuvres*, we took precautions with the cunning of hunters. The tunics of the dragoons, normally navy blue, had been made of black cloth. The sets were done in gray-beige tints; the furniture was chosen because it was black or lacquered white; those items that were not black or white originally were carefully repainted. The women's dresses and the civilians' suits were allowed a limited range of colors running from black to white through beige and maroon. The only touch of color, which appeared like a leitmotiv throughout the film, was the red of the military trousers. Thanks to these restrictions limiting the palette to neutral tints, a simple patch of color was enough to draw attention to an object possessing dramatic or comic value, such as the gramophone with the red horn that emits a comic song to fill the embarrassed silence of a flagging reception. Similarly the color orange attracts attention to the wheel of chance, the blind instrument of destiny. Again, color is the basis for the gag of the two coquettes who meet one another and notice, only long after the audience, that they are wearing the same yellow hat. The set for the provincial main street, built on the studio lot, was treated in the same range of beige-gray and whites. We even had to spray yellow the leaves of the real trees, in order to tone down their crude green.

In France, the years 1955–56 saw the greatest number of color films made, some of them in combination with Cinemascope. Among the most interesting were Renoir's *French Cancan* (1954), with sets by Max Douy; Claude Autant-Lara's *Marguerite de la nuit* (1955), also with sets by Douy; Gérard Philipe's *Les Aventures de Till l'Espiègle* (1956), with sets by Barsacq; Renoir's *Paris Does Strange Things* (1956), with sets by Jean André; Henri-Georges Clouzot's short, *The Picasso Mystery* (1956), and Albert Lamorisse's *The Red Balloon* (1956).

When the New Wave appeared in 1958–59, it seemed that perhaps color should be reserved for spectaculars: Camus's *Black Orpheus* or swashbuckler adventures like d'Hunebelle's *The Captain*. A few Franco-Italian co-productions, like René Clément's *Plein Soleil* (*Purple Noon*, 1959), also used color. Two productions which used color to good effect were Jacques Tati's *Mon Oncle* (1959) and Jacques Baratier's *Goha* (1959), shot in Tunisia. The white Moorish architecture proved extremely photogenic, thanks to the Agfacolor process.

American directors seemed more at ease with color when they were working in Europe, outside the rigid framework of Hollywood. For *Moulin Rouge*, John Huston drew his inspiration from the most famous paintings of Toulouse-Lautrec. The sets are by the illustrator–designer Marcel Vertès and Paul Sheriff. This was one of the first films to use color with discrimination. In 1955 King Vidor filmed Tolstoy's *War and Peace* in Italy, with American actors. The sets were by Mario Chiari and Mario Garbuglia and included some fine sequences, especially battle scenes.

The Soviet director Pudovkin's last film was *The Return of Vasily Bortnikov* (1953). It opens with a man walking at night through a snow-covered landscape. The spectator is convinced that the film is in black and white until the moment when the camera picks up the lit window of a house. The yellow patch of light has shock force, multiplied tenfold because it is unexpected. After *The Great Warrior Skanderberg* (1954), a film dealing with a medieval Albanian hero in skillfully orchestrated color, Yutkevich made a more classical *Othello* (1955). In 1954, Sergei Vasiliev, the co-director of *Chapaiev*, tackled a very important film about an incident of the Russo-Turkish War, *The Heroes of Shipka*. It contains an unexpected color effect: we see the Russian troops in a snowy landscape; suddenly the firing of an artillery salvo changes the color of the trees before our eyes by shaking the snow from the branches.

The contribution of Japanese color films is significant. The first one shown in Europe, Kinugasa's *Gate of Hell*, was a revelation. The vividness and, at the same time,

159

the subtlety of the color harmonies were undoubtedly inspired by eighteenth-century woodblock prints, but this effect had to be translated on the cinematic plane, which, as we have seen, is not at all easy. The sets for *Gate of Hell* are remarkable for the choice of colors and the skillful use of traditional Japanese architecture. The film was shot on Eastmancolor stock. The art director was Kisaku Itoh, and the production was designed by Kosaburo Nakajima, greatly aided by color consultant Sanzo Wada, a painter and professor of art who arranged the sets. Contrary to general opinion, it was not the first Japanese film in color, but the first Japanese film to be made in a reliable color process.

After a transitory crisis, lasting seven or eight years, color once more became an inseparable part of most films that were at all ambitious. Musicals especially—*West Side Story* and *My Fair Lady,* for instance—were conceived in terms of color and are difficult to imagine in black and white.

Thanks to color, costume films like Sergei Bondarchuk's *War and Peace* (1964–67), with sumptuous sets by Mikhail Bogdanov and Gennady Myasnikov,

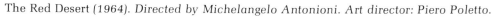

The Red Desert *(1964). Directed by Michelangelo Antonioni. Art director: Piero Poletto.*

acquire a certain resemblance to a kind of historical painting, especially in the battle scenes. David Lean's *Dr. Zhivago* (1965), with fine interior sets by John Box, derives from color certain effects—the hallucinatory presence of red flags, for example—that are inconceivable in black and white. Fellini and his designer Gherardi stressed the strange, dreamlike aspect of *Juliet of the Spirits* (1965) by their extreme use of wildly clashing colors in alternation with sequences dominated by milky whites enlivened by patches of pure color.

The desire to utilize color, to make it participate in the style of the film, even if it is shot out of doors, is apparent in Antonioni's *The Red Desert* (1964), in which designer Piero Poletto had even the grass of the landscape painted. This practice culminated in Antonioni's *Blow-Up* (1966), which reaches a sort of perfection in abstraction. Nothing remains entirely real, because this time the British designer Assheton Gorton, in order to keep to the director's style, entirely re-created existing interiors with color. The result is surprisingly fresh scenes of London.

Color is now used with greater freedom than it was in the early and mid-fifties. Technical progress and more adventurousness on the part of directors and designers have given color films both a richness and a style that are different from black-and-white films and that will unquestionably become stronger. In Vadim's *La Curée* (*The Game Is Over,* 1966), with strange sets by Jean André derived from art deco, Robert Hossein's *I Killed Rasputin* (1967), in which Barsacq, while respecting the Russian setting, evolved his sets in terms of the dominant colors, and Jean-Pierre Melville's *Le Samourai* (1967), with highly stylized interiors by François de Lamothe, color was undeniably a determining factor in evolving a visual style.

The great majority of American filmmakers, however, employ color in a rather impersonal manner, although with great technical vigor. There are of course exceptions. One of the most interesting American films from the point of color is Arthur Penn's *Bonnie and Clyde,* in which everything is transformed, down to the red of the blood, which becomes rose pink, making the gory scenes bearable.

Although the color films by Alan Resnais, Claude Lelouch, Robert Enrico, and François Truffaut do not seem to be based on a clear aesthetic postulate, Jean-Luc Godard, true to his collage theory, seems to draw inspiration from Pop Art painting, that is, from giving significance through the use of color to the most utilitarian and commonplace utensils of our consumer culture. His films from *Pierrot le Fou* (1965) to *La Chinoise* (1967) are shot in real exteriors and interiors, which are generally small and look much the same: white walls from which stand out brightly painted doors, violently colored objects (especially plastic utensils in acid tints), posters, reproductions of pictures, and the like.

9 Creating the Set

The Studios

The main tool of the motion picture industry is the studio. In 1907 France, which initially dominated world film production, had nine studios, all situated in Paris or its outskirts: Méliès, Pathé, Gaumont, Eclair, Théophile Pathé, Georges Hattot, Désirée Weiss, Galland, Lux. But in the wake of World War I, the industry developed only fitfully. None of the big French firms wanted or could afford to build a major cinematic center like the UFA studios near Berlin or the major companies in Hollywood. The few existing studios grew without any overall plan on lots that were too small. With the coming of sound, companies were content to install sound equipment as best they could in the glazed sheds of their original studios. The only French studios built specifically for the production of sound film were those erected by Paramount at St. Maurice. Even the few studios established after 1930 were set up in buildings intended for quite different purposes: coach-building workshops, antiques display rooms, etc.

During World War II, several studios in the Paris region and Nice, which had become France's second film center, were destroyed. Between 1950 and 1960 a new group of studios was built at Boulogne-sur-Seine, while others were extended. But at the same time small studios like Neuilly or Photosonor were expropriated, while the old Gaumont and Pathé studios became television studios. Paris has no studio complex like those at Pinewood near London, Cinecittà in Rome, Bavaria in Munich, Barrandov in Prague, or Universal or MGM in Hollywood.

A look at a typical French studio would be worthwhile. Some visitors entering this supposedly magical domain for the first time may be disappointed. The studio looks like a combination music hall backstage, electrical factory, and demolition site. The corridors are full of people dressed up in the most unexpected costumes: the king's musketeers chat with SS officers, and charming Carmelite nuns mix with vice squad detectives. A dull clamor comes from the acting area where the set is being built. When the door opens, visitors are assailed by a deafening pounding of hammers. Stagehands, carpenters, painters, and electricians work on the set at one time or another, while in the background men are dismantling a set where filming has just

162

finished. Walls come tumbling down in a cloud of plaster while property men hurriedly bring out furniture. It all looks a bit like a cataclysm.

In marked contrast, the set in use seems a haven of peace. The silence is broken only by the brief orders of the director or the cameraman. An impressive battery of projectors lights up at the sound of a whistle; a camera on a dolly moves toward the actors; movements are rehearsed. Makeup artists and dressers stand by to give the actors a final touch of comb or brush before shooting begins. Everything has a technical, even scientific look, yet a single unplanned detail may halt everything. What strikes visitors most is this feverish haste coupled with apparent nonchalance—many people seemingly unoccupied but all ready to participate the moment they are needed.

The shooting of a French film of average budget takes between six and ten weeks, say about fifty days. If, for simplicity's sake, one figures a budget of $500,000, an average day's filming costs around $10,000. This is the most expensive time in the cinema. In France the shooting area measures an average of 100 x 50 feet. For some years newly built areas have measured 130 x 100 feet. In other countries they are as large as 260 x 130 or even 165 feet. In addition to shooting areas, the number of which can vary from two to seven, each studio contains all the ancillary services: electrical generating station; metallurgical reheating furnace; electrical warehouses that store the projectors, cables, and other equipment; set warehouses, in which are kept the frames and other standard elements used in set construction (doors, windows, staircases, and so on). The workshops (carpentry, painting, plastering, modeling, mechanical, etc.) are located in neighboring buildings. Close to the shooting area are furniture warehouses and upholstery and costume shops. Then there are the design studios, production offices for the administrative personnel, actors' dressing rooms, a large makeup room, and so on. Elsewhere, the cutting rooms, one or two projection rooms, an auditorium, and the darkrooms for the assistant cameramen and the photographers complete the studio. Although there used to be a small lot next to each studio on which exterior sets could be constructed, little by little these lots have vanished, making way for new buildings. Eclair is the only company in Paris with a studio lot for exteriors.

Building a set takes between five days and three weeks of work, but a single day is often enough to shoot the scenes for which the sets are intended. This is why, during peak periods, French production suffers from the lack of new studios. Unfortunately there are slack periods, especially in winter.

Preparation for Filming

Often the director is permitted to select his collaborators—designer, director of photography, cutter, script supervisor—especially if they habitually work as a team. Otherwise, the producer hires the technicians. The major film companies stopped hiring their own production "teams" by the year in 1945.

Consider a designer just hired for a film. After reading the scenario, or more often the synopsis, he has an interview with the producer or his representative, the director of production. The film's director, who probably hasn't yet established the final shooting script, discusses with the designer the needs of the film, the main sets, the general style, and so on. The producer consults the designer on more material details: the estimated cost of the sets, the number of shooting areas required, the possibility of filming certain scenes in natural settings or out of doors, and the like.

As for the sets, preparations for the film depend in part on the working methods of the director. There are directors who, after writing their adaptation or shooting script, have a precise vision of the general arrangement of the sets—the position of doors, windows, and stairs—as well as of the movements of the camera and actors. This simplifies the work of the designer. Other directors give no thought to placing the elements of the set and trust to the imagination of the designer, who, through his ideas, will influence their directing. Finally there are some directors (very few in France) who work on their shooting script in collaboration with the designer and sometimes the cameraman.

The designer's first task is to draw up the plans of the main sets, keeping in mind the requirements of the scenario. In so doing, he has to imagine a certain way of staging the scene, visualizing the movements of the camera and the actors within his sets. The following is a concrete example, an attempt to decide the movements of the camera and the actors in terms of a shooting script and, with this as the point of departure, the layout of the set.

HOTEL CORRIDOR   Broadcast of a soccer game

131 MEDIUM SHOT. *Camera moves back, pans.* Pierre reaches the top of the stairs. On the landing he hesitates, seems to be looking for something, then comes toward the camera.
Camera dollies back, farther. Pierre walks along the corridor, looking right and left, then stops and turns toward the door to right of camera.
Camera pans to the right.
132 MEDIUM CLOSE SHOT. The door seen by Pierre, No. 19; the key is in the door.

HOTEL ROOM

133 MEDIUM SHOT. *The camera pans left-right.* The door opens slowly, revealing Pierre, who enters the room.
Camera pans slowly, revealing the whole room, the empty bed, the window at the far end on the right, the venetian blinds closed.

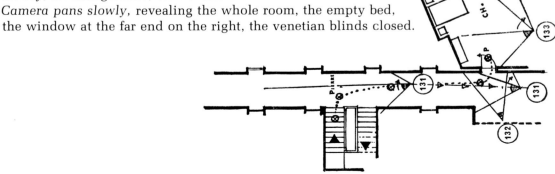

164

Once this very schematic plan has been established, a few facts emerge: It would be better to replace the straight corridor, at the end of which nothing happens, by a curved corridor giving an impression of length but occupying little space; there is no need to build the right side of the room; and the half-flight of stairs could go down into a pit, which would make it unnecessary to mount the set on a raised platform.

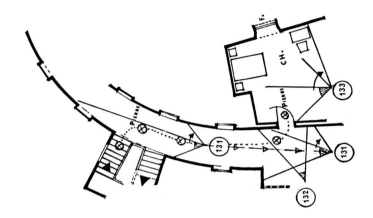

This is the point at which the designer has to look through photographic references, or at real buildings, for a hotel corridor with approximately the same atmosphere, in order to find typical details that will place the set precisely in its country, its town, and even its district, as well as in the period and, naturally, its class.

After drawing up the systematic plans and checking references on the interior to be depicted (especially photographs, but also engravings, paintings, or even detailed descriptions), the designer must give concrete shape to his vision of the framework for the film by drawing the set from the most interesting angles. He begins by making countless thumbnail sketches. The idea has to take shape, often starting from a detail seen in a reference or dredged up from the depths of his memory. Little by little the whole thing sorts itself out, the vision clarifies: light and shade begin to bring the volumes to life, or a touch of color brings out the whites and grays. Every designer has his own way of working, looking for an idea, preparing a sketch, or drawing or painting. The style of the drawing may vary with the subject or the style of the film; it may be loose or exact, sketched in pen, charcoal, wash, pastel, or painted in gouache, watercolor, colored inks, or oils. The essential thing is to convey the idea that governed the initial development of the set so that it is clear and comprehensible to the director, the producer, and all the other artists who will have to carry out this idea.

Armed with sketches and layout plans, the designer meets with the director. This interview is very important and, as a rule, fruitful, because the discussion now relates to concrete elements. For the first time images of the film appear. It is useful for the cinematographer to take part in this discussion, as certain problems may come up that should be solved before shooting starts.

After any modifications by the designer, the final plans for the sets are drawn up by his assistants. They base their work on the schematic plans but try to keep as close

165

Set still for Conquest *(MGM, 1937). Art directors: William Horning and Cedric Gibbons.*

as possible to the sketches. (The graphic method devised by Jean Perrier makes it possible to work out the plan of a set from a perspective sketch or a photograph.) The construction plans for a film set, with sections and elevations, are true architects' drawings, generally drawn to a scale of 1:50 with details at 1:20 or 1:10, and sometimes life size. Prints of all these drawings, as well as photographs of the sketches, are distributed to the various department heads as required. The assistant designers (generally two for the average film, though for major films there may be many more) supervise set construction; they are recruited from among the most gifted assistants with at least ten years of studio experience. The work of preparing the sets is much the same in all European film-producing countries.

In the United States, things are organized rather differently. At the major studios the supervising art director (who is the top person in his department) is assisted by one or several unit art directors.* At an enormous organization like MGM, which during a quarter of a century turned out a few dozen films a year, the name of the studio's supervising art director, Cedric Gibbons, eventually appeared on the credits of hundreds of films. Now, while Gibbons personally designed an occasional prestige production (*David Copperfield, Marie Antoinette, Ben Hur, Camille, A Tale of Two*

* This and the following paragraph are by Elliott Stein.

Cities), or most of it, he may have merely supervised many of the other films that bear his name, and the actual designing would have been done by the unit art director assigned to the picture, working with a crew of draftsmen—subject, of course, to Gibbons's approval. When MGM became the biggest studio in the world, its organization differed from that of the other major studios: it was the only studio where the props, costume, process photography, miniature and special effects departments were so tightly centralized under one head. That head was Gibbons. On productions that he worked on personally, he exerted much more control than other art directors, and he often was a brilliant designer. On the other hand, his name appears as art director on the credits for dozens of films he did not work on; his habit of taking credit for them does not facilitate the work of film historians.

The first official thoroughgoing job of production design may be dated from the work of William Cameron Menzies on *Gone with the Wind*. Menzies was a many-faceted genius of impeccable taste who had entered the motion picture industry in 1918. He designed dozens of films and directed several himself (notably the remarkable science-fiction fantasy *Things to Come*). He retained independence and integrity throughout his career and avoided being dictated to by the "house rules" of any one studio. *Gone with the Wind* was a giant project, and Menzies's work on it exceeded the usual scope of a studio art director. (Lyle Wheeler was art director for *Gone with the Wind* and received a separate Oscar for "interior decoration.") At one point, Selznick considered letting Menzies direct the film, and he actually did direct at least ten per cent of it. In a letter to company executives, dated September 1, 1937, Selznick wrote:

*I feel that we need a man of Menzies's talent and enormous experience on the sets of this picture, and on its physical production. I hope to have Gone with the Wind prepared almost down to the last camera angle before we start shooting, because on this picture really thorough preparation will save hundreds of thousands of dollars. . . . When he gets the complete script, he can then do all the sets, set sketches, and plans during my absence, for presentation to me upon my return, and can start on what I want on this picture and what has only been done a few times in picture history (and these times mostly by Menzies)—a complete script in sketch form, showing actual camera setups, lighting, etc. This is a mammoth job that Menzies will have to work on very closely with Cukor. There is also the job of the montage sequences, which I plan on having Menzies not merely design and lay out but also, in large degree, actually direct. In short, it is my plan to have the whole physical side of this picture, with many phases that I have not dealt with in this paragraph (such as the handling of the process shots) personally handled by one man who has little or nothing else to do—and that man, Menzies. Menzies may turn out to be one of the most valuable factors in properly producing this picture. One of the minor problems in connection with this arrangement is the matter of Menzies's credit. Menzies is terribly anxious not to get back to art direction as such, and of course his work on this picture, as I see it, will be a lot greater in scope than is normally associated with the term "art direction." Accordingly, I would probably give him some such credit as "Production Designed by William Cameron Menzies." **

* David O. Selznick, *Memo from David O. Selznick,* ed. Rudy Behlmer (New York: Viking, 1972), pp. 151–52.

Menzies not only directed the Atlanta fire and other scenes, but he also worked on the script with Selznick. When any dispute arose with the representatives from Technicolor about lighting the set, Selznick ordered that Menzies have the final word.

Today the production designer functions as a coordinator of the film's disparate components well before shooting starts. With all minor problems solved on paper, the director has more time to devote to the actors, and delays in shooting can be reduced by twenty-five per cent. This presupposes that the producer, script writer, director, production designer, and director of photography work together for at least a few weeks after the initial work on the scenario. A daily script board is set up indicating the scenes, the music, and a series of drawings called continuity sketches to give

La Bayadère *in crinolines.* Gone with the Wind *(Selznick–MGM release, 1939). Production designed by William Cameron Menzies—the first such credit to appear on a major American film. Art director: Lyle Wheeler; interiors: Joseph Platt; interior decoration: Edward G. Boyle. The huge gate from* King Kong's *Skull Island, redecorated as a row of housefronts, made its final screen appearance during the burning of Atlanta sequence.*

physical shape to the action. This work involves four or five people, including the director. Starting from these sketches, the production designer conceives the sets and the illustrators render the shooting script sequence by sequence.

American directors are now accustomed to this system of using an illustrated shooting script that they follow faithfully during shooting. There is no doubt that it results in an appreciable saving in shooting time. However, it produces in the director a certain detachment regarding the purely visual part of his work, something like atrophy of his personal vision. Henri-Georges Clouzot, Claude Autant-Lara, and designer Max Douy have used a similar but far less rigid method in France.

American unit art directors, who often have under their orders an assistant responsible for research, another concerned with color and light, the costume designer, and the set builders (the studio's architecture department), create the sets for a given film. The major American companies have had to create a cumbersome administrative apparatus to manage all the ancillary services that make up a studio: furniture and costume stores, numerous workshops (especially those concerned with special effects),

Helen Walker as Lilith Ritter, crook-psychologist, and in his finest performance, Tyrone Power as Stan Carlisle, candidate for geekdom, in Nightmare Alley (20th Century–Fox, 1947). Cinematographer: Lee Garmes; art director: J. Russell Spencer; supervising art director: Lyle Wheeler. As psychological design, this scene is ahead of its time. The prison bar motif, which was to become a cliché of film noir in the 50s, makes an early genre appearance in this scene in Walker's office when it becomes clear that she does, indeed, have Power in a trap.

Three examples of engaging decorative clutter in Vincente Minnelli films. Opposite, top: Kirk Douglas in Lust for Life (MGM, 1956). The screen credits read, "Art directors—Cedric Gibbons, Hans Peters, Preston Ames"—but, as was often the case at MGM, there is no evidence that Gibbons designed any part of the film. Because of the unstable quality of Metrocolor the original release prints have faded. Opposite, bottom: Penn Station set still for The Clock (MGM, 1945). Art director: William Ferrari; set decorators: Mac Alper and Edwin B. Willis. Above: set still for Madame Bovary (MGM, 1949). Art director: Jack Martin Smith; set decorators: Richard A. Pefferle, Edwin B. Willis. This set was used during a sequence in which Emma (Jennifer Jones) is dallying indoors with Rodolphe (Louis Jordan), while in the marketplace Bovary (Van Heflin) addresses the villagers on the merits of fertilizer.

and book, photograph, and record libraries. Nothing is left to chance, to the inspiration of the moment. Advisers of all kinds—literary, artistic, technical, military, and so on—are there to watch out for mistakes. Under these conditions, only a few people of exceptional temperament can make a film that retains a personal touch.

In Hollywood, the large number of shooting areas makes it possible not only to leave the sets in place during the whole shooting of the film, but even to construct duplicates for rehearsals. But in Europe, particularly in France, the shooting schedule has to be established on the basis of rotation of sets. Once each set has been used, it is dismantled to make way for the next. It is not unusual for a film to involve fifteen to thirty sets that must be built on just three or four shooting areas. Some of these sets are used for a week, others for half a day. Large complexes sometimes occupy two adjacent areas, while several small interiors can be erected in the same area.

171

The shooting schedule must take account of both the possibility of rotating sets (which depends on the size of the shooting areas and the time needed for construction, shooting, and dismantling the sets) and the dates on which the leading actors are free—frequently a real headache for the production manager and the designer, who are responsible for the schedule. In any case, the chronological order of the scenes as written in the shooting script is practically never followed, since one set has to be removed to make way for another; or else arrangements have to be made to accommodate an actor who has to be free by a certain date, meaning that all his scenes must be filmed together. Thus one sequence that follows another in the shooting script may be filmed after an interval of three weeks or even more.

Continuity is the responsibility of the script supervisor, who notes details of costume, gestures, the position of the furniture, the length of partially smoked cigarettes, and the like, so that each scene exactly matches up with the one before. As well as script notes, continuity photographs are helpful.

Having prepared drawings for the first sets, the designer and his assistants hire the personnel necessary for their execution. Studio workers are specialists used to putting together the elements of a set quickly and easily. Fitters, carpenters, plasterers, masons, metalworkers, painters, electricians, and others—from fifty to two hundred workers depending on the film—help to construct and equip the sets. Special props not in stock are manufactured in the various workshops. Craftsmen practice trades analogous to those on a construction site, but adapted to the building of film sets.

Once the set has been built, it must be dressed—draperies hung, furniture installed. At the major studios, the designer supervises this work, which is carried out by the prop department. A designer at a small studio may do some dressing himself. Most interiors have to be dressed in a few hours. The problems are different from those involved in work in the theater. Actors—usually actors in motion followed by a tracking camera—may form elements of the set dressing since the decoration was conceived to be photographed with them. What looked great on paper may get cluttered once the actors and the camera are going through their paces, if the art director has not thought these problems through.

Set Construction

A film set should enhance reality. The main problem during set construction is how to reconcile authenticity of appearance with great mobility of the elements of the set. It would be just as unreasonable to employ real gold ingots for a scene in a film as to build the wall of a set with real blocks of granite. Thanks to years of experiments and adjustments, film set design has reached the point where it can reproduce in a more or less satisfactory manner materials that are too cumbersome, too difficult to make, or too expensive. Thus film doors, windows, tiling, and flooring are more or less the same as real ones, but walls are replaced by flats.

The following, in broad terms, is the way sets are constructed. Once the plans and elevations have been drawn up, the best way of placing the set or sets in the given shooting area has to be determined. The most economical method of using the available space is established by drawing a scale plan. This can be complicated, since it involves not only placement of the set or sets, but also easy access, sufficient space for the vistas (ten to sixteen feet), and sufficient room behind the movable frames for rapid evacuation in case of fire. To satisfy all these demands, some sets may have to be reduced in size, or, if there are several sets in one area, one set may have to be built after shooting in the preceding set has been finished.

Once the placement has been worked out, the chief set dresser and his assistants trace the plan of the set on the studio floor and then paint over the tracing to make it clearly visible. There is still time for the designer, or occasionally the director, to modify the proportions, now that the layout is clearly indicated in outline.

The sets are constructed in exact conformity to the plans, sections, and elevations. The first job is to assemble on the set the elements chosen from stock or manufactured in the workshops (doors, windows, stairs, alcoves, and so on); then scaffolding is built as necessary. To avoid creaking or an echo that would interfere with the sound recording, great care must be taken to insulate the scaffolding. Strips of insulating material are placed on the upper surfaces of the truss and the crossbeams. The planks are also lined with insulating material before the floor covering is applied.

The walls are made from frames that are stocked in various sizes, to conform to the measurements in the plans, leaving spaces for doors, windows, bays, and alcoves. Once in place, the frames are covered with light canvas to which packing paper is glued, and the joints are masked prior to papering. These laminated walls must be fiinished with great care to create the illusion of stone, brick, wood paneling, or metal sheets, as required. Occasionally there are advantages in using real wood paneling or wallpaper or in covering the frames with molded or sculpted panels, cornices, dados, frame linings, plinths, and so on. For rustic walls, the frames are covered with a mixture of plaster and sand or with plastic, which can be roughened by scratching. Stones and bricks are molded on real walls, and the sheets taken from the molds (about six by three feet) are attached to the walls and the joints flushed so as to be invisible.

Staff (plaster reinforced with vegetable fiber) has long been useful to designers; it can be molded to imitate any shape or material. But for the past few years, it has frequently been replaced by polystyrene as a surface finish. Plastic possesses considerable advantages: because of its stability, lightness, and suppleness it can be sawed or screwed or bent for curved surfaces. In addition, architectural motifs in plastic—ornaments, fireplaces, and others—can be re-covered, unlike objects of the heavier, more fragile, more easily soiled staff, which almost always finish in the garbage. Another plastic material, styrofoam, is light, porous, and friable, and can be used to make blocks of stone or old bricks.

The metal parts of a construction are made of real metal if the elements are light enough to handle, or if the frame has to support considerable weight. Wood, less resistant to traction and flexion, cannot reproduce sections or profiles as finely as

It Started with Eve (Universal, 1941). Directed by Henry Koster. Art director: Jack Otterson. Anne (Deanna Durbin) and Jonathan (Robert Cummings) sit down and try to determine how they can break the news to his father—that Anne has posed as Jonathan's fiancée.

metal. For a long time the price and weight of such materials limited their use in film sets. Now several sectional metals are on the market, as well as smooth, striped, hammered, and corrugated sheets of aluminum and other materials that facilitate surfacing modern sets. The designer's task is also simplified by a considerable choice of lightweight panels clad with plastic. There are relatively cheap materials made for walls, floors, and ceilings. As a general rule real materials are used wherever imitations are unsatisfactory because of appearance, shooting difficulties, safety, or sound problems. But wood, plywood, staff, and plastic are always the foundation materials, because they are adaptable, light, and easy to use.

The paintwork, especially patina, is most important and must be done with great care. Paintwork may be matte, satin finish (oil paint), or high gloss (lacquer or varnish), as required. Sets are no longer painted in a range of grays for black and white films, as they were in the early days of the cinema (orthochromatic film was insensitive to red and almost insensitive to yellow). The colors used are beige, cream,

Merle Oberson and Alan Marshal in Lydia *(United Artists, 1941). Produced by Alexander Korda. Sets designed by Vincent Korda and Jack Okey; set decorator: Julia Heron.*

blue-gray, gray-green, and, for more striking effects, even red, blue, yellow, black, and white. The resulting surroundings please the eye and harmonize with the costumes, curtains, chairs, and pictures (which are always in color)—an important factor because actors are sensitive to the atmosphere of the set. Moreover, the range of grays obtained this way is richer in photographic value than tones of pure gray. Color films have different problems, and color should be used with economy and deliberation. This does not necessarily imply that sets have to be dull or uniform; recent sets have shown that bright colors can contribute significantly to the atmosphere of a film, if used with discernment.

Patina enriches the surface texture of materials—brick and slate, for example—and brings sets to life by reproducing the wear and tear of time. To apply patina, specialists need the skills of scene painters and a talent for observation and

"Claire Trevor and Lionel Banks, art director of Columbia Pictures, have a preview of the decorative fabrics to be used in Miss Trevor's new picture to go into production shortly. . . . Miss Trevor is admiring the 'Monticello' pattern, inspired by a wood carving in Thomas Jefferson's enshrined home."—caption on original 1940s photo release.

invention. Rusty iron, worn, soiled, or torn wallpaper, crackling paint and cracks in walls, dirt, damp, or just a slight yellow glaze applied to woodwork are the responsibility of the patina expert.

Decorative artists handle all the painted decoration such as decorative panels, curtains, stage scenery, and textured floors; but they are most frequently called in to produce vistas. Sometimes painted or built as scale models, vistas most often consist of enlarged photographs usually depicting rural or urban landscapes. The decorator always touches them up and, for a color film, colors the entire surface of any photograph. When the decorative artists work on floors, they prefer to wait for the painting and patina to be finished before laying the floors, unless they are using real tiles, which are laid in plaster and are easy to clean. For real parquet floors, the walls of the set are wedged up to the thickness of the parquet blocks, which are then slipped

Greensman from the Goldwyn art department hammering leaves on a tree for Wuthering Heights *(1939).*

under the frames. Parquet or tile floors laid in decorative patterns must be specially built. The patterns are painted on slabs of plastic, the joints are cut, and then the cut slabs are varnished and laid. If the budget permits, fitted carpets are real; if it does not, they can easily be replaced by coarse cloth, either patterned or plain.

When the set is almost finished, the upholsterer goes to work. He lays the fitted carpet and the stair carpet and hangs the draperies, which he has made in advance, as well as all other hanging fabrics included in the set. He also covers the chairs with fabric specially chosen to harmonize with the interior decoration.

Nurserymen install the corners of gardens, a difficult task in a studio. Green plants and winter gardens work well, but trees in leaf do not last on the sets; and then there is the problem of filming in winter. Bare trees are used, their branches decked out with artificial leaves. Plastic flowers are often used instead of real ones, which fade quickly under the arc lamps.

177

Before the set that has been constructed, painted, and patinaed can be furnished, it must be equipped electrically. Electricians' catwalks, about a yard wide, run around the whole upper part of the set. For large-scale sets, supplementary walks run from side to side, lengthwise or crosswise above the set, to divide up the surfaces that need lighting. These catwalks hold lights of all shapes and sizes. While incandescent light from projectors of 1, 2, 5, and 10 kilowatts light the actors and the set, arc lights of 150 or 225 amps are used for special effects: sunlight, moonlight, lightning, conflagrations, and so on. In addition to the projectors on the catwalks, many small projectors, basin-shaped reflectors holding 5-kilowatt reflectors equipped with six 500-watt lamps, ceiling lights, and others, are set up out of camera range, suspended or fixed on special stands and hidden behind projecting parts of the set.

All that remains is to install the furniture, pictures, tapestries, chandeliers, and knicknacks. The choice of furniture and properties needed on the set, as well as properties that are necessary in the script, is up to the interior decorator in consultation with the designer. Some decorators with outstanding knowledge and taste make a personal contribution to the film set.

The word "property" describes the whole range of unlikely objects used in the film. A bishop's crozier is a property, and so is a machine gun or an iron lung. A period bicycle or a shrunken head can be rented from an antique dealer as easily as a Regency commode; but there are some objects and pieces of furniture that are available only from specialists and must be tracked down. When various objects, pieces of furniture, and other props cannot be found through furniture renters or antique dealers—most likely to happen in films about the remote past or the future—it becomes the responsibility of the set designer or the interior decorator to design and have manufactured the missing article.

So far, this chapter has covered only sets representing interiors, but scenarios frequently call for the construction of exterior sets. Filming in existing exteriors may be ruled out for various reasons: their remoteness (in films whose action takes place abroad, for example), difficulty of access, weather conditions, traffic, the need for a great deal of filming by night, the refusal of permission. For historical films these difficulties may be compounded by the presence of modern buildings, telephone poles, trolley wires, billboards, or other anachronistic objects making a given exterior unusable. That is why major constructions such as the Boulevard du Crime, the Barbès Métro station, the open square in front of Notre Dame, a district on the outskirts of town, or even modern buildings of glass and concrete can be seen going up on the lots beside film studios. It may also be necessary, in the absence of a suitable existing structure, to build a set in the middle of a forest, the desert, or the mountains, or on the banks of a lake.

In drawing up the plans for an exterior set, the designer has to take account of the least encumbered views or, for a landscape, the most interesting views. He must place the set so as to make maximum use of sunlight, bearing in mind the time of year and the height of the sun. The ideal orientation is on a north–south axis, avoiding constructions facing north, where they would have the light behind them, and making maximum use of positions facing east, south, and west.

Constructing exterior sets differs from building sets in the studio. These temporary buildings, generally large, have to stand up to wind and weather, demanding a stable framework of metal or timber scaffolding with firm wind braces. Floors and roofs, if required, are calculated in terms of the weight they must carry: crowds, snowfalls, violent winds, and so on. The various levels are served by concealed stairs giving easy access. Wall surfaces are made of resistant materials, such as plaster tiles, slabs of conglomerate, planks, or wattle coated with staff or plaster that is then whitewashed. Streets are paved (preferably with real paving stones), asphalted, or cemented as required, including curbs and gutters. The painting is done with oil or acrylic paint or any other water-resistant product. In sunny countries colored washes are used.

The patina of exterior sets has to be even more carefully applied than that of studio sets. Sunlight makes it impossible to cheat, to "paint" the set as can be done in artificial light. House fronts are patinaed with a spray, a hard brush, or rags, using oil sludge, dirty or strongly dyed water, or acid. Excess patina can be washed off by throwing buckets of water at it or by hosing it down. "Old" housefronts and doors

A replica of New York's Amsterdam Avenue in 1914, during filming of The Pride of the Yankees *(produced by Sam Goldwyn for RKO release, 1942). Directed by Sam Wood. Camera crew is concentrating on Douglas Croft (in front of bakery wagon) who portrays young Lou Gehrig on his way to sandlot baseball game behind billboards. Production designer: William Cameron Menzies; art directors: Perry Ferguson and McClure Capps; set decorator: Howard Bristol.*

John Ford's How Green Was My Valley (20th Century–Fox, 1941). Art directors: Nathan Juran and Richard Day; set decorator: Thomas Little. The Welsh mining village was constructed in a California valley named Brent's Crags, where it spread over 86 acres.

undergo a process that makes their paint peel. Other parts of the set can be made shiny with varnish, encaustic, or silicate. For street sets the walls—especially walls of individual houses—are brought to life with painted signs and half-obliterated graffiti. In general, it is advisable to use many details—streetlamps, balconies, signs, chimney stacks, neon signs, traffic lights, television antennas—everything that enriches the image, moves, shines, or casts shadows. Trees and other vegetation, curtained windows, smoking chimneys, busy traffic, are all assets to this kind of set, which, despite lavish attention, is liable to look artificial.

Apart from special kinds of films such as ballets or musicals, exterior sets are ill adapted to stylization or simplification. For this reason it is important to find a plan, a distribution of buildings that provides the most variety in shots. Long shots, false perspectives, and scale models are a great help in extending the set and giving a more interesting appearance to the buildings, which are less numerous than in real exteriors.

In France, exterior location sets, which are generally quite expensive, are often erected on rented scaffolding in lots that do not belong to the studio. This means that the sets have to be dismantled as soon as the film is finished, even if they have to be re-erected a few months later for another film requiring similar sets. The major German, Italian, and American companies often owned large tracts of land and were thus able to preserve and re-use large-scale constructions over a period of years. The

180

The turn-of-the-century Welsh village of How Green Was My Valley *was transformed into a Norwegian village occupied by the Nazis for* The Moon Is Down *(20th Century–Fox, 1943). Directed by Irving Pichel. Art directors: James Basevi and Maurice Ransford; set decorators: Walter M. Scott and Thomas Little. Sir Cedric Hardwicke is the German colonel in the center, with next to him, Henry Travers as the mayor.*

major American companies had permanent constructions on their back lots—the New York street, the western street, often the side of an ocean liner, and so on. The framework for these sets was sometimes built of reinforced concrete or metal, almost impervious to the destruction of time. It was sufficient to modify a few architectural details or to change the look of the store fronts to use the same sets for different films.

This is an appropriate moment to say a word about the cost of constructing sets, an important factor, especially for low-budget productions, which often tilts the scales in the direction of real sets. This is a false consideration from the start, since it takes no account of the technical quality of the film, especially the sound track. For equal quality, studio construction demands a greater initial outlay but is less expensive in the long run.

The estimated cost of the sets, based on previous films of the same type, is somewhat empirical. The figure is based upon the number of workmen required by construction during the period of filming. The work sheet gives the total number of man hours involved in constructing, maintaining, and changing the sets and the wage levels of various categories of workers. The cost of the raw material for the sets generally amounts to about fifty per cent of the wages. To the total thus arrived at must be added miscellaneous decoration costs, which include photographic vistas, plants, fabrics, metalware, and generally all the expenses that fall outside the actual construction. The cost of furniture and properties naturally varies with the type of furniture, the duration of shooting, and the rarity of the objects required, and can range from $2,000 to $50,000, depending on the film. As a general rule the cost of the sets works out to be approximately ten per cent of the total cost of the film. It is interesting to note that the overall cost of a film has increased far more than the cost of sets. Sets generally amounted to twenty per cent of the budget during the years 1946–50 in France; the percentage currently spent on them is usually about half that.

The designer is often involved in films shot on location. What is his role in such films? First a distinction must be made between a real interior whose original purpose corresponds to the set required by the scenario, and an anonymous place enclosed by walls and a ceiling that has to be adjusted to fit the situation and spirit of the film. The latter is possibly the most frequent case, and under these circumstances the designer has to do almost everything. The walls have to be dressed, an unnecessary door or staircase must be concealed, a counter, partition, or glass case installed, the whole set repainted and furnished. A real bookstore may be transformed into a tailor's shop, a real nightclub into a hotel lobby, a real lobby into an auto showroom, and so on. (In 1974, the New York street on Universal's back lot was converted into the Hollywood Boulevard seen—and destroyed—in *Earthquake.*) Even when the real interior conforms to the script, modifications are almost always needed in color, furniture, or fittings.

A designer may have to build an entire café or restaurant in the shelter provided by a covered market, a garage, or a narrow street covered with tarpaulin to keep out rain and light. Even the appearance of a landscape may be modified by building a wall or door, erecting the outlines of castles or churches in the distance, or adding hedges, wayside shrines, fountains, or ruins. The main advantage to using natural settings in some cases lies in the possibility of seeing a landscape animated, for example, by the waves of the sea, the traffic in the street, and so on. It is true that sets built in the studio, despite rear projection and vistas (even when these are full of life), and despite cutting in exteriors shot through windows, rarely create the illusion of bustling life outside the walls.

More sensitive film, new portable cameras, and lighter and more powerful lighting equipment (quartz lamps) have facilitated the use of natural settings. The quality of sound recording, however, still leaves a great deal to be desired, and it is often unfortunately necessary to resort to post-synchronization. Filming on location, far from the studio, also introduces the problems of transportation, housing, and other costs that reduce the profitability of the undertaking far more than might be guessed.

10 Special Effects

This chapter examines in detail only those special effects applied to sets or used during shooting. The other special effects that were carried out "while turning the handle" in the days of silent films—slow motion, accelerated motion, fading in or out, double exposure, freeze frame, reverse motion, and so forth—are now done in the laboratory. Modern motor-operated cameras do not perform direct special effects (except for some cameras specially designed for slow or accelerated motion).

Modern special effects would be all but impossible without the optical printer, which was developed about the same time as the early talking pictures. The printer is based on the principle of a film projector which, instead of projecting positive images onto a screen, projects them onto an unused negative. Once the image has been produced on it, this is known as the dupe negative. A process camera and a projector are then set up to face one another; the process camera holds the dupe negative, the movie projector the master positive. They are then synchronized by the printer, so that a single frame of positive is projected, timed to the exposure of a single frame of negative. Printers may be manipulated to achieve all sorts of special effects—dissolves, fade-ins or fade-outs, wipes, freeze frames, split-screen effects. Trick shots containing matte paintings may also be accomplished with the printer—this is often used to do away with the cost of building sets. Other processes make it possible to place scenes shot in the studio against a background of landscapes or sets shot separately.

A constant problem is representing, within a limited area, a set that would normally extend far beyond the modest dimensions available in a studio. An example is a street or a very long gallery, such as the Gallery of Mirrors at Versailles. The designer almost always has to construct the set in perspective, increasing the perspective effect by progressively diminishing the size of the elements making up the set. A door close to the camera will be a normal height, but a similar door at the far end of the set may be only three feet high. The vanishing point must be calculated exactly, which means that the floor rises up toward the back of the set. And of course, all the other props, such as furniture or cars, must be built on a diminishing scale.

183

A large miniature designed by Léon Barsacq for Carmine Gallone's Michael Strogoff *(1956).*

There is also the problem of how the cast moves around in this kind of set. A line marks the limit beyond which the actors must not step, and it is often necessary to "people" the far end of the set with children dressed and made up as adults, to preserve the overall scale. In *Maya*, a film adapted from the famous stage play by S. Gantillon, the set representing a street in a red-light district was built in perspective. The prostitutes at the far end of the street were played by little girls of six or eight in pleated skirts and high-heeled shoes.

To represent an exterior upon which the windows or doors of a set open, the only solution is a vista (unless it is a street or a narrow courtyard, in which case it is built at the same time as the interior). For a long time vistas were painted in trompe-l'oeil, fixed for an area seen from a window or a terrace, or revolving if it was a moving panorama seen from a train, ship, or car. Photographic enlargements have been used since 1935 for stationary vistas. This process, long perfected, involves enlarging to a specific size photographs of the area in question. These are printed on sheets of photographic paper three feet long. The problem is to obtain a uniform print so that the joins between the different sheets will not be visible. Photographic vistas often measure 60 by 18 feet and give excellent results if placed about 15 feet from the windows or the actors. The effect of depth is improved by arranging the vistas in several planes: for example, first plane in silhouette, second plane in silhouette, and the background. For color films, the prohibitive price of enlargements makes it necessary to color photographic vistas by hand, and sepia prints are preferable to black and white, being much warmer. The tinting has to be done with transparent glazes. In the United States, photographic vistas printed on a transparent base like gelatine are used. The sheets are gummed together and the resulting background is lit by rear projection, unlike photographic vistas on paper, which are lit from the front. The American method often gives greater depth, but the process is very expensive.

When a basically urban setting must be shown (houses, roofs, chimneys, skyscrapers, and so on), especially if this landscape serves as a background for moving elements on a reduced scale (overhead railway, cars, ships, for example), sometimes a three-dimensional vista replaces the photographic vista. The architectural elements are constructed on a predetermined reduced scale. This kind of special effect demands

Edward Carrere with scale model of set of The Adventures of Don Juan *(Warner Bros., 1949), for which he received an Academy Award nomination for best color art direction. Directed by Vincent Sherman.*

great care. To achieve the appearance of aerial perspective (the background less clear than the foreground), screens of gauze are used. Photographic enlargements may be used in a three-dimensional vista. If a landscape in movement is involved, rear projection is employed. This procedure, widely used today, will be discussed further, following an examination of older special effects that involve sets.

For a long time designers searched for a process that would make it possible to produce a set cheaply and to add to it, as required, a richly decorated ceiling, one or more upper stories, roofs, and even a sky. The earliest such process was first used in 1907 by Norman O. Dawn and was developed by Ferdinand P. Earle. The set was constructed up to a predetermined height; then Earle placed between the set and the camera, about eight feet from the latter, a sheet of plate glass on which he had painted the missing part of the set. This method made it possible to complete or to alter either a set or a landscape, but the camera could not be used till the painted glass was ready.

In France, M. P. Day, an English painter, was the first to paint sets on glass. Jean Perrier perfected the method, creating perspective by utilizing the angle of the camera shots, a system that enabled him to determine in advance the outlines of the constructed set and the painted segment topping the set. Following this development, trompe-l'oeil painting was done in the studio on cardboard, instead of on glass in front of the constructed set, significantly reducing the time during which the camera was not used. Nevertheless, it took three to four hours to adjust the lighting on the set and the painting.

Charles Assola, a painter and designer who concentrated on special effects, adopted Perrier's system but thought of using a matte. This matte, a silhouette exactly the height of the set and covering all the part to be painted, was placed in front of the lens. The constructed set was lit and filmed normally, with no need to trouble about the part to be filled in. Protected by the matte of black cardboard, the upper part of the frame was not photographed. A few frames of the film were then developed, and Assola, with the aid of a fixed projection, was able to integrate the perspective and lighting of the set into his trompe-l'oeil painting. When the painting was finished, Assola adjusted the lighting, then his camera, to which he applied a counter-matte to protect the part of the set already photographed, and photographed the painting. The results were very satisfactory if the same camera was used for shooting both the set as a whole and the painted silhouette.

In 1924 the three-dimensional model appeared. First came the ceilings, and finally very large models were placed between the constructed set and the camera. The distance of the model from the camera, about 10 feet, determines its scale. For a set 45 feet long, the model will be made to a scale of one in five, but for a set 180 feet long, it will be only one-twentieth of the real size, and so on. A special platform attached to the camera support makes it possible to execute tilts and pans and even certain traveling shots, impossible with the painted screen. The models must be constructed with great care. All the architectural details, sculpture, chandeliers, electrical wall fittings, draperies, and so on, must be built to the exact scale of the model. Often small human figures, some movable, are introduced. The main difficulty is adjusting the lighting of the model to that of the real set by using small projectors on the same scale

Goodbye, Mr. Chips (MGM, 1939). Directed by Sam Wood. Art director: Alfred Junge. Although exteriors were filmed at Repton College, some of the largest sets ever built for a British-made film were constructed for Chips. In this shot, though the bottom sections of the buildings were built to scale, they were then combined with a glass shot of the roof and tower at the left and of the sky and landscape backgrounds. A glass shot is an effect which combines live actions (and constructed sets) and a painting—or paintings—on sheets of glass, generally placed about 10 feet in front of the camera.

as the model. Minine and Wilcke introduced and perfected the use of the three-dimensional model in France.

Another method of using models, the Schüfftan process, was invented in 1923 and first used in two films of Fritz Lang's—*Die Niebelungen* (1924) and *Metropolis* (1926). Eugen Schüfftan, architect, painter, and later a great cinematographer, invented the process which bears his name and combines live action with reflected miniatures. For this trick shot, miniature sets are reflected onto a mirrored glass. The glass is positioned in front of the camera at a 45-degree angle. Where the live action is to occur, portions of the glass are scraped away, and bits of real sets are built to be viewed behind the holes. The reflected miniatures and the pieces of real sets are lit to match one another. With this process, it is easier to light the miniature than with an effects shot using hanging miniatures placed in front of the camera.

When a film's budget permits, massive special effects such as disasters, cataclysms, and explosions are sometimes shot in a life-size set using existing elements. Naturally it is possible to derail a real train, sink an out-of-service liner, or blow up a bridge or a house; but the complications, the expense, and the risks are such that, for the most part, it is better to use a scale model. Using one, it is equally easy to film a battle between pirate ships, the bombing of Tokyo, a vision of the end of the

187

world, or a fight between prehistoric monsters in a landscape of giant ferns. By intercutting these effects with related sequences shot in the studio or in outdoor settings, by using rear projection and a few shots from newsreels, it is often possible to create an illusion of reality. The secret of success lies in the scale of the model: the larger it is, the more precise the details and the more convincing the result.

Some moving elements, such as water, fire, and smoke, scarcely lend themselves to a change of scale. A slight ripple, enlarged even fifty times, will never possess the majestic motion of a wave, just as a cigarette does not smoke like a factory chimney. Using slow motion to overcome this problem works well only if the model is large enough: one-tenth life size, for example. A sailing frigate 15 feet long will yield satisfactory results, but a naval battle in a bath tub with 20-inch vessels will look ridiculous. And of course, a large model allows a man concealed on one side to maneuver the ships and fire the cannon. For some years electronically controlled models have been available.

Now consider matte work, one of the ways in which scenes shot separately may be combined in one frame. The matte is simply a mask of some sort which prevents some light from passing through the lens. Early matte shots were done in-the-camera; traveling mattes were used as early as *Ben Hur* (1925). Traveling mattes can change shape—they do not rigidly limit the live action to fixed areas. The spectacular temple collapse in De Mille's *Samson and Delilah* (1949) was engineered by Gordon Jennings, who had been the head of Paramount's special effects department for many years. This mammoth mayhem scene had to be filmed three times before it met with De Mille's approval. This one sequence required a year's work and an outlay of $150,000. In it, Samson knocks down two temple pillars and brings down a giant idol which destroys every person and thing in sight. The "miniature" idol was 17 feet tall—it appeared over 100 feet tall. It seemed to crash down on the heads of real people—the actors had been matted into the shot.

The early Dunning process was another method for combining studio shots with background footage filmed elsewhere. It was a blue-backing process.

Rear projection, invented in the United States and introduced into Europe around 1932, has the advantage of making visible the background against which the action takes place. The process can be traced back to Norman Dawn's work on *The Drifter* (1913). His system projected an image which did not move. Fifteen years passed before a satisfactory system was developed, combining live action with moving projections. *Just Imagine* (1930), a wacky futuristic science-fiction musical, is the first movie credited with making extensive use of the perfected system. The undisputed emperor of rear projection was Paramount's Farciot Edouart. He achieved amazing results at his studio during the thirties with this process—far superior to the process shots used at Hollywood's poshest studio, MGM.

At first rear projection was reserved for landscapes in motion. The landscape alone is filmed with a camera placed in a car, train, or boat. The resulting reel is projected from behind onto a translucent screen in front of which stands part of the car, train, or boat. The scene required takes place inside the moving vehicle, and it is enough to film the combination of the set and the projected landscape to obtain an

Cecil B. De Mille's Samson and Delilah (Paramount, 1949). Its art directors (Walter Tyler, Hans Dreier) and set decorators (Ray Moyer, Sam Comer) received Academy Awards for their work on the film. The special effects were the work of Gordon Jennings, Paul Lerpae, and Devereaux Jennings. The "miniature" of the temple was 17 feet high, that of the idol 17 feet—both built at ⅓ scale. Gordon Jennings had to demolish the temple three times before De Mille was satisfied with the result. The crushed extras were real people—matted into the shot—and miniature dolls.

illusion of movement. The effect of a swell, vibration, or jolt can be accentuated by mounting the set on springs, a pivot, or a pulley block.

French studios have only limited technical resources, but in the United States, the special effects department has assumed considerable importance and become almost autonomous. Fred W. Jackman, A.S.C., one of the first special effects technicians, who organized one of the best special effects departments in Hollywood, once described the requirements of his department along the following lines: A special effects plant, properly directed and established either by the department of a major studio or by an independent special effects contractor, must be an organization comprising many specialists. Practically every phase of a studio's activity should be represented. Apart from the film crew—a highly competent cameraman and his assistants, electricians, carpenters, and mechanics, all of them experienced not only in production but also in special effects, and led by a director of photography expert in special effects—there must also be specialists in the design and painting of sets and properties in miniature and life size, staffers, fitters, designers, draftsmen, and others. There must also be laboratory technicians, specialists in the development of negative and positive films and in ordinary printing, multiple printing, color printing, and sensitometry. There should also be fitters, projectionists, and office staff, all familiar not only with usual studio work but also with special effects work. To direct everyone there must be a fully experienced chief, who must be at the same time a highly competent technician, a businessman, a manager, and an executive. He must have at his disposal not only the services of this varied and highly qualified staff, but also a sufficiently large physical plant to cope with the demands of the task. This organization makes the difference between the early days of special cinematic effects and the art of the modern special effects engineer.

In practice, in the United States, the special effects department looks after all the special effects in a film. The list and budget are established as soon as the scenario is completed. The special effects crew is also responsible for building and installing special equipment necessary for rain, snow, air attacks, and other effects.

No chapter on special effects would be complete without a passing homage to the four masters in that field: Willis O'Brien, Ned Mann, James Basevi, and John P. Fulton.*

O'Brien was supreme in three-dimensional stop-motion model animation. His finest work is to be seen in *Mighty Joe Young* (1949) and *King Kong* (1933). The giant monsters in *King Kong* were actually steel-armatured rubber models a few feet tall—except for Kong's head and one arm which were built to scale for certain scenes. O'Brien's patience was limitless; often a good day's work meant twenty-five feet of action in the can. Kong's brawl with a pterodactyl, brief as it appears on the screen, required weeks of shooting. The highly atmospheric scenes of the jungle on Skull Island (they are reminiscent of Gustave Doré engravings) were achieved by painting on three separate planes of 9-by-12-foot sheets of glass for each set-up.

Ned Mann dropped his career as a professional roller skater to take up movie special effects. He worked on the Fairbanks *Thief of Bagdad* (1924) and was later summoned by Alexander Korda, for whom he worked in England on René Clair's *The Ghost Goes West* (1935), *The Man Who Could Work Miracles* (1936), and above all the superb political science-fiction extravaganza based on H. G. Wells, *Things to Come* (1936), directed by William Cameron Menzies, with breathtaking designs by Vincent Korda. During his stay in England, Mann's influence on British special effects men was incalculable; he trained most of the top artists working in England in the field today.

James Basevi enjoyed a varied career as both art director and special effects man. His accomplished designs for *Wuthering Heights* (1939), *Tobacco Road* (1941), *The Black Swan* (1942), *Son of Fury* (1942), *The Gang's All Here* (1943), two Hitchcock films—*Lifeboat* (1943) and *Spellbound* (1945), *Mighty Joe Young*, *East of Eden* (1955), and John Ford's *The Searchers* (1956), are but a fraction of his art director's credits. But Basevi's most striking film legacy was two memorable disasters. He collaborated with Arnold Gillespie on the great earthquake in *San Francisco* (1935), an astounding sequence which lasts two full reels. (Incidentally, Basevi's tremor, made thirty years ago, is considerably more convincing and beautiful than the Sensurround gimmickry and effects of Universal's *Earthquake* of 1974.) Basevi's major solo achievement is to be seen in John Ford's *The Hurricane* (1937)—a storm which took four months to design and film. This, the finest tempest sequence ever filmed in a studio, utilized a 600-foot set of an island village. All was demolished by a tidal wave to end all tidal waves, produced by the release of tens of thousands of gallons of water pouring down huge high chutes onto the giant miniature.

* This and the following five paragraphs are by Elliott Stein.

190

John P. Fulton was in charge of special effects at Universal during the thirties. Fulton's excellent miniature work for John Ford's *Air Mail* (1932) was topped by his masterpiece—the justly famous effects for James Whale's *The Invisible Man* (1933).

The 1968 Oscar for special effects was, not surprisingly, awarded to Stanley Kubrick for *2001: A Space Odyssey*. The director had personally designed the effects he wanted, but accepted the award on behalf of the four technicians who had executed them: Tom Howard, Wally Veevers, Douglas Trumbull, and Con Pederson. Volumes have appeared devoted to this film and its complicated and apparently seamless effects.* In passing, it should at least be noted here that one of the film's triumphs is the convincing use of *front* projection in several passages. The settings for the Dawn of Man prologue, for instance, were created by frontally projected footage originally shot in South Africa, projected to surround the man–apes onto a 90-foot-long screen in the English studio.

The same specialization as in Hollywood has been pursued in the Soviet studios. The special effects department is very important and several young cameramen and designers specialize in combined shots, the Russian term for shots using painted or three-dimensional models, rear projection, traveling mattes, and so on. Many war films, such as *The Battle of Stalingrad*, or historical films like *Glinka*, *Admiral Uchakov*, *The Great Warrior Skanderberg*, *Othello*, and *The Mexican*, make wide use of combined shots. The major studios such as Mosfilm and Lenfilm also have centers for technical research.

Let us look at an original Soviet process for filming a model in the water of an aquarium. To obtain the effects of atmospheric perspective, or of a layer of mist or fog, the water is slightly tinted with gouache. Rear projection behind the aquarium produces the effect of clouds in the sky. In Yutkevich's *The Great Warrior Skanderberg*, the mountain landscape—a scale model—was filmed in the water of an aquarium tinted with orange paint to obtain the effect of a misty sunset. When the overall set has been shot with the painted or three-dimensional models, the resulting background is rear projected to film the middle distance with actors. This guarantees the photographic unity of the backgrounds.

The traveling matte process has fostered the development of a few effects previously impossible to create. These may involve changing the scale of the background compared to the foreground, or slowing down or speeding up the movement of clouds or waves in the background, or they may involve the effects of colors that lend an unreal appearance to the background without detracting in any way from the reality of the actors in the foreground.

Despite differences in the sophistication of the installations and equipment used for special effects in various countries, the basic elements are more or less identical everywhere. Rain comes from sets of pierced copper tubes, fire hoses, vaporizers, and the like, which control the amount of rainfall from a fine drizzle to a downpour. Fans of various types, even airplane propellers or a wind-tunnel, are used for wind effects. Lightning is obtained by rapidly switching on and off naked arcs (with visible carbon filaments). Windowpanes are frosted with yellow soap or liquid glue, squirted on. For

* E.g. *The Making of Kubrick's 2001*, ed. by Jerome Agel (New York: Signet, 1970).

some years, small aerosol bombs have been used to frost or dull shiny surfaces. Borax, fiberglass, cotton wool, white sand, or plastics such as polyesters produce different snow effects: falling snow, snow resting on ledges, balconies, or branches, ground covered with snow showing footprints or tire tracks. Artificial fog and heavy smoke are created with an ingenious apparatus using paraffin and ice. Spectacular flames are produced with a chemical product which produces no smoke; but there is a whole range of smokes—white, black, gray, or yellow—for conflagrations, explosions, and so on. In war films, small mines are adjusted for various kinds of explosions, detonators represent the impact of bullets or gun flashes, and electric vibrators cause the set to shake. Parts of the set, arranged in advance, come crashing down, pulled by invisible threads of fine steel or nylon. Rocks or beams that fall on the actors are made of cork or light balsa wood, which is also used to make break-away furniture for fight scenes. To avoid all danger, windows, bottles, and glasses broken in the course of the action are made from a sugar base or plastic. Studio visitors always enjoy the cobweb machine. This is a simple apparatus whose basic elements are a bell-shaped container attached to an electric fan. The container is filled with a rubber solution, and the fan, when turned on, blows forth the liquid in a spray which forms cobwebs.

Special effects, requiring great care, patience, and especially inventiveness, are contributing to the perfection of the cinematic idiom. They stimulate a search for ingenious solutions that re-create reality with new and relatively inexpensive means, and therein lies the whole drama of the cinema. René Clair's observation remains true: "The cinema to-day is still exposed to the same danger which threatened it from its very beginning, namely—money. Money was needed for creating and developing the film industry, and the laws of money still govern and oppress it." *

Every new school or style instinctively tries to free itself from this yoke and find a fresh approach by a vow of poverty. Once the surprise effect has worn off, however, the cinema has to return to a certain level of technical perfection, in order to satisfy the critical eye of the spectator. The right balance must be found between spontaneity of inspiration and quality of execution. The essential thing is that the governing idea of the film be defended throughout production against all obstacles, and often against the zeal of those involved in making it. Feyder has summarized perfectly the constraints of creative work in the cinema: "What a struggle to obtain, in the service of an idea, the material means that it demands; and what a new struggle to avoid becoming their prisoner." †

* Clair, pp. 108–09.

† Quoted in Charles Spaak, "Jacques Feyder," Cine-Club (Nov. 1948).

Conclusion

Although it is difficult to predict the directions the cinema of tomorrow will take, it is evident that small-scale "human interest" reporting is a genre henceforth more appropriate to television; it would be foolish for the cinema to attempt to dispute this territory with the small screen.* The cramped melancholy poverty of the so-called natural settings of *cinéma-vérité* is now outmoded; a swing back to sets created in studios or out of doors is already well under way.

The American motion picture industry turned up with few masterpieces in 1974, but that year marked a spectacular comeback for the industry on several levels. It was the best year at the box office since the record year of 1946. The public returned to the movies—at least to certain movies—to see and resee spectacular productions of the ilk of *The Exorcist*, *The Towering Inferno*, *Earthquake*, and *Airport 75*. None of these productions achieved, or even attempted, any depth—they were programmed to make noise and money—and did so—but they gave the public something unavailable on television: spectacular (though not very artful) sets, and complicated, ingenious special effects projected on large screens. The art of illusion had come back in force.

It was no accident that few or hardly any of the younger technicians available were possessed of the knowledge and experience to concoct these mammoth junkyard fantasies. The year 1974 was marked by the return to activity of veteran special effects men who had retired or taken up other work. A nearly lost art was, if not reborn, rehashed on a giant scale—larger, noisier, but generally inferior to the *Hurricanes*, the *San Franciscos*, the *Deluges*, the *Good Earths* of yore.

The sound stage, reviled by many younger directors in recent years as an artificial ambiance, is returning to favor in 1975. Unfortunately, most of the major studios have already razed most of their back lots—the New York street, the western frontier towns, Old Chicago, Cedric Gibbons's Versailles are all gone with the bulldozers.

But it is probable that more spectacular film sets will be designed and constructed in the coming years than went up during the entire previous decade. For, contrary to the dictum "truth is stranger than fiction," the set designer is called to demonstrate that fiction transcends truth.

* By Elliott Stein.

193

Papillon (Allied Artists, 1973), Directed by Franklin J. Schaffner. Production designer: Anthony Masters; art director: Jack Maxsted; set decorator: Hugh Scaife. The French penal colony at Devil's Island was recreated at Montego Bay, Jamaica.

FILMOGRAPHIES OF ART DIRECTORS AND PRODUCTION DESIGNERS

by Elliott Stein

Although what follows is, to my knowledge, the most comprehensive muster of design filmographies yet published, it is far from complete. Everyone has not been included, and some entries are partial—simply for lack of space. For the same reason, it has not been possible to list every collaboration or published reference. It would have been an easy task to concentrate on the big names. My intention has been to provide an extensive, international cross section of the careers of those who created sets for motion pictures, not only for super-productions where sets were costly and conspicuous, but also for the B pictures, genre films and quickies which for many years were the industry's bread and butter. Dave Milton and Edward C. Jewell have their place here as much as Hans Dreier and Cedric Gibbons.

The apparently simple task of correctly itemizing "who did what" is in fact not that simple. Screen credits are often misleading, and at times downright false. For years, it was deplorable common practice at the major studios (with the exception of Warner Bros.) to credit the supervising art director with the sets of every picture made at his studio whether his own contribution was creative or merely supervisory. The unit art director who usually did the lion's share of the creative work was, at times, not even mentioned. (For more on this, see the quoted interview with Boris Leven, and on pages 245–247 the letters of Wiard Ihnen.) The task of unraveling "who did what" is further complicated by the fact that the "art director" credit on English films often refers to what is called "set decoration" in the United States.

Barsacq's original text did not demarcate the work of the art director under the old studio system from that of the production designer as it has developed in recent years. The added excerpt from the Selznick correspondence (page 167) dealing with William Cameron Menzies's credit as production designer on *Gone with the Wind* sheds some light on the inevitability of such an evolution, but I felt it would be useful to ask a contemporary production designer to trace it in his own words. Leo Kerz* obliged with the following text, written for this book:

The term production designer seems to have come into use since the emergence of the independent producer–director, vis-à-vis the in-house producer and the staff director of the major companies. It coincides with the independent director's quest for a distinctive style, an approach to the filming of a script which will make the result unmistakably the work of a specific team. At least that is the intent.

---

* Leo Kerz was born in Berlin in 1912. He started work in the theater at 14, studied architecture, then worked as assistant to Erwin Piscator in Berlin, and on several films in collaboration with Maurischat. He left Germany in 1933 and worked for a year at the Barrandov Studios, Prague, notably on one of the most famous films of the 30s—Gustav Machaty's *Ecstasy* (33). He spent five years in South Africa where he was art director for the J. Walter Thompson Empire Exhibit. Arrived in the U.S. in 1941; much work for the N.Y. stage (*Rhinoceros*); art director with CBS for five years. His film design credits include: *Guilty Bystander* (50), Fred Zinnemann's *Teresa* (51), *Mr. Universe* (51), Robert Wise's *Odds Against Tomorrow* (59).

In order to achieve that characteristic something—in terms of overall grain and atmosphere—the art director, whose work is substantially that of a set designer (of sets for which he often does not personally create the dressing) is inadequate. So a new figure emerges, with a new title, a new creative responsibility: the production designer. For him, the designing and drafting of the settings is only part of the job—and that part is often now done by another—the acting art director who works under the guidance of the production designer.

The main function of the production designer is to create, in collaboration with the film's director and the director of photography, a distinct mood, a graphic approach, which in color, in texture, in overall image produces a characteristic style intended to set this particular film apart from the work of any other given team of film-makers. The production designer determines the keyshots and sketches them out for cameraman and director. These sketches ideally incorporate everything, from lighting to position of characters, the choice of lenses—his work thus really becomes the point of departure for the shooting of the film.

One of the rewards of compiling these lists has been the occasional emergence of meaningful patterns in art director–director teaming (e.g. Glasgow–Aldrich, Oliver–Borzage, MacDonald–Losey, Muraki–Kurosawa, Charbonnier–Bresson, Ames–Minnelli, Tavoularis–Coppola, Kuter–Daves, Grot–Curtiz). These fruitful, often long-lived alliances and others like them were not formed solely through contemporary contractual obligations at the same studio, but resulted from compatabilities of directorial and architectural style which can be traced from film to film.

Film dates are those of release in country of origin unless otherwise stated. In addition to standard abbreviations, these are used: AA, Academy Award; a.d., art director; des., designed or designing; dir., directed or director; prod., produced or producer or production; stud., studied; UA, United Artists; WB, Warner Bros.

Aaes, Erik   Danish. 1899–1966. Began as asst. designer at Nordisk Films. 1920–22 worked in Berlin with the Danish dir. Sven Gade. 1925–30 worked on avant-garde films in France. Sets for Renoir, Cavalcanti, Dreyer, de Toth. *Yvette* (27), *En Rade* (27), *The Little Match Girl* (28), *Tire-au-flanc* (28), *Le Capitaine Fracasse* (29), *La P'tite Lili* (29), *Cocktail* (37), *Day of Wrath* (43), *Ordet/The Word* (55), *Herr Puntila und sein Knecht Matti* (56), *Amor i Telefonen* (57), *Hidden Fear* (57), *Sult/Hunger* (66). A's vigorous, poetic style is very much in evidence in *En Rade*, *Day of Wrath*, and *Ordet*.

Adam, Ken   b. 1921 Berlin. To England 1934, stud. Bartlett School of Architecture. War service in RAF. Entered films 1947; draftsman on several pictures, notably *The Queen of Spades* (48). Asst. a.d. *Helen of Troy* (55). A.d. (European scenes) *Around the World in 80 Days* (56). As a.d.: *Night of the Demon/Curse of the Demon* (57), *Gideon's Day/Gideon of Scotland Yard* (58), *10 Seconds to Hell* (59), *The Angry Hills* (59), *The Trials of Oscar Wilde* (60), *Sodom and Gomorrah* (61), *Dr. No* (62), *Dr. Strangelove, or How I Learned to Stop Worrying and Love the Bomb* (64), *Goldfinger* (64), *Thunderball* (65), *The Ipcress File* (65), *You Only Live Twice* (67), *Chitty Chitty Bang Bang* (68), *Goodbye, Mr. Chips* (69), *Diamonds Are Forever* (71), *Sleuth* (72), *The Last of Sheila* (73), *Barry Lyndon* (75). A has, time and again, organized the vast expensive spaces in which the gadgetry of James Bond and assorted foes can operate in style; the best film he has worked on to date, however, is Jacques Tourneur's modestly budgeted *Night of the Demon*. See Hudson, "Three Designers"; St. John Marner, *Film Design*.

Ames, Preston   US. Stud. architecture France. 1936 hired by Gibbons for MGM art dept. Most of his work has been at MGM, some recent work for Universal. His finest work has been for *Vincente Minnelli. *Crisis* (50), **An American in Paris* (51), *The Wild North* (52), **The Band Wagon* (53)—in collab. Oliver Smith, **Brigadoon* (54), **Kismet* (55), **The Cobweb* (55), **Lust for Life* (56), **Designing Woman* (57), **Gigi* (58), *Green Mansions* (59), **The Bells Are Ringing* (60), **Home from the Hill* (60), *Billy Rose's Jumbo* (62), *Penelope* (66), *Made in Paris* (66), *Airport* (70), *Brewster McCloud* (70), *Lost Horizon* (73), *The Don Is Dead* (74), *Earthquake* (74), *Rooster Cogburn* (75), *The Prisoner of 2nd Avenue* (75). See Ames, "Art Direction: The Technical Approach to Design and Construction," *IATSE Official Bulletin*, no. 436 (Winter 1963). See also interview with A in Steen, *Hollywood Speaks! An Oral History*; Minnelli, *I Remember It Well*; Fordin, *The World of Entertainment!*

Anderson, Roland   US. Worked mostly at Paramount, often in collab. Dreier (on many films dir. by Cecil B. De Mille), later with Pereira. *A Farewell to Arms* (32), *This Day and Age* (33), *4 Frightened People* (34), *Cleopatra* (34), *The Lives of a Bengal Lancer* (35), *The Plainsman* (37), *Spawn of the North* (38), *The Buccaneer* (38), *Disputed Passage* (39), *North West Mounted Police* (40), *Reap the Wild Wind* (42), *To Each His Own* (46), *The Big Clock* (48), *Carrie* (52), *The Country Girl* (54), *The Space Children* (58), *Will Penny* (67), *The Sterile Cuckoo* (69). See "Mr. Roland Anderson . . . Defines His Job," *What's Happening in Hollywood*, no. 18 (Jan. 12, 1942), in which A elucidates his visualization of De Mille's *Reap the Wild Wind*.

André, Jean   *Paris Does Strange Things* (55), *Et Dieu créa la femme/And God Created Woman* (56), *Sait-on jamais?* (57), *Et Mourir de plaisir/Blood and Roses* (60), *La Vérité* (60), *Les Félins/The Love Cage/The Joy House* (64), *La Curée/The Game Is Over* (66), *Don Juan 1973 ou si Don Juan était une femme* (73). Accomplished, conventionally chic designer in his films for *Vadim.

Andrejew, Andrei   1886 Russia–1966 France. *Raskolnikoff* (23), *Thérèse Raquin* (28), *Pandora's Box* (28), *Die Dreigroschenoper/Threepenny Opera* (31), *Don Quichotte* (34), *The Dictator/The Loves of a Dictator* (34), *Mayerling* (36), *Beloved Vagabond* (36), *The Golem* (36), *Dark Journey* (37), *Storm in a Teacup* (37), *Tarakanova* (38), *Jeunes Filles en détresse* (39), *L'Assassin habite au 21* (42), *La Symphonie fantastique* (42), *Le Corbeau* (43) —in collab. Warm, *Anna Karenina* (48), *The Man Between* (53), *Melba* (53), *Mambo* (55), *Anastasia* (56). One of the great international a.ds., A worked in Germany, England, France, and Czechoslovakia—for Pabst, Wiene, Clouzot, and Victor Saville. In nearly every film his own original gloomy visions emerge.

Anger, Kenneth   b. California. *La Lune des lapins/Rabbits' Moon* (50)—dir., costumes, editing, hand-made sets, *Inauguration of the Pleasure Dome* (54)—dir., sets, editing. *Rabbits' Moon* is the most stunning film ever des. by an American in Paris.

Arnold, C. Wilfred   GB. *The Pleasure Garden* (25), *The Lodger* (26), *The Ring* (27), *Blackmail* (29), *Rich and Strange* (32), *Number 17* (32). A's sets for these early Hitchcock films are all of quality; those for *Blackmail* are memorable.

Asakura, Setsu   Teaches at Tokyo School of Design. Much theater work. *Bara no Soretsu/Funeral Parade of Roses* (70), *Shura/Pandemonium* (71?). Both films dir. by Toshio Matsumoto. ". . . One of Japan's outstanding and innovative set designers. The unusual calligraphic character for her first name, Setsu, is derived from the combination used in 'Prince Regent,' as her birth coincided with the ascent to power of the present emperor. To have given this name to a girl expressed the advanced views of her father, sculptor Fumio Asakura. Her development into a woman of independent spirit and intellect in a culture which discourages these qualities in women was aided by her father's enlightened attitudes."—Joan Mellen, *Voices from the Japanese Cinema* (NY, 1975), pp. 153–62.

Autant-Lara, Claude   b. 1903 France. This prolific dir. began in films as an a.d. Films as designer only: *Le Carnaval des vérités* (19), *L'Homme du large* (20), *Villa Destin* (21), *Don Juan et Faust* (22), *L'Inhumaine/The New Enchantment* (23), *Nana* (26). A-L's comparatively brief career as an a.d. did include 2 extraordinary films: *L'Inhumaine* and Renoir's *Nana*. Though the New Wave considered him a hack, he dir. some of the finest films made in occupied Paris, one of which—*Douce*, with sets by Jacques Krauss—is a masterpiece.

Ballin, Hugo   1879 NY–1956 California. Stud. art in Rome. A noted painter, with architectural training, B came to Hollywood in 1915, shortly after Buckland. (This first wave of set designers is largely forgotten today, since many of their films no longer exist, although the reputations of the major designers who arrived a bit later, in the 20s—Gibbons, Menzies, etc.—are firmly established.) Dir. many films starring his wife, Mabel Ballin, though his most elaborate sets were done for a Gloria Swanson picture he did not dir.: *The Love of Sunya*. Its oriental lavishness made it an ideal choice as first film to play New York's "Cathedral of the Motion Picture," the Roxy Theatre. He executed murals in Griffith Park Observatory and for the 1939 Golden Gate Exposition. The National Gallery of Art possesses several of his paintings. *Baby Mine* (17), *Jane Eyre* (20), *Vanity Fair* (23), *The Love of Sunya* (27). "In *Baby Mine*, Hugo Ballin, the mural decorator, began to introduce simplified

197

settings. He eliminated useless detail. He used large spaces of clear wall with restrained detail. In the decoration he began to suggest more of the habits and nature of the characters of the story than had until that time been attempted."—Kenneth MacGowan, "The Artist Enters the Closeup," *Vanity Fair* (Sept. 1920).

Barsacq, Léon 1906 Russia–1969 France. Stud. architecture, decorative arts in Paris. From 1941 asst. designer in films, working under Perrier and Andrejew. Renoir's *La Marseillaise* (38) was one of B's first major assignments as full-fledged a.d. *Lumière d'été* (43), *Les Enfants du paradis* (45)—in collab. Trauner, Raymond Gabutti, *Boule de suif* (45), *The Idiot* (46), *Les Dernières Vacances* (47), *Le Silence est d'or* (47), *Pattes blanches* (48), *La Beauté du diable* (49), *Le Château de verre* (50), *Belles de nuit/Night Beauties* (52), *Roma, Ore 11* (52), *Bel Ami* (54), *Les Grandes Manoeuvres/Summer Maneuvers* (55), *Les Diaboliques/Diabolique* (55), *Les Aventures de Till l'Espiègle* (56), *Porte des Lilas/Gates of Paris* (57), *Pot Bouille* (57), *The Longest Day* (62), *Trois Chambres à Manhattan* (65).

For B, décor was never to be considered a spectacle in itself—he saw its purpose as, above all, a means to create atmosphere. In his best, earlier work, the results were interesting enough to clash with his own doctrine of sets as mere self-effacing means to an end. If, as Sadoul states (p. 17), B's "work in the Sixties was of considerably less interest," it should also be noted in fairness that the work of the dirs. he was des. for—Carné, Clair—was also in decline.

Basevi, James b. Plymouth, England. Stud. architecture; colonel in WWI. Moved to Canada, then Los Angeles and started in films as draftsman at MGM. Superv. a.d. 20th–Fox 1943–44. Films as special effects dir.: *The Mysterious Island* (29), *San Francisco (36)*–in collab. Gillespie, *History Is Made at Night* (37), *The Hurricane* (37). Art dir.: *The Big Parade* (25) —as asst. to Gibbons, *Confessions of a Queen* (25), *The Tower of Lies* (25), *The Temptress* (26), *Wuthering Heights* (39), *The Long Voyage Home* (40), *Tobacco Road* (41), *The Black Swan* (42), *Son of Fury* (42), *Dancing Masters* (43), *The Gang's All Here* (43), *The Song of Bernadette* (43), *The Lodger* (44), *Spellbound* (45), *My Darling Clementine* (46)—in collab. Wheeler, *Duel in the Sun* (46), *Captain from Castile* (47), *Fort Apache* (48), *3 Godfathers* (49), *Mighty Joe Young* (49), *She Wore a Yellow Ribbon* (49), *Wagonmaster* (50), *East of Eden* (55)—in collab. Malcolm Bert, *The Searchers* (56)—and many more.

A long, glorious career, both as designer and effects dir.—B's cataclysm in *The Hurricane* is one of the wonders of the Seventh Art. Has often worked in collab. with other great designers (Day) and for great dirs. (Vidor, Seastrom, Hitchcock—and, notably, *John Ford).

Bérard, Christian 1902 Paris–1949. Best known as a painter and stage designer, B conceived the strikingly stylish and appropriate sets for 3 Cocteau films: *La Belle et la Bête/Beauty and the Beast* (46), *L'Aigle à deux têtes* (48)—in collab. Wakhévitch, and *Les Parents terribles* (48).

Berger, Ralph b. 1904 Los Angeles. Stud. architecture. Entered films 1924 as draftsman at Universal. Worked for several studios; in 40s unit a.d. RKO. 1953 superv. a.d. all Desilu Prods. *White Zombie* (32), *Flash Gordon* (36), *The Brighton Strangler* (45), *Back to Bataan* (45), *Partners in Time* (46), *Trail Street* (47), *The Miracle of the Bells* (48), *The Boy with Green Hair* (48), *The Big Steal* (49), *Where Danger Lives* (50), *Macao* (made 50, rel. 52).

Bertrand, Paul b. 1915 France. Started in films as an asst. to Trauner. *Félicie Nanteuil* (42), *Les Maudits* (47), *Jeux interdits/Forbidden Games* (52), *Gervaise* (56), *Une Vie* (58), *Plein Soleil/Purple Noon* (59). His best work (for Clément and Astruc) is imbued with a powerful poetic realism.

Bogdanov, Mikhail b. 1914. Usually works in collab. with another Soviet designer, G. Myasnikov. *The Stone Flower* (46), *Michurin* (48), *Przhevalsky* (51), *The Heroes of Shipka* (55), *The First Echelon* (56), *The Communist* (58), *War and Peace* (66). B is gifted with a fine sense of color. He is extremely adroit in designing for vast crowd scenes.

Borg, Karl Oscar (or Carl Oscar) 1878 Sweden–1947. To US 1904 as merchant seaman; jumped ship in San Francisco and took refuge in the Southwest. Self-taught, became a noted painter, esp. for scenes of Indian life. Works in Phoenix Art Museum; California State Library, Sacramento; de Young Museum, San Francisco; Los Angeles Public Library. *The Black Pirate* (26), *The Winning of Barbara Worth* (26), *The Magic Flame* (27), *The Night of Love* (27), *The Gaucho* (27). B did not work on many films (3 prod. by Goldwyn, 2 for

Fairbanks), but they were all elaborate prods., des. with *maestria*. *The Black Pirate* was the first important 2-color Technicolor feature; many scenes were des. to show off the process. *The Night of Love*, dir. by Fitzmaurice, is one of the most rousing swashbucklers of the 20s; its rich but unfussy pictorialism is in the lineage of *The Thief of Bagdad*.

Borsody, Julius von *Heimkehr* (28), *Narkose* (29), *Berlin–Alexanderplatz* (31), *Komödianten* (41)—the best-looking film dir. by Pabst in Germany during the war.

Box, John b. 1920 London. Brought up in Ceylon; stud. architecture in England; WWII service. First film work as draftsman at Denham Studios 1947. Worked as asst. a.d. to Sherrif, Dillon, and Vetchinsky. First work as solo a.d. 1953. *Fire Down Below* (57), *The Inn of the Sixth Happiness* (58), *Our Man in Havana* (60), *Lawrence of Arabia* (62), *Dr. Zhivago* (65), *A Man for All Seasons* (66), *Oliver!* (68), *Nicholas and Alexandra* (71), *Travels with My Aunt* (72), *The Great Gatsby* (73), *Rollerball* (75), *Sorcerer* (76). Considered Britain's most distinguished designer. 4-time AA winner.

Boyle, Robert b. 1910 Los Angeles. B. Arch. Univ. Southern California, 1933. "My first jobs in the industry were that of acting extra in order to earn my bread while one architectural firm after another for which I worked, went broke. Then Hans Dreier of Paramount hired me to work for Wiard Ihnen, Art Director on a film whose title eludes me [Leisen's *Cradle Song*, 1933] but in which I do recall Dorothea Wieck, playing a nun in a Spanish convent. We worked a feverish weekend to finish that convent set—which was cancelled. After that, I worked variously as sketch artist, draftsman, assistant Art Director. My first film as a full-fledged Art Director was with Alfred Hitchcock—*Saboteur*. World War II interrupted my career and I did a stint overseas as combat photographer for the Signal Corps. Upon my return, I started a film with Hitchcock at RKO. A young woman, Bess Taffel, was writing the script. The production soon fell apart for those mysterious front office reasons. However, the writer and the art director stayed together. They got married. I remained at RKO to do one or two films—then returned to Universal. I worked at all the going studios—Columbia, Warners, MGM, Sam Goldwyn. Now—about working for Hitchcock—nothing makes things easier for the art director. Art Direction is by its very nature very difficult work. It is not any easier to work with Hitchcock. It is, however, extremely rewarding and instructive—but not because he preplans or cuts-in-the-camera. (Rigid planning could be an inhibitive headache to an art director.) I find Hitch a catalyst to my own creative functioning, and on each picture I recognized again, as if for the first time, that I was working with a master. He is one of the few who really knows the materials of his craft and their effect—and he will use anything—in any combination—in any form, conventional or not—to make his statement, to tell his story. To tell the story in a way that involves his audience is his main objective and his preplanning consists in selecting those elements and techniques that will best accomplish that goal. About *Marnie*—we were aware of the impact of that matte shot and the diminished perspectives of the Baltimore Street and it was a conscious decision to leave it that way."—letter from B to Eliott Stein, March 30, 1976.
  *Films dir. by Hitchcock. *Saboteur* (42), *Flesh and Fantasy* (43), *Shadow of a Doubt* (43), *Ride the Pink Horse* (47), *Another Part of the Forest* (48), *Mystery Submarine* (50), *Bronco Buster* (52), *The Beast from 20,000 Fathoms* (53), *It Came from Outer Space* (53), *Lady Godiva* (55), *The Brothers Rico* (57), *Buchanan Rides Alone* (58), *The Crimson Kimono* (59), *North by Northwest* (59), *The Birds* (63), *Marnie* (64), *The Russians Are Coming, The Russians Are Coming* (66), *How to Succeed in Business Without Really Trying* (67), *In Cold Blood* (67), *The Thomas Crown Affair* (68), *Gaily, Gaily* (69), *The Landlord* (70), *Fiddler on the Roof* (71), *Mame* (74), *Bite the Bullet* (75), *Leadbelly* (76), *W. C. Fields and Me* (76), *The Shootist* (76). The matte paintings and unrealistic vistas in *Marnie* which bothered so many critics in 1964 have already been absorbed into the mainstream.

Bridgeman, Ken GB. *Smashing Time* (67), *A Nice Girl Like Me* (69), *Vampyres* (74)—the best, in fact the only soft-core porn-cum-horror film with lush, appropriately luxuriant, and oppressive décors.

Brinton, Ralph b. 1895. Architect 1928–33; began working in UK film industry 1934. *Wings of the Morning* (37)—the first English 3-strip Technicolor prod., *Odd Man Out* (47), *Uncle Silas* (47), *Eye Witness* (50), *The Knave of Hearts/M. Ripois/Lovers, Happy Lovers* (54), *Moby Dick* (56), *The Gypsy and the Gentleman* (58), *A Taste of Honey* (61), *The Loneliness of the Long Distance Runner* (62), *Tom Jones* (63), *Isadora/The Loves of Isadora* (68). B's best work often borders on the fantastic world of the expressionists.

Brown, Hilyard b. 1910 Nebraska. Stud. architecture, Univ. Southern California. Entered films 1937 as draftsman at WB. Asst. a.d. *Citizen Kane* (41). *A Guy, A Gal, A Pal* (45), *Valley of the Zombies* (46), *The Exile* (47), *All My Sons* (48), *Has Anybody Seen My Gal* (52), *Take Me to Town* (53), *The Creature from the Black Lagoon* (54), *The Night of the Hunter* (55), *Fear Strikes Out* (57), *Man of the West* (58), *Man in the Net* (59), *Al Capone* (59), *Cleopatra* (63)—in collab. De Cuir, etc., *Shock Treatment* (64), *Von Ryan's Express* (65), *Finian's Rainbow* (68), *Skullduggery* (70), *Fuzz* (73), *Freebie and the Bean* (74), *Hustle* (75). Much of B's work has been eclectic (a fancy way of saying: what the studio thinks it wants this season). But on at least one occasion, prodded by a cameraman (Stanley Cortez) and a dir. (Charles Laughton) of genius, he came up with superb designs—the stylized and very Germanic *Caligari*-revisited sets for *The Night of the Hunter*. This brilliant film was received with indifference in 1955, but posterity has been busy making amends ever since. See entry on B in *Film Dope*, no. 5 (July 1974).

Bryan, John 1911 London–1969. Began as theater set designer. In films, at first collab. with Vincent Korda on several pictures, notably *Major Barbara* (41). Then: *The Adventures of Tartu* (43), *Millions Like Us* (43), *Fanny by Gaslight/Man of Evil* (44), *Caesar and Cleopatra* (45), *Great Expectations* (46), *Oliver Twist* (48), *Blanche Fury* (48), *Pandora and the Flying Dutchman* (51), *Becket* (64). B's love of old London resulted in a splendidly romantic job of period restoration for the 2 Dickens pictures he designed for David Lean; a more flamboyant component in the designer's nature responded gamely, but in vain, to the sympathetic but humorless insanity of Lewin's *Pandora*.

Buckland, Wilfred US. 1866–1946 Hollywood. *The Ghost Breaker* (14), *The Virginian* (14), *Carmen* (15), *The Cheat* (15), *Joan, the Woman* (16), *Romance of the Redwoods* (17), *Stella Maris* (18), *The Whispering Chorus* (18), *Male and Female* (19), *The Grim Game* (19), *The Deuce of Spades* (22), *The Masquerader* (22), *Robin Hood* (22), *Omar the Tentmaker* (22), *Adam's Rib* (23), *The Forbidden Woman* (27), *Almost Human* (27).

B left NY for California in 1914, to work for De Mille and other dirs. at Famous Players–Lasky. "Cecil [De Mille] and I began to think an art director might be an asset to a picture company, and his mother recommended Wilfred Buckland, who had been responsible for the scenic beauty . . . in Belasco's plays. We brought Buckland to the Coast to head a staff of designers and draftsmen. . . . As the first bona fide art director in the industry, and the first to build architectural settings for films, Buckland widened the scope of pictures tremendously by throwing off the scenic limitations of the stage."—Jesse Lasky, *I Blow My Own Horn* (London, 1957), p. 107. "He accepted the very small sum of $75 a week in return for his services, a salary that was not increased even three years later. From the beginning, he collided with De Mille. He wanted to group the figures on the screen, while De Mille felt that the function of the art director was only to design the backgrounds. This was entirely against Belasco's concepts. Not only Buckland but the entire workshop involved in the construction of sets was bitterly dissatisfied in that early period. [They were] quite often required to work 18-hour stretches, 7 days a week. . . . "—Higham, *De Mille*.

In some important respects US film set design may be dated before and after Buckland. His first sets were built in an old barn at what is now the corner of Vine and Selma. What the world knows as Hollywood was born in that barn—the first California film studio. B dressed his sets with real furniture (before, most movie furniture had been painted flats on the walls). The fantastic bathrooms which he des. for a succession of De Mille heroines were described by William De Mille as "shrines." One of B's greatest innovations was the use of the klieg light for exterior and interior sets. "Lasky Lighting" (by cameraman Alvin Wyckoff) of B sets created chiaroscuro effects as famous in 1915–22 as those of *Citizen Kane* a quarter of a century later. "My best friend, Bill Buckland, was son of the first film art director. . . . Buckland was the man who originated interior lighting in the infant film industry. Until then, directors relied on natural sunshine controlled by metal-foil-covered reflectors and canvas sails. . . . The innovation of arc lamps produced dramatic lighting and opened a new world for film makers. I have seen Wilfred Buckland tie a couple of actors to the camera with ropes so that they could be kept in focus as they were drawn along by one of the first cameras to be placed on a 'dolly' or platform on wheels. A man who had made suns rise and set on a theater stage was not likely to leave our early films to the whims of weather. Artificial lighting made it possible to tell day from night without the aid of the title 'Came the dawn!' "—Jesse Lasky, Jr., *Whatever Happened to Hollywood?* (NY, 1975), pp. 10–11. See also Kenneth MacGowan in *Photoplay* (Jan. 1921), p. 73, on lighting.

In 1941 B was given a testimonial dinner by the Society of Motion Picture Art Directors. In his later years he worked for MGM, and even when past 80 went to work at the studio every day. "The buzzer snarled on [De Mille's] desk. Wilfred Buckland, now retired and in his mid-eighties [sic], had stopped by to see him. . . . The old gentleman made a shuffling appearance, blinking at the models of sets and the sketches which he might himself have prepared, long ago. . . . He was a bulky man, with a fine crest of silver-white hair and lively blue eyes behind pince-nez that gave him the look of a somewhat ancient Theodore Roosevelt. In other lands he would have been weighted down with honors for his contribution to film art and industry. He was in fact neglected, jobless, left virtually penniless by the Depression." —Lasky, Jr., p. 197. On July 18, 1946, he killed his mentally ailing son and shot himself. "The Bucklands had been one of filmland's first families and who now would ever know or care? I'm not even sure whether Hollywood's first art director had his name on one of those brass stars on Hollywood Boulevard."—Ibid., p. 201.

Bumstead, Henry   US. *Saigon* (48), *My Own True Love* (48), *Song of Surrender* (49), *The Furies* (50), *No Man of Her Own* (50), *Come Back, Little Sheba* (52), *The Man Who Knew Too Much* (56), *I Married a Monster from Outer Space* (58), *Vertigo* (58), *Cinderfella* (60), *The War Lord* (65), *Topaz* (69), *Tell Them Willie Boy Is Here* (69), *High Plains Drifter* (73), *The Sting* (73), *The Front Page* (74), *The Great Waldo Pepper* (75), *Family Plot* (76). B has been acclaimed for his recent 20s and 30s designs, but his best work to date has been for *Hitchcock (esp. *Vertigo*) and in his evocative settings for the medieval fantasy Brittany of Schaffner's *The War Lord*. See extensive interview with B in "Academy Award-Winning Art Direction for *The Sting*," *American Cinematographer* (May 1974).

Burns, Robert A.   US. *The Texas Chainsaw Massacre* (74).

Cain, Syd   GB. In films since 1956. *Fahrenheit 451* (66), *Billion Dollar Brain* (67), *Frenzy* (72), *Shout at the Devil* (76).

Carré, Ben   b. 1883 Paris. Stud. painting at Atelier Amable, then worked there as scenic painter, often on sets of immense scale (Paris Opéra, Comédie Française, Covent Garden). Entered films 1901 at Pathé Gaumont Studios. To US 1912, and worked as designer at the Eclair Studios at Fort Lee, for this French company making films in NJ. There began his long assoc. with Tourneur. A founding member of the Motion Picture Academy, C has an impressive list of firsts on his credits. He worked on the first feature with a synchronized musical score (*Don Juan*), the first part-talking picture with several song sequences (*The Jazz Singer*), the first all-talking western made on location (*Riders of the Purple Sage*), and the first Charlie Chan picture (*The Black Camel*). In 1937 he stopped working as an a.d. and went back to des. scenic backgrounds, some of them 100 feet long, at MGM. Des. 3 murals for General Motors Pavilion at 1964 NY World's Fair. Retired in 1965, after 64 years in films, and has since devoted much of his time to easel painting.
*Films dir. by Maurice Tourneur. *La Course aux potirons* (07), *The Dollar Mark* (12), *Mother* (14), *The Man of the Hour* (14), *The Wishing Ring* (14), *The Pit* (14), *Camille* (15), *La Vie de Bohème* (15), *Alias Jimmy Valentine* (15), *The Cub* (15), *Trilby* (15), *The Ivory Snuff Box* (15), *A Butterfly on the Wheel* (15), *The Pawn of Fate* (15), *The Hand of Peril* (16), *The Closed Road* (16), *The Rail Rider* (16), *The Velvet Paw* (16), *A Girl's Folly* (16), *The Whip* (17), *The Pride of the Clan* (17), *The Poor Little Rich Girl* (17), *The Undying Flame* (17), *The Law of the Land* (17), *Exile* (17), *Barbary Sheep* (17), *The Rise of Jenny Cushing* (17), *Rose of the World* (18), *A Doll's House* (18), *The Blue Bird* (18), *Prunella* (18), *Sporting Life* (18), *Woman* (18), *The White Heather* (19), *The Life Line* (19), *The Broken Butterfly* (19), *Victory* (19)—in collab. Floyd Mueller, *Bob Hampton of Placer* (21), *My Lady's Garter* (20), *The Light in the Dark* (22), *Wife in Name Only* (23), *The Red Lily* (24), *Tarnish* (24), *The Phantom of the Opera* (25)— only the scenes under the opera house, *The Masked Bride* (25), *Don Juan* (26), *Mare Nostrum* (26), *Old San Francisco* (27), *The Red Dance* (28), *Hot for Paris* (29), *The Cock-Eyed World* (29), *The Iron Mask* (29), *City Girl* (30), *The Black Camel* (31), *Riders of the Purple Sage* (31), *Women of All Nations* (31), *Sailor's Luck* (33), *Dante's Inferno* (35)—inferno scenes only, *A Night at the Opera* (35), *Let's Sing Again* (36), *The Mine with the Iron Door* (36), *Great Guy* (36), *23 1/2 Hours Leave* (37). C painted backgrounds for *The Wizard of Oz* (39), *Meet Me in St. Louis* (44), *An American in Paris* (51).
"Carré was a pioneer in the field of scenic design for motion pictures, and long before the term 'art director' had been established, he and Maurice Tourneur had brought a new standard of beauty to the American screen. His work was so imitated that others have won

201

the praise that belongs to him; his Gothic catacombs of the Paris opera house seem to belong to a much later period of Universal horror films. But the style can be dated back to the earliest days at Eclair.''—Kevin Brownlow, *Film Dope*, no. 6 (Nov. 1974), p. 26.

Carrere, Edward   US. Unit a.d., mostly at WB. *The Fountainhead* (49), *The Adventures of Don Juan* (49), *White Heat* (49), *The Breaking Point* (50), *Young Man with a Horn/Young Man of Music* (50), *The Flame and the Arrow* (50), *South Sea Woman* (53), *Dial M for Murder* (54), *Helen of Troy* (55), *Separate Tables* (58), *Camelot* (67), *The Wild Bunch* (69).

Carrick, Edward (Edward Craig)   b. 1905 London. Son of Gordon Craig. *Laburnum Grove* (36), *Jump for Glory/When Thief Meets Thief* (37). During WWII, a.d. for Crown Film Unit for which he des. several documentaries, notably *Target for Tonight* (41) and *Western Approaches* (44). Then: *Captain Boycott* (47), *The Red Beret/The Paratrooper* (53), *Blind Date/Chance Meeting* (59), *The Nanny* (65). C is a skilled designer and theoretician who has often written on the problems of film set design. He founded the first school in England specialized in the study of cinema (1937); author of *Designing for Moving Pictures*. See his *Gordon Craig* (NY, 1968).

Cartwright, Robert   GB. *The Devils* (71), *The Optimists of Nine Elms* (74).

Cavalcanti, Alberto   b. 1897 Brazil. Dir., set designer, screenwriter. Stud. architecture in Geneva. Started in films as a.d.: *L'Inhumaine/The New Enchantment* (23), *L'Inondation* (24), *La Galerie des monstres* (24), *The Little People* (26).

Caziot, Jean-Jacques   *Le Souffle au coeur/Murmur of the Heart* (71), *La Scoumone* (72), *Le Trio infernal* (74).

Charbonnier, Pierre   All films listed were dir. by Robert Bresson. *Le Journal d'un curé de campagne/Diary of a Country Priest* (50), *Un Condamné à mort s'est échappé/A Man Escaped* (56), *Pickpocket* (59), *Le Procès de Jeanne d'Arc/The Trial of Joan of Arc* (62), *Au Hasard, Balthasar/Balthazar* (66), *Une Femme douce/A Gentle Creature* (69), *Quatre Nuits d'un rêveur/4 Nights of a Dreamer* (71), *Lancelot du Lac* (74).

Chiari, Mario   b. 1909 Italy. Stud. architecture. Entered cinema as asst. dir. to Blasetti. Des. theater sets and costumes for prods. by Visconti. 1942–43 dir. 3 documentary films. As a.d.: *Vulcano* (50), *Le Carrosse d'or/The Golden Coach* (52), *I Vitelloni* (53), *Carosello Napolitano* (54), *War and Peace* (56)—in collab. Franz Bachelin, *Le Notti bianche/White Nights* (57), *La Battaglia di Maratona/The Giant of Marathon* (59), *Barabbas* (62), *Il Commissario* (62), *The Bible (. . . in the Beginning)* (66), *Doctor Dolittle* (67), *Ludwig* (73).

Clark, Carroll   US. 1894–1968. Worked at Pathé; signed in 1932 by RKO, where he remained as unit a.d. for many years. Worked for Disney on live-action features in last decade of his life. *The Magic Garden* (27), *Hell's Angels* (30), *A Bill of Divorcement* (32), *What Price Hollywood?* (32), *Hell's Highway* (32), *The Most Dangerous Game* (32), *King Kong* (33)—in collab. Herman, *Flying Down to Rio* (33), *Top Hat* (35), *Mary of Scotland* (36), *Swing Time* (36), *Shall We Dance* (37), *Carefree* (38), *Suspicion* (41), *Joan of Paris* (42), *Youth Runs Wild* (44), *The Spanish Main* (45), *Notorious* (46), *I Remember Mama* (48), *A Woman's Secret* (49), *Vice Squad* (53), *While the City Sleeps* (56), *Beyond a Reasonable Doubt* (56), *Darby O'Gill and the Little People* (59), *Mary Poppins* (64). See also Van Nest Polglase entry.

Clark, John   GB. *The Railway Children* (71), *Performance* (71), *The Offence* (72), *Jesus Christ Superstar* (73), *Tommy* (75).

Clatworthy, Robert   US. *Christmas Holiday* (44), *Variety Girl* (47), *Woman in Hiding* (49), *Apache Drums* (51), *Horizons West* (52), *Written on the Wind* (57), *The Incredible Shrinking Man* (57), *Touch of Evil* (58), *Psycho* (60), *Report to the Commissioner* (75).

Clavel, Robert   b. 1912 Paris. In 1942–47 worked as assoc. a.d. with Barsacq and Trauner. Films as full-fledged designer: *La Valse de Paris* (49), *L'Homme à l'imperméable* (57), *Le Passage du Rhin* (60), *Belle de Jour* (67), *Verdict* (74). His sets are rich in carefully noted details; for Buñuel's masterpiece, *Belle de Jour*, the designs were worthy of the occasion.

Colasanti, Veniero   b. 1910 Italy. Stud. architecture in Rome. Much work des. sets and costumes for ballet and opera at La Scala and Rome Opera. *Fabiola* (48). Since 1958 his film work has been in close collab. with John Moore: *A Farewell to Arms* (58), *El Cid* (61), *55 Days at Peking* (63), *The Fall of the Roman Empire* (64), *A Matter of Time/Nina* (76). His period reconstructions have been marked by real grandeur. *Films prod. by Samuel Bronston at his studios near Madrid.

Colasson, Maurice   b. 1911 France. *Eugénie Grandet* (46), *Dédée d'Anvers/Dédée* (48), *Une Si Jolie Petite Plage* (49), *Un Homme marche dans la ville* (49), *Le Dialogue des Carmélites* (59), *Mayerling* (68).

Crawley, Paul   US. *The Fire Brigade* (27), *The Bat Whispers* (30). C is not yet a household word. He deserves to be one: he des. one of the few really exciting films prod. by MGM and—in the late 20s—Roland West's masterpiece, *The Bat Whispers*, where, in certain scenes, the sets are used in a way which prefigures *Citizen Kane*.

Crisanti, Andrea   *Uomini Contro* (70), *Il Caso Mattei/The Mattei Affair* (72), *A Proposito di Lucky Luciano/Lucky Luciano* (73), *Cadaveri Eccellenti/The Context* (76). Her work on these 4 films—all dir. by Francesco Rosi—is evidence enough that C is one of the most talented a.d.s working in the Italian cinema today.

D'Agostino, Albert   1893 NY–1970. Entered films as asst. a.d. MGM. In the 30s worked for Universal until 1936; then with RKO 1936–58. *Films prod. by Val Lewton, with a.d. by Dag in collab. Walter E. Keller. *Salvation Nell* (21), *Ramona* (28), *Blood Money* (33), *I Cover the Waterfront* (33), *The Werewolf of London* (35), *The Mystery of Edwin Drood* (35), *The Raven* (35), *Dracula's Daughter* (36), *The Invisible Ray* (36), *The Stranger on the 3rd Floor* (40), *The Cat People* (42), *I Walked with a Zombie* (43), *The Leopard Man* (43), *The 7th Victim* (43), *The Ghost Ship* (43), *This Land Is Mine* (43), *The Curse of the Cat People* (44), *Mademoiselle Fifi* (44), *None but the Lonely Heart* (44), *Isle of the Dead* (45), *The Body Snatcher* (45), *Bedlam* (46), *The Spiral Staircase* (46), *Notorious* (46), *Jet Pilot* (50), *The Thing* (51), *Macao* (52), *Clash by Night* (52), *Angel Face* (52), *Run of the Arrow* (57). Whatever his other accomplishments—and they are often exemplary, e.g. *The Spiral Staircase*—or his work with the greatest dirs.—in one year (1952) RKO released films for which he had done sets for Sternberg, Lang, Preminger, and Hawks—Dag will always be remembered for his contribution to the series of hauntingly intimate low-budget thrillers prod. by Lewton at RKO in the 40s.

"To create his set designs for the classic Universal horror films of the 1930s . . . D'Agostino took tentative advice from Charles D. Hall, Universal's chief art director. D'Agostino's style was his own, however . . . an example can be seen when comparing Hall's sets for the original *Dracula* (1931) with D'Agostino's in *Dracula's Daughter* (1936). Hall's designs were indeed magnificent in their gothic magnitude, but they showed very little more than huge exterior and interior decor. D'Agostino used these same Hall sets, but he also found reason to develop purpose and realism behind them. The characters in the film blended into the surroundings. This in itself is the quality I find in D'Agostino's designs. The realism is incorporated into a personification of the character. There is a human quality involved in a completely fantastic circumstance, and D'Agostino's sets assisted in this transition."—Gary Dorst, "Albert S. D'Agostino—A Tribute," *Cinefantastique* (Summer 1971), p. 35.

Darling, William   1882 Austria-Hungary–1963. Stud. at Hungarian Academy of True Arts. To US 1905; set up a studio in NY where he painted portraits of celebrities—among them F. W. Woolworth and Billy Sunday. In 1922 joined Fox Films; within a year named chief art and technical dir. Remained with Fox for most of his career. *Films dir. by John Ford. *Her Mad Bargain* (21), *What Price Glory* (26), *Paid to Love* (27), *Fazil* (28), *A Girl in Every Port* (28), *4 Devils* (28)—sets executed by D from sketches by Herlth and Röhrig, *The Black Watch* (29), *City Girl* (30), *Men Without Women* (30), *Bad Girl* (31), *The Yellow Ticket* (31), *While Paris Sleeps* (32), *Hoop-la* (33), *Cavalcade* (33), *Pilgrimage* (33), *Zoo in Budapest* (33), *The World Moves On* (34), *Steamboat Round the Bend* (35), *The Prisoner of Shark Island* (36), *Lloyds of London* (36), *Seventh Heaven* (37), *Wee Willie Winkie* (37), *Wake Up and Live* (37), *In Old Chicago* (38)—in collab. Sternad, *Jesse James* (39), *Stanley and Livingstone* (39), *Hangmen Also Die* (43), *The Song of Bernadette* (43), *Anna and the King of Siam* (46). Despite D's AA-winning, elaborately academic designs for big-budget spectaculars, his most impressive work is on a smaller scale, at Fox in the early 30s—the amazing studio re-creation of a murky Paris for Dwan's low-budgeted *While Paris Sleeps*, and his superb sets for Rowland Lee's exquisite *Zoo in Budapest*.

Davis, George W.   b. 1914 Indiana. Worked at 20th–Fox in the 50s. After the retirement of Gibbons, went over to MGM; superv. a.d. there for several years from 1959. *The Ghost and Mrs. Muir* (47), *Daisy Kenyon* (47), *Deep Waters* (48), *House of Strangers* (49), *No Way Out* (50), *All About Eve* (50), *The Robe* (53), *The Egyptian* (54), *The 7 Year Itch* (55), *Funny Face* (57), *The Diary of Anne Frank* (59), *The Time Machine* (60), *2 Weeks in Another*

Town (62), *How the West Was Won* (62), *Mutiny on the Bounty* (62), *7 Women* (66)—in collab. Eddie Imazu, *Point Blank* (67).

Day, Richard 1895 Canada–1972. To Hollywood 1920, worked briefly as a set painter. Collab. with the dir. on sets for Stroheim films (1922–28) for various studios; also worked for MGM in late 20s. With Goldwyn and UA in 30s until 1938; with 20th in 1939–47. In WWII commissioned a major in Marine Corps; des. and built models of assault areas where marines were planning to land. Superv. a.d. at 20th–Fox 1940–42 and 1945–Feb. 1947; 1949–50 worked on Goldwyn films rel. by RKO; after 1950 worked for WB, UA, and other studios.

Foolish Wives (22), *Merry-Go-Round* (23), *Greed* (24), *Sinners in Silk* (24), *Bright Lights* (25), *The Merry Widow* (25), *Bardelys the Magnificent* (26), *Beverly of Graustark* (26), *Adam and Evil* (27), *The Enemy* (27), *The Unknown* (27), *The Student Prince* (27), *Mr. Wu* (27), *The Show* (27), *Tea for 3* (27), *Rose-Marie* (28), *Wickedness Preferred* (28), *The Wedding March* (28), *The Hollywood Revue of 1929* (29), *Whoopee* (30), *Arrowsmith* (31), *Street Scene* (31), *The Front Page* (31), *Rain* (32), *The Kid from Spain* (32), *Hallelujah, I'm a Bum* (33), *Roman Scandals* (33), *The Bowery* (33), *The House of Rothschild* (34), *The Last Gentleman* (34), *The Wedding Night* (35), *Barbary Coast* (35), *Dark Angel* (35), *Dodsworth* (36), *Come and Get It!* (36), *Dead End* (37), *The Hurricane* (37), *Stella Dallas* (37), *The Goldwyn Follies* (38), *The Adventures of Marco Polo* (38), *Drums Along the Mohawk* (39), *Hound of the Baskervilles* (39), *Young Mr. Lincoln* (39), *The Mark of Zorro* (40), *The Grapes of Wrath* (40), *How Green Was My Valley* (41)—in collab. Juran, *Blood and Sand* (41), *Weekend in Havana* (41), *Tobacco Road* (41), *This Above All* (42), *The Black Swan* (42), *The Razor's Edge* (46), *Captain from Castile* (47), *Force of Evil* (49), *Edge of Doom* (50), *A Streetcar Named Desire* (51), *On the Waterfront* (54), *Solomon and Sheba* (59)—in collab. Alfred Sweeney, *Exodus* (60), *Something Wild* (61), *Goodbye Charlie* (64), *Cheyenne Autumn* (64), *The Greatest Story Ever Told* (65)—in collab. William Creber, *The Chase* (66), *Valley of the Dolls* (67), *The Boston Strangler* (68), *Tora! Tora! Tora!* (70)—and many more.

"There have been very few really successfully versatile art directors, in fact I only know of one, Richard Day. It was he who designed the stinking beetle-ridden staircase in the tenement house for *Dead End*, and he also designed that most beautiful 'Nymph Ballet' sequence with a white horse sculptured against a blue sky in *Goldwyn Follies*, but I do not know of any other artist who can be so convincing in two such different spheres."—Carrick, *Designing for Moving Pictures*, p. 19. Viewing D's long, prolific career from another angle: how amazing the life work which created the settings in the midst of which promenaded the varied forms of Lon Chaney, Eddie Cantor, Shirley Temple, Holmes and Watson, Carmen Miranda, and Marlon Brando!

D'Eaubonne, Jean 1903 France–1971. Stud. with the sculptor Bourdelle. Trained by Meerson. *Le Sang d'un poète/Blood of a Poet* (32), *Jenny* (36), *Fahrendes Volk/Les Gens du voyage* (38), *La Chartreuse de Parme* (47), *Orphée* (49), *La Ronde* (50), *Le Plaisir* (51), *Casque d'or* (52), *Madame de/The Earrings of Madame de* (53), *Lola Montès* (55)—in collab. Schatz, *Crack in the Mirror* (60), *The Big Gamble* (61). One of the most talented French designers, he fits neatly in no pigeonhole. D could adapt himself so well to Cocteau's style that most people assume Cocteau did the sets for *Poète* and *Orphée*; he could provide exquisite designs which harmonized with Ophüls's unrelentingly baroque tracking shots. And, when the occasion called for it, he was capable of the most tactful poetic naturalism in his re-creation of turn-of-the-century Belleville, just right for Becker's *Casque d'or*. If this is a great film, not just a period gangster movie, D's contribution to its greatness is not small.

De Cuir, John b. 1918 San Francisco. Stud. Chouinard Art School, Los Angeles. At Universal 1938–49, a.d. 20th–Fox 1949; much work at Fox, mostly on big prods., since then. *White Tie and Tails* (46), *Brute Force* (47), *Time out of Mind* (47), *The Naked City* (48), *Curtain Call at Cactus Creek* (50), *My Cousin Rachel* (52), *The Model and the Marriage Broker* (52), *The Snows of Kilimanjaro* (53), *Call Me Madam* (53), *3 Coins in the Fountain* (54), *There's No Business Like Show Business* (54), *Daddy Long Legs* (55), *The King and I* (56), *South Pacific* (58), *A Certain Smile* (58), *Cleopatra* (63)—in collab. Hilyard Brown, etc., *Circus World* (64), *The Agony and the Ecstasy* (65), *The Taming of the Shrew* (67), *The Honey Pot* (67), *Hello, Dolly!* (69), *On a Clear Day You Can See Forever* (70), *The Great White Hope* (70), *Jacqueline Susann's Once Is Not Enough* (75). Earlier work at Universal more vigorous than the later elaborate designs at Fox and elsewhere. De C is responsible for the only décor in a 1975 US film which evokes an audible response from audiences—the gaudy bedroom of George Hamilton's bachelor pad in *Once Is Not Enough*. Its deliberate heavy vulgarity is, however, not all that markedly unlike sets in some other films by De C where the effect was not deliberate.

Dillon, Carmen b. 1908 London. Stud. Architectural Association School. Dissatisfied with architecture, in 1934 D became an asst. to Brinton (an architectural school colleague) at Wembley Studios. Set dresser/a.d. on many pictures for Two Cities and Rank, often in collab. with prod. designers Sheriff or Furse. *The 5 Pound Man* (37), *Quiet Wedding* (41), *Henry V* (44)—as asst. to Sheriff, *Hamlet* (48)—des. by Furse, sets decorated by D, even though English credit for her reads a.d., *The Rocking Horse Winner* (49), *The Browning Version* (51), *The Importance of Being Earnest* (52), *The Iron Petticoat* (56), *Carry On Cruising* (62), *Accident* (67), *The Go-Between* (71), *Lady Caroline Lamb* (73), *Butley* (74). For nearly a quarter of a century D was the only woman a.d. working in English films. There are a few others today: Maggie Pinhorn, Julia Trevelyan Oman, and Peggy Glick. See Dillon, "The Function of the Art Director," *Films and Filming* 3 (May 1957).

Donati, Danilo b. 1926 Italy. First work in theater was as costume designer for Visconti opera prods. Costumes for theater revues and for several early Pasolini films. Became best-known costume designer in Italy; 1968 won AA for costumes for Zeffirelli's *Romeo and Juliet*. *Porcile* (69), *Fellini Satyricon* (69)—also costumes; sets in collab. Scaccianoce, some based on sketches by Fellini, *Fellini Roma* (72), *Amarcord* (74), *Gore Vidal's Caligula* (76). See Stanley J. Solomon, *The Classic Cinema* (NY, 1973), pp. 326–27, 336–37, on *Satyricon* sets; Charles Choset and Stuart Byron, "From Rimini to Roma: An Exclusive Interview with Federico Fellini," *The Real Paper* (Boston; Dec. 18, 1974).

Douy, Max b. France 1914. Started as asst. to Perrier, Meerson, and Trauner. *La Règle du jeu/Rules of the Game* (39)—as asst. to Lourié, *Lumière d'été* (43), *Adieu Léonard* (43), *Les Dames du Bois de Boulogne* (45), *Falbalas* (45), *Le Diable au corps/Devil in the Flesh* (47), *Quai des orfèvres/Jenny Lamour* (47), *Manon* (48), *Occupe-toi d'Amélie* (49), *Le Rouge et le Noir* (54), *French Cancan* (54), *Cela s'appelle l'Aurore* (55), *Topkapi* (64), *Le Franciscain de Bourges* (67), *Castle Keep* (69), *Le Moine* (72), *Section Spéciale* (75). Though D has often worked on lavish productions, his most memorable sets are those for the small, intense, closed world of Bresson's *Les Dames du Bois de Boulogne*.

Dreier, Hans 1885 Germany–1966. Stud. architecture in Munich. Superv. architect of the German Imperial Government in the Cameroons, West Africa. Entered films 1919 at UFA, Berlin. To US 1923 to work for Paramount, and spent rest of career with that studio, where he was superv. a.d. until his retirement in 1950. A large share of D's most striking designs were for von Sternberg films.
*Films dir. by Lubitsch. *Der Reigen* (20), *Kurfürstendamm* (20), *Peter der Grosse/Peter the Great* (23), *Forbidden Paradise* (24), *East of Suez* (25), *Underworld* (27), *The Last Command* (28), *The Dragnet* (28), *The Patriot* (28), *The Docks of New York* (28), *The Case of Lena Smith* (29), *Thunderbolt* (29), *The Love Parade* (29), *Morocco* (30), *Dishonored* (31), *An American Tragedy* (31), *The Smiling Lieutenant* (31), *Dr. Jekyll and Mr. Hyde* (31), *Love Me Tonight* (32), *The Man I Killed* (32), *One Hour with You* (32), *Trouble in Paradise* (32), *Shanghai Express* (32), *Design for Living* (33)—in collab. Fegté, *Song of Songs* (33), *Cleopatra* (34), *The Scarlet Empress* (34), *The Crusades* (35), *The Devil Is a Woman* (35), *Desire* (36)—in collab. Usher, *Angel* (37)—in collab. Usher, *Easy Living* (37)—in collab. Fegté, *Bluebeard's 8th Wife* (38)—in collab. Usher, *Union Pacific* (39), *Midnight* (39), *Bahama Passage* (41), *The Glass Key* (42), *Lady in the Dark* (44)—in collab. Raul Pène Du Bois who des. costumes and most of sets, and dir. Leisen, *Frenchman's Creek* (44), *The Emperor Waltz* (48), *Samson and Delilah* (49), *Sunset Boulevard* (50), *A Place in the Sun* (51).
"He was as influential as Cedric Gibbons at MGM and his elegant, witty designs, which took in all forms of Americana as well as simulated foreign settings, were realized by a talented team of associate designers. Dreier had a special affinity with European-oriented directors, working notably with Lubitsch over many years."—Gillett, *International Encyclopedia of Film*, p. 181. "Under the control of Hans Dreier . . . the studio's product achieved an opulence of surface never equalled by others. . . . If Metro's films had polish, Paramount films had a glow. The best of them seem gilded, luminous, as rich and brocaded as Renaissance tapestry. Décor in a Paramount production was seldom, as in Metro films,

merely a background; settings, draperies, gowns insinuated themselves into the action, guiding and occasionally dictating the feel of a film."—Baxter, *Hollywood in the Thirties*, p. 46. For Du Bois's work on *Lady in the Dark*, see Chierichetti, *Hollywood Director*.

Eatwell, Brian   GB. *Just Like a Woman* (66), *Here We Go Round the Mulberry Bush* (67), *The Shuttered Room* (67), *The Abominable Dr. Phibes/Dr. Phibes* (71), *Walkabout* (71), *Dr. Phibes Rises Again* (72), *Godspell* (73), *The 3 Musketeers* (73), *The 4 Musketeers* (74), *The Man Who Fell to Earth* (76), *Billy Jack Goes to Washington* (76). There has not been a resident genius designer on the British film scene since the death of Junge—there has certainly never been a resident English one. E's work, which turned up on those occasionally stuffy premises shortly after the death of Junge, came as a cool, insidiously outrageous, and very welcome breath of fresh air. It is too early to tell how far his talent for camp, color, and clutter will take him—but the first decade has been more than promising. See "The Making of *Godspell*," *Filmmakers Newsletter* (May 1973).

Egidi, Carlo   b. 1918 Rome. Stud. architecture. *Caccia Tragica* (47), *Non c'è Pace tra gli Ulivi* (49), *Il Ferroviere/The Railroad Man* (56), *Divorce, Italian Style* (61), *Seduced and Abandoned* (63), *La Noia/The Empty Canvas* (64), *Investigation of a Citizen Above Suspicion* (70). After his appropriate designs for the earlier De Santis neorealist films, E's later sets for Germi's more commercial films are marked by the beautiful authenticity of the interiors.

Enei, Yevgeni   1890 Austria-Hungary–1971. Stud. Fine Arts Academy, Budapest. Entered Soviet film industry 1923. *Films dir. by Grigori Kozintsev (the first 4 of these were co-dir. by Ilya Trauberg). *The Cloak* (26), *The New Babylon* (29), *Fragment of an Empire* (29), *The Youth of Maxim* (35), *The Return of Maxim* (37), *Pavlov* (49), *Don Quixote* (57), *Hamlet* (64), *Katerina Izmailova* (67), *King Lear* (70). "Enei . . . assisted both the spirit and the functioning of the film [*The Cloak*] by sharply characterized interiors and street scenes."—Jay Leyda, *Kino* (NY, 1970), p. 202. Though he has des. for several dirs., E's career will always be assoc. with that of Kozintsev—their collab. lasted 40 years. His fine work on the first 2 parts of the *Maxim* trilogy is perhaps only slightly overshadowed by the marvelous heaps of bric-a-brac assembled for the eponymous Parisian department store in *The New Babylon*. See *Designers of the Soviet Cinema*.

Ericksen, Leon   US. *Films dir. by Robert Altman. *Wild Angels* (66), *Psych-Out* (68), *The Savage 7* (68), *That Cold Day in the Park* (69), *Futz* (69), *Medium Cool* (69), *The Rain People* (69), *McCabe and Mrs. Miller* (71), *Images* (72), *Cinderella Liberty* (73), *California Split* (74), *Mahogany* (75).

Evein, Bernard   b. 1929 France. Stud. fine arts at Nantes where he met Jacques Demy for whom he later des. several films. Stud. film design at IDHEC. In collab. Saulnier: *Les Amants* (58), *A Double Tour/Leda* (59). Then: *Les 400 Coups* (59), *Zazie dans le Métro/Zazie* (60), *Cléo de 5 à 7* (61), *Une Femme est une femme* (61), *La Baie des anges* (62), *Le Rendezvous de minuit* (62), *Vie privée/A Very Private Affair* (62), *Le Feu follet/The Fire Within* (63), *The Umbrellas of Cherbourg* (64), *Viva Maria* (65), *L'Aveu* (70), *L'Evenement le plus important depuis que l'homme a marché sur la lune/The Slightly Pregnant Man* (73). E's poetic vision of décor brightened up the New Wave—a bit.

Fegté, Ernst   b. 1900 Germany. Left with advent of Hitler. Unit a.d. Paramount for many years, first at its Astoria, NY, studio, then in Hollywood from 1932. Later work for RKO, Republic, UA; mid-40s superv. a.d. for Goldwyn. *Design for Living* (33)—in collab. Dreier, *Death Takes a Holiday* (34), *Murder at the Vanities* (34), *The General Died at Dawn* (36), *Swing High, Swing Low* (37), *Easy Living* (37)—in collab. Dreier, *College Swing* (38), *You and Me* (38), *The Lady Eve* (41), *I Married a Witch* (42), *The Palm Beach Story* (42), *5 Graves to Cairo* (43), *The Great Moment* (44), *The Miracle of Morgan's Creek* (44), *The Uninvited* (44), *Frenchman's Creek* (44), *And Then There Were None/10 Little Niggers* (45), *Wonder Man* (45), *I've Always Loved You* (46), *Specter of the Rose* (46), *On Our Merry Way/A Miracle Can Happen* (48), *Destination Moon* (50), *Superman and the Mole Men* (51), *The Amazing Transparent Man* (60), *Beyond the Time Barrier* (60). Leisen, *Sturges, Clair, Wilder—for over a decade F des. for some of the best men in the business.

Ferguson, Perry   b. 1901 Texas—deceased. Worked mostly for RKO and Goldwyn. *Films in collab. with Jenkins. *Hooray for Love* (35), *Bringing Up Baby* (38), *The Story of Vernon and Irene Castle* (39), *Citizen Kane* (41), *Ball of Fire* (42), *The North Star* (43), *The Best Years of*

Our Lives (46), *The Stranger* (46), *The Kid from Brooklyn* (46), **The Secret Life of Walter Mitty* (47), **The Bishop's Wife* (47), *Desert Fury* (47), *A Song Is Born (48), *Rope* (48), *711 Ocean Drive* (50), *The Sound of Fury/Try and Get Me* (51), *The Big Sky* (52), *Ready for the People* (64).

Citizen Kane's credits read: "Art Director—Van Nest Polglase, Associate Art Director—Perry Ferguson." In most sources, F is omitted altogether and Polglase gets all the credit. But in the only writing on *Kane*'s sets yet published to which any credence can be lent—by the film's cameraman, Gregg Toland (*The American Cinematographer*, Feb. 1941)—the situation is reversed. In Toland's tribute, he speaks of his work with "art director Perry Ferguson" and does not even name Polglase. Without getting into a Welles *vs.* Mankiewicz dispute over the matter, it must be noted that F's contribution to the art direction of *Citizen Kane* was, at the least, considerable. In another Welles film, *The Stranger* (where F was solo a.d.), lies further evidence of his singular talents.

Fisk, Jack US. *Badlands* (73), *The Phantom of the Paradise* (74).

Fitzgerald, Edward All films listed were dir. by Buñuel in Mexico. *Los Olvidados/The Young and the Damned* (50), *La Hija del Engaño* (51), *Subida al Cielo/Mexican Bus Ride* (52), *El/This Strange Passion* (53), *La Ilusión viaja en Tranvía* (54), *Abismos de Pasión/Wuthering Heights* (54), *Robinson Crusoe* (made 52, rel. 54), *El Río y la Muerte* (55), *La Muerte en este Jardín/La Mort en ce jardin/Evil Eden* (56), *Nazarín* (59).

Fuest, Robert b. 1927. Art school, London. Exhibited paintings Royal Academy. A.d. and dir. of *The Avengers* (TV). F is known as a dir.—for *The Abominable Dr. Phibes* (71) and his remake of *Wuthering Heights* (72). But *The Final Programme/The Last Days of Man on Earth* (74)—dir., written, and des. by him—is a real achievement, the sauciest and best-looking sci-fi fantasy in quite some time.

F, on *The Final Programme*: "I asked for $600,000. Only $50,000 of this would be used on the sets. Everyone told me that the film could not be done for that small a budget. They all said—It has got to have a James Bond-type image. I told them that they were wrong, and I convinced them that in my hands, it could be done. I decided to design the sets myself, because I knew what I wanted, and I knew how they could be done economically. I did need someone to actually build my designs, so I called Philip Harrison whom I had known from my days in television. Philip had done the film 'How I Won the War' and had been the art director on a couple of Ken Russell films. I asked him to assist me on 'The Final Programme.' I told him that I was going to dictate what the sets would be. I knew it was the most rotten and insulting thing to do to an art director, and I told him this. He understood the situation I was in, and he was marvellous. He came in, listened to every word I told him, and came up with the built sets I designed. He put up with me, and I admire him for this. I decided that the only way to do the sets was to build huge, reusable building blocks. In one scene, one of these blocks might be used as a wall, and then in the next it might be the ceiling. We made them 30 or 40 feet wide; they were huge. We used them over and over again throughout the film. There were 6 main pieces. Another way in which I saved money was making sets very simple. For instance, there is a scene when Jon Finch is in the hospital. All there was for that set was a bed and a door. The viewer assumes the rest is there. It is surprising what little is needed."—Interview with F in *Bizarre*, no. 4 (1975). See also Tim Lucas, "*The Last Days of Man on Earth*," *Cinefantastique* 4, no. 2 (1975).

Fuller, Leland b. 1899 California. An architect for many years; entered films 1942 as unit a.d. 20th–Fox. **Films dir. by Otto Preminger. Heaven Can Wait* (43), *Laura (44), *Where Do We Go from Here?* (45), *Fallen Angel (46), **Centennial Summer* (46), *The Dark Corner* (46), *The Fan (49), *Whirlpool (50), *Hell and High Water* (54), *Desirée* (54), *Will Success Spoil Rock Hunter?* (57).

Furse, Roger 1903 England–1972 Corfu. Stud. Eton, Slade School of Art; 5 years as portrait painter in NY; stage designs for Old Vic. *Odd Man Out* (47), *Hamlet* (48), *Ivanhoe* (52), *Richard III* (55), *The Prince and the Showgirl* (57), *St. Joan* (57), *Bonjour Tristesse* (58), *The Roman Spring of Mrs. Stone* (61), *The Road to Hong Kong* (62).

Gabourie, Fred Des. most of the great silent *Buster Keaton features. *Our Hospitality (23), **3 Ages* (23), *The Navigator (24), *The Sea Hawk* (24)—des. and executed ships, **Sherlock Jr.* (24), **7 Chances* (25), *Wild Justice* (25), *The General (26), *College (27), *The Cameraman (28), **Steamboat Bill, Jr.* (28).

Gailling, Hans *Jonathan* (71). G's sets for this one film—Geissendörfer's romantic-political vampire fable—place him among the half-handful of first-rate West German designers.

Garbuglia, Mario *Films dir. by Luchino Visconti. Barrage contre le Pacifique/This Angry Age/The Sea Wall* (57), *A Farewell to Arms* (57), *La Grande Guerra* (59), *Rocco and His Brothers* (60), *The Leopard* (63), *Vaghe Stelle dell'Orsa/Sandra* (65), *Lo Straniero/The Stranger* (67), *Barbarella* (67), *Waterloo* (70), *Valdez* (73), *Gruppo di Famiglia in un Interno/Conversation Piece* (75), *Polvere di Stelle* (75), *Der Richter und sein Henker/End of the Game* (75), *The Killer Whale* (76). G is at ease concocting sets either sumptuous or sordid—the ideal designer for Visconti. "The only region of the outside world viewed in *Conversation Piece* is a rooftop vista of the domes of Rome as seen from high up in the Palazzo—a marvelous artificial panoramic decor, and the best studio *trompe-l'oeil* set made in recent years for any film. I hope it has been preserved at Cinecittá."—Elliott Stein, *Film Comment* (Nov.–Dec. 1975).

Gherardi, Piero 1909 Italy–1971. Self-taught artist. Entered films 1946. Des. for Fellini, Pontecorvo, Monicelli, and Lumet. *Eugenia Grandet* (46), *Senza Pietà* (48), *Anni Facili* (53), *The Nights of Cabiria* (56), *I Soliti Ignoti/Big Deal on Madonna Street* (58), *Kapò* (59), *La Dolce Vita* (60), *8 1/2* (63), *La Ragazza di Bube* (63), *Juliet of the Spirits* (65), *L'Armata Brancaleone* (65), *The Appointment* (69), *Infanzia, Vocazione e Prime Esperienze di Giacomo Casanova Veneziano* (69), *¡Queimada!/Burn!* (70). A great designer whose work was both witty and serious.

Gibbons, Cedric 1893 Brooklyn–1960 California. "My first exposure to the art department [of MGM] as a director was the first in a running series of battles. It was a medieval fiefdom, its overlord accustomed to doing things in a certain way . . . his own. Few directors took exception to this. I did."—Vincente Minnelli, *I Remember It Well*, p. 122. G stud. at Art Students League, NY, worked in his father's architectural firm; 1915 entered films as asst. to Ballin at Edison Studios. Worked briefly as full-fledged a.d. for Goldwyn (NY) before joining navy. After discharge followed Goldwyn to California, worked for him until 1923. When MGM was formed in 1924, became superv. a.d. and remained there 32 years. After 1925 most of his films were des. in collab. After heart attack in 1946 delegated much work to his staff; suffered stroke in 1956 and retired. Nominated for 37 AAs and won 11, only one for a film he had des. alone (*Bridge of San Luis Rey*). Credited with having des. the "Oscar" statuette.

Thais (17), *The World and Its Woman* (19), *The Woman and the Puppet* (20), *The Return of Tarzan* (20), *Madame X* (20), *Doubling for Romeo* (21), *The Christian* (23), *The Green Goddess* (23), *He Who Gets Slapped* (24), *His Hour* (24), *Ben Hur* (25), *The Big Parade* (25), *The Student Prince* (27), *The Patsy* (28), *The Big City* (28), *Our Dancing Daughters* (28), *West of Zanzibar* (28), *The Kiss* (29), *Dynamite* (29), *The Hollywood Revue of 1929*, *Hallelujah* (29), *The Bridge of San Luis Rey* (29), *Our Modern Maidens* (29), *The 13th Chair* (29), *The Sea Bat* (30), *Anna Christie* (30), *The Big House* (30), *Our Blushing Brides* (30), *Susan Lenox—Her Fall and Rise* (31), *Grand Hotel* (32)—in collab. Toluboff, *Kongo* (32), *Dinner at 8* (33), *Gabriel over the White House* (33), *The Merry Widow* (34)—in collab. Scognamillo, Frederic Hope, *Men in White* (34), *David Copperfield* (35)—in collab. Merrill Pye, *Mad Love* (35), *Born to Dance* (36), *Romeo and Juliet* (36)—in collab. Oliver Messel, *San Francisco* (36), *Fury* (36)—in collab. Horning, *The Great Ziegfeld* (36), *The Gorgeous Hussy* (36), *Maytime* (37), *Madame X* (37), *Camille* (37), *Conquest* (37), *Captains Courageous* (37)—in collab. A. Gillespie, *Marie Antoinette* (38), *The Girl of the Golden West* (38), *Blossoms in the Dust* (41), *Girl Crazy* (43), *Little Women* (49), *Julius Caesar* (53)—in collab. Edward Carfagno, *The Blackboard Jungle* (55)—in collab. Randall Duell.

In 1924 G inserted a clause in his contract to have his name listed as a.d. on every MGM film made in the US. (In spite of this, he is quoted as disliking the term art director—he considered his staff as the studio's "architectural and engineering" dept.) His name appears as a.d. on 1,500 films—all of which he obviously did not personally design. In 1924 the advertising for *Greed* read, "Art Director—Cedric Gibbons"—but G did no work on the film, which was des. by Day and Stroheim. G got solo dir. credit for *Tarzan and His Mate* (34)—the best Tarzan film ever made—which he did not dir. Prod. had been halted when the footage shot by G proved unsatisfactory; it was reshot from scratch, with cast changes, by Jack Conway, who received no credit. This is put forth for purposes of deobfuscation, not to deny G a place as one of the most important figures in the history of the US film industry. "The credit to Cedric Gibbons on almost all of Metro's major films of the Thirties and Forties indicates that Gibbons, admittedly a great designer, exercised a supervisory control over the designs. Where a credit is shared, it often means that he relinquished this control to another designer, who himself organised the team. There are notable exceptions, but in almost all cases film design was a group activity."—Baxter, *Hollywood in the Thirties*, p. 13. "The distinct Metro style was set up by Cedric Gibbons. . . . Whether it fit the story or not, he was going to have his sets paramount. In *Young Man* we were supposed to have a dinner party at a golf club in Billings, Montana. I picked out a set that was standing and we had the people all ready to go in business suits, but, oh no, that was not MGM. Gibbons did the most elaborate country club you've ever seen, all bright white and everybody dressed to the teeth in white tie and tails. Then one scene took place in a bookie joint. We used some tacky real estate office on Washington Boulevard for the exterior, but when Gibbons did the interior, it looked like something out of *House and Garden*. He had copper lamps with plants growing out of them. In a bookie joint! He was God out there. He wanted it a certain way, that was the MGM style and that's what you got."—Mitchell Leisen in Chierichetti, *Hollywood Director*, pp. 291–92.

Early in his career, G proved himself an innovator when, after a year at Edison, he curtailed painted scenery and insisted on the use of 3-dimensional furnishings. He had a fetish for white sets—the ballroom in *Conquest* which should have been gilded and heavily damasked was unhistorically but beautifully white. His deco sets for *Our Dancing Daughters* and some later films were a strong influence on interior decoration throughout the country. G was largely responsible for the MGM "look"—basically a brightly lit soft gray-white, never harsh—almost the exact opposite of the WB "look." He hated wallpaper and always preferred clean white walls (the frilly sets for *Camille* are a notable exception). The white-walled house he designed for himself in Santa Monica was a Gibbons set, meant to be lived in. He may not have been a great artist (an independent designer of genius like Menzies could permit himself this luxury), but his great ego belonged to a great engineer, a great executive. For an adulatory assessment, see George P. Erengis, "Cedric Gibbons," *Films in Review* (April 1965); see also Morton Eustis, "Designing for the Movies—Gibbons of MGM," *Theatre Arts Monthly* (Oct. 1937).

Gillespie, A. Arnold   b. Texas 1899. Stud. Art Students League, NY. Entered films as draftsman for Paramount, on De Mille's *Manslaughter* (22). Went over to MGM, where he worked for rest of career, at first as unit a.d. under Gibbons. In 1936 named head of MGM's special effects dept.—miniatures, process, and full-sized effects. As a.d. only: *Ben Hur* (25), *The Road to Mandalay* (26), *La Bohème* (26), *The Blackbird* (26), *Upstage* (26), *London after Midnight* (27), *The Divine Woman* (28), *The Crowd* (28), *Eskimo* (33), *Tarzan and His Mate* (34), *Mutiny on the Bounty* (35), *Captains Courageous* (37)—in collab. Gibbons. Worked in both *Ben Hurs* (25, 59), and both *Mutiny on the Bountys* (35, 62), each time as a.d. for the first, and effects dir. for the second version. Over 200 a.d. and 300 SPFX credits at MGM. Most of G's work as a.d. fitted neatly into the MGM factory mould—standardized sets, no personal style required or manifested. (The one notable exception are the larger-than-life-size sets for *The Crowd*, where G was taking his cues from dir. King Vidor, then strongly under the spell of Lang's *Metropolis*.) An accomplished technician, G des. all sorts of movies with dexterous anonymity. His later work as purveyor of earthquakes (*San Francisco*, 36), tornadoes (*The Wizard of Oz*, 39), bombings (*30 Seconds over Tokyo*, 44), robots, ray guns, and flying saucers (*Forbidden Planet*, 56) has been more truly creative. See the G chapter in Steen, *Hollywood Speaks!* His work as FX man is examined in detail in Brosnan, *Movie Magic*.

Giovannini, Giorgio   *La Dolce Vita* (60), *Esther and the King* (60), **La Maschera del Demonio/Black Sunday* (60), **Gli Invasori/Erik the Conqueror* (61), **La Ragazza che Sapeva Troppo/The Evil Eye* (62), **I Tre Volti della Paura/Black Sabbath* (63), **Terore nello Spazio/Planet of the Vampires* (65), *Operation St. Peter's* (68). G worked as asst. to Gherardi on *La Dolce Vita*, but he came into his own as a first-rate solo designer with the fantasy films subsequently made for dir. *Mario Bava. *La Maschera del Demonio* is a classic—spectral nightmare landscapes and superb black-and-white photography: arguably the best horror film made in Europe since WWII.

Glasgow, William   US. 1906–72. A star player on *Robert Aldrich's "team." *The Hat Box Mystery* (47), **World for Ransom* (54), *Bait* (54), **Kiss Me Deadly* (55), **The Big Knife* (55), **Autumn Leaves* (56), **Attack!* (56), *Timbuktu* (58), *The 4 Skulls of Jonathan Drake* (59),

*What Ever Happened to Baby Jane? (62), The Black Zoo (63), *4 for Texas (63), *Hush, Hush, Sweet Charlotte (64), *The Flight of the Phoenix (66), A Guide for the Married Man (67), *The Legend of Lylah Clare (68), *The Killing of Sister George (68), Whatever Happened to Aunt Alice? (69), Tick . . . tick . . . tick (70). ". . . Glasgow did a marvellous job on Four for Texas. He did an even better job on Charlotte which doesn't show because it's in black-and-white. I believe I gave him his first credit as an art director, and we've been associated ever since. I give him a concept. He comes back with the drawings. . . . As I approve or disapprove of his suggestions, his ideas snowball and gradually become better and better."—Aldrich quoted in Higham & Greenberg, Celluloid Muse, p. 37.

Gliese, Rochus   b. Berlin 1891. Stud. architecture. Eventrude, die Geschichte eines Abenteurers (14), Der Golem (14), Rübezahls Hochzeit (16), Der Rattenfänger von Hameln/The Pied Piper of Hamelin (16), Der Yogi (16), Der Golem und die Tänzerin (17), Malaria (19), Der Verlorene Schatten (21)—also dir., *Der Brennender Acker (22)—also costumes, *Die Austreibung (23), *Die Finanzen des Grossherzogs (23), *Sunrise (27). G dir. films, acted in them, prod. plays, worked on special effects, and did costumes. Although the earlier part of his career is linked with the films of actor–dir. Paul Wegener, he will always be assoc. with the films he des. for *Murnau, above all Sunrise and its incredible trompe-l'oeil sets—the greatest German film ever made in Hollywood and, in spite of critical raves, a total financial flop. "In some ways this American film was the apogee of the German Expressionist cinema. The designs of Rochus Gliese . . . evoke an atmosphere no less distinct and haunting than Murnau's Nosferatu had done."—Robinson, Hollywood in the Twenties, p. 63.

Golitzen, Alexander   b. 1907 Moscow. To US 1923, stud. architecture at Univ. Wisconsin. Entered films as illustrator at MGM on Queen Christina (33). First important work as a.d. with Goldwyn/UA. In 1954 succeeded Herzbrun as superv. a.d. at Universal. The Call of the Wild (35), The Hurricane (37), Foreign Correspondent (40)—in collab. Menzies and Richard Irvine, Sundown (41), That Uncertain Feeling (41), The Phantom of the Opera (43), Scarlet Street (45), The Magnificent Doll (46), Letter from an Unknown Woman (48), Bagdad (49), All I Desire (53), This Island Earth (55)—in collab. Riedel, Written on the Wind (56), Tarnished Angels (57), Imitation of Life (59), Spartacus (60), Tammy Tell Me True (61), Flower Drum Song (61), Back Street (61), To Kill a Mockingbird (63), Thoroughly Modern Millie (67), Coogan's Bluff (68), The Forbin Project (70), Slaughterhouse 5 (72), Earthquake (74).

   G is one of the great all-purpose Hollywood designers. Working for a strong dir. who knows what he wants (Hitchcock, Lang, Siegel), the results will be high up to the mark or even great—as with the superb turn-of-the century Vienna he created for Ophüls's masterpiece Letter from an Unknown Woman. When the boss was a producer of the ilk of Ross Hunter (as it has often been since G became superv. a.d. at Universal), things turned out slick and glossy-to-specification: department-store-chic backgrounds for wax dummy actors—but it was always one of the better stores. G is very much at home with sci-fi, horror, and fantasy projects—his planet Metaluna in the classic This Island Earth is quite credibly surreal and marked by tragic grandeur, which is more than can be said of most distant planets. See American Cinematographer (Nov. 1974), p. 1326, on the prod. design for Earthquake, a film for which G and a.d. Preston Ames had to design 96 separate sets twice—before and after the quake.

Goodman, John B.   b. 1901 Denver. Stud. architecture. Joined Paramount 1920 as a.d. In 1943–49 with Universal (superv. a.d. 1943–part of 46), where he often worked in collab. Golitzen. G left Universal in 1946 to work for other studios, mostly Paramount. It's a Gift (34), Wells Fargo (37), If I Were King (38), Frankenstein Meets the Wolf Man (43), Flesh and Fantasy (43), Shadow of a Doubt (43), The Phantom of the Opera (43), The Climax (44), Cobra Woman (44), The Frozen Ghost (45), Good Sam (48), The Great Missouri Raid (50), The Trouble with Harry (55), The Mountain (56).

Goosson, Stephen   1889 Michigan–1973. Stud. architecture Syracuse Univ. In 1915–19 practiced architecture in Detroit. Entered films in early 20s; worked for Mary Pickford Prods., Frank Lloyd, De Mille Pictures, and Fox, before settling down at Columbia in early 30s, where he became superv. a.d. and remained rest of career. Little Lord Fauntleroy (21), Oliver Twist (22), The Hunchback of Notre Dame (23)—in collab. E. E. Sheeley, The Sea Hawk (24), The Patent Leather Kid (27), The Wreck of the Hesperus (27), Skyscraper (28), Wild Company (30), Just Imagine (30), Movietone Follies of 1930, American Madness (32),

One Night of Love (34), *It Happened One Night* (34), *Crime and Punishment* (35), *The Black Room* (35), *The King Steps Out* (36), *Pennies from Heaven* (36), *Lost Horizon* (37), *The Awful Truth* (37), *The Little Foxes* (41), *Tonight and Every Night* (45), *Gilda* (46)—in collab. Polglase, *The Lady From Shanghai* (made 46, rel. 48), *Dead Reckoning* (47).

G will be forgiven the vast ghastliness of the Shangri-La reared for Frank Capra's *Lost Horizon* for his work on another silly but visually ravishing Capra film, *American Madness*. Nearly all of it takes place in an enormous bank, beset by a run during the Depression. The décor is an art deco Temple of Mammon—a superset cathedral–forest of grilles, clocks, and columns: one of the most beautifully des. and lit films of the 30s. *The Black Room* seems the only first-rate horror film ever made by Columbia. G's contribution to its success was a minatory Gothic picture-book castle, and stylized exteriors, with misshapen trees against murky painted skies. What a career! G started with Mary Pickford, des. most major films at Columbia in the 30s, and went on to upholster the depth-focused dramatics of Bette Davis in *The Little Foxes* for Goldwyn, to concoct networks of plexiglass shrubbery for the Dionysiac samba revels of Rita Hayworth in *Tonight and Every Night*, and the crazy hall of mirrors in the deserted amusement park of Orson Welles's *The Lady from Shanghai* where a more somber Rita Hayworth would shoot it out with her husband in this great "fun" movie which Columbia executives so loathed they shelved it for 2 years.

Gorton, Assheton   GB. *The Knack* (65), *Blow-Up* (66), *The Bliss of Mrs. Blossom* (68), *The Magic Christian* (69), *The Bed Sitting Room* (69), *Zachariah* (71), *Get Carter* (71), *The Pied Piper* (72).

Grau, Albin   *Nosferatu* (22), *Schatten/Warning Shadows* (23), *Der Korsar* (25), *Das Haus der Lüge* (26).

Groesse, Paul   b. 1906 Austria-Hungary. Stud. at Yale. Architect in Chicago 1930–31, designer Chicago Century of Progress Exhibition. Worked mostly at MGM, often in collab. Gibbons. A specialist in 19th-century décors. *The Firefly* (37), *The Great Waltz* (38), *Madame Curie* (43), *Lassie Come Home* (43), *The Valley of Decision* (45), *The Yearling* (46), *Little Women* (49), *Annie Get Your Gun* (50), *King Solomon's Mines* (50), *The Merry Widow* (52), *Lili* (53), *The Catered Affair* (56), *Bye Bye Birdie* (63).

Grot, Anton   Né Antocz Franziszek Groszewski, 1884 Poland–1974 California. Stud. illustration Krakow Art School. To US 1909. In 1913 hired by producer Sigmund Lubin to des. sets for the Lubin Co. (1913–17). Worked on Gasnier serials shot in NJ, and des. Fitzmaurice films shot in NY area. To Hollywood 1922. Worked for Fairbanks, then De Mille; 1927 signed by First Nat.–WB and remained with WB until retirement 1948. Invented and patented a "ripple machine" to create weather and light effects on water scenes—first used in *The Sea Hawk*—and received for it a special AA in 1940. After retirement, G devoted himself to painting.

*Films dir. by Michael Curtiz. *The Mouse and the Lion* (13), *Arms and the Woman* (17), *The 7 Pearls* (18), *The Naulahka* (18), *Bound and Gagged* (19), *Velvet Fingers* (20), *Tess of the Storm Country* (22), *The Thief of Bagdad* (24)—in collab. Menzies, *Don Q, Son of Zorro* (25), *The Road to Yesterday* (25), *The Volga Boatman* (26)—in collab. Leisen, *The King of Kings* (27)—in collab. Leisen, *White Gold* (27), *The Barker* (28), *Show Girl* (28), *Smiling Irish Eyes* (29), *Noah's Ark* (29), *Lilies of the Field* (30), *Song of the Flame* (30), *No, No, Nanette* (30), *Surrender* (31), *Body and Soul* (31), *Svengali* (31), *Little Caesar* (31), *The Mad Genius* (31), *Alias the Doctor* (32), *Dr. X* (32), *Scarlet Dawn* (32), *2 Seconds* (32), *Big City Blues* (32), *Hatchet Man* (32), *Footlight Parade* (33), *The Mystery of the Wax Museum* (33), *Mandalay* (34), *British Agent* (34), *The Firebird* (34), *Captain Blood* (35), *Bright Lights* (35), *Dr. Socrates* (35), *Gold Diggers of 1935* (35), *A Midsummer Night's Dream* (35), *White Angel* (36), *Anthony Adverse* (36), *Stolen Holiday* (37), *Confession* (37), *The Life of Emile Zola* (37), *Tovarich* (37), *The Great Garrick* (37), *The Private Lives of Elizabeth and Essex* (39), *Juarez* (39), *A Dispatch from Reuter's* (40), *The Sea Hawk* (40), *The Sea Wolf* (41), *Thank Your Lucky Stars* (43), *Rhapsody in Blue* (45), *Mildred Pierce* (45), *Deception* (46), *The Unsuspected* (47), *Possessed* (47), *The 2 Mrs. Carrolls* (47), *Nora Prentiss* (47), *June Bride* (48), *Romance on the High Seas* (48), *One Sunday Afternoon* (48), *Backfire* (50).

An extensive collection of G's drawings and designs (for films of 1925–42) is in the UCLA Special Collections. A BBC-TV film surveys G's career; homage to this outstanding designer is long overdue in the US. "Despite his disastrous work on *A Midsummer Night's Dream*, the cycle [of historical biographies, dir. by Dieterle] also furthered the reputation of the marvelously talented Polish art director Anton Grot, whose deliberately exaggerated Germanic sets fitted the mood of Dieterle's sombre direction. Grot had first come to prominence with his work on Archie Mayo's *Svengali* in 1931, a masterpiece of bizarre foreshortened set design, influenced by German models. Later, his sets for *The Mystery of the Wax Museum* developed, in the two-color system, his theories of expressionist set construction. More creatively involved in his films than the equivalent set directors Hans Dreier at Paramount and Cedric Gibbons at Metro–Goldwyn–Mayer, he could range all the way from the dream-like surrealistic sets of *Gold Diggers of 1933* to the intricate San Franciscan Chinatown of William Wellman's film of the tong wars, *Hatchet Man*; at all times he worked with a free imagination, deliberately departing from 'realism.' A master of illusion, he created a world: he even painted in shadows, or superimposed special imitation ceilings to cause patterns of shadows to fall on the walls."—Higham, *Warner Brothers*, pp. 118–119. See also Balshofer & Miller, *One Reel a Week*, for G in his Fitzmaurice period and his special methods of designing; Higham & Greenberg, *Hollywood in the Forties*, p. 113; Donald Deschner, "Anton Grot, Warners Art Director," *The Velvet Light Trap*, no. 15 (Fall 1975).

Guffroy, Pierre *Le Testament d'Orphée* (60), *Mouchette* (67), *Le Charme discret de la bourgeoisie* (72), *Le Fantôme de la liberté* (74).

Gys, Robert b. 1901 France. First film work 1922 in collab. Mallet-Stevens. *Un Fil à la patte* (22), *Le Fantôme du Moulin Rouge* (25), *Le Voyage imaginaire* (25), *Prix de beauté* (30), *L'Agonie des aigles* (33), *Madame Bovary* (34), *Pasteur* (35), *Bonne Chance* (35), *Le Mot de Cambronne* (36), *Carmen* (42), *Fanfan la Tulipe* (52), *Lucrèce Borgia* (52), *Quand tu liras cette Lettre* (53), *Si tous les gars du monde* (55). One of the first "modernist" a.d.s in French cinema, and one of a handful who helped advance the art of film design there. Two early films for Clair, several in the 30s for Guitry; from 1948 on, he has des. most of Christian-Jaque's films.

Haas, Robert 1887 Newark, NJ–1962 California. Stud. architecture Univ. Pennsylvania. Practicing architect 1912–20. Art manager Famous Players–Lasky 1920–22, NY. Inspiration Pictures, Italy and NY, 1922–24. Moved to the coast in 1927 and worked for the old Fox studio for 2 years. Joined WB in 1929 and remained with them until retirement 1950.
  *Films dir. by Henry King. *Sentimental Tommy* (21), **Fury* (22), **White Sister* (23), **Romola* (24), **Sackcloth and Scarlet* (25), **She Goes to War* (29), **Hell Harbor* (30), **Merely Mary Ann* (31), *3 on a Match* (32), *Bureau of Missing Persons* (33), *Lady Killer* (33), *The Key* (34), *A Modern Hero* (34), *Page Miss Glory* (35), *The Story of Louis Pasteur* (36), *Black Legion* (37), *They Won't Forget* (37), *The Prince and the Pauper* (37), *Jezebel* (38), *Angels with Dirty Faces* (38), *Dark Victory* (39), *The Old Maid* (39), *City for Conquest* (40), *The Maltese Falcon* (41), *Strawberry Blonde* (41), *In This Our Life* (42), *Now, Voyager* (42), *Edge of Darkness* (43), *Uncertain Glory* (44), *Devotion* (46), *A Stolen Life* (46), *Life with Father* (47), *Johnny Belinda* (48), *Beyond the Forest* (49), *The Glass Menagerie* (50), *The Damned Don't Cry* (50). This accomplished craftsman whose sets were usually marked by restrained good taste and dramatic aptness contributed much to the entertainment of millions through his work on WB films of the 30s and 40s—many "weepies" starring Bette Davis, fine work for dirs. Huston, Walsh, and Curtiz. For H in his Lasky period, see Balshofer & Miller, *One Reel a Week*, p. 147. For H at work with King in Italy on *White Sister* and *Romola*, see the chapter on King in Brownlow, *The Parade's Gone By*, which includes stills of the superb *Romola* sets.

Hagegard, Anne Terselius Swedish. Stud. set design Accademia de Belle Arti, Rome, then worked in the art dept. of the Swedish State television. First major assignment: asst. to prod. designer Henny Noremark on Bergman's *The Magic Flute*. All films dir. by Bergman: *The Magic Flute* (75), *Il Ballo* (75), *Face to Face* (76)—in collab. Anna Asp and Maggie Strindberg.

Hall, Charles D. b. 1899 England. Stage designer Fred Karno shows. Principal a.d. at Universal late 20s and most of 30s (*films dir. by James Whale) and for the 4 features made by Chaplin 1924–36. Some late work for Roach, UA. *The Lying Truth* (22), *The Gold Rush* (25), *The Cohens and the Kellys* (26), *The Cat and the Canary* (27), *The Man Who Laughs* (28)—in collab. Joseph Wright, *The Circus* (28), *Broadway* (29), *The Last Warning* (29), *All Quiet on the Western Front* (30), *City Lights* (31), **Frankenstein* (31)—in collab. Rosse, *Dracula* (31), **The Old Dark House* (32), **By Candlelight* (33), **The Invisible Man* (33), *Little Man, What*

Now? (34), *The Black Cat* (34), *Remember Last Night?* (35), *The Magnificent Obsession* (35), *Diamond Jim* (35), *The Good Fairy* (35), *The Bride of Frankenstein* (35), *Show Boat* (36), *Modern Times* (36), *The Road Back* (37), *Captain Fury* (39), *One Million B.C.* (40), *Not Wanted* (49), *The Vicious Years* (50), *Red Planet Mars* (52).

H is a household word for horror buffs, chief architect of all the greater Transylvanias reared on Universal's back lot: Dracula's incredible staircase; Chaplin's teetering *Gold Rush* cabin; the extraordinary machinery of *Modern Times* in a factory which was the largest set ever built for a Chaplin film; the vast nightclub in *Broadway*, so huge that the "*Broadway* crane"—largest ever—had to be built to encompass it all; the trenches of *All Quiet*; the *Old Dark House* itself (Universal later rented this set to other companies for cheap thrillers unworthy to be housed in it); the Bauhaus-like black mass room where Karloff presided in *The Black Cat*; the superb stylized cemetery in *Bride*. Late in his career, H des. (for designer-turned-director Harry Horner) the definitive paranoid McCarthyist sci-fi howler, *Red Planet Mars*.

Hall, Walter L. *Intolerance* (16). It has often been said and printed that Griffith's gigantic film was produced without an a.d., or with Lillian Gish's "modest genius of a carpenter," Huck Wortman, acting in lieu of a designer. The publication of *Adventures with D. W. Griffith* by Karl Brown (NY, 1973) seems to have settled the matter once and for all. An entire chapter, "The Towers of Babylon" is devoted to the construction of the sets for *Intolerance*. Brown states (pp. 150–56): "Griffith required a worthy organizer who could bring to full fruition all the grandiose dreams that were bursting for realization in his imagination. Huck Wortman was the best in his line, but there are limits to what even the best of stage carpenters can do. Somebody had to design the show, and this somebody had to be the very best of all. Griffith found him and his name was Hall. I later heard that his full name was Walter L. Hall, but nobody around the lot knew it at the time. He was *Mr.* Hall, if you please, . . . The designing of theatrical spectacles was Hall's life work . . . [he] . . . combined the great gift of an imaginative creative artist with the needlepoint accuracy of a fine architect. . . . [His preliminary drawings were all done with pencil on specially surfaced heavy cardboard, like title cards]. . . .

"He could look at a pictured fragment of a recently unearthed archaeological find and from it reconstruct the entire subject, whatever it might have been. A partial remnant of a stairway at Persepolis became the entire great stairway to the great palace of Belshazzar. . . . What was his secret? Perspective, always perspective. . . .

"'How'd you learn all this?' I asked one day.

"'*Learn?* Learn *this?* . . . Nobody can learn this. It's something you *have* to *do*. . . .' A great deal of this work was the making of stencils for the guidance of our painters, who had somehow to put Hall's pictures on the great walls. There were also friezes that had to run here, there, and everywhere along the walls, high and low—some of them 80 or 90 feet above the ground. . . ."

Haller, Daniel b. 1929 Los Angeles. Des. TV commercials, entered films 1955. Until recently worked as a.d. mostly on garish schlocky horror films dir. by *Roger Corman, released by AIP. In 1967 started dir. his own schlock. *War of the Satellites* (58), *Machine Gun Kelly* (58), *A Bucket of Blood* (59), *The House of Usher* (60), *The Little Shop of Horrors* (60), *The Premature Burial* (62), *The Raven* (63), *The Terror* (63), *X—The Man with the X-Ray Eyes* (63), *The Comedy of Terrors* (64). "Daniel Haller's sets [for *Usher*] are a brilliant attempt to appear spacious, on only the most limited means."—David Pirie, in *Roger Corman* (Edinburgh Film Festival, 1970), p. 51. Corman wrapped up *The Raven* ahead of schedule; H's sets were still standing. *The Terror* was conceived and shot—script all but improvised—to make use of the *Raven* sets, in a few days.

Haller, Michael US. *THX 1138* (71), *Harold and Maude* (71), *The Last Detail* (73), *Rancho DeLuxe* (75).

Hamada, Tatsuo *Scandal* (50), *The Moderns* (52), *Tokyo Monogatari/Tokyo Story* (53), *Soshun/Early Spring* (56), *Ohayo/Good Morning* (59), *Late Autumn* (60), *Samma no Aji/An Autumn Afternoon* (62). H was *Ozu's preferred a.d. For Ozu's later work his sets tended to more and more simple volumes in keeping with this dir.'s ascetic style.

Hartley, Esdras US. WB unit a.d. in 30s where he des. few great but many entertaining movies: *The Show of Shows* (29), *The Millionaire* (31), *Taxi* (32), *Wild Boys of the Road* (33), *The House on 56th Street* (33), *Convention City* (33), *Jimmy the Gent* (34), *Special Agent* (35), *The Return of Dr. X* (39).

Hasler, Emil b. 1901 Berlin. Stud. at Königliche Kunstschule; worked as painter of theater sets. Entered films 1919, some work for Lubitsch (*Der Bergkatze*) and for pioneer prod. Oskar Messter. In 1933–40 H des. 10 films dir. by †Geza von Bolvary. Did sets for West Berlin TV 1962–66; retired 1966. An inventive technician, usually employed by the best German dirs.—*Lang, Pabst, and after the war, Käutner. *Monica Vogelsang* (19), *Die Bergkatze* (21), *Tagebuch einer Verlorenen/Diary of a Lost Girl* (29), *Die Frau im Mond/Woman in the Moon* (29), *Der Blaue Engel/The Blue Angel* (30), *M* (31), *Das Testament des Dr. Mabuse/The Last Will of Dr. Mabuse* (made 32, banned by Nazis, rel. US 43)—in collab. Vollbrecht, †*Abschiedswalzer* (34), †*Stradivari* (35), *Pygmalion* (35), †*Schloss in Flandern* (36), †*Lumpazivagabundus* (37), *The Blum Affair* (48), *Epilog* (50), *Die Hexe* (54), *Ein Mädchen aus Flandern* (56), *Das Totenschiff* (59), *Die Grosse Reise* (61), *Die Schneekönigin* (64). See Eisner, *Haunted Screen* (pp. 253, 248) for a fine sketch for *M* and fascinating photos of the sets under construction for *Frau im Mond*. See also Kaul, *Schöpferische Filmarchitektur.*

Haworth, Ted US. *Strangers on a Train* (51), *Invasion of the Body Snatchers* (56), *The Friendly Persuasion* (56), *Sayonara* (57), *The Goddess* (58), *I Want to Live* (58), *Some Like It Hot* (59), *Pepe* (60), *The Longest Day* (62), *What a Way to Go!* (64), *Seconds* (66), *The Professionals* (66), *The Beguiled* (71), *The Getaway* (72), *Jeremiah Johnson* (72), *Pat Garrett and Billy the Kid* (73), *Harry and Tonto* (74), *Claudine* (74), *The Killer Elite* (76).

Heckroth, Hein 1898 Germany–1970 Holland. Sets for Jooss Ballet, then left Germany 1933. In WWII interned in England as enemy alien and sent to concentration camp in Australia. Afterward, taken on by Junge to work on his staff in England on films dir. by *Michael Powell. Also des. for †Powell & Pressburger. †*The Red Shoes* (48), †*The Elusive Pimpernel* (50), †*Gone to Earth/The Wild Heart* (51), †*The Tales of Hoffman* (51), †*Oh, Rosalinda!!* (55), *The Sorcerer's Apprentice* (55), *Bluebeard's Castle* (64), *Torn Curtain* (66). Of all the major designers who worked for Powell & Pressburger, it is H whose sets have most dated. See Gough-Yates, *Michael Powell* (1973); Heckroth and Powell, "Making Colour Talk," in Gough-Yates, *Michael Powell* (1971).

Hedrick, Earl b. 1896 Los Angeles. A.d. at Paramount from 1933, where he often worked in collab. Dreier, and after Dreier's retirement, with Hal Pereira. *The Great McGinty* (40), *Christmas in July* (40), *Dr. Cyclops* (40), *Sullivan's Travels* (41), *Wake Island* (42), *So Proudly We Hail* (43), *The Lost Weekend* (45), *M. Beaucaire* (46), *Sorry, Wrong Number* (48), *The File on Thelma Jordon* (49), *Union Station* (50), *Detective Story* (51), *Ace in the Hole/The Big Carnival* (51), *Jivaro* (54).

Hennesy, Dale b. 1926 Washington, D.C. Father was layout artist for Disney, and one of key designers for *Snow White, Pinocchio*. Stud. painting and motion picture illustration at School of Allied Arts, Glendale. Entered films 1952 as illustrator at 20th–Fox. Illustrator on *The King and I, South Pacific*, and other major prods. First film as full-fledged a.d. in 1963. *Under the Yum Yum Tree* (63), *Good Neighbor Sam* (64), *John Goldfarb, Please Come Home* (65), *Fantastic Voyage* (66), *In Like Flint* (67), *Adam at 6 AM* (70), *The Christian Licorice Store* (71), *Dirty Harry* (71), *Everything You Always Wanted to Know about Sex* (72), *A Time to Run* (72), *Slither* (73), *Battle for the Planet of the Apes* (73), *Sleeper* (73), *Young Frankenstein* (74), *Logan's Run* (76).

   "It seems that I have developed a reputation for science-fiction because of *Fantastic Voyage* and *Sleeper* and while I am very proud of the look of those films, I am equally pleased with *Dirty Harry, Adam at Six AM*, and *Slither* for their very real look. I also enjoyed the fun and craziness of *Young Frankenstein*. The designer in film should be qualified to design the total visual look no matter what the subject and sometime I would love to do a western. It is a most rewarding position in our industry."—letter, H to Elliott Stein, May 28, 1975. Filmographies make strange bedfellows: the film H des. immediately after *Everything You Always Wanted to Know about Sex* was *A Time to Run*—prod. by Billy Graham.

Herlth, Robert 1893 Germany–1962 Germany. Met Warm in WWI and des. sets with him for their army theater. Often collab. with Röhrig. One of the greatest German designers, H was an important influence on expressionism and the *Kammerspiel*. His brother Kurt, also a set designer, made a few films in collab. with him. *Films dir. by Murnau and des. by H and Röhrig. *Die Toteninsel* (20), *Der Müde Tod/Destiny* (21), *Der Schatz/The Treasure* (23), *Der Letzte Mann/The Last Laugh* (24), *Zur Chronik von Grieshuus* (25), *Tartuffe* (25),

*Faust (26), *4 Devils (28), Hokuspokus (30), Der Kongress Tanzt/Congress Dances (31), Morgenrot/Dawn (33), Prinzessin Turandot (34), Olympiad (38)—technical designs, Film ohne Titel (48), Das Doppelte Lottchen (50), Der Letzte Mann (55), Magic Fire (56), Buddenbrooks (59), Gustav Adolfs Page (60). See the invaluable chapter by H about his work with Murnau in Eisner, Murnau. See also Kaul, Schöpferische Filmarchitektur.

Herman, Alfred Unit a.d. RKO in 30s and 40s. Captain Blood (24), King Kong (33)—in collab. Carroll Clark, Son of Kong (33), Anne of Green Gables (34), Room Service (38), Love Affair (39), Once Upon a Honeymoon (42), From This Day Forward (46), Crossfire (47), The Locket (47), Berlin Express (48), They Live by Night (48), Easy Living (49), The Company She Keeps (50), The Lusty Men (52). It should be noted that the unique visual style of King Kong is at least as much to the credit of "art technicians" Mario Larrinaga and Byron Crabbe who des. the glass and background paintings as to that of the a.ds. who des. the non-trick sets.

Herzbrun, Bernard b. 1891 NY. Member American Institute of Architects. Joined Paramount 1926. Late 30s at Fox; from 1947 superv. a.d. at Universal until 1954. Skippy (31), The Devil and the Deep (32), Belle of the 90s (34), Poppy (36), The Texas Rangers (36), Make Way for Tomorrow (37), Kidnapped (38), Alexander's Ragtime Band (38), Temptation (46), The Egg and I (47), Winchester '73 (50), Abbott and Costello Meet Dr. Jekyll and Mr. Hyde (53), The Far Country (55).

Hitchcock, Alfred b. London 1899. Entered films 1920 as title writer and artist for the Islington studio of Famous Players–Lasky. When Lasky stopped prod. in England, kept on by the studio and hired by Michael Balcon's new unit. Films prod. by Balcon, dir. by Graham Cutts, with a.d. by H: Woman to Woman (23), The White Shadow (23), The Passionate Adventure (24), The Blackguard (25), The Prude's Fall (25). "Whilst filming the final Squibs picture in the Islington studio, we often went during the lunch break to the little office of the studio Art Director, a very friendly young man, to gamble with pennies on a little toy race-game he had contrived. In the studio, at work, he always seemed oblivious to his surroundings, deep in thought, pondering. How little we foresaw then that he was destined to achieve fame as a film director of world status . . . that his name would rank with the few great ones of the Motion Picture medium—Alfred Hitchcock."—Pearson, Flashback, p. 120.

Holsopple, Theobald Bomba, the Jungle Boy (49), *The Steel Helmet (51), *Park Row (52), Daughter of Dr. Jekyll (57), Kronos (57), The Fly (58), The Bamboo Saucer (67). Though somewhat specialized in fantasy films, H's best work is to be seen elsewhere—in the 2 pictures for *Sam Fuller, especially Park Row, a lovely period newspaper story—and a complete flop. Its cramped but convincing sets provide an excellent example of what talent can squeeze from a low budget.

Horner, Harry b. 1910 in what is now Czechoslovakia. Stud. architecture in Vienna; apprentice designer with Otto Preminger there. Worked as actor with Max Reinhardt and came to the US with him in 1935. Much designing for NY stage in late 30s, and opera sets at the Met. Brought to Hollywood by Sol Lesser to assist Menzies on designs for Our Town. Has done as many as 1,000 preliminary sketches for a single film. Started dir. in the 50s—notably the greatest crackpot film of that decade, Red Planet Mars (52). Our Town (40), Stage Door Canteen (43), Winged Victory (44), A Double Life (48), The Heiress (49), Born Yesterday (50), Outrage (50), He Ran All the Way (51), Separate Tables (58), The Wonderful Country (59), The Hustler (61), The Black Bird (75). See Herbert G. Luft, "Production Designer Horner," Films in Review (June–July 1959), pp. 328–35.

Horning, William A. Right-hand man of Gibbons at MGM. Ah, Wilderness! (35), Mad Love (35)—in collab. Gibbons, Fury (36), Conquest (37), Marie Antoinette (38)—in collab. Gibbons, The Wizard of Oz (39), Quo Vadis (51), The Wings of Eagles (57), Les Girls (57), Gigi (58), Party Girl (58), Ben Hur (59), The World, the Flesh, and the Devil (59)."Cedric Gibbons was my art director, aided by William Horning. It was their province to conceive and build the two main areas where we would film, Munchkinland and Oz itself. For the former, Gibbons and his team built a model that was one-fourth life size. They fabricated an entire model town, 122 buildings. It took months to finish that alone, and some of the statistics boggle the mind. For example, there were 150 painters and they ultimately used 62 shades of colors on the models. When the full set was built, it covered 25 acres of the studio back lot, or would have if all the sets were up at once. We had 65 different sets in the picture, and each one of them was concocted out of whole cloth and hard work."—Mervyn Leroy, Take One (NY, 1974), pp. 137–38.

215

Hotaling, Frank   US. Dozens of pictures at Republic, many pictures for *John Ford and others. At other studios after 1957. *Home in Oklahoma* (46), *The Gay Ranchero* (48), *I Shot Jesse James* (49), **Rio Grande* (50), **The Quiet Man* (52), **The Sun Shines Bright* (54), **The Searchers* (56)—in collab. Basevi, *3:10 to Yuma* (57), *The Big Country* (58), **The Horse Soldiers* (59).

Hunte, Otto   1883 Germany–1947. **Die Spinnen*, part 1/*Der Goldene See*/*The Golden Lake* (19)—in collab. Warm, **Die Spinnen*, part 2/*Das Brillantenschiff*/*The Slave Ship* (20)—in collab. Warm, *Das Indische Grabmal* (21), **Dr. Mabuse der Spieler*/*Dr. Mabuse, the Gambler* (22), **Die Niebelungen* (24), **Metropolis* (26), *Die Liebe der Jeanne Ney* (27), **Spione* (28), **Die Frau im Mond*/*Woman in the Moon* (29), *Der Blaue Engel*/*The Blue Angel* (30), *Gold* (34), *Der Mann der Sherlock Holmes War* (37), *Jud Süss* (40), *Die Mörder Sind unter Uns* (46), *Razzia* (47).

H's skill was assoc. with nearly all of the major *Fritz Lang films of the 20s—the trapdoors and underground chambers of *Spinnen*, the caves, vast studio forests, and massive architecture of *Niebelungen*, the lunar caverns in *Frau*. During the Hitler period, his last fling at invigorating design was the extraordinary underwater laboratory for Karl Hartl's anti-British sci-fi superproduction, *Gold*. The lab came complete with an atomic reactor—quite a few years *avant la lettre*. Because of it, all available prints of the film were seized after the war by alarmed Allied authorities. The reactor was, however, simply a product of H's fertile imagination. His next big "job" was on the most notorious film of the Third Reich. *Jud Süss* is the only known film in the history of the cinema from which members of the audience emerged to trample elderly Jews to death (see Hull, *Film in the Third Reich*, pp. 160–72). It was shown to SS units before they were sent to round up Jews; on Himmler's order, it was required viewing for police, SS, and concentration camp guards. More than any other film, it prepared the ground for Dachau and Buchenwald: H is as close as cinema art directorship has come to furnishing an accomplice to genocide. A grotesque final touch—the last film of quality he worked on was Staudte's anti-Nazi *Die Mörder Sind unter Uns*/*The Murderers Are Amongst Us*.

Ihnen, Wiard   b. 1897 NJ. Stud. architecture at Columbia, Paris Ecole des Beaux Arts, and under father, Henry S. Ihnen, NY architect; painting, Art Students League, NY. Worked for Berg and Co. and des. manor houses NJ and Pelham Manor, NY. Entered films 1919; first worked for Adolph Zuckor at Famous Players–Lasky studio in Manhattan, then at that company's Astoria studio when it opened in late 1920. Work for George Fitzmaurice on pictures starring Houdini, Irene Castle, and for Mae Murray's independent company. Early 20s artistic dir. of pageant lighting for Westinghouse. Co-founder of Tilford Co., an independent prod. outfit which made films with Irene Castle, dir. by Alan Crosland. 1928 received offer from his old associate, Polglase, to work as a.d. at Paramount; with Paramount 1928–34. Late 30s–mid 40s several RKO films, but mainly at 20th–Fox until 1944. In WWII coordinator of camouflage division of US Office of Civilian Defense. 1945–53 worked on several films prod. by *William Cagney starring James Cagney. Married to Edith Head, the industry's top costume designer, whom he met while both were working on *Cradle Song*; both have assembled an impressive array of AAs. Ihnen has des. and built sets for Goulding, Preminger, Dupont, Lang, Leisen, Hathaway, McCarey, Ford, Mamoulian, Lubitsch, Walsh, King, Dorothy Arzner, Cromwell, Von Sternberg—and a dozen other dirs. of note. His is a staggering list of major r credits on important films, beautifully designed—especially for someone who confesses: "For me, making pictures was a means of making money. Exciting, yes, but my plan was to save enough so I could devote all of my time to painting."—letter, I to Elliott Stein, Feb. 4, 1976.

Idols of Clay (20), *On with the Dance* (20), *Dr. Jekyll and Mr. Hyde* (20), *School Days* (21), *Peacock Alley* (22), *Slim Shoulders* (22), *The Fighting Blade* (23), *The Bright Shawl* (23)—in collab. Everett Shinn, *Potash and Perlmutter* (23), *Monte Carlo* (30), *City Streets* (31), *If I Had a Million* (32), *Blonde Venus* (32), *Shanghai Express* (32)—train interiors only, *Cradle Song* (33), *Duck Soup* (33), *Becky Sharp* (35), *Dancing Pirate* (36), *Go West, Young Man* (36), *On Such a Night* (37), *Every Day's a Holiday* (38), *Doctor Rhythm* (38), *Stagecoach* (39), *Return of the Cisco Kid* (39), *Hollywood Cavalcade* (39), *Maryland* (40), *The Return of Frank James* (40), *Johnny Apollo* (40), *The Blue Bird* (40), *Tall, Dark, and Handsome* (41), *Remember the Day* (41), *Hudson's Bay* (41), *Confirm or Deny* (41), *Man Hunt* (41), *Moon over Miami* (41), *Western Union* (41), *Iceland* (42), *Secret Agent of Japan* (42), *Roxie Hart* (42), *China Girl* (42), *The Magnificent Dope* (42), *Crash Dive* (43), *Wilson* (44), *Jane Eyre* (44), *Along Came Jones* (45), *It's a Pleasure* (45), **Blood on the Sun* (45), *Tomorrow Is*

216

Forever (46), *The Time of Your Life* (48), *Kiss Tomorrow Goodbye* (50), *Only the Valiant* (51), *Rancho Notorious* (52), *A Lion Is in the Streets* (53), *War Paint* (53), *I, The Jury* (53), *This Is My Love* (54), *The Indian Fighter* (55), *The King and 4 Queens* (56), *The Gallant Hours* (60).

"The Paris cabaret in *Blonde Venus*, a bizarre collaboration between Sternberg and designer Wiard Ihnen . . . the baroque extravagance of her [Marlene Dietrich's] number . . . a figure in glittering white tailcoat reviewing with Lesbian arrogance a group of veiled beauties, strolling as she sings among leaning gothic arches, crouching monsters and nude female torsos."—John Baxter, *The Cinema of Josef von Sternberg* (NY, 1971), pp. 105–06. See Balshofer & Miller, *One Reel a Week*, pp. 147–52, for I's early work on Mae Murray films.

Iribe, Paul   d. 1935. Collab. with Dufy and Cocteau on the review *Le Mot*. Book illustrator. *The Affairs of Anatol* (21), *Manslaughter* (22)—also costumes, *The 10 Commandments* (23), *The Golden Bed* (25), *The Road to Yesterday* (25), *The King of Kings* (27)—6 elaborate Cecil B. De Mille prods. "Above all, though, he [De Mille] had the help [for *Anatol*] of Paul Iribe, a brilliant French designer with a leaning toward Art Nouveau, who arranged the entire picture like a series of Beardsley illustrations to Oscar Wilde. Lasky sent the suave and elegant Iribe to De Mille following Wilfred Buckland's inevitable resignation, with instructions De Mille use him; correcting De Mille's vulgar streak, Iribe created an ambience so dazzling, so intoxicating, that many art critics discussed the picture in serious journals. And when De Mille saw it, after the long discussions and wranglings during the production, he embraced Paul Iribe in gratitude."—Higham, *Cecil B. De Mille*, p. 86.

Itoh, Kisaku   *Jigokumon/Gate of Hell* (53)—in collab. Kosabura Nakajima, *Ugetsu Monogatari/Ugetsu* (53), *Sansho Dayu/Sansho the Bailiff* (54), *Narayama Bushi-Ko/The Ballad of the Narayama* (58). Designer of 2 of *Mizoguchi's finest films.

Jenkins, George   b. Baltimore. Des. many Broadway shows. Brought to Hollywood by Sam Goldwyn in 1945 to work on *Best Years*. Much TV work. *Films in collab. with Ferguson for Goldwyn/RKO. †Films dir. by Arthur Penn. *The Best Years of Our Lives* (46), *The Secret Life of Walter Mitty* (47), *The Bishop's Wife* (47), *A Song Is Born* (48), *At War with the Army* (50), †*The Miracle Worker* (62), †*Mickey One* (65), *Up the Down Staircase* (67), *Wait Until Dark* (67), *No Way to Treat a Lady* (68), *The Angel Levine* (70), *Klute* (71), *The Paper Chase* (73), *The Parallax View* (74), *Funny Lady* (75), †*Night Moves* (75), *All the President's Men* (76).

Jewell, Edward C.   *His Dog* (27), *The King of Kings* (27), *Red Hot Rhythm* (29), *Brothers* (30), *Tol'able David* (30), *The Criminal Code* (31), *Once Upon a Time* (44), *Detour* (45), *Counter-Attack* (45), *Club Havana* (45), *White Pongo* (45), *The Strangler of the Swamp* (45), *The Mask of Dijon* (46), *Her Sister's Secret* (46), *Alimony* (49), *One Man's Way* (64).

As one of the team of artists who worked on *King of Kings*, J participated in one of the more expensive acts of cinematic prestige piety of the 20s. Twenty years later, after some time with Columbia, he was churning out sets for lurid cheapies by the dozen—at PRC which was almost to Monogram what Monogram was to UFA. From UFA came Frank Wisbar, whose *Fährmann Maria* (36) had been one of the few first-rate German films of the 30s, a more than honorable descendant of Lang's *Destiny*. *Strangler of the Swamp* was a remake of *Maria* at PRC, directed by Wisbar on a budget so low that for some scenes J had to make do with painted flats and a handful of tacky vines. The result was a little miracle—the most intriguing movie made on Gower Gulch in the 40s. "Like most of the old German fantasies, the film is totally stylized, and virtually all studio made. For the basic set of the deserted ferry . . . the twisted trees, the lack of either sunlight or moonlight, the constant ground mist, all contrive to hide the boundaries of what must have been a very small set indeed, and to give it real style."—Everson, *Classics of the Horror Film*, p. 176. Hats off to E. C. Jewell—the Dreier of Poverty Row!

Job, Enrico   b. 1934 Italy. Stud. architecture Milan. Des. sets and costumes for Piccolo Teatro di Milano. *Nel Nome del Padre* (71), *Film d'Amore e d'Anarchia/Love and Anarchy* (73), *Tutto a Posto e Niente in Ordine/All Screwed Up* (74), *Blood for Dracula* (74), *Travolti da un Insolito Destino nell'Azzurro Mare d'Agosto/Swept Away . . .* (74), *Andy Warhol's Frankenstein* (74), *Pasqualino Settebellezze/7 Beauties* (76). She Married Her Art Director—not another movie: *films were dir. by Signora Lina Wertmuller Job. See Robb Baker, "Enrico Job: Images and Iconoclasms," *Soho Weekly News* (Jan. 29, 1976).

217

Junge, Alfred   1886 Germany–1964. Five years of work in German cinema (1923–28). Late 20s des. several British prods. dir. by E. A. Dupont; 1932 settled in Britain permanently. In 30s worked on 3 films for Hitchcock, often on Victor Saville prods., many delightful musicals starring Jessie Matthews, and a few films dir. by †Michael Powell. Late 30s–40s work on several films prod. and dir. by ‡Powell and Emeric Pressburger, among them his masterpiece, *Black Narcissus*. Nearly all the pictures J worked on 1949–57 were MGM films made in England; headed MGM's art dept. in England for most of 50s. *Dir. by Dupont.

   Das Alte Gesetz (23), *Die Grüne Manuela* (23), *Mensch gegen Mensch* (24), *Waxworks* (24)—in collab. Leni and Ernst Stern, *Athleten* (25), *Spitzen* (26), *Brennende Grenze/The Jackals* (26), *Mata Hari* (27), *Moulin Rouge* (28), *Picadilly* (28), *Atlantic* (29), *After the Ball* (32), *Midshipmaid* (32), *The Good Companions* (33), *The Ghoul* (33), *Waltzes from Vienna* (33), †*The Fire Raisers* (33), *I Was a Spy* (33), *Just Smith* (33), *Britannia of Billingsgate* (33), *Channel Crossing* (33), *The Constant Nymph* (33), *Sleeping Car* (33), *Waltz Time* (33), †*The Night of the Party/The Murder Party* (34), *Evergreen* (34), *Evensong* (34), *Jew Suss* (34), *The Clairvoyant* (34), *The Man Who Knew Too Much* (34), †*Red Ensign* (34), *Lady in Danger* (34), *Road House* (34), *Dirty Work* (34), *Jack Ahoy* (34), *Chu Chin Chow* (34), *Little Friend* (34), *The Iron Duke* (35), *The Guv'nor* (35), *Bulldog Jack* (35), *Me and Marlborough* (35), *Car of Dreams* (35), *Everything Is Thunder* (36), *It's Love Again* (36), *Head over Heels* (36), *Young and Innocent/The Girl was Young* (37), *King Solomon's Mines* (37), *Gangway* (37), *The Great Barrier* (37), *The Citadel* (38)—in collab. Meerson, *Sailing Along* (38), *Goodbye, Mr. Chips* (39), *Contraband/Blackout* (40), *Busman's Holiday/Haunted Honeymoon* (40), *He Found a Star* (41), ‡*The Life and Death of Colonel Blimp/Colonel Blimp* (43), ‡*The Volunteer* (43), ‡*A Canterbury Tale* (44), ‡*I Know Where I'm Going* (45), ‡*A Matter of Life and Death/Stairway to Heaven* (46), ‡*Black Narcissus* (47), *Edward My Son* (49), *Conspirator* (49), *The Miniver Story* (50), *Calling Bulldog Drummond* (51), *Ivanhoe* (52), *The Hour of 13* (52), *Mogambo* (53), *Time Bomb/Terror on a Train* (53), *Never Let Me Go* (53), *Knights of the Round Table* (54), *Beau Brummel* (54), *Crest of the Wave* (54), *The Flame and the Flesh* (54), *Quentin Durward* (55), *That Lady* (55), *The Barretts of Wimpole Street* (57), *Invitation to the Dance* (made 52, rel. 56—parts 1 and 2 only (part 3 des. by Randall Duell), *A Farewell to Arms* (57).

   In Gough-Yates's invaluable *Michael Powell*, the dir. often refers to J: "[I had] respect for the Germans as film-makers—the best technicians personally that I had ever seen. . . . First of all the early great days of UFA and then the people who came over to British International Pictures in those early days like Dupont . . . and Alfred Junge, his art director with this fabulous control of the whole organization . . . of making films . . . Hollywood couldn't hold a candle to them. . . . Junge . . . had a lot to do with the first British film that I made for Mickey Balcon, *The Night of the Party*. He was head art director at Balcon's Lime Grove . . . he ran it like a machine. . . . *A Matter of Life and Death* . . . was a very happy film from start to finish and there'd been nothing like it since the big UFA days—films like *Destiny* and *Nibelungen*." In another Gough-Yates interview with Powell (Brussels Film Museum, 1973), the dir. speaks of his break with J at the time of *Red Shoes* (subsequently designed by Heckroth): "K. G-Y: . . . you refer to the future and look forward to a period when the art director will assume a role of major creative importance in the cinema. Do you think it is a prophesy that has been fulfilled? M. P.: No . . . although I still believe in it . . . as much now as I did then. . . . I'd seen Junge's work at Elstree when I first went there in 1928. . . . It was the first time in England that they had a supervising art director. Junge was a good organizer, a tremendous disciplinarian, and a very good trainer of young people. He had all the qualities that made for a head of department, besides being a very great designer himself. . . . It was only after I discussed *The Red Shoes* with Junge and told him what I wanted to do and he said 'Well Mickie, I think you want to go too far.' That's all. I immediately decided I would drop him as I was not going to be told by my own designer that I wanted to go too far. I wanted a designer who told me I didn't go far enough. . . . So I sent for Hein. . . . I realized that I was treating Alfred very badly because he *was* the chief designer. But he shouldn't have said that I wanted to go too far. Even though he was probably quite right, that wasn't the point." See Junge, "The Art Director and His Work," *Artist* (May-June 1944); see bibliography for J material in Paris.

Juran, Nathan   b. 1907 Austria-Hungary. Stud. M.I.T. Practiced architecture NY, entered films 1937. A.d. 1937–52; in early 40s many films at Fox, often in collab. Day. With OSS in WWII. Since 1952 has dir., notably: *20 Million Miles to Earth* (57), *The 7th Voyage of Sinbad* (58), *First Men in the Moon* (64)—all fantasy films with 3-dimensional animation by Ray

Harryhausen. As a.d. only: *How Green Was My Valley* (41)—in collab. Day, *Belle Starr* (41), *Charley's Aunt* (41), *I Wake Up Screaming* (41), *The Loves of Edgar Allen Poe* (42), *Dr. Renault's Secret* (42), *The Razor's Edge* (46), *Body and Soul* (47), *The Other Love* (47), *Kiss the Blood off my Hands* (48), *Tulsa* (49), *Deported* (50), *Winchester '73* (50), *Thunder on the Hill* (51).

Kaplunovsky, Vladimir   1906 Russia–1969. Stud. at Kiev Film and Theater Institute. *Revolt of the Fishermen* (34), *Lone White Sail* (37), *Tractor Drivers* (39), *Yakov Sverdlov* (40), *Dream* (43), *Glinka* (46), *The Fall of Berlin* (49), *The Unforgettable Year 1919* (52), *Revizor/The Inspector General* (52). K was perhaps obliged by circumstances to be more eclectic than his obvious natural bent for lyricism and poetry would have had it. Was at his best in work for Piscator's extraordinary experimental *Revolt of the Fishermen* and in Legoshin's charming and invigorating *Lone White Sail*. His later work, on overblown Stalinist pageants of the ilk of *Unforgettable Year* and *Fall of Berlin*, now seems to belong to the category of grotesque pop art iconography.

Keller, Walter E.   Best work was at RKO 1942–46, where, in collab. D'Agostino, he des. the superior series of B thrillers prod. by *Val Lewton. *Irish Luck* (25), *The New Klondike* (26), **The Cat People* (42), *This Land Is Mine* (43), **I Walked with a Zombie* (43), **The Leopard Man* (43), **The 7th Victim* (43), **The Ghost Ship* (43), **The Curse of the Cat People* (44), **Mademoiselle Fifi* (44), **Isle of the Dead* (45), **The Body Snatcher* (45), **Bedlam* (46), *The Woman on the Beach* (47), *Born to Kill* (47), *Dick Tracy Meets Gruesome* (47), *Blood on the Moon* (48), *The Window* (49), *I Married a Communist/The Woman on Pier 13* (50), *Bunco Squad* (50), *Private Hell 36* (54), *Son of Sinbad* (55). See Joel E. Siegel, *Val Lewton: The Reality of Terror* (NY, 1973).

Kettelhut, Erich   b. 1893 Germany. *Die Nibelungen* (24), *Metropolis* (26), *Berlin, die Symphonie der Grossstadt/Berlin, Symphony of a Great City* (27), *Ungarische Rhapsodie* (28), *Asphalt* (29), *FPI Antwortet nicht/FPI* (32), *Schlussakkord* (36), *Eine Liebesgeschichte/A Love Story* (58), *Die 1000 Augen des Dr. Mabuse/The 1000 Eyes of Dr. Mabuse* (60). The great studio-built landscapes of *Niebelungen* were apparently des. by Hunte and K, and constructed by Vollbrecht. See Kaul, *Schöpferische Filmarchitektur.*

Kiebach, Jürgen   *Der Fall X701/Frozen Alive* (64), *The Corrupt Ones/The Peking Medallion* (67), *De Sade* (69), *The Dead Are Alive* (72), *Cabaret* (72).

Kimball, Russell   *Home in Wyomin'* (42), *Ice Capades Review* (42), *Someone to Remember* (43), *The Lady and the Monster* (44), *Storm over Lisbon* (44), *Murder in the Music Hall* (46)—all Republic films. One of art direction's kings of the Bs, K des. some of Republic's best attempts in the 40s. *Lady* is an interesting curiosity—a successful but overproduced B horror film (Republic was then seeking acceptance as a major). Kimball was given a largish budget—enough, at any rate, to run out and put fancy chandeliers in motel rooms!

Kirk, Charles M.   A.d. for most of *D. W. Griffith's 1921–26 films. Early 30s at Paramount's NY (Astoria) studio; mid–30s at RKO. **Dream Street* (21), **Orphans of the Storm* (21), **One Exciting Night* (22), **The White Rose* (23), **America* (24), **Sally of the Sawdust* (25), **That Royle Girl* (25), **The Sorrows of Satan* (26), *Aloma of the South Seas* (26), *Jealousy* (29), *Christopher Strong* (33), *Ann Vickers* (33), *The Informer* (35)—in collab. Polglase. K's Revolutionary France for *Orphans of the Storm* (particularly the vast exterior décors) is one of the great creations in US cinema of the early 20s.

Kirk, Mark-Lee   Deceased. Entered films 1936; at Fox (1936–40), RKO (1940–44), Fox (1945–59). Early work at Fox often in collab. Day, later work there often with Wheeler. *Films des. in collab. Day, dir. by John Ford. *Wake Up and Live* (37), **Young Mr. Lincoln* (39), **Drums Along the Mohawk* (39), **The Grapes of Wrath* (40), *My Favorite Wife* (40)—in collab. Polglase, *Kitty Foyle* (40), *They Knew What They Wanted* (40), *The Magnificent Ambersons* (42), *Journey into Fear* (43), *I'll Be Seeing You* (44), *A Bell for Adano* (45), *A Royal Scandal* (45), *Moss Rose* (47), *The Iron Curtain* (48), *Prince of Foxes* (49), *Way of a Gaucho* (52), *Kangaroo* (52), *White Witch Doctor* (53), *Prince Valiant* (54), *The Tall Men* (55), *Prince of Players* (55), *The Revolt of Mamie Stover* (56), *Bus Stop* (56), *The Sun Also Rises* (57), *The Bravados* (58), *The Best of Everything* (59), *Compulsion* (59). K was a fine craftsman and all-round designer, but, unlike others with somewhat similar careers (e.g. Herzbrun), he nearly always managed to inject a measure of personality into his work—and in Welles's *The Magnificent Ambersons*, which he des. alone, superbly, he proved himself a great master of period atmosphere.

Kita, Takeo *Bijo to Ekitai Ningen/The H-Man* (58), *Mosura/Mothra* (61), *Furankenshutain tai Baragon/Frankenstein Conquers the World* (66), *Kaiju Soshingeki/Destroy All Monsters* (68). Kita des. most of the giant Toho teratologosities which were popular all over the world in the 50s and 60s—most of them (and all of the above) were dir. by Inoshiro Honda and engineered by the great Japanese special effects dir., Eiji Tsuburaya, who died in 1970. *Mothra* is the least mechanical of the lot—a strikingly beautiful, graceful, and poetic monster movie.

Korda, Vincent b. 1896 Austria-Hungary. WWI served in Hungarian army. Stud. painting in Paris and settled there early 30s. When London Films was founded in 1932 by K, his brother Alexander, and Lajos Biro, and Denham Studios built, K settled in England and des. most of the lavish films prod. by London. They were the first great English successes on the world film market in the 30s.

   Marius (31), *The Girl from Maxim's* (33), *The Private Life of Henry VIII* (33), *Catherine the Great* (34), *The Private Life of Don Juan* (34), *The Scarlet Pimpernel* (34), *Sanders of the River* (35), *The Ghost Goes West* (35), *Things to Come* (36), *Rembrandt* (36), *Men Are Not Gods* (36), *I, Claudius* (37)—unfinished, *The Squeaker* (37), *Over the Moon* (37), *The Man Who Could Work Miracles* (37), *Elephant Boy* (37), *The Drum/Drums* (38), *Prison Without Bars* (38), *Q Planes* (39), *The 4 Feathers* (39), *The Lion Has Wings* (39), *The Spy in Black/U-Boat 29* (39), *The Thief of Bagdad* (40)—in collab. Menzies, *21 Days/21 Days Together* (40), *Major Barbara* (41), *Lady Hamilton/That Hamilton Woman* (41), *To Be or Not to Be* (42), *The Jungle Book* (42), *Perfect Strangers/Vacation from Marriage* (45), *An Ideal Husband* (48)—in collab. Joseph Bato, *The Fallen Idol* (48), *Bonnie Prince Charlie* (48), *The Third Man* (49), *The Sound Barrier/Breaking the Sound Barrier* (52), *Outcast of the Islands* (52), *Fire over Africa* (54), *The Deep Blue Sea* (55), *Summer Madness/ Summertime* (55), *Scent of Mystery* (60), *The Longest Day* (62).

   During first 15 years of his career, K's sets for the historical spectacles prod. by his brother were marked by extravagant opulence; since *Fallen Idol*, sobriety and simplification have set in. Whether this corresponds to an inner impulse or to trends in the British film industry is a moot question. What is not moot is that K, with Junge and Andrejew—all of whom came from the Continent—were *the* major designers of that industry. See Korda, "The Artist and the Film," *Sight and Sound* 3 (Spring 1934), pp. 13–15, with sketches for *Catherine* and *Henry* and stills of the sets as they appear in the films; Karol Kulik, *Alexander Korda* (New Rochelle, NY, 1975).

Kozlovsky, Sergei 1885 Russia–1962. Stud. painting Odessa. Entered films 1913 (*A Hunting Drama*). *Polikushka* (made 19, rel. 22), *Aelita* (24)—in collab. Isaac Rabinovich and Victor Simov, **Mother* (26), *The Girl with the Hatbox* (27), **The End of St. Petersburg* (27), **Storm over Asia/The Heir to Jenghis-Khan* (28), *A Living Corpse* (29), **A Simple Case* (32), **Deserter* (33), *Okraina/Outskirts/Patriots* (33), *The New Adventures of Schweik* (43). *Films dir. by Vsevolod Pudovkin. One of the pioneers of Soviet film design; often inspired by 19th-century Russian painting.

Krauss, Jacques 1900 Paris–1957. Entered films as asst. designer to Aguettand. **Le Paquebot Tenacity* (34), **Marie Chapdelaine* (34), **La Bandera* (35), **La belle Equipe/They Were 5* (36), **Pépé le Moko* (36), *Entrée des artistes* (38), **La Fin du jour* (39), **La Charrette fantôme* (39), *Le Baron fantôme* (42), *Le Mariage de chiffon* (42), *Lettres d'amour* (42), *Douce* (43), *Sylvie et le fantôme* (45), *Du Guesclin* (48), *Caroline Chérie* (50), *Gibier de Potence* (51), *La Fille Elisa* (56). The poetic realism of K's sets for the **Duvivier films of the 30s is in perfect keeping with the mainstream of tristful, naturalistic, prewar French cinema. But the only great film he was ever assoc. with, Autant-Lara's *Douce*, is a searing, rather Jamesian study of the French middle-class and betrayed love, set during the Second Empire, and all the more astonishing for having been prod. under Pétain. K's period atmosphere is oppressively right for the movie. Its opening pan shot—the bottom part of the Eiffel Tower, with the top not yet there (it is being built)—as seen from a *hôtel particulier* window in the snow—is unforgettable.

Kuter, Leo US. 1897–1970. Unit a.d.; mostly at Universal in 20s, at WB from early 40s. A conscientious artisan, skilled at des. adventure films, K often worked on pictures dir. by **Delmer Daves. Late 60s, president of Hollywood Art Directors Local 876 (IATSE). *Trifling Women* (22), *Smouldering Fires* (25), *Sporting Life* (25), *Captain Salvation* (27), **Destination Tokyo* (43), *Northern Pursuit* (43), **Hollywood Canteen* (44), *Confidential Agent* (45), **Pride of the Marines* (45), *The Unfaithful* (47), **To the Victor* (48), *Key Largo* (48), **Task Force* (49), *Flamingo Road* (49), *Chain Lightning* (50), *I Was a Communist for the F.B.I.* (51),

This Woman Is Dangerous (52), *Trouble Along the Way* (53), *The Boy from Oklahoma* (54), *Toward the Unknown* (56), *The Deep 6* (58), *A Summer Place* (59), *Rio Bravo* (59), *Parrish* (61), *Rome Adventure* (62), *House of Women* (62), *PT 109* (63), *Ensign Pulver* (64). See Kuter, "Art Direction," *Films in Review* 8 (June–July 1957), pp. 248–58.

Larsen, Tambi *Secret of the Incas* (54), *Artists and Models* (55), *The Rose Tattoo* (55), *The Scarlet Hour* (56), *Spanish Affair* (57), *The Rat Race* (60), *It's Only Money* (62), *The Counterfeit Traitor* (62), *Too Late Blues* (62), *Hud* (63), *Nevada Smith* (66), *The Molly Maguires* (70), *The Life and Times of Judge Roy Bean* (72), *Thunderbolt and Lightfoot* (74). Many films at Paramount since the mid-50s, often in collab. Pereira, generally on pictures with modern settings, but best work was the splendid period reconstruction for *The Molly Maguires*.

Lawson, Arthur b. 1908 England. Entered films 1932. *The Way Ahead* (44)—in collab. David Rawnsley (44), *This Happy Breed* (44), *A Matter of Life and Death/Stairway to Heaven* (46)—asst. to Junge, *Oh, Rosalinda!!* (55)—in collab. Heckroth, *The Battle of the River Plate/The Pursuit of the Graf Spee* (56), *Harry Black and the Tiger* (58), *Peeping Tom* (59), *H.M.S. Defiant/Damn the Defiant!* (62), *The Double Man* (67), *The Lost Continent* (68). L has been overshadowed by the more spectacular designers (Heckroth and Junge) who also often worked on films dir. by *Powell & Pressburger. His work, however, has consistently been of high quality; alone, he designed a film which Powell dir. alone and is possibly his greatest—*Peeping Tom*—in which L's restrained but unforgettable décors beautifully characterize every aspect of Karl-Heinz Böhm's singular activities—the large sound stage at the film studio, the small tacky porno posing rooms in Soho, and above all, the congested "secret" flat-cum-film lab where the psycho *cinéphile* screens movies of his crimes.

Lee, Robert E. US. *The Tigress* (27), *The Matinee Idol* (28), *So This Is Love* (28), *That Certain Thing* (28), *The Great Gabbo* (29), *The Costello Case* (30). *3 of Frank Capra's early films at Columbia.

Leisen, Mitchell 1898 Michigan–1972 Hollywood. Stud. architecture Washington Univ.; draftsman for architectural firm. Entered films 1919 as costume designer of Cecil B. De Mille's *Male and Female*. Worked as principal a.d. and top asst. to *De Mille for 12 years, except for a period when he was fired and des. the costumes for *Robin Hood* and *The Thief of Bagdad*, both for Fairbanks. In 1932 began dir. his own films, working mostly at Paramount. Dir. some of the most delightful and entertaining romantic comedies ever made. For years, L was taken for granted as a competent hack—for *Cahiers du Cinéma* he was merely "un grand couturier," for Andrew Sarris, he was "lightly likable." But cinema auteurism is basically a question of who sees what when—and then has a column to push his favorites. The dir. of *Murder at the Vanities*, *Swing High—Swing Low*, *Hold Back the Dawn*, and 2 masterpieces—*Easy Living* and *Midnight*—began to come into his own critically about the time of his death, after a decade (47–57) of interesting but unsuccessful pictures, an unhappy private life, an amputated leg. L's background as an a.d. partially accounts for the constant presence of visual charm in his films, an element often lacking in the work of other contract dirs. of the period who had been assigned similar material. His last theatrical feature, *The Girl Most Likely* (made RKO 56, rel. Universal 57) was both L's last film and the last film to be made at the dying studio. When the costumes for *Girl* were finished, the costume dept. for the entire studio was shut down—forever. When the film's sets had been built, RKO's art dept. closed down for good. In the 60s, L did some TV work and ran a dance studio in Hollywood.

As a.d.: *The Road to Yesterday* (25)—in collab. Grot, *The Volga Boatman* (26)—in collab. Max Parker and Grot, *His Dog* (27), *The Angel of Broadway* (27), *The Fighting Eagle* (27), *The Wise Wife* (27), *Dress Parade* (27), *The Forbidden Woman* (27), *The King of Kings* (27)—in collab. Grot and Jewell, *Chicago* (27), *Power* (28), *Show Folks* (28), *Celebrity* (28), *Lover Over Night* (28), *The Godless Girl* (29), *Dynamite* (29)—in collab. Gibbons, *Madame Satan* (30)—in collab. Gibbons, *The Squaw Man* (31), *The Sign of the Cross* (32)—also costumes and asst. dir. Most of the other films (27–28) were De Mille–Pathé prods. See Higham, *Cecil B. De Mille*; Chierichetti, *Hollywood Director*; James Kelley & John Schultheiss, "Hollywood Contract Director—Mitchell Leisen," *Cinema* 8 (Spring 1973); Leonard Maltin, "A Visit with Mitchell Leisen," *Action* (Nov.–Dec. 1969); Leonard Maltin, "FFM Interviews Mitchell Leisen," *Film Fan Monthly* (Jan. 1970).

In the Maltin interview, L, in speaking of his work on the 2 De Mille films at MGM—*Dynamite* and *Madame Satan*—gives an idea of how frenzied early sound shooting must have been, even at the largest studio: "Those were very hectic days, because they only had one sound stage. Our sets were put in and ready at 9 in the morning, they were snatched out from under us at 6. At 6:30 there was a set in for a short subject, which quit at 7. At 7:30, that was gone, and the set was in for a company that worked all night. So the sets had to be very flexible to be brought back in a hurry." In the *Cinema* article, L remarks: "The art director in the ideal case very often sets the camera line for the Director because he knows the best angle to shoot from." In the same article, speaking of his career as contract director: "Every problem strikes me as one in construction. I think it all stems from the fact that my entire training was as an architect. What is your foundation going to be? What is your structure? What are you going to use on the outside for trimmings? Everything in motion pictures comes up as a new subject and has to be handled in a new way. That's why I like directing better than architecture. You can get stuck in architecture . . . sometimes you discover you left out the bathroom. Of course, in pictures, you find you left out the plot once in a while." Kelly & Schultheiss make the interesting observation: "The ensuing years forced Leisen to emphasize the visual aspects of his films in order to compensate for the deficiencies in the scripts he received. His shift in orientation is reflected in the remarkable phenomenon that of the 13 Oscar nominations for Interior Decoration won by Paramount films (by Hans Dreier and his staff) during the quintessential Leisen period from 1940 to 1949, *seven* were for Leisen-directed pictures." When the authors remarked to L, "There are so many factors involved in the look and style of your pictures, but there is a special elegance to the sets and the costumes, he replied, "Well, having been an art director . . . but as a result of that fact, my big problem was to get the art department to design it. They wanted me to do it all the time."

Leni, Paul   1885 Germany–1929 Hollywood. Stud. Academy of Fine Arts and Art Metalwork College, Berlin. Set designer for Max Reinhardt stage prods. Entered films as a.d. 1914, started dir. 1916. L des. nearly all of the films he dir. in Germany from 1917 on (*), plus many films for other dirs. His *Kammerspiel* picture *Backstairs* and *Waxworks* were 2 of the most notable and influential German films of the 20s.

   Das Panzergewolbe (14), *Das Achte Gebot* (15), **Das Tagebuch des Dr. Hart* (16), **Dornröschen* (17), **Primavera* (17), **Prinz Kuckuck* (19), **Patience* (20), *Der Weisse Pfau* (20), **Hintertreppe/Backstairs* (21)—co-dir. with Leopold Jessner, *Frauenopfer* (22), *Lady Hamilton* (22)—in collab. Dreier, *Tragödie der Liebe* (23), **Das Wachsfigurenkabinett/Waxworks* (24), *Der Farmer aus Texas* (25), *Manon Lescaut* (26), *Fiaker no. 13* (26)—dir. by Michael Kertesz (later Curtiz), *Die Goldene Schmetterling* (26)—dir. by Kertesz. Films dir. by L in US: *The Cat and the Canary* (27), *The Chinese Parrot* (27), *The Man Who Laughs* (28), *The Last Warning* (29).

   Waxworks was a great success; it brought L an invitation from Carl Laemmle to work at Universal. The macabre melodramas he dir. in Hollywood (a.d. Charles D. Hall, who followed L's concepts) were something new in US cinema: an odd, often brilliant alloy of semi-expressionist sets, nervous mobile camerawork, much use of distorted shadows, and (save for *The Man Who Laughs*) low comedy effects which were Universal's idea of box office insurance but which work against the films' total effectiveness. *The Man Who Laughs* is an incredible picture—made in Hollywood, based on a French novel set in 17th-century England, it is one of the most German-looking films ever made west of the Mississippi. See the excellent chapter on *The Man Who Laughs* (with stills of the sets) in Everson, *Classics of the Horror Film*. "If Paul Leni, the Expressionist painter and film-maker, patterned the essence of his *Waxworks* on the title of *Das Kabinett des Dr. Caligari*, he did so deliberately, for he was to amplify, in his own playful manner and using a more skillful technique, the fairground ambience which had already proved so conducive to mystery. In *Waxworks* . . . the main action is set at night in a fairground booth. Tents with mysterious shadows, innumerable electric signs, the merry-go-round and a gigantic wheel turning in a welter of lights, the whole multiplied by the superimpositions which thread across the screen like spiders' webs, show how far the German cinema had come since the rather arid abstraction of the *Caligari* fairground. . . . The puffy dough-like settings in the episode of the baker's wife are full of rotundities and cockled walls and seem to have no interior framing: the corridors, staircases . . . and the soft, yielding arches seem to anticipate the creations of Antonio Gaudí. Architectural details in the first two episodes reveal Leni's skill as a designer. . . . Eisenstein's *Ivan the Terrible* shows the influence of the decorative stylization in Leni's film. Eisenstein used *Waxworks* as a model, particularly in the disposition of the figures on the screen, and the way in which they are reduced to ornaments, their gestures frozen to the point of a carefully elaborated abstraction."—Eisner, *Haunted Screen*, p. 115.

Leven, Boris   b. Moscow. Stud. Univ. Southern California, degree in architecture; several awards in architectural competitions. Entered films 1933 as a sketch artist at Paramount, where he worked, uncredited, on *Cleopatra*, *The Scarlet Empress*, other films. Unemployed in the Depression, L took film work originally as a stopgap: "Architecture was my life, and at that time I could not imagine myself devoting the rest of my professional career to films." 1938–47 mostly at Fox; 1947–48 Universal; free lance since 1948.

   *Films dir. by Robert Wise. *Alexander's Ragtime Band* (38), *Just Around the Corner* (38), *Second Chorus* (40), *The Shanghai Gesture* (41), *Tales of Manhattan* (42), *Life Begins at 8:30* (42), *Hello, Frisco, Hello* (43), *Shock* (46), *Home Sweet Homicide* (46), *The Shocking Miss Pilgrim* (47), *I Wonder Who's Kissing Her Now* (47), *The Senator Was Indiscreet* (47), *Mr. Peabody and the Mermaid* (48), *Criss Cross* (49), *Dakota Lil* (50), *House by the River* (50), *The Prowler* (51), *A Millionaire for Christy* (51), *Sudden Fear* (52), *The Star* (52), *Invaders from Mars* (53), *Donovan's Brain* (53), *The Long Wait* (54), *The Silver Chalice* (54), *Giant* (56), *Anatomy of a Murder* (59), *West Side Story* (61), *2 for the Seesaw* (62), *The Sound of Music* (65), *The Sand Pebbles* (66), *Star!* (68), *The Andromeda Strain* (71), *Happy Birthday, Wanda June* (71), *The New Centurions* (72), *Jonathan Livingston Seagull* (73), *Shanks* (74), *Mandingo* (75).

   Stylistically, 2 of the most striking films were apparently director-dominated. *Shanghai Gesture* looks more like other Sternbergs than any other film des. by Leven, and *Invaders from Mars* (a striking job on a small budget) is marked by typically Menzian perspectives. A fine hand at science fiction, L also had a real flair for film noir—*Criss Cross* and *Sudden Fear* make one regret he ventured into this genre so seldom. *Tales of Manhattan* is one of the few really handsome Fox prods. of the early 40s. Architecture's loss has meant over 40 years of strongly des. motion pictures. See Higham & Greenberg, *Hollywood in the Forties*, p. 45; "Rene L. Ash Interviews Boris Leven," *Film Index*, no. 15; Mike Kaplan, "The $325,000 Core—Production Design for *The Andromeda Strain*," *Today's Film Maker* 1 (Aug. 1971). The Ash interview is required reading for decipherers of a.d. credits:

   "When you worked at Fox, why did Zanuck assign two art directors to a feature film?

   "At that time it was the custom for the head of the art department whether he contributed to the design of sets or not, to receive top credit above the name of the so-called unit art director, who was handling the particular film. In this way the head of the art department had his name on all the films produced by the studio where he worked.

   "Was each director responsible for specific scenes?

   "No. I have already explained the reason for two names. Occasionally two unit art directors were assigned to a technically involved film. In this case three names would appear on the screen. The head of the art department, and the two unit art directors. I would like to add that before this period and for a long time, only the name of the head of the art department was used. The unit art directors who actually were responsible for the design of the sets rated no screen credit.

   "At Fox, did you have a choice on the films you wished to work?

   "Not really. However the head of the department if he had any sense, would assign an art director to a film for which he was best suited."

Lonergan, Arthur   b. 1906 NY. Stud. architecture Columbia. Entered films 1938 as illustrator in MGM art dept. *Intrigue* (48), *Maneaters of Kumaon* (48), *A Life of Her Own* (50), *Ride, Vaquero!* (53), *The Actress* (53), *It's Always Fair Weather* (55), *Forbidden Planet* (56), *On the Double* (61), *Robinson Crusoe on Mars* (64), *Red Line 7000* (65), *How Sweet It Is!* (68), *Che!* (69), *M*A*S*H* (70). See Steve Rubin, "Retrospect—*Forbidden Planet*," *Cinefantastique* 4, no. 1 (1975), which contains many prod. sketches by L for this film and a detailed essay on its production: " . . . the studio gave them [the prod. unit] the cold shoulder. Arthur Lonergan was pulled away from Cedric Gibbons' art department and was given virtually no departmental assistance on the film. As Arnold Gillespie put it: 'Everybody thought we were nuts.' 'The interesting thing,' says Lonergan, 'is how to research a project like this. There is simply no place to go. You have to reach up to the stars and grab onto something. The art department was used to having a particular field of research. The only way to start on this film was to field a lot of ideas, let some go and latch onto the rest'. . . . Like the starship set, the futuristic house had its own soundstage, complete with forested vegetation and entrances to the Krel laboratories and underground complex. Like Ken Adam, who much later became acclaimed for the scope and complexity of his futuristic set design on the James Bond films, Lonergan on *Forbidden Planet* dispensed with the customary plans for Earth houses. Says Lonergan: 'I made the assumption, which isn't too far-fetched now, that there need be no separation between the house and the forest. We had no windows in the

223

Morbius home. . . . We tried to avoid using anything that would resemble an earthly appliance.'"

Lourié, Eugène b. 1905 Russia. To Paris 1921; des. ballets. In US since 1943 where he has worked as a.d. on many films, special effects dir. of several (*Krakatoa—East of Java*, 69), and dir. of a few sci-fi pictures (only one, *The Beast from 20,000 Fathoms*, of quality). *Napoléon* (27)—in collab. Alexandre Benois and Schildknecht, *Le Bossu* (34), *Crime et châtiment/Crime and Punishment* (35), *Sous les yeux d'Occident/Under Western Eyes* (36), *Les Bas Fonds/The Lower Depths* (36), *Alibi* (37), *La grande Illusion* (37), *Werther* (38), *La Bête humaine* (38), *La Règle du jeu/The Rules of the Game* (39), *Sans Lendemain* (39), *This Land Is Mine* (43), *3 Russian Girls* (43), *The Imposter* (44), *Abbott and Costello in Society* (44), *The Southerner* (45), *The House of Fear* (45), *The Strange Adventure of Uncle Harry* (45), *The Diary of a Chambermaid* (46), *The Long Night* (47), *Song of Scheherezade* (47), *A Woman's Vengeance* (48), *The River* (51), *Limelight* (52), *The Beast from 20,000 Fathoms* (53), *So This Is Paris* (54), *Shock Corridor* (63), *The Naked Kiss* (64), *The Battle of the Bulge* (65), *A Crack in the World* (65), *Bikini Paradise* (67), *Custer of the West* (68), *The Royal Hunt of the Sun* (69), *What's the Matter with Helen?* (71). A singular career which has often veered from the sublime to the ridiculous and back again. L stands to be best remembered for his sets on 8 *Jean Renior films; his finest later work has been for 2 by Samuel Fuller—*Shock Corridor* and *Naked Kiss*—good low-budget films noirs with stark, harshly unfussy, effective settings.

Lundgren. P. A. b. 1911 Sweden. Before entering films worked in advertising as a commercial artist. *Films dir. by Ingmar Bergman. *It Rains on Our Love* (46), *A Ship to India* (47), *Night Is My Future/Music in Darkness* (47), *Prison/The Devil's Wanton* (49), *Monika/Summer with Monika* (53), *A Lesson in Love* (54), *Smiles of a Summer Night* (55), *Vildfaglar/Wild Birds* (55), *The 7th Seal* (57), *The Magician/The Face* (58), *The Virgin Spring* (60), *The Devil's Eye* (60), *Through a Glass Darkly* (61), *Pleasure Garden* (61), *Winter Light* (63), *The Silence* (63), *Now about These Women/All These Women* (64), *491* (64), *Ön/The Island* (made 64, rel. 66), *People Meet and Sweet Music Fills the Heart* (67), *Shame* (68), *The Passion of Anna* (69), *Utvandrarna/The Emigrants* (71), *The Night Visitor* (71), *The Touch* (71)—in collab. Ann-Christin Lobraten. "Jonas Sima: In *The Virgin Spring* . . . you make use of models . . . the farmhouse in the film was a model. Bergman: That's something we do now and again. P. A. Lundgren, our art director, is a specialist and incredibly clever at it. Did you know it was originally a Swedish invention? Julius Jaenzon invented it in 1919. Afterwards it was forgotten and the French took it over. Later, little by little, we re-invented it again. It's known as mirroring in."—*Bergman on Bergman* (NY, 1973), p. 122.

McCleary, Urie Unit a.d. MGM many years, then *Patton* at 20th–Fox. *Blossoms in the Dust* (41), *National Velvet* (44), *Adventure* (46), *Command Decision* (48), *The Secret Garden* (49), *Any Number Can Play* (49), *3 Little Words* (50), *Pat and Mike* (52), *Plymouth Adventure* (52), *Kiss Me Kate* (53), *Young Bess* (53), *Jupiter's Darling* (55), *Some Came Running* (58), *2 Weeks in Another Town* (62), *4 Horsemen of the Apocalypse* (62), *The Prize* (63), *The Split* (68), *Where Were You When the Lights Went Out?* (68), *Patton* (70).

MacDonald, Richard b. Scotland. Stud. Royal College of Art, London. Began his long collab. with *Joseph Losey as des. consultant on *The Sleeping Tiger* (54). *The Gypsy and the Gentleman* (58)—in collab. Brinton, *Blind Date/Chance Meeting* (59), *The Criminal/The Concrete Jungle* (60)—as des. consultant, *The Damned/These Are the Damned* (61)—as des. consultant in collab. Bernard Robinson, *Eva/Eve* (62), *The Servant* (63), *King and Country* (64), *Modesty Blaise* (66), *Far from the Madding Crowd* (67), *Boom* (68), *Secret Ceremony* (68), *Bloomfield* (70), *A Severed Head* (71), *The Assassination of Trotsky* (72), *Jesus Christ Superstar* (73), *Galileo* (75), *The Day of the Locust* (75), *The Romantic Englishwoman* (75). See Hudson, "Three Designers." For Losey's comments on M's sets for *Galileo*, see Richard Combs, "Losey, Galileo and the Romantic Englishwoman," *Sight and Sound* (Summer 1975).

MacGregor, Scott b. 1914 Scotland. Stage designer, entered films 1941 as asst. to Carrick. A.d. since 1946. Much work on fantasy and horror films, recently mostly at Hammer. His most inventive work has been for Robert Young's richly surreal *Vampire Circus*. *Action of the Tiger* (57), *The Million Eyes of Su-Muru* (67), *Taste the Blood of Dracula* (70), *Scars of Dracula* (70), *The Vampire Lovers* (70), *Burke and Hare* (71), *Vampire Circus* (71), *Blood from the Mummy's Tomb* (71). See St. John Marner, *Film Design*, pp. 120–23.

Mackay, John Victor *Manhattan Merry-Go-Round* (37), *Man of Conquest* (39), *The Dark Command* (40). A Republic film was hardly ever nominated for an Oscar—in any category—and when it was, it did not win the award. These 3 are oddities in the annals: they were produced by the minor studio which specialized in oaters, and all 3 earned Mackay nominations for best a.d.

Mallet-Stevens, Robert 1886 Paris–1945. Architect of many International Style town houses in Paris, and of the St.-Jean-de-Luz casino. *Le Secret de Rosette Lambert* (23), *L'Inhumaine/The New Enchantment* (23)—in collab. Fernand Léger, Autant-Lara, and Cavalcanti, *Le Miracle des loups* (24), *Le Tournoi* (29). In France, credited with the first use of modern architecture in the cinema—in *L'Inhumaine*. The movies' only a.d. with a street named after him—Rue Mallet-Stevens, Paris.

Mann, Roman 1911 Russia–1960. *Ostatni Etap/The Last Stage* (48), *Mlodosc Szopin/The Young Chopin* (52), *Pokolenie/A Generation* (54), *Celuloza/A Night of Remembrance* (54), *Czlowiek na torze/The Man on the Track* (56), *Kanal* (56), *Popiol i diament/Ashes and Diamonds* (58), *Matka Joanna od Aniolow/Mother Joan of the Angels/Joan of the Angels?* (61). Although inclined to "artiness" on his films for *Wajda, M was the film designer of his generation in Poland.

Mano, Shigeo *Moju/The Blind Beast/Warehouse* (69). Brilliant design for Yasuzo Masumura's unusual love story, especially the sculptor's studio with its wall frieze of giant navels.

Marchi, Virgilio 1895 Italy–1960 Italy. Stud. architecture; much work des. for theater and opera. Architect of many theaters and movie houses in Italy—the Odeon Cinema, Livorno, is the largest. Taught at the Centro Sperimentale di Cinematografia—the Rome film-training center founded by Mussolini, where M formed a generation of young a.ds. A member of the Futurist movement and author of *Architettura Futurista* (1924). *Milizia Territoriale* (35), *I Due Sergenti* (36), *Un'Avventura di Salvator Rosa* (39), *La Corona di Ferro/The Iron Crown* (40), *La Conquista dell'Aria* (40), *Un Pilota Ritorna* (42), *La Cena delle Beffe* (42), *Maria Malibran* (42), *Quattro Passi fra le Nuvole/4 Steps in the Clouds* (42), *Cielo sulla palude* (49), *Olivia/The Pit of Loneliness* (50), *Francesco, Giullare di Dio/The Flowers of St. Francis* (50), *Umberto D* (52), *Europa 51* (52), *Don Camillo* (52), *Il Ritorno di Don Camillo* (53), *Stazione Termini/Indiscretion of an American Wife* (54), *La Tua Donna* (56). M's best work is to be seen in the films dir. by *Alessandro Blasetti; although the charming *4 Steps* is a significant precursor of neorealism, the masterpiece of both dir. and designer is the Byzantine western, *The Iron Crown*, that delirious tournament of bric-a-brac, one of the rare films of the Mussolini era to attain real grandeur.

Marsh, Terence Specialist in elaborate period reconstructions, often in collab. with *Box. *Lawrence of Arabia* (62), *Dr. Zhivago* (65), *A Man for All Seasons* (66), *Oliver!* (68), *Scrooge* (70), *Mary, Queen of Scots* (71), *The Abdication* (74), *Juggernaut* (74), *Royal Flash* (75), *The Adventures of Sherlock Holmes' Smarter Brother* (75).

Masters, Anthony (Tony) b. 1919 England. *The Bespoke Overcoat* (55), *The Story of Esther Costello* (57), *The Spaniard's Curse* (58), *The Doctor from 7 Dials/Corridors of Blood* (made 58, rel. 62), *Expresso Bongo* (59), *Stop Me Before I Kill* (61), *The Day the Earth Caught Fire* (61), *The Moon-Spinners* (64), *The Heroes of Telemark* (65), *2001: A Space Odyssey* (68)—in collab. Harry Lange and Ernest Archer, *The Adventurers* (70), *Z.P.G.* (72), *Papillon* (73), *That Lucky Touch* (75). See Jerome Agel, ed., *The Making of Kubrick's 2001* (NY, 1970), p. 64: "The art department, which occupies a nearby building, is presided over by Tony Masters, a tall, Lincolnesque man who was busy working on the Jupiter drawings when we appeared. . . ."

Matsuyama, So *Drunken Angel* (48), *Stray Dog* (49), *Rashomon* (50), *The Idiot* (51), *Ikiru/To Live/Living* (52), *7 Samurai* (54). Although he has des. for other dirs., M will be best remembered for his work on these 6 great films, all dir. by Akira Kurosawa.

Maurischat, Fritz b. 1893 Berlin. First film work 1922. *Films dir. by Detlef Sierck (later Douglas Sirk). *Geschlecht in Fesseln* (28), *Mädchen in Uniform/Girls in Uniform* (31), *Im Banne des Eulenspiegels* (32), *Anna und Elisabeth* (33), *S.O.S. Eisberg* (33), *Der Alte und der Jünge König* (35), *Das Hofkonzert* (36), *Zu Neuen Ufern/Life Begins Anew/To New Shores* (37), *The Devil Makes 3* (52), *For the First Time* (59). Period biography, period musicals, period melodramas, homosexual dramas in claustrophobic settings—and Frank Wysbar's extraordinary *Anna und Elisabeth* which fits into no category. See Kaul, *Schöpferische Architektur.*

Medin, Gastone b. 1905 Italy. 1929–33 in charge of set construction for the Cines company. *Films dir. by Mario Camerini. *Sole* (29), *Figaro e la sua Gran Giornata* (31), *La Tavola dei Poveri* (32), *Gli Uomini, che Mascalzoni!/Men Are Such Rascals* (32), *Acciaio/Steel* (33), *Ma Non è una Cosa Seria* (36), *Il Signor Max* (37), *Una Romantica Avventura* (40), *L'Assedio dell'Alcazar* (40), *Piccolo Mondo Antico/Little Old-fashioned World* (41), *I Promessi Sposi* (41), *Un Colpo di Pistola/A Pistol Shot* (41)—in collab. Nicolà Benois, *Malombra* (42), *Zazà* (43), *Due Lettere Anonime* (45), *Davanti a Lui Tremava Tutta Roma* (46), *Messalina/The Loves of Messalina* (51), *Puccini/2 Loves Had I* (53), *L'Oro di Napoli/The Gold of Naples* (54), *Il Tetto/The Roof* (56), *A Farewell to Arms* (57), *Anna di Brooklyn* (58), *The Enemy General* (60). M was one of the chief designers of the Italian cinema's "calligraphic" (formalist) period, 1941–43. See *La Scenografica Cinematografica in Italia* (Rome, 1955).

Meehan, John b. 1902 California. Stud. architecture Univ. Southern California. At Paramount 1935–50; since 1951 at Columbia, Disney, Universal. *The Virginian* (46), *The Bride Wore Boots* (46), *The Strange Love of Martha Ivers* (46), *Suddenly It's Spring* (47), *Golden Earrings* (47), *Dream Girl* (48), *Sealed Verdict* (48), *The Heiress* (49), *Sunset Boulevard* (50)—in collab. Dreier, *The Marrying Kind* (52), *Salome* (53), *It Should Happen to You* (54), *20,000 Leagues Under the Sea* (54), *Cult of the Cobra* (55).

Meerson, Lazare 1900 Russia—1938 London. After the Revolution emigrated to Germany, then to Paris in 1924 and worked in France for 12 years. M was the foremost designer in French cinema in the first half of the 30s, working with several dirs., principally Feyder, Clair, and L'Herbier. In 1936 brought to England by Korda for London Films. M's influence on set design was as strongly felt in England as in France. The Italian *Filmlexicon* considers M and Warm the two greatest designers in the history of European cinema.
*Films dir. by Feyder. †Films dir. by Clair. *Gribiche* (25), *Feu Mathias Pascal* (25), *Carmen* (26), †*La Proie du vent* (26), †*Un Chapeau de paille d'Italie/An Italian Straw Hat* (27), †*Les 2 Timides* (28), *Cagliostro* (28), *Les nouveau Messieurs* (29), †*Sous les Toits de Paris/Under the Roofs of Paris* (30), *David Golder* (30), *Le Parfum de la dame en noir* (31), †*Le Million* (31), †*A Nous la liberté* (31), *Der Ball/Le Bal* (31), *Jean de la Lune* (31), †*Quatorze Juillet* (32), *Ciboulette* (33), *Le grand Jeu* (34), *Amok* (34), *Lac aux dames* (34), *Pension Mimosas* (35), *La Kermesse héroïque/Carnival in Flanders* (35), *Les beaux Jours* (35), *As You Like It* (36), *Fire over England* (37), *Knight Without Armour* (37), †*Break the News* (37), *The Return of the Scarlet Pimpernel* (37), *South Riding* (38), *The Citadel* (38)—in collab. Junge, *The Divorce of Lady X* (38)—in collab. Sheriff.
". . . a designer whose studio-built street scenes and sets for Feyder and Clair broke completely away from expressionism, impressionism, and conventional studio 'naturalism' to create an ambience at once realistic and poetic. He is undoubtedly one of the major contributors to the development of French poetic realism. His early death ended a remarkable career, but even in the 60s many French designers (some of them his former assistants) were still profiting from his lessons."—Sadoul, *Dictionary of Film Makers*, p. 172. Carrick, *Designing for Motion Pictures* reproduces several M sketches; "Meerson, who was very keen on 'detail,' put most of his work into his sets while they were being built; he used plaster work very lavishly" (p. 35). The décors of Autant-Lara's peculiar filmed opéra-comique, *Ciboulette*, which is hardly known outside of France, are among M's most impressive. See "Lazare Meerson," *Sight and Sound* 7 (Summer 1938).

Méliès, Georges 1861 France–1938 France. Magician, cartoonist, automaton maker, and designer at the Théâtre Robert Houdin. First films 1896. Made over 500 films in 1896–1912, of which fewer than 90 have survived. Bankrupt after WWI, in later years M sold toys in a Paris subway station. *Une Partie de cartes/Playing Cards* (1896), *Le Voyage dans la lune/A Trip to the Moon* (02), *La Légende de Rip van Winkle/Rip's Dream* (05), *L'Éclipse du soleil en pleine lune/The Eclipse* (07), *A la Conquête du Pôle/The Conquest of the Pole* (12).
Genius and pioneer, M was the first dir. of narrative films. He des. and made sets and costumes, was his own cameraman and principal actor, and invented many of the movies' basic special effects. Specialized in fantasy and sci-fi films. His designs were marked by an inexhaustible imagination; far from being "primitive" as has often been claimed, M was fully aware of the entertaining tensions producible through distortions in perspective. See George Franju's film *Le Grand Méliès* (1952); Paul Hammond, *Marvellous Méliès* (NY, 1975)—the first book on M in English and more reliable than any of the volumes in French on the great man.

Ménessier, Henri 1904 first film work, painting backdrops at Pathé. 1905 hired by Gaumont, Paris, to direct des. dept. In 1910 to US to work for Lewis Selznick and on several Maurice Tourneur films; 1915 head of Metro art dept. Brought back to Europe by Pearl White for whom he worked in Paris. Several films for the US dir. *Rex Ingram who had settled at the Nice studios in the 20s. *La Passion—La Vie du Christ* (06), *Lest We Forget* (17), *Koenigsmark* (23), *The Magician* (26), *The Garden of Allah* (27), *L'Aiglon* (31), *Le Puritain* (37). M's sets for *Magician* are about the best thing in the film—the stark Parisian operating room, the sorcerer's castle-lab on a jagged cliff (precursor of the 30s lairs of *Dracula* and *Frankenstein* at Universal)—a jolly mixture of Gothic gloom and Arthur Rackhamesque quaintness.

Menzies, William Cameron 1896 New Haven, Conn.–1957 California. Stud. at Yale; in AEF in WWI; stud. at Art Students League, NY A.d. Famous Players; to Hollywood as a.d. First Nat., then des. for Mary Pickford, Goldwyn, Selznick in mid–late 30s as prod. designer.
  *Films dir. by Sam Wood. *The Naulahka* (18)—as asst. to Grot, *Serenade* (21), *Kindred of the Dust* (22), *Rosita* (23), *The Thief of Bagdad* (24)—in collab. Grot, Irvin J. Martin, and Park French, *Cobra* (25), *The Eagle* (25), *Her Sister from Paris* (25), *The Bat* (26), *The Son of the Sheik* (26), *Fig Leaves* (26), *The Beloved Rogue* (27), *The Dove* (27), *2 Arabian Knights* (27), *Sorrell and Son* (27), *The Awakening* (28), *Drums of Love* (28), *The Garden of Eden* (28), *Sadie Thompson* (28), *The Loves of Zero* (28), *Tempest* (28), *The Woman Disputed* (28), *The Iron Mask* (29), *Alibi* (29), *Bulldog Drummond* (29), *Condemned* (29), *Lady of the Pavements* (29), *The Rescue* (29), *The Taming of the Shrew* (29), *Abraham Lincoln* (30), *The Bad One* (30), *Be Yourself* (30), *DuBarry, Woman of Passion* (30), *The Lottery Bride* (30), *Lummox* (30), *One Romantic Night* (30), *Puttin' on the Ritz* (30), *Raffles* (30), *Reaching for the Moon* (30), *Alice in Wonderland* (33)—also costumes and collab. on script, *Cavalcade* (33)—a.d. and SPFX of war scenes only, *Things To Come* (36)—in collab. V. Korda, also dir., *The Young in Heart* (38), *The Adventures of Tom Sawyer* (38)—cave sequence, *Made for Each Other* (39), *Gone with the Wind* (39)—in collab. Wheeler, also dir. at least 10% of the film, *Foreign Correspondent* (40)—in collab. Golitzen, *The Thief of Bagdad* (40)—co-dir. and des. in collab. V. Korda, *Our Town* (40), *So Ends Our Night* (41), *The Devil and Miss Jones* (41), *Kings Row* (42), *The Pride of the Yankees* (42), *For Whom the Bell Tolls* (43), *Address Unknown* (44)—also prod. and dir., *Ivy* (47)—also des. costumes and co-prod., *Arch of Triumph* (48), *Reign of Terror/The Black Book* (49), *Drums in the Deep South* (51)—also dir., *The Whip Hand* (51)—also dir., *The Maze* (53)—also dir., *Invaders from Mars* (53)—also dir.
  M worked with an impressive number of Hollywood's great figures—Griffith, Walsh, Lubitsch, Hitchcock, Goldwyn, Selznick, Fairbanks, Pickford, Barrymore, Valentino, and the remarkably idiosyncratic Roland West for whom he des. 3 films—*The Bat*, *The Dove* (which earned him the first a.d. AA ever awarded), and *Alibi*, with its weird deco-cum-*Caligari* sets. Identifiably Menziesian perspectives run as visual leitmotifs through nearly 40 years of design (e.g. a predilection for broken diagonal barriers which cross the frame like jagged slashes and usually turn up during scenes of tension, grief, and separation in the form of fences, walls, palisades, railings). They can be seen in the Murnau-like designs for *Tempest* (the wall against which Barrymore is cashiered), in Griffith's *Lincoln*, *Kings Row*, *Our Town*—and in both the lavish *Gone with the Wind* and the fine low-budgeter *Invaders from Mars*.
  "Probably the most influential designer in the Anglo-American cinema (and virtually an *auteur* in his own right), Menzies became known in the 20s with his elaborate fairy-tale settings in *The Thief of Bagdad*, *Beloved Rogue* with its great vista of rooftops . . . and other historical spectaculars."—Gillett, *International Encyclopedia of Film*, p. 361. "Often Anton Grot and I would have dinner together at a restaurant . . . called Hendricks . . . on the north side of 56th Street . . . several art students who had part-time jobs in the neighborhood were frequent customers. One of them was William Menzies, to whom Anton introduced me. . . . Our next picture, *The Naulahka*, starred Antonio Moreno . . . it was laid in India so Anton Grot designed a set representing the interior of a huge Hindu temple, with the foreground 30 feet deep where the action was to take place. The remaining depth of the set was built in 'forced perspective.' Although the actual depth of the entire set was no more than 50 or 60 feet, it appeared on the screen to extend for at least 200 feet. When Fitzmaurice looked at a test of the set on the screen, he urged Grot to use the same method to build other sets in the picture. This gave Anton an opportunity to ask for an assistant. I knew he had Billy Menzies in mind . . . Fitz agreed, and it wasn't long before Anton had taught Billy the trick of

making drawings, using his dimension scale, which Menzies used throughout his long and distinguished career as a production designer."—Miller & Balshofer, *One Reel a Week*, pp. 131–34. "An 8-foot mutant from Mars; Rhett Butler driving a terrified horse against a sky reddened by burning Atlanta; Douglas Fairbanks jnr. trying to date Paulette Goddard in an incredibly 30s-impressive office; Fairbanks snr. piloting his ship across the dark, slow-motion waves; Paris Mitchell illuminated by the lightning flash that shows the tree-root distorted streets of Kings Row; actors like ants in an H. G. Wells city of the future; Valentino sinisterly eyeing belly-dancer Agnes Ayres in a desert night-dive . . . most moviegoers carry some of these images and they are all largely the work of one man. William Cameron Menzies was possibly the greatest visual talent to work in films. Yet his name is little known because so-called 'serious criticism' revolves almost exclusively on the work of directors, whereas Menzies' greatest achievements are the films he designed for others to direct."—John Howard Reid, "Address Unknown," *Film Index*, no. 14.

See the chapter on M in John Baxter, *Science Fiction in the Cinema* (NY, 1970); "The Layout for Bulldog Drummond," *Creative Art* 5 (Oct. 1929); Menzies, "Cinema Design," *Theatre Arts Monthly* (Sept. 1929); notes on the set design of *The Thief of Bagdad* in "Pictorial Beauty in the Photoplay," *Cinematographic Annual* 1 (1930). For *Things to Come* and *The Thief of Bagdad* see Brosnan, *Movie Magic*, and Chris Steinbrunner & Burt Goldblatt, *Cinema of the Fantastic* (NY, 1972). *Motion Picture* 33 (Apr. 1927), pp. 20–21, contains 6 superb sketches by M for *The Beloved Rogue* in a style still strongly influenced by Grot.

Metzner, Ernö   1892 Austria-Hungary–1954. Stud. Budapest Fine Arts Academy. From 1920 worked as a set designer in Germany. Career in 1926–33 is notable for superb designs for 7 films dir. by *G. W. Pabst. Dir. several films himself, including the avant-garde *Uberfall*. 1933 left Germany; worked in England for several years, then settled in US.

Salome (22)—also co-dir., *I.N.R.I.* (23), *Fridericus Rex* (23)—in collab. Dreier, *Arabella* (24), *Ein Sommernachtstraum/A Midsummer Night's Dream* (25), *Geheimnisse einer Seele/Secrets of a Soul* (26), *Man Steigt Nach* (27)—also co-scripted, *Uberfall/ Accident* (28)—also dir. and photographed, *Hotelgeheimnisse* (28), *Das Tagebuch einen Verlorenen/The Diary of a Lost Girl* (29), *Die Weisse Hölle von Piz Palü* (29), *Westfront 1918* (30), *Rivalen im Weltrekord* (30)—dir. and co-scripted, *Kameradschaft* (31), *Die Herrin von Atlantis/L'Atlantide* (32), *Du Haut en bas* (33), *Chu Chin Chow* (33), *The Robber Symphony/La Symphonie des Brigands* (36), *It Happened Tomorrow* (44), *The Macomber Affair* (47).

The Pabst–Metzner collab. was extremely fruitful. *Westfront* and *Kameradschaft* are triumphs of design in the service of direction; in *Secrets of a Soul*, the surrealist architectural phantasmagoria of the dream episodes contrast strikingly with the cleanly contemporary 20s interiors. Although he did work in Hollywood in the 40s (where his last important film was Clair's turn-of-the-century fantasy *It Happened Tomorrow*), M's only really notable work after his last film for Pabst was *The Robber Symphony*, one of the great and delightful eccentricities of European cinema in the 30s, shot in England in French and English versions. This musical fable (hardly known in the US) was dir. by Friedrich Feher (M had previously des. *Hotelgeheimnisse* for him), who can also be seen as one of the principal actors in *Caligari*. See *Graham Greene on Film* (NY, 1972), pp. 76–78, for a review of *Robber Symphony*, accompanied by a fine still of one of M's sets. See also Roger Manvell & Heinrich Fraenkel, *The German Cinema* (NY, 1971), pp. 47–48, on *Uberfall*; Metzner, "On the Sets of the Film *Atlantis*," *Close Up* (Sept. 1932), much of which is reprinted in Carrick, *Designing for Motion Pictures*, pp. 77–78; Metzner, "The Travelling Camera," *Close Up* (June 1933).

Milton, Dave   The Cedric Gibbons of Monogram. Astonishingly prolific—des. 16 films for Monogram in 1946, des. 29 films in 1950 (still mostly for that B studio). In the late 50s kept up the pace—more than 20 films a year, many for Allied Artists (Monogram's new moniker after 1953). *Films dir. by Phil Karlson. 'Neath Brooklyn Bridge (42), *The Ape Man* (43), *Voodoo Man* (44), *Live Wires (46), *Dark Alibi (46), *Wife Wanted (46), *The Face of Marble* (46), *Sensation Hunters* (46), *Louisiana (47), *Black Gold (47), *Rocky (48), *Jiggs and Maggie in Society* (48), *The Feathered Serpent* (49), *The Whipped* (50), *Sideshow* (50), *The Steel Fist* (52), *Fangs of the Arctic* (53), *Riot in Cell Block 11* (54), *The Adventures of Hajji Baba* (54)—in collab. prod. designer Gene Allen and color consultant George Hoyninge-Huene, *Wichita* (55), *The Disembodied* (57), *Dino* (57), *The Beast of Budapest* (58), *The Bat* (59), *The Hypnotic Eye* (60), *Hell to Eternity (60), *King of the Roaring 20s* (61).

Mizutani, Hiroshi   Des. several films for one of the great artists of world cinema, *Kenji Mizoguchi. *Zangiku Monogatari/The Story of the Last Chrysanthemums (39), *Genroku Chushingura/The Loyal 47 Ronin of the Genroku Era (41, 42), *Saikaku Ichidai Onna/The Life of O-Haru (52), *Chikamatsu Monogatari/A Story from Chikamatsu/The Crucified Lovers (54), *Yokihi/Yang-Kwei-Fei (55), *Akasen Chitai/Street of Shame (56), Yoru no Tsuzumi/Night Drum (58), Bridge to the Sun (61). The unity of style which pervades the Mizoguchi masterpieces—O-Haru, Chikamatsu—is so impeccable that it is not easy to discern a line separating designer from the dir.—who had been a painter himself and designer of kimonos, and was possessed of an exquisite "painter's eye." From such invisible marriages, great films were once made.

Mogherini, Flavio   b. 1922 Italy. Stud. architecture. Eleonora Duse (48), Guardie e Ladri (51), La Provinciale/The Wayward Wife (53), Dov'è la Libertà (53), Ulisse/Ulysses (54), La Romana/The Woman of Rome (54), Attila (54), Le Fatiche di Ercole/Hercules (57), Giovani Mariti (58), Era Notte a Roma (60), La Ragazza con la Valigia/The Girl with a Suitcase (60), La Viaccia (61), Cronaca Familiare/Family Diary (62), La Freccia d'Oro/The Golden Arrow (62), Mamma Roma (62), Rogopag (63), Diabolik (67), Kemek (70), Anche se Volessi Lavorare, Che Faccio? (72)—also dir. Paolo Barca, dir. by M, was one of the greatest successes of 1975 in Italy. A major talent, whose years of glory were 1960–62 with the breathtaking designs for Bolognini's La Viaccia which seemed inspired by late ottocento painting (Giuseppe de Nittis, Pellizza da Volpedo), and for the 2 Zurlini films, Girl with a Suitcase and above all Family Diary, the most moving Italian film of the 60s, des. and dir. with the simplest and most affecting pointillism, avoiding the crudeness of neorealism and the extravagances of Fellini and Co.

Monteiro, Regis   A Falecida/The Deceased (65), Toda Nudez Será Castigada/All Nudity Shall Be Punished (73). The only design talent of note who seems to have surfaced in Brazil in recent years. Witty, "tropicalist" sets for a bitter sex comedy.

Morahan, Jim   b. 1902 London. *Films dir. by Alexander Mackendrick. Frieda (47), Saraband for Dead Lovers/Saraband (48), *Whisky Galore/Tight Little Island (49), The Blue Lamp (50), *The Man in the White Suit (51), *Mandy/The Crash of Silence (52), His Excellency (52), The Cruel Sea (53), *The Maggie/High and Dry (54), *The Ladykillers (55), Out of the Clouds (55), Dunkirk (58), Satan Never Sleeps (62), The Mind Benders (63), Witchfinder General/The Conqueror Worm (68).

Morahan, Tom   b. 1906 London. Stud. architecture. *Films dir. by Alfred Hitchcock. St. Martin's Lane/Sidewalks of London (38), *Jamaica Inn (39), Next of Kin (42), The Foreman Went to France (42), Went the Day Well? (42), On Approval (44), Men of 2 Worlds (46), *The Paradine Case (47), So Evil My Love (48), *Under Capricorn (49), Treasure Island (50), Captain Horatio Hornblower (51), Decameron Nights (53), Sons and Lovers (60), Those Magnificent Men in Their Flying Machines (65).

Muraki, Yoshiro   Since 1955 has des. most of the films dir. by *Akira Kurosawa. *Ikimono no Kiroku/Record of a Living Being/I Live in Fear (55), *Kumonosu-jo/The Throne of Blood (57), *Donzoko/The Lower Depths (57), *Kakushi Toride no San-Akunin/The Hidden Fortress (58), *Warui Yatsu Hodo Yoku Nemuru/The Bad Sleep Well (60), *Yojimbo (61), *Tsubaki Sanjuro/Sanjuro (62), *Tengoku to Jigoku/High and Low (63), *Akahige/Red Beard (65), Joi-Uchi/Rebellion (67), *Dodeska-den (70), Kaigun Tokubetsu Nenshohei/The Heroes of Iwo Jima (72), Nippon Shinbotsu/Tidal Wave (75).

Though not completely successful, Dodeska-den, with its comic-strip style and junkyard pop art effects, was a remarkable new direction for both dir. and designer. The sets for Kumonosu-jo (Kurosawa's version of Macbeth) remain M's most striking achievement to date. "What [Kurosawa] did do, once he knew he was to direct the picture, was to begin a study of the traditional Japanese musha-e—those early picture scrolls of battle scenes. At the same time he asked Kohei Esaki—famous for continuing this genre—to be the art consultant. The designer, Yoshiro Muraki, remembers: 'We studied old castle layouts, the really old ones, not those white castles we still have around. And we decided to use black and armored walls since they would go well with the suiboku-ga (ink-painting) effect we planned with lots of mist and fog. That also is the reason we decided that the locations would be high on Mount Fuji, because of the fog and the black volcanic soil. But . . . we created something which never came from any single historical period. To emphasize the psychology of the hero, driven by compulsion, we made the interiors wide with low ceilings and squat pillars to create the effect of oppression.' Kurosawa remembers that 'first, we built an open set at the base of Fuji with a flat castle rather than a real 3-dimensional one. When it was ready, it just didn't look right. For one thing, the roof tiles were too thin and this would not do. I insisted and held out, saying I could not possibly work with such limitations, that I wanted to get the feeling of the real thing from wherever I choose to shoot.' Consequently . . . the entire open set was dismantled. 'About sets,' Kurosawa has admitted: 'I'm on the severe side. This is from *Ikiru* onward. Until then we had to make do with false-fronts. We didn't have the material. But you cannot expect to get a feeling of realism if you use, for example, cheap new wood in a set which is supposed to be an old farm-house. I feel very strongly about this. After all, the real life of any film lies just in its being as true as possible to appearances.' After a further argument with Ezaki, who wanted a high and towering castle while Kurosawa wanted a low and squat one, the set eventually used was built—to Kurosawa's specifications (which were extreme: even the lacquer-ware had to be especially made, from models which he found in museums). 'It was a very hard film to make. I decided that the main castle set had to be built high up on Fuji and we didn't have enough people and the location was miles from Tokyo. Fortunately there was a U.S. Marine Corps base nearby and they helped a lot. We all worked very hard, clearing the ground, building the set, and doing the whole thing on this steep, fog-bound slope. An entire MP battalion helped most of the time. I remember it absolutely exhausted all of us—we almost got sick.' Actually, only the castle exteriors were shot here. The castle courtyard (with volcanic soil brought all the way from Fuji so that the ground would match) was constructed at Toho's Tamagawa studios in the suburbs, and the interiors were shot in a smaller Tokyo studio. In addition, the forest scenes were a combination of actual Fuji forest and studio in Tokyo, and Washizu's mansion was miles away from anywhere, in the Izu peninsula."—Donald Richie, *The Films of Akira Kurosawa* (Berkeley, 1965), pp. 12–23.

Murton, Peter *Billy Budd* (62), *The Ipcress File* (65), *Thunderball* (65), *Funeral in Berlin* (66), *Half a Sixpence* (67), *The Lion in the Winter* (68), *The Ruling Class* (72), *The Possession of Joel Delaney* (72), *The Man with the Golden Gun* (74), *The Black Windmill* (74), *Man Friday* (75). Best work to date: the stunning Edwardian sets for George Sidney's exuberant musical, *Half a Sixpence*.

Nishioka, Yoshinobu *Enjo/Conflagration* (58), *Bonchi* (60), *Hakai/The Sin* (61), *Yukinojo Henge/An Actor's Revenge/The Revenge of Yukinojo* (63), *Kaidan Botan Doro/A Tale of Peonies and Stone Lanterns* (68), *The Wanderers* (72). All except *Kaidan* dir. by Kon Ichikawa. *Yukinojo* alone would suffice to assure N a place among the Japanese cinema's greatest designers. It made the same sort of visual breakthrough as, several years earlier, *Lola Montès* had in Europe. Both proved that, on occasion, dir. and designer could overcome the ungainly proportions of the wide screen. The restrained use of the Kabuki stage in *Yukinojo*, and the stunning nocturnal exteriors blocked out by Ichikawa and N are akin to the means Ophüls used to resolve the problem in *Lola*—taming Scope, muting sections of the screen at times, reserving total width for privileged moments.

Novi, Charles Stud. architecture Italy. WB unit a.d.; worked with Grot for many years. *Crime School* (38), *King of the Underworld* (39), *Singapore Woman* (41), *Underground* (41), *The Mysterious Doctor* (43), *Shine On, Harvest Moon* (44), *The Desert Song* (44), *To Have and Have Not* (44).

Obzina, Martin Specialized in melodrama and horror films at Universal late 30s–mid 40s; left Universal 1947 to work for other studios. Early 60s des. several TV films dir. by John Ford, then worked for *Alfred Hitchcock Presents*. *First Love* (39), *The Invisible Man Returns* (40), *The Flame of New Orleans* (41), *Son of Dracula* (43), *Dead Man's Eyes* (44), *Sherlock Holmes and the Spider Woman* (44), *House of Frankenstein* (44), *The Suspect* (45), *House of Dracula* (45), *The Killers* (46), *Black Angel* (46), *Heaven Only Knows* (47), *Jungle Goddess* (48), *The Green Promise* (49), *M* (51), *Lady in the Iron Mask* (52).

Odell, Cary Mid-40s until 1962 at Columbia, later at other studios. *My Sister Eileen* (42), *Cover Girl* (44), *Johnny O'Clock* (47), *To the Ends of the Earth* (48), *The Dark Past* (48), *The Loves of Carmen* (48), *We Were Strangers* (49), *The Reckless Moment* (49), *No Sad Songs for Me* (50), *The Member of the Wedding* (52), *From Here to Eternity* (53), *Storm Center* (56), *20 Million Miles to Earth* (57), *Bell, Book and Candle* (58), *They Came to Cordura* (59), *Homicidal* (61), *Mr. Sardonicus* (61), *The Notorious Landlady* (62), *Kid Galahad* (62), *7 Days in May* (64), *The Patsy* (64), *Hawaii* (66), *Cool Hand Luke* (67), *The Gypsy Moths* (69), *Mr. Majestyk* (74).

Odell, Robert A. b. 1896 Los Angeles. Stud. architecture. Entered films 1919, worked for Lew Cody Prods., Jack Pickford, Astra Studio. Later work mostly at Paramount. *Tom Sawyer* (30), *King of the Jungle* (33), *The Eagle and the Hawk* (33), *Torch Singer* (33), *3-Cornered Moon* (33), *Alice in Wonderland* (33), *Ruggles of Red Gap* (35), *Beau Geste* (39).

Okey, Jack US. A formidable career: 20s and 30s at First Nat.–WB; with RKO in 40s and 50s. Exuberant, outlandish sets for Busby Berkeley musicals. Several of the early First Nat. films were dir. by *Maurice Tourneur who had worked with Rodin and was blessed with a unique visual flair. Two decades later at RKO, O was des. impressive films dir. by his son, †Jacques Tourneur. *Torment* (24), *The White Moth* (24), *Old Loves and New* (26), *Sally* (29), *Showgirl in Hollywood* (30), *The Dawn Patrol* (30), *5 Star Final* (31), *The Last Flight* (31), *I Am a Fugitive from a Chain Gang* (32), *Tiger Shark* (32), *The Crowd Roars* (32), *Private Detective 62* (33), *Female* (33), *The Kennel Murder Case* (33), *42nd Street* (33), *Footlight Parade* (33)—in collab. Grot, *Central Airport* (33), *Lilly Turner* (33), *The Merry Frinks* (34), *Fashions of 1934* (34), *Flirtation Walk* (34), *Wonder Bar* (34), *Bordertown* (35), *Johnny Come Lately* (43), †*Experiment Perilous* (44), *The Spiral Staircase* (46), *Deadline at Dawn* (46), *Crack-Up* (46), †*Out of the Past* (47), *Rachel and the Stranger* (48), *The Set-Up* (49), *Born to Be Bad* (50), *The Racket* (51), *Blackbeard the Pirate* (52), *Devil's Canyon* (53), *A Bullet for Joey* (55), *Bengazi* (55), *Screaming Eagles* (56), *Run of the Arrow* (57), *The Missouri Traveler* (58), *The Young Land* (59). In Sept. 1934 O was brought to London by A. Korda. O chose the site for and then des. Korda's vast Denham studio. Construction began in June 1935 and lasted nearly a year. Later O worked with the Kordas on 2 of their US prods.: *Lydia* (41) and *The Jungle Book* (42), both in collab. V. Korda.

Oliver, Harry 1888 Minnesota–1973 California. Worked at Universal 1910–14, Roach 1914–16, early 20s for Mary and Jack Pickford. Greatest period of his career was late 20s at Fox, where he des. several films dir. by *Frank Borzage. At MGM most of 30s. *Face of the World* (21), *The Hill Billy* (24), *Don Q, Son of Zorro* (25)—as consulting artist, *Little Annie Rooney* (25)—in collab. Schulze, *Sparrows* (26), *7th Heaven* (27), *Street Angel* (28), *The Gaucho* (28), *The River* (28), *Lucky Star* (29), *Sunny Side Up* (29), *They Had to See Paris* (29), *City Girl* (30), *Lightnin'* (30), *Liliom* (30), *Song o' My Heart* (30), *Scarface* (32), *Tillie and Gus* (33), *White Woman* (33), *The Cat's Paw* (34), *Viva Villa!* (34), *Mark of the Vampire* (35), *Vanessa, Her Love Story* (35), *The Good Earth* (37), *Of Human Hearts* (38).

In the 40s, with an exemplary career and several AA nominations behind him, O became bored with the movie business and moved to the Coachvella Valley desert, where he lived most of the time as a hermit, earning a reputation as one of Southern California's most colorful characters. He wanted to die on a July 4, and did. O's work for Borzage was influenced by Murnau, whose style was endemic in most of Hollywood's serious prods. of the late 20s. O des. for Murnau himself (*City Girl*), but even before that, Murnau is to be felt in the distinctly Germanic cold gray expressionistic expanses of *Street Angel*—a murky Naples of the mind which could have been born only in a film studio. O's sets for *Sparrows* were lit by Murnau's cameramen—this film is dir. William Beaudine's masterpiece, the finest Mary Pickford vehicle of the 20s, and one of the most richly atmospheric and expertly des. US films of that decade.

Osua, Osmo Finnish. *Valkoisen Peuran/The White Reindeer* (52).

Otterson, Jack b. 1881 Pittsburgh. Stud. architecture at Yale. 1929–30 among the architects who des. decoration of Empire State Bldg. Entered films 1932 as a sketch artist at Fox. 1936 to Universal, where he remained for rest of film career, and became superv. a.d. after the departure of Charles D. Hall. 1943 John Goodman replaced O as superv. a.d., but O continued to work at Universal until 1946 when he resigned to devote himself to painting. Since then has had several one-man shows. *Carolina* (34), *One More Spring* (35), *The Magnificent Brute* (36), *3 Smart Girls* (37), *You're a Sweetheart* (37), *The Rage of Paris* (38), *Sinners in Paradise* (38), *Son of Frankenstein* (39), *You Can't Cheat an Honest Man* (39), *Tower of London* (39), *7 Sinners* (40), *The Bank Dick* (40), *My Little Chickadee* (40), *The Wolf Man* (41), *It Started with Eve* (41), *Hellzappopin* (42), *The Spoilers* (42), *Arabian Nights* (42), *The Mad Doctor of Market Street* (42), *The Killers* (46), *Song of Scheherezade* (47).

Ozaki, Chiyo *Kurutta Ippeiji/A Page of Madness* (26). Superb sets for the most unusual Japanese silent film to have come down to us. Quite Caligaresque, in spite of the fact that O and dir. Kinugasa had not seen *Caligari*.

231

Parker, Max In the 20s with De Mille Prods., then worked mostly for Fox until 1935; thereafter with WB. *The Road to Yesterday* (25), *Eve's Leaves* (26), *The Volga Boatman* (26), *Turkish Delight* (27), *The Hawk's Nest* (28), *The Yellow Lily* (28), *Gold Diggers of Broadway* (29), *Public Enemy* (31), *The Warrior's Husband* (33), *The Power and the Glory* (33), *The Worst Woman in Paris* (33), *Grand Canary* (34), *I am Suzanne* (34), *Satan Met a Lady* (36), *Marked Woman* (37), *Sh! The Octopus* (37), *Green Light* (37), *A Slight Case of Murder* (38), *Men Are Such Fools* (38), *Each Dawn I Die* (39), *The Roaring 20s* (39), *Devil's Island* (40), *Invisible Stripes* (40), *It All Came True* (40), *Brother Orchid* (40), *Manpower* (41), *The Hard Way* (43), *Princess O'Rourke* (43), *Cloak and Dagger* (46), *Deep Valley* (47), *The Secret Beyond the Door* (48). See Parker, "The Art Director," in *Opportunities in the Motion Picture Industry* (Los Angeles, 1922), bk. 3, pp. 55–63.

Parrondo, Gil *The 7th Voyage of Sinbad* (58), *The 3 Worlds of Gulliver* (60), *Hamelin* (67), *Dr. Coppelius* (67), *The Valley of Gwangi* (69), *The Battle of Britain* (69), *Patton* (70), *Nicholas and Alexandra* (71), *The Wind and the Lion* (75), *The Girl from Red Cabaret* (75).

Pereira, Hal 1933–40 des. for the theater. Entered films as unit a.d. at Paramount (1942–46), often working with Dreier. When Dreier retired, P succeeded him in April 1950 as superv. a.d. of all Paramount films. Worked in collab. Albert Nozaki (AN), Roland Anderson (RA), Walter Tyler (WT), Franz Bachelin (FB), Joseph McMillan Johnson (JJ), Henry Bumstead (HB), Tambi Larsen (TL). *Double Indemnity* (44), *Ministry of Fear* (44), *And Now Tomorrow* (44), *Blue Skies* (46), *The Goldbergs/Molly* (50), *When Worlds Collide* (51, AN), *Carrie* (52, RA), *The Greatest Show on Earth* (52, WT), *Shane* (53, WT), *The Naked Jungle* (54, FB), *Rear Window* (54, JJ), *The Rose Tattoo* (55), *To Catch a Thief* (55, JJ), *The 10 Commandments* (56, WT, AN), *Vertigo* (58, HB), *Ladies' Man* (61), *Love with the Proper Stranger* (63), *The Nutty Professor* (63, WT), *Hud* (63, TL), *The Odd Couple* (68). The superb period décor of Wyler's *Carrie* was the Paramount art dept.'s finest accomplishment of the 50s.

Peters, Hans Mid- to late 30s at 20th–Fox. 1943 invited by Gibbons to work for MGM, where he remained 20 years. *Dressed to Thrill* (35), *The Road to Glory* (36), *Heidi* (37), *Rebecca of Sunnybrook Farm* (38), *Submarine Patrol* (38), *The Little Princess* (39), *The Hound of the Baskervilles* (39), *Tarzan's Desert Mystery* (43), *Music for Millions* (44), *The Picture of Dorian Gray* (45), *The Green Years* (46), *Easy to Wed* (46), *Song of Love* (47), *If Winter Comes* (47), *Act of Violence* (48), *The Great Sinner* (49), *Battleground* (49), *The Red Danube* (49), *Kim* (50), *The Red Badge of Courage* (51), *Scaramouche* (52), *The Prisoner of Zenda* (52), *Small Town Girl* (53), *Diane* (55), *Moonfleet* (55), *High Society* (56), *Lust for Life* (56), *Tip on a Dead Jockey* (57), *Man on Fire* (57), *High School Confidential* (58), *The Miracle* (59), *Girls Town* (59), *Bachelor in Paradise* (61), *Boys' Night Out* (62), *The Hook* (63). One of the industry's most tasteful craftsmen. Somewhat specialized in period spectacles, but equally at home with *Small Town Girl*, a neat, modern, low-budget musical. His most memorable work was for *Dorian Gray*, with its impeccably clean-limned *fin-de-siècle* interiors and superbly malevolent exteriors for the Blue Gates Fields sequence.

Peterson, Robert Late 40s several films at 20th, then worked almost exclusively for Columbia. Many westerns and films noirs. P has des. for an impressive number of top dirs.—Boetticher, Fuller, Lang, Siegel, Ford, Edwards, Ray. *Arizona* (40)—in collab. Lionel Banks, *The Devil's Mask* (46), *Backlash* (47), *The Wreck of the Hesperus* (48), *Leather Gloves* (48), *Ladies of the Chorus* (48), *Knock on Any Door* (49), *In a Lonely Place* (50), *Scandal Sheet* (52), *The Big Heat* (53), *Human Desire* (54), *5 Against the House* (55), *The Long Gray Line* (55), *The Last Frontier* (55), *Hot Blood* (56), *The Garment Jungle* (57), *Decision at Sundown* (57), *The Last Hurrah* (58), *Edge of Eternity* (59), *Ride Lonesome* (59), *2 Rode Together* (61), *Underworld USA* (61), *Zotz!* (62), *Experiment in Terror* (62), *The Outlaws Is Coming!* (65).

Poelzig, Hans 1869 Berlin–1936 Berlin. Before WWI, an industrial architect (e.g. chemical factory, Posen, Poland). Taught architecture, Berlin. Remodeled Grosses Schauspielhaus theater, Berlin, for Max Reinhardt (1919). Des. administrative buildings I. G. Farben works, Frankfurt (1930). *Der Golem: Wie Er in die Welt Kam* (20), *Lebende Buddhas* (24), *Zur Chronik von Grieshuus* (25).

"One cannot lose interest in a work so strangely engrossing and with such power as *The Golem* has in many of its scenes. This power is derived mainly from a combination of exceptional acting and the most expressive settings yet seen in this country. Resembling somewhat the curious constructions of *The Cabinet of Dr. Caligari*, the settings may be called expressionistic, but to the common man they are best described as expressive, for it is their eloquence that characterises them. They give impressions of distance, of compactness, of massiveness, of old-world unearthiness that could not be conveyed in any other way. They are as active a part of the story as any of its characters, and afford another striking illustration of how much constructed scenery, furniture, buildings and the like may mean in a photodramatic composition. It is not because they are weird, but because they vivify the action of the story that they are cinematographic works of art."—Unsigned review of *The Golem, New York Times,* June 20, 1921 (*Caligari* had been released in NY 3 months earlier). For discussion and illustrations of P's *Golem* sets see Eisner, *Haunted Screen,* pp. 56–62, 64–68. See John R. Clark, "Expressionism in Film and Architecture," *Art Journal* 34 (Winter 1974–75), p. 115.

Pogany, William Andrew (Willy)   1882 Austria-Hungary—1955. Stud. Univ. of Budapest, art school in Budapest: then to Munich, Paris, US. Member Architectural League NY. Much work des. opera sets in Europe; also costume designer, mural painter, sculptor, architectural designer (swimming pool of St. George Hotel, Brooklyn, and the People's Home for the Niagara Falls Power Co.), portrait painter, book illustrator (over 150 titles). *The Devil Dancer* (27), *Palmy Days* (31), *Tonight or Never* (31), *Unholy Garden* (31), *The Mummy* (32), *Dames* (34), *Wonder Bar* (34)—in collab. Okey, *Fashions of 1934* (34), *Dante's Inferno* (35).

Poletto, Piero   *L'Avventura* (60), *Teseo contro il Minotauro/The Minotaur* (61), *L'Eclisse/The Eclipse* (62), *Il Deserto Rosso/The Red Desert* (64), *La Decima Vittima/The 10th Victim* (65), *Le Streghe/The Witches* (66)—in collab. Garbuglia, *Questi Fantasmi/Ghosts, Italian Style* (67), *C'Era una Volta/More Than a Miracle* (67), *Gli Amanti/A Place for Lovers* (68), *The Technique and the Rite* (71), *The Black Belly of the Tarantula* (71), *The Passenger* (75). P's work for *Antonioni has never been less than remarkable; but a case could be made for him as the top Italian designer of his generation on the basis of one quite dissimilar production—the sets for Francesco Rosi's medieval fairy tale, *C'Era una Volta,* are the most ravishing of any Italian film of the 60s.

Polglase, Van Nest   1898 Brooklyn–1968. Stud. architecture, Beaux Arts, NY. Practicing architect with Berg and Orchard, NY. A year in Cuba working on designs for Presidential Palace, Havana. Entered films 1919 a.d. Famous Players–Lasky. 1927–32 des. for Paramount, MGM. 1932 hired by Selznick as superv. a.d. all RKO films, position he retained until 1942 when his alcoholism led to friction with studio heads. After 1943 des. for several studios and worked on 8 Allan Dwan films (P had des. for Dwan at Paramount in 20s; the dir. never lost faith in him). All but one of the late Dwan films were independently prod. and rel. by RKO. *Films dir. by Dwan. †Films for which the assoc. a.d. was Carroll Clark.
   A Kiss in the Dark (25), *Lovers in Quarantine* (25), *Stage Struck* (25), *Untamed* (29), *Little Women* (33), †*Flying Down to Rio* (33), *The Lost Patrol* (34)—in collab. Sidney Ullman, †*The Gay Divorcee* (34), †*Roberta* (35), *The Informer* (35)—in collab. Charles Kirk, *The Last Days of Pompeii* (35), †*Top Hat* (35), †*Follow the Fleet* (36), †*Mary of Scotland* (36), *Mummy's Boys* (36), *The Plough and the Stars* (36), †*Swing Time* (36), †*Shall We Dance* (37), *Stage Door* (37), †*Carefree* (38), *Love Affair* (39), *The Hunchback of Notre Dame* (39), *The Story of Vernon and Irene Castle* (39)—in collab. Ferguson, *Gunga Din* (39), *Abe Lincoln in Illinois* (40), *Dance, Girl, Dance* (40), *Citizen Kane* (41)—in collab. Ferguson, *All That Money Can Buy* (41), †*Suspicion* (41), *A Song to Remember* (45), *Gilda* (46)—in collab. Goosson, *The Crooked Way* (49), *The Fireball* (50), *The Man Who Cheated Himself* (50), *Johnny One-Eye* (50), *Silver Lode* (54), *Passion* (54), *Cattle Queen of Montana* (54), *Escape to Burma* (55), *Pearl of the South Pacific* (55), *Tennessee's Partner* (55), *Slightly Scarlet* (56), *The River's Edge* (57).
   The degree of P's personal involvement in the design of the RKO prods. credited to him (1932–42) is disputed, and varies depending on the source consulted. What is indisputable is that P was one of the great superv. a.ds. in the US film industry. During his RKO period the art dept. there was second to none in stylishness, tasteful flights of fancy, and an enjoyably identifiable studio imprint; one would be less hasty to make such a generalization about 20th under Wheeler or Universal under Golitzen. The Astaire–Rogers films are known and admired the world over—not only for the song-and-dance routines, but also for the way they look. But *Mary of Scotland, Hunchback, Abe Lincoln,* and *All That Money Can Buy* are equally magnificent achievements in their overall sweep of atmospheric design, reinforced by excellence of detail. "Cameramen . . . exploited maximum contrasts in black and white photography to produce a rich visual mood for musical sequences. RKO went farther in this direction than any of the other studios. There, scenic designers Van Nest Polglase and Carroll Clark introduced the fixed architectural institution that soon became known as the

B.W.S. (Big White Set). It appears in one form or another in nearly every Astaire–Rogers film: as the Carioca Casino, as the Brighton Beach esplanade in *The Gay Divorcee*, as Roberta's salon, and as Venice in *Top Hat*."—Arlene Croce, *The Fred Astaire and Ginger Rogers Book* (NY, 1972), p. 25. "Polglase did not personally design the sets in this [*Top Hat*] or any other RKO picture. His name on the films is an inclusive term standing for the RKO art department. It has also come to stand for the style in décor that was this department's specialty in the Astaire–Rogers musicals. . . . As head of his department at RKO, Polglase read scripts, estimated budgets and handed out assignments. He undoubtedly collaborated in an advisory capacity on designs, but the actual designing was done by draftsmen under the supervision of a unit art director. On all but one of the Astaire–Rogers films the unit art director was Carroll Clark. . . . We probably should use Clark's name instead of Polglase's when we speak of the décor in these movies (the name Polglase just seems to call it all up), although no single person appears to have been responsible for it."—Ibid., p. 77.

The above is somewhat at variance with Baxter, *Hollywood in the Thirties* (pp. 188–89): "Set design was a field in which Hollywood produced more than its fair share of geniuses. . . . Among the most imaginative of these was RKO's major designer during the 30s, Van Nest Polglase. Mainly responsible for the glossy décor of the Fred Astaire–Ginger Rogers musicals, he perfected the huge brightly lit night club sets which, in one form or another, appeared in every musical for the next twenty years. His black glass floors and looping chromium-plated banisters set a style perfectly appropriate to Astaire's fashion-plate elegance, the two elements reaching complete harmony in George Stevens's *Swing Time*, that most perfect evocation of the New York never-never-land where all Hollywood musical stars live. Polglase, however, did not restrict himself to modern décor. His period work is faultless, particularly that recalling the middle ages. Dieterle's *The Hunchback of Notre Dame* has some of the most realistic re-creations ever engineered for an American film, with crooked rooftops and leaning shop-fronts the design of which is impeccably judged, though equally dramatic are the sets for John Ford's *Mary of Scotland*, where the décor of Mary's Scottish castle reflects perfectly the complexities of her position. His towering judges' dais in the trial scene, the painted panels of the ceilings which loom over Mary, the tortuous castle corridors with their shadowy doorways are all elements bearing directly on the nature of the film. Less comfortable in the design of conventional sets, Polglase's cobbled run-down Dublin in *The Informer* is probably his best effort at contemporary construction, but as a designer for grand occasions he has no equal."

"Darrell Silvera, Polglase's chief set decorator on at least 5 of the Astaire–Rogers pictures, at times had as many as 110 set decorators, including furniture men, carpet men . . . working under him. Silvera recalled in a recent interview how Polglase had 5 unit art directors (including Carroll Clark, with whom he created the Art Deco style of the Astaire–Rogers series) among whom he divided his duties. John Mansbridge, one of the few of these unit directors still living, told me that in fact each of the lavish sets required its own art director, who answered only to Polglase. Polglase himself, according to both Silvera and Mansbridge, got the first and last words, but seldom stayed around in between. Thus, it does not seem unfair that the name Van Nest Polglase has come to symbolize the décor of the Astaire–Rogers films. . . . Polglase had a fondness for thin double parallel lines, a motif he borrowed from streamlined vehicles and which he applied to whole rooms, with the lines running from the door to the walls to the couches to the lampshades to Ginger Rogers' dress. This sort of total, smooth environment—used especially for private dancing clubs, salons, and dressing rooms—gave a feeling of stark elegance. . . . What interested Polglase was the relationship between curved and flat surfaces . . . and the opposition of the circle and the angle. These two shapes suggest the springs and spokes of a machine, or, more abstractly, the contrast between movement and stillness, which is the source of tension in the films. Round tables meet long vertical wall panels, curving double staircases have sharp-cornered steps, sinuous mouldings end in angular corners, and straight lines, whether on walls, dresses, or furniture, clash with unexpected semicircles. It is a motif, like black-and-whiteness and streamlining, which infuses Polglase's work, or at least work he supervised."—Ellen Spiegel, "Fred and Ginger Meet Van Nest Polglase," *The Velvet Light Trap*, no. 10 (Fall 1973).*

* This article prompted the following letter to the editor from Maurice Zuberano: "Your RKO issue was especially interesting to me because I was there. I came to work in the art dept. in 1935, and stayed for 16 years. I had been with Norman Bel Geddes in NY right after school and jumped right into the Rogers/Astaire pictures. . . . As knowledgeable as your piece was I could see that you did not quite know where to place the credit (or blame) for those sets. Allan Abbott was their chief designer then. He would make a sketch of the

From an interview with Dwan: " 'You kept the same crew on all those pictures, Van Nest Polglase as art director, John Alton as cameraman.'—'Van Polglase was head of that department at RKO and he'd had a misfortune. Started to hit the bottle pretty hard and by the time he got off it, people had lost confidence in him. But I'd known him to be a very fine art director and a practical one, which is the kind I like. A lot of them are very arty and cost you too much money. This was a great guy to take one set and transform it into another one for you with very little money. So I approved of him highly when he was proposed. RKO wouldn't employ him but we would.' "—Peter Bogdanovich, *Allan Dwan, The Last Pioneer* (NY, 1971), pp. 155–56. See also A. B. Laing, "Designing Motion Picture Sets," *Architectural Record* (July 1933).

Proud, Peter   In his most noteworthy reincarnation turned up as an English a.d. who worked for *Hitchcock on 3 occasions. *Murder (30)—in collab. J. F. Mead, *Waltzes from Vienna (33)—in collab. Junge, *The Man Who Knew Too Much (34)—in collab. Junge, *Green for Danger* (46), *The Woman in the Hall* (47), *The League of Gentlemen* (60), *Candidate for Murder* (62), *Fanatic/Die! Die! My Darling!* (65).

Rakhals, Vasili   1890 Russia–1942. *Films dir. by Eisenstein. *Luch Smerti/The Death Ray* (25)—in collab. Pudovkin, *Stachka/Strike (25), *Bronenosets Potyomkin/Battleship Potemkin (25), *Predatel/Traitor* (26), *Tretya Meshchanskaya/Bed and Sofa* (27)—in collab. Yutkevich, *Staroye i Novoye/The Old and the New* (29).

Rambova, Natacha   Née Winifred Shaunessy, 1897 Salt Lake City–1966 California. Taken to Europe by her stepfather Richard Hudnut, the millionaire perfumer. Stud. dance, returned US with Ted Kosloff's Imperial Ballet Co. Went to Hollywood to design *Camille*, starring her friend Nazimova, married the film's leading man, Rudolph Valentino. *Camille* (21), *Salome* (22)—also costumes, *Monsieur Beaucaire* (24).

Known as the "Ice Maiden," R was probably the most disliked woman in Hollywood in the 20s. She dir. her husband's career; no decision could be made without her approval. Finally, no studio would employ him, despite his popularity, without an agreement that R be barred from the set. This talented designer (atypical deco sets for *Camille*, Beardsley-like trappings for *Salome*) worked on only 3 films in that capacity. She played the leading role in *When Love Grows Cold* (25) and wrote the script of *What Price Beauty* (28).

William K. Everson, notes for a showing of *Camille* at the New School, NY: "The major contribution is made by the much-maligned Natacha Rambova, whose bizarre sets are eye-popping and dramatic. Sets and props are full of obligatory German symmetry, a fireplace that looks like a Christmas pudding and a bedroom window like a goldfish bowl." See "Life with Natacha" in Jack Scagnetti, *The Intimate Life of Rudolph Valentino* (Middle Village, NY, 1975); here R is seen in a more favorable light than anywhere else. In Melville Shavelson's egregiously fictional (and highly entertaining) *The Legend of Valentino* (TV, 1975), R, portrayed by Yvette Mimieux, appears as a monster of egotism and ambition. Shavelson's film did attempt a faithful reconstruction of several of R's singular sets for *Camille*.

Ransford, Maurice   b. 1896 Indiana. Stud. Univ. Illinois. Architect 1920–30. Unit a.d. 20th–Fox; retired 1961. *The Pied Piper* (42), *The Moon Is Down* (43), *Lifeboat* (44), *Hangover Square* (45), *Leave Her to Heaven* (45), *Somewhere in the Night* (46), *The Foxes of Harrow* (47), *Road House* (48), *The 13th Letter* (51), *Niagara* (53), *Titanic* (53), *King of the Khyber Rifles* (53), *Black Widow* (54), *The Bottom of the Bottle* (56), *Love Me Tender* (56), *Desk Set* (57), *From the Terrace* (60), *Snow White and the 3 Stooges* (61). The eerie Edwardian London created for John Brahm's *Hangover Square* was one of the rare major accomplishments of 20th's art dept. in the 40s.

---

set in charcoal pencil and invariably Carroll Clark, the unit art director, would then take it into the draughting room and they would make working drawings of the set. The design originated with Abbott every time and of course the art director and the unit art director would approve the design. I originally did stage sets and murals and anything of a "strange" nature such as dreams, hallucinations, and fantasy. My offbeat approach continued until they made *Citizen Kane* and Perry Ferguson and Welles said from then on my approach was considered normal. Of course those low setups and way out-size sets were nothing more than the Ufa school of designing."—*Velvet Light Trap*, no. 12 (Spring 1974). Since 1951 Zuberano has worked elsewhere, notably: in England, as prod. designer of *So Well Remembered* (47); with Boris Leven on *The Sand Pebbles* (20th, 66); with Robert Wise; as second unit dir. on Mike Nichols's films; and as prod. illustrator.

Rasch, Kai Danish. *Ditte Menneskebarn/Ditte, Child of Man* (46), *Gertrud* (64), *Once Upon an Island* (65).

Ree, Max b. Copenhagen. Stud. architecture. Worked for Nordisk Films, Copenhagen, during the heroic period of Scandinavian cinema. In Hollywood much work des. costumes for various studios (*The Scarlet Letter, The Wedding March, Queen Kelly, A Midsummer Night's Dream*) and distinguished work at RKO, where he was superv. a.d. for sets and costumes 1929–32. *Rio Rita* (29)—also costumes, *7 Keys to Baldpate* (29), *Tanned Legs* (29), *The Case of Sergeant Grischa* (30), *Dixiana* (30), *Hit the Deck* (30)—also costumes, *Leathernecking* (30), *Beau Ideal* (31)—also costumes, *Cimarron* (31), *Girl Crazy* (32), *Carnegie Hall* (47). See Ree, "Costumes and Sets as Mediums of Expression," *Cinematographic Annual* (1931), pp. 291–300.

Reimann, Walter Expressionist painter, member of *Der Sturm* group. His first work des. for the cinema was on *Caligari* (he had been working for Decla–Bioscop as a scene painter) with his *Sturm* colleagues Warm (the two met while working in an army theater in WWI) and Röhrig. *Das Cabinet des Dr. Caligari* (20), *Die Pest in Florenz* (19), *Algol* (20), *Genuine* (20), *Vanina* (22), *Ein Walzertraum* (25), *Alraune* (28), *Elisabeth und ihr Narr* (33)—also co-scripted, *Hanneles Himmelfahrt* (34), *Das Mädchen Irene* (36).

Relph, Michael b. 1915 England. A.d. and prod. designer at Ealing until 1947. Since then has written several films and prod. many. *They Drive by Night* (38), *They Came to a City* (44), *Champagne Charlie* (44), *Dead of Night* (45), *The Captive Heart* (46), *Nicholas Nickleby* (47).

Remisoff, Nicolai b. 1887 Russia. Stud. Fine Arts Academy, St. Petersburg. Des. for Max Reinhardt in Europe; worked on US films since 1939. *Films dir. by Lewis Milestone. *Of Mice and Men* (39), *Turnabout* (40), *My Life with Caroline* (41), *The Corsican Brothers* (41), *Guest in the House* (44), *Young Widow* (46), *The Strange Woman* (46), *Lured* (47), *No Minor Vices* (48), *The Red Pony* (49), *The Big Night* (51), *The Moon Is Blue* (53), *Apache* (54), *Please Murder Me* (56), *Pork Chop Hill* (59), *Ocean's 11* (60).

Reticker, Hugh WB unit a.d. *Stranded* (35), *The Walking Dead* (36), *Dangerously They Live* (41), *Across the Pacific* (42), *Background to Danger* (43), *Between 2 Worlds* (44), *In Our Time* (44), *The Horn Blows at Midnight* (45), *Nobody Lives Forever* (46), *Of Human Bondage* (46), *Shadow of a Woman* (46), *Humoresque* (46), *April Showers* (48), *Night Unto Night* (49), *This Side of the Law* (50).

Richter, Kurt All films listed except *Der Student von Prag* and *Monna Vanna* were dir. by Lubitsch. *Der Student von Prag* (13), *Schuhpalast Pinkus* (16), *Ich Möchte kein Mann Sein* (18), *Die Augen der Mummie Ma* (18), *Carmen/Gypsy Blood* (18), *Meine Frau, die Schauspielerin* (19), *Madame Dubarry/Passion* (19), *Die Puppe* (19)—also costumes, *Sumurun/One Arabian Night* (20), *Anna Boleyn/Deception* (20), *Das Weib des Pharao/The Loves of Pharaoh* (21)—in collab. Ernst Stern, *Monna Vanna* (22), *Die Flamme/Montmartre* (23).

Riedel, Richard H. US 1907–1960 Italy. Unit a.d. at Universal who worked under superv. a.ds. Herzbrun and Golitzen. Killed in an automobile accident near Rome while scouting set locations for Universal's remake of *Back Street* (61). *Son of Frankenstein* (39)—in collab. Otterson, *The Bank Dick* (40), *The House of the 7 Gables* (40), *Never Give a Sucker an Even Break* (41), *Night Monster* (42), *Flesh and Fantasy* (43), *Ali Baba and the 40 Thieves* (44), *Destiny* (44), *Sudan* (45), *Canyon Passage* (46), *Idea Girl* (46), *The Time of Their Lives* (46), *The Ghost Steps Out* (46), *Pirates of Monterey* (47), *Ivy* (47)—in collab. Menzies, *Larceny* (48), *Family Honeymoon* (48), *Illegal Entry* (49), *Abbott and Costello Meet the Killer, Boris Karloff* (49), *Calamity Jane and Sam Bass* (49), *Francis* (49), *South Sea Sinner* (50), *Comanche Territory* (50), *Saddle Tramp* (50), *Outside the Wall* (50), *No Room for the Groom* (52), *Red Ball Express* (52), *The Lawless Breed* (53), *Drums Across the River* (54), *Saskatchewan* (54), *This Island Earth* (55)—in collab. Golitzen, *I've Lived Before* (56), *The Land Unknown* (57), *Imitation of Life* (59), *Pillow Talk* (59)—in collab. Golitzen, *Portrait in Black* (60), *Hell Bent for Leather* (60). With the death of R at his prime, the US film industry lost one of its most talented and original a.ds. He had des. nearly every genre of film, but his forte was fantasy, horror, and sci-fi. *Son of Frankenstein* is the most extraordinarily des. of all the films ever inspired by that illustrious house; R's sets for *Flesh and Fantasy* and *This Island Earth* are marked by solid workmanship and unexpected, striking detail.

Robinson, Bernard GB. *Crimes at the Dark House* (40), *Reach for the Sky* (56), *The Revenge of Frankenstein* (58), *The Curse of the Werewolf* (61), *Nightmare* (64), *Rasputin—The Mad Monk* (66), *The Devil Rides Out/The Devil's Bride* (68).

Röhrig, Walter b. 1892. First des. for theater in Zurich. A member of the *Der Sturm* group, as were his co-designers on *Caligari*. Many films in collab. with Herlth (4 of them for *Murnau); later, often worked on films dir. by Gustav Ucicky. In the late 30s des. mostly Nazi entertainment and propaganda pictures. *Das Cabinet des Dr. Caligari* (20), *Der Müde Tod/Destiny* (21), *Satansketter* (21), *Der Schatz* (23), **Der Letzte Mann/The Last Laugh* (24), *Zur Chronik von Grieshuus* (25), **Tartuffe* (25), **Faust* (26), *Luther* (27)—in collab. Herlth, **4 Devils* (28), *Das Flötenkonzert von Sanssouci* (30), *Der Kongress Tanzt/Congress Dances* (31), *Morgenrot/Dawn* (33), *Walzerkrieg* (33), *Das Mädchen Johanna* (35), *Amphitryon* (35), *Hans im Glück* (36)—also script and co-dir. with Herlth, *Patrioten* (37), *Unternehme Michael* (37), *Heimkehr* (41), *Rembrandt* (42), *G.P.U.* (42). *Der Schatz* is not one of Pabst's great films, but the Herlth–Röhrig sets are most impressive: squat, heavy, oppressive interiors, locales where the young lovers are constrained by the greedy family, in contrast to the dazzling *Jugendstil* storybook vineyard outside wherein they are free to court. See Hull, *Film in the Third Reich*, pp. 220–21, for R's work on *Rembrandt*.

Rosse, Herman 1887 Holland–1965 Nyack, NY. Stud. Kensington School of Art, London. Arrived US 1908, stud. architecture at Stanford. Taught design at Univ. California and for a period was dir. of the design dept. of Art Institute, Chicago. In 20s and 30s des. for Broadway stage. Last theater work *Ulysses in Nighttown* (58). At his death was editor and art editor of *Chapter One*, periodical of the American National Theater and Academy. *King of Jazz* (30), *Frankenstein* (31)—uncredited, *Murders in the Rue Morgue* (32), *The Emperor Jones* (33). See "Cinema Design," *Theatre Arts Monthly* (June 1932), which includes sketches by R for the above films.

Saulnier, Jacques b. 1928 Paris. Stud. architecture at Beaux Arts, then went to IDHEC. First film work 1948, asst. to Douy and Trauner; later des. several films in collab. Evein. Saulnier is probably the a.d. most assoc. with French New Wave dirs. *Films dir. by Alain Resnais. A Double Tour/Leda* (59), **L'Année dernière à Marienbad* (61), *Landru/Bluebeard* (62), **Muriel* (63), *Marco Polo/Marco the Magnificent* (64), *Mademoiselle* (65), *What's New, Pussycat?* (65), **La Guerre est finie* (66), *Le Voleur* (67), *La Prisonnière* (68), **Stavisky* (74), *French Connection II* (75).

Scaccianoce, Luigi b. 1914 Venice. Stud. architecture. *Il Ladro di Venezia/The Thief of Venice* (51), *Othello* (52)—in collab. Trauner (dir. Welles), *Senilità* (62), *Mare Matto* (63), *Il Vangelo secondo Matteo/The Gospel According to St. Matthew* (64), *La Donna del Lago* (65), *Uccellacci e Uccellini* (66), *La Strega in Amore/The Witch in Love* (66), *Edipo Re* (67), *Fellini Satyricon* (69)—in collab. Donati, *Una Breve Vacanza/A Brief Vacation* (74). Wonderfully evocative period sets for Bolognini's *Senilità*, based on the Svevo novel, and for Damiani's underrated *La Strega in Amore*.

Schatz, Willi German. *Lola Montès* (55)—in collab. d'Eaubonne, *Der Tiger von Eschnapur* (58), *Das Indische Grabmal* (58). The last 2 features, Fritz Lang's 2-part Indian adventure story, while shown complete on the Continent, were shortened and released in England as *The Tigress of Bengal*. The US distributor whittled down over 3 hours of footage to 90 garbled minutes which were released here as *Journey to the Lost City* in 1960.

Schildknecht, Pierre Sometimes credited as Schilzneck, sometimes as Schild. b. Russia. Des. films in France, later in Spain and Portugal. *Napoléon* (27)—in collab. Alexandre Benois, W. Meinhardt, and Lourié, *Un Chien andalou* (28), *L'Age d'or* (30), *Les Disparus de St.-Agil* (38), *Camoëns* (46).

Schulze, Jack Some films credited John Ducasse Schulze. 1867–1943. Most of 20s at First–Nat., 1929 to Fox for several years. Later worked for independent prod. Edward Small (films distrib. by UA). *Films dir. by Edwin Carewe. *The Invisible Fear* (21), **Mighty Lak' a Rose* (23), **Madonna of the Streets* (24), **A Son of the Sahara* (24), **Joanna* (25), **The Lady Who Lied* (25), *Little Annie Rooney* (25)—in collab. Oliver, **My Son* (25), *Irene* (26), *My Best Girl* (27), *Happy Days* (29), *Born Reckless* (30), *On Your Back* (30), *So This Is London* (30), *The Brat* (31), *The Count of Monte Cristo* (34), *The Last of the Mohicans* (36), *The Man in the Iron Mask* (39), *My Son, My Son!* (40), *The Son of Monte Cristo* (41), *Cheers for Miss Bishop* (41).

Scognamillo, Gabriel 1906 NY–1974. Stud. Royal Academy of Fine Arts, Italy. 1928 returned US to work at Paramount's Astoria studios. Early 30s in France, where he des. 2 films for *Renoir. 1934 to Hollywood; many years as unit a.d. MGM. For TV: Ozzie and Harriet show. *On purge bébé (31), *La Chienne (31), Fanny (32), The Merry Widow (34)—in collab. Gibbons and Frederic Hope, Andy Hardy Meets Debutante (40), For Me and My Gal (42), Thousands Cheer (43), High Barbaree (47), Love Happy (49), Black Hand (50), The Great Caruso (51), The Story of 3 Loves (53)—in collab. Ames, Twist All Night (62), The Balcony (63), The 7 Faces of Dr. Lao (64), Angel, Angel, Down We Go (69).

Scott, Elliot GB. Beyond Mombasa (56), Odongo (56), I Accuse (58), Tom Thumb (58), Gorgo (61), The 4 Horsemen of the Apocalypse (62)—in collab. McCleary, The Haunting (63), The Americanization of Emily (64), Dark of the Sun (68), No Blade of Grass (70), Pope Joan (72), A Doll's House (73), Mr. Quilp (75), Permission to Kill (76), Sarah (76). "The sinister nooks and corners of the distorted rooms [in The Haunting] are a credit to . . . Elliot Scott, in particular the library with its spiral staircase which, with apparent intent, shakes and gradually disintegrates while two of the characters are standing at the top."—Butler, Cinema in Britain, p. 252.

Scotti, Ottavio b. 1904 Italy. Stud. architecture, and at Centro Sperimentale, Rome. Ettore Fieramosca (38), Teresa Venerdi (41), Fedora (42), Black Magic (49), Senso (54), Nella Città l'Inferno (59), L'Assedio di Siracusa (59), Arrivano i Titani (62), La Frusta e il Corpo/Night Is the Phantom (63)—under the pseudonym Dick Grey. Specialist in costumers. His tasteful work is best seen in Fieramosca, Blasetti's superb Renaissance adventure film; in Visconti's Senso, in which the lavish ottocento settings are always integrated with the action; and in the rousing Titani "peplum" of Duccio Tessari.

Shampan, Jack b. London. Interior decorator in 30s; entered films as draftsman, Ealing Studios. Much TV work, notably The Prisoner. Circus of Horrors (60), Night of the Eagle/Burn, Witch, Burn (61), Modesty Blaise (66), The Adding Machine (69), Persecution/The Terror of Sheba (74), The Ghoul (75). See St. John Marner, Film Design.

Sheriff, Paul Né Shouvalov, 1903 Russia–1965 London. Stud. architecture, Oxford. Entered cinema 1935 as asst. to Meerson and Andrejew. From 1939 a.d. at Two Cities. The First of the Few/Spitfire (42), The Demi-Paradise (43), Henry V (44)—in collab. Dillon, The Black Rose (50), The Crimson Pirate (52), Moulin Rouge (53)—in collab. Marcel Vertès, Pickup Alley (57), The Doctor's Dilemma (59), Bluebeard's 10 Honeymoons (60). The sets for Henry V and Moulin Rouge are world famous; those for The Crimson Pirate, possibly the most beautifully designed swashbuckler ever made, are, in their own way, fully as good.

Shindo, Kaneto b. 1912 Hiroshima. Son of a farmer, entered films 1934 as a.d.; later scriptwriter and dir. Onibaba (65)—a.d., script, and dir.

Shpinel, Isaac Also Iosif Aronovich Shpinel. b. 1892 Russia. Stud. Art Academy, Kiev. Arsenal (29)—in collab. Vladimir Muller, Pyshka/Boule de suif (34), Alexander Nevsky (38), Semya Oppenheim/The Oppenheim Family (39), Mashenka (42), Ivan the Terrible, part 1 (44), Conspiracy of the Doomed (50), The Great Warrior Skanderbeg (54), Ivan the Terrible, part 2 (finished 46, rel. 58). Best-known work has been for Eisenstein films; his designs for Romm's Boule de suif are equally fine. Many films for Grigori Roshal. See Artists of the Soviet Cinema for sketches by S for Ivan and other films.

Simm, Ray GB. *Films dir. by Bryan Forbes. Abandon Ship! (57), The Rising of the Moon (57), Saint Joan (57), The Angry Silence (60), *Whistle Down the Wind (61), *The L-Shaped Room (62), *Seance on a Wet Afternoon (64), A Hard Day's Night (64), Help! (65), Darling (65), Hennessy (75), The Slipper and the Rose (76).

Smith, Jack Martin 15 years at MGM, where he worked on many of the studio's grandest prods., specializing in musicals prod. by Arthur Freed, often dir. by *Vincente Minnelli. In 1955 to 20th–Fox. The Wizard of Oz (39)—uncredited, *I Dood It (43)—musical numbers des. by Merrill Pye, *Meet Me in St. Louis (44), *Yolanda and the Thief (45), *Ziegfeld Follies (46), *The Pirate (48), Words and Music (48), Easter Parade (48), Summer Holiday (48), On the Town (49), *Madame Bovary (49), Summer Stock (50), Royal Wedding (51), Show Boat (51), *An American in Paris (51)—uncredited, in collab. Irene Sharaff (uncredited) and Ames, The Belle of New York (52), Million Dollar Mermaid (52), I Love Melvin (53), Dangerous When Wet (53), Valley of the Kings (54), Bandido (56), Carousel (56), Bigger Than Life (56), Peyton Place (57), Can-Can (60), Cleopatra (63)—in collab. De Cuir, etc., *Goodbye Charlie (64)—in collab. Day, Planet of the Apes (68)—in collab. William Creber, Justine (69)—in collab. Creber, Butch Cassidy and the Sundance Kid (69)—in collab. Philip Jefferies, Emperor of the North Pole (73), Bug (75), The Reincarnation of Peter Proud (75).

At MGM S participated in the des. of a half-dozen of the most stylish and remarkable musicals ever made. The glorious failure, Yolanda, with designs inspired by Tiepolo and Dali, the rousing Pirate, and Meet Me in St. Louis are classics. The least of his films at MGM were marked by a robust vulgarity. The 20 years later spent at Fox may have been in a more superv. capacity, but work there has been heavier, marked with less flair and originality. See Fordin, The World of Entertainment!, which contains sketches for Oz, Yolanda, and Ziegfeld Follies; Mel Gussow, Don't Say Yes Until I Finish Talking (NY, 1971).

Smith, Oliver   b. 1918 Wisconsin. Stud. architecture Penn. State Univ. Des. for Ballets Russes de Monte Carlo, American Ballet Theater, many Broadway prods. The Band Wagon (53)—in collab. Ames, Oklahoma! (55), Guys and Dolls (55), Porgy and Bess (59). See Fordin, The World of Entertainment!, pp. 397–419, for S's work on Band Wagon.

Smith, Ted   Stud. architecture. WB unit a.d. Many westerns. *Films dir. by Raoul Walsh. Gold Is Where You Find It (38), Dodge City (39), Torrid Zone (40), *High Sierra (41), *Gentleman Jim (42), Captains of the Clouds (42), Action in the North Atlantic (43), The Mask of Dimitrios (44), *San Antonio (45), *Objective Burma (45), 3 Strangers (46), The Verdict (46), Her Kind of Man (46), *Pursued (47), *Cheyenne (47), *Silver River (48), *Fighter Squadron (48), *Colorado Territory (49).

Speer, Albert   b. 1905. German architect and Nazi politician. Triumph des Willens/Triumph of the Will (35). See Leni Riefenstahl, Hinter den Kulissen des Reichparteitag-Films (Munich, 1935).

Spencer, J. Russell   Unit a.d., mostly at 20th–Fox. The Great Dictator (40), Nob Hill (45), Cluny Brown (46), Margie (46), Dragonwyck (46), Nightmare Alley (47), The Late George Apley (47), That Lady in Ermine (48), A Letter to 3 Wives (49), An American Guerrilla in the Philippines (50), Where the Sidewalk Ends (50), Les Misérables (52), Lydia Bailey (52).

Stepanov, Ivan   1887–1953 Moscow. Book illustrator. *The great Gorky trilogy dir. by Marc Donskoi. The Road to Life (31), Nightingale, Little Nightingale (36), *The Childhood of Gorky (38), *V Lyudyakh/My Apprenticeship/Among People (39), *My Universities (41), The Young Guard (48).

Sternad, Rudolph   b. 1905 NY. Stud. architecture Cooper Union. Unit a.d. at 20th in 30s, later at Columbia. 1948–62 prod. designer for films dir. and/or prod. by *Stanley Kramer. In Old Chicago (38)—in collab. Darling, Suez (38), Young People (40), You'll Never Get Rich (41)—in collab. Lionel Banks, The Talk of the Town (42), You Were Never Lovelier (42), The More the Merrier (43), Up in Mabel's Room (44), 1,001 Nights (45), The Bandit of Sherwood Forest (46), Down to Earth (47), Dead Reckoning (47), *Champion (49), *The Men (50), *High Noon (52), *The 5,000 Fingers of Dr. T (53), *Not as a Stranger (55), *The Defiant Ones (58), *On the Beach (59), *Inherit the Wind (60), *Judgment at Nuremberg (61), *Pressure Point (62), *It's a Mad, Mad, Mad, Mad World (63), Lady in a Cage (64).

Suvorov, Nikolai Georgievich   b. 1889. Stud. Saratov Art School. *Films dir. by Friedrich Ermler. Adres Lenin/Lenin's Address (29), Golden Mountains (31), Groza/The Storm (34), *Peasants (35), Baltic Deputy (37), Peter the Great, parts 1 and 2 (37, 39), *The Great Citizen (38), *She Defends Her Country (43), *The Great Turning Point (46), The Soldiers (57). Artists of the Soviet Cinema contains sketches by S for The Storm, Baltic Deputy.

Svidetelyev, Yevgeny Vasilievich   1921–1971 USSR. Stud. State Institute of Cinema. Sadko (53), Ilya Murometz/The Sword and the Dragon (56), The Cranes Are Flying (57). Wildly imaginative sets for Ilya Murometz, one of the rare great Soviet fantasy adventure films. For designs for Cranes see Artists of the Soviet Cinema.

Sylos, Frank Paul   b. 1900 Brooklyn. Stud. at Yale. Mural painter, des. covers for Liberty magazine. Entered films 1935. Bank Alarm (37), The Moon and Sixpence (42), Corregidor (43), When Strangers Marry (44), Machine Gun Mama (44), Dillinger (45), The Great Flamarion (45), The Enchanted Forest (45), Jealousy (45), Suspense (46), A Scandal in Paris (46), Return of Rin Tin Tin (47), Private Affairs of Bel Ami (47), Ruthless (48), Caught (49), Baron of Arizona (50), Bride of the Gorilla (51), 99 River Street (53), The Steel

Lady (53), *The Mad Magician* (54), *Men in War* (57). Although he has worked for several studios, and at times for name dirs. on quality prods., S will be best remembered for his heroic toil on Poverty Row pictures churned out in the 40s at PRC, Monogram, Republic. His contribution to *When Strangers Marry*, *The Great Flamarion*, *Enchanted Forest*, etc.—interesting credible sets, albeit with cut corners—supplied a good deal of the atmosphere which made these "quickies" works of considerable artistic merit. S died in 1976 in Hollywood.

Tavoularis, Dean   b. 1932 Lowell, Mass. Stud. architecture Otis Art Institute. Worked at Disney Studios in the animation dept., later moved to live production; then at Columbia and Warners as an asst. a.d. *Films for which T was prod. designer and Angelo Graham was a.d. †Films dir. by Francis Ford Coppola. Asst. a.d.: *Ship of Fools* (65), *Inside Daisy Clover* (66). A.d.: *Bonnie and Clyde* (67), *Candy* (68). Prod. designer: *Zabriskie Point* (70), *Little Big Man* (70), †*The Godfather* (72), †*The Conversation* (74), *†*The Godfather, Part II* (74), **Farewell, My Lovely* (75), *†*Apocalypse Now* (77).

"A production designer should be involved in all visual aspects of the film. An art director, if he is also employed on the film, is your assistant and probably involved with the construction of sets, etc. I suppose each designer works differently with his assistants. Angelo Graham and I have worked together on *Little Big Man*, *Godfather, Part II*, *Farewell, My Lovely* and *Apocalypse Now*. He also worked with me on the aborted start of *The Great Gatsby* [postponed a year, then eventually filmed with designs by Box]. Angelo makes sure all the drafting and construction of sets is carried out and is involved in the selection of locations. If I can not be with the camera while the shooting is taking place, Angelo would be there to check on last minute details.

"It is 4 p.m. in Manila as I write this letter. This morning Angelo and I were swimming in a river 200 miles from here placing sampans in the water for a helicopter shot. So you do what has to be done.

"About the pre-production stages of the work. I usually get involved quite early on with the director even if it is a talking out thing. Angelo comes on after I have some kind of program and idea of what we are going to do.

"As for Antonioni. We first worked together on *Zabriskie Point* and since then we have met and talked about other projects. In fact, I did work with him in Rome late 1971 to March 1972 on a film titled *The Spiral*. We were working on many interesting ideas with video, laser beams, holographs and theatrical scrims. The film, unfortunately, did not reach the filming stages. Antonioni, I consider to be a friend, and look forward to working with him again."—letter from T, on location in the Philippines with the *Apocalypse Now* company, to Elliott Stein, March 31, 1976.

Farewell, My Lovely was one of the rare US films of 1975 marked by superlative design. T accomplished a near-impossible task: recreating a 40s film noir in the mid-70s—and in color. The means: a muted palette, used with impeccable taste. No better designer is working in the US film industry today.

Toda, Jusho   The a.ds. for Nagisa Oshima's early films (1959–66) were Koji Uno and Yasutaro Kon. Since 1966 most of Oshima's films have been des. by T: *Violence at Noon* (66), *A Treatise on Japanese Bawdy Songs* (67), *Japanese Summer: Double Suicide* (67), *Koshikei/Death by Hanging* (68), *3 Resurrected Drunkards* (68), *Diary of a Shinguku Thief* (68), *Shonen/Boy* (69).

Toluboff, Alexander   1882 Russia–1940 Hollywood. Stud. architecture, St. Petersburg. 1926–34 unit a.d. MGM; from 1935 he superv. the a.d. of Walter Wanger prods. *Love* (27), *Mockery* (27), *The Cossacks* (28), *Diamond Handcuffs* (28), *Grand Hotel* (32)—in collab. Gibbons, *Rasputin and the Empress* (32), *Queen Christina* (33), *The Painted Veil* (34), *The Cat and the Fiddle* (34), *Shanghai* (35), *Mary Burns, Fugitive* (35), *Every Night at 8* (35), *Trail of the Lonesome Pine* (36)—the first 3-strip Technicolor feature shot on location, with natural exteriors, *Big Brown Eyes* (36), *Spendthrift* (36), *History Is Made at Night* (37), *You Only Live Once* (37), *Vogues of 1938* (37), *Stand-In* (37), *Algiers* (38), *Blockade* (38), *Trade Winds* (38), *Stagecoach* (39)—listed here for the record, but principally des. by "associate" Ihnen.

Trauner, Alexandre   b. 1906 Budapest. Stud. painting. Entered French cinema as asst. to Meerson, who trained him and with whom he worked until 1935, on films mostly dir. by Clair (*Le Million*, *Quatorze Juillet*) and Feyder (*Pension Mimosas*, *La Kermesse* héroïque/*Carnival in Flanders*). 1937–50 des. 9 films for *Marcel Carné, most based on Jacques Prevert scripts. Nazi racial laws obliged T to work clandestinely during the Occupation—he des. films at home, but could not appear at the studio. Since 1952 work on international and US prods., esp. on films dir. by †Billy Wilder. Some theater work, notably sets for Sartre's *Kean* (1953).

Gribouille (37), **Drôle de drame/Bizarre, Bizarre* (37), **Quai des brumes/Port of Shadows* (38), *Entrée des artistes* (38), **Hôtel du Nord* (38), **Le Jour se lève* (39), *Mollenard* (39), *Remorques/Stormy Waters* (41), **Les Visiteurs du soir/The Devil's Envoys* (42)—in collab. Wakhévitch, **Les Enfants du paradis* (45)—in collab. Barsacq and Raymond Gabutti, **Les Portes de la nuit* (46), *Voyage surprise* (47), **La Marie du port* (49), *Manèges* (49), **Juliette ou la clef des songes* (50), *Othello* (52)—in collab. Scaccianoce (dir. Welles), *Du Rififi chez les hommes* (54), *Land of the Pharaohs* (55), †*Love in the Afternoon* (57), †*Witness for the Prosecution* (58), *The Nun's Story* (59), *Once More, with Feeling* (60), †*The Apartment* (60), *Aimez-vous Brahms?/Goodbye Again* (61), †*One, Two, Three* (61), *Paris Blues* (61), †*Irma la Douce* (63), †*Kiss Me, Stupid* (64), *Night of the Generals* (67), *Uptight* (68), *La Puce à l'oreille/A Flea in Her Ear* (68), †*The Private Life of Sherlock Holmes* (70), *Promesse à l'aube/Promise at Dawn* (71), *The Man Who Would Be King* (75), *Mr. Klein* (76).

A major designer, largely in the "poetic realism" tradition of his mentor Meerson, with an occasional Utrillo-like touch of his own in his sketches. T is responsible for several great studio-built sets which have become icons of "movie Paris" for *cinéphiles* the world over—the fairground (*Quai des brumes*), the Canal St. Martin (*Hôtel du Nord*), the banlieu (*Le Jour se lève*), the elevated Métro station (*Les Portes de la Nuit*). See the section on T in *La Scenografia nel Film* (Rome, 1956); Martin Gray, "On Alexander Trauner," *Films and Filming* 3 (Jan. 1957).

Urban, Joseph 1872 Vienna–1933 NY. Des. New Town Hall, Vienna; the Czar's Bridge, St. Petersburg; Austrian Pavilion, 1904 St. Louis Fair (Grand Prix); Ziegfeld Theatre and New School for Social Research, NY; one of the team of architects who planned Rockefeller Center. Stud. architecture Vienna, and at an early age became known as an eminent member of the Austrian Sezession. First stage work 1906, for Burgtheater, Vienna. Children's book illustrator. 1909–11 stage and opera sets in Austria, Germany. 1912 invited to become stage dir. for Boston Opera Co., settled US. Florenz Ziegfeld, enthused by his sets for the Broadway show *Garden of Paradise*, signed him for the 1915 Follies. U des. succeeding Follies until 1931—and sets for *Sally*, *Rio Rita*, and *Show Boat*, historic Ziegfeld prods. 1920–25 a.d. of William Randolph Hearst's prod. company, Cosmopolitan. Most of the Cosmo films were showcases for Hearst's mistress, ex-Ziegfeld Follies girl Marion Davies. Many were period spectacles—often in medieval dress—with costumes des. by U's daughter Gretl. U was the only designer working in US films in the early 20s whose name was a household word. In 1921—when most a.ds. did not even receive screen credit—his name bulked large in the advertising for *Enchantment* (the first US film with modern interiors). Artistic dir. of Metropolitan Opera 1917–33. Cookie manufacturer F. H. Bennett, impressed by U's *Hansel and Gretel* at the Met, commissioned a remarkable gingerbread castle (1930) in Hamburg, NJ (now open to the public). Although U's sets for Ziegfeld and Hearst were often elaborate in detail, they were given backbone by the synthesis and rigor of his designs. He was a pioneer of "The New Stagecraft"—and, with fellow designers Lee Simonson and Norman Bel Geddes, helped spread the theories of Appia and Craig in the US. The Ziegfeld Theatre (54th St. and 6th Ave., opened in 1927 with *Rio Rita*)—a striking egg-shaped auditorium with medieval decor, "Urban blue" skies, and rich curved facade—was a masterpiece, its demolition in 1967 a crime.

All of the films listed are Cosmopolitan Prods., except those of 1931, which are Fox. *Films starring Marion Davies, most of them dir. by Robert Vignola. *The World and His Wife* (20), **The Restless Sex* (20), **The Bride's Play* (21), **Buried Treasure* (21), **Enchantment* (21), *Get-Rich-Quick Wallingford* (21), *Back Pay* (22), **Beauty's Worth* (22), **When Knighthood Was in Flower* (22), **The Young Diana* (22), **Little Old New York* (23), **Adam and Eva* (23), *The Enemies of Women* (23), *Under the Red Robe* (23), *The Great White Way* (24), **Janice Meredith* (24), **Yolanda* (24), *Never the Twain Shall Meet* (25)—dir. Tourneur, **Zander the Great* (25), *The Man Who Came Back* (31), *Doctors' Wives* (31), *East Lynne* (31).

"Urban's aim was always to find the over-all tone, color and atmosphere by emphasizing essentials, working for effect by the simplest means and dispensing with hackneyed tricks

241

of decoration and false perspective. . . . Ziegfeld was well aware of Urban's enormous contribution, and during the rest of his career had an almost superstitious fear of attempting any production without Urban's collaboration."—Randolph Carter, *The World of Flo Ziegfeld* (NY, 1974), pp. 38–63. See ibid. for U's pre-1912 career. See also Urban, "The Cinema Designer Confronts Sound," in Oliver M. Sayler, ed., *Revolt in the Arts* (NY, 1930); articles on U by Otto Legan and others in *Architecture* (May 1934); Marjorie Farnsworth, *The Ziegfeld Follies* (NY, 1956); W. A. Swanberg, *Citizen Hearst* (NY, 1967); Harry and Janine Mahnken, "An Appreciation of Joseph Urban," *Educational Theatre Journal* (March 1963); Brownlow, *The Parade's Gone By* for U's work on *The World and His Wife* and other films; Charles Higham, *Ziegfeld* (Chicago, 1972). Columbia University owns a large collection of U sketches.

Usher, Robert US. Unit a.d. Paramount early 30s until 1945 (often in collab. with Dreier), later work for other studios. Many films for major dirs.: Lubitsch, Cukor, Sturges, and for pictures with Mae West and Shirley Temple. That he was an art director's art director is evident from his designs for 6 films dir. by *Mitchell Leisen. *She Done Him Wrong* (33), *Now and Forever* (34), *Peter Ibbetson* (35), *Rumba* (35), *Goin' to Town* (35), *Desire* (36)—in collab. Dreier, *The Big Broadcast of 1937* (36), *Angel* (37)—in collab. Dreier, *Artists and Models* (37), *Zaza* (38), *Bluebeard's 8th Wife* (38), *Midnight* (39), *The Ghost Breakers* (40), *Arise, My Love* (40), *Hold Back the Dawn* (41), *I Wanted Wings* (41), *China* (43), *No Time for Love* (43), *Till We Meet Again* (44), *Practically Yours* (44), *The Chase* (46), *The Sin of Harold Diddlebock* (47), *Vendetta* (50). U seems to have specialized in the recreation of Paris on Paramount sound stages: his different versions of the French capital appear in Lubitsch's *Angel* and *Bluebeard's 8th Wife,* in Cukor's *Zaza,* in Leisen's *Arise, My Love* and *Midnight.* The best of all these back-lot Parises can be seen in *Midnight*—one of the cleverest comedies ever made. Excellent atmospheric designs for Hathaway's romantic fantasy, *Peter Ibbetson*—one of the French surrealists' favorite films.

Verity, Terence GB. b. 1913. Stud. architecture London. *Corridor of Mirrors* (48), *The Hasty Heart* (49), *Stage Fright* (50), *24 Hours of a Woman's Life/Affair in Monte Carlo* (52), *1984* (56), *The Devil's Disciple* (59).

Vetchinsky, Alex b. 1905 London. Entered films 1928. Several early films for Victor Saville; 30s and 40s worked mostly at Gainsborough. One of the longest des. careers in British cinema. *Films dir. by Carol Reed. *Jack and Jill* (29), *Sunshine Susie/The Office Girl* (31), *The Faithful Heart* (32), *The Phantom Light* (35), *Tudor Rose* (36), *The Man Who Changed His Mind/The Man Who Lived Again* (36), *Oh, Mr. Porter!* (37), *Alf's Button Afloat* (38), *Bank Holiday/3 on a Weekend* (38), *The Lady Vanishes* (38), *Night Train to Munich/Night Train* (40), *The Girl in the News* (40), *Kipps* (41), *The Young Mr. Pitt* (42), *Waterloo Road* (44), *Tawny Pipit* (44), *Beware of Pity* (46), *The October Man* (47), *Escape* (48), *Hunted* (52), *Singlehanded/Sailor of the King* (52), *The Colditz Story* (54), *A Town Like Alice* (56), *Ill Met by Moonlight/Night Ambush* (56), *A Night to Remember* (58), *Northwest Frontier/Flame over India* (59), *Carry On, Nurse* (59), *The Singer Not the Song* (61), *Victim* (61), *A Study in Terror* (65), *Amorous Adventures of Moll Flanders* (65), *Gold* (74).

Wakhévitch, Georges b. 1907 Russia. At early age immigrated to France, stud. painting Paris. Entered films as asst. to Meerson. Much work (sets and costumes) in theater, opera, ballet. *Baroud* (32), *La Tête d'un homme* (32), *Madame Bovary* (34), *Prison sans barreaux* (38), *Louise* (39), *Pièges* (39), *Les Visiteurs du soir/The Devil's Envoys* (42)—in collab. Trauner, *L'eternel Retour* (43), *L'Homme au chapeau rond* (46), *La Danse de mort* (46), *Martin Roumagnac* (46), *Ruy Blas* (47), *L'Aigle à deux têtes* (48)—in collab. Bérard, *Dédée d'Anvers* (48), *Miquette et sa mère* (50), *The Medium* (51), *The Beggar's Opera* (53), *Me and the Colonel* (58), *King of Kings* (61), *Le Journal d'une femme de chambre* (64), *Les Fêtes galantes* (65), *Mayerling* (68), *King Lear* (71)—dir. Peter Brook. Des. for a pleiad of notable dirs.: Rex Ingram, Renoir, Siodmak, Ray, Duvivier, Gance, Buñuel. A bent for lushness; work often heavy with rich theatrical detail. Many period costumers. Also capable of the appropriately gloomy but divergent naturalism on view in Allegret's fine *Dédée* and in Bunuel's masterful *Journal.*

Walton, Tony For the Broadway stage: *Chicago. Mary Poppins* (64)—as des. consultant, *A Funny Thing Happened on the Way to the Forum* (66), *Fahrenheit 451* (66), *Petulia* (68), *The Sea Gull* (68), *The Boy Friend* (71), *Murder on the Orient Express* (74). Brilliantly whimsical designs for Ken Russell's *The Boy Friend.*

242

Warm, Hermann b. 1889 Germany. Trained at Kunstgewerbeschule, Berlin. Theater sets for Berlin Schillertheater, Düsseldorf. Expressionist painter, member of *Der Sturm* group. Entered films 1912, working for Vitascop, then Decla–Bioscop. Des. several early films for one of the forgotten pioneers of German cinema, dir. Max Mack, and 2 masterpieces for Dreyer in France—*Jeanne d'Arc* and *Vampyr*. In 30s free-lance designer and architect in France, Hungary. 1941–44 in Switzerland, 1947 returned to Germany.

Die Blaue Maus (12), *Der Shylock von Krakau* (13), *Der Hund von Baskerville* (14), *Die Spinnen, part 1/Der Goldene See/The Golden Lake* (19)—in collab. Hunte, *Die Spinnen, part 2/Das Brillantenschiff/The Slave Ship* (20)—in collab. Hunte, *Das Cabinet des Dr. Caligari* (20)—in collab. Reimann, Röhrig, *Der Müde Tod/Destiny* (21)—Arabian and Venetian sequences, *Schloss Vogelöd* (21), *Phantom* (22), *Der Student von Prag/The Man Who Cheated Life* (26), *La Passion de Jeanne d'Arc* (28)—in collab. Jean Hugo, *Eine Nacht in London* (28), *Dreyfus* (30), *Vampyr* (32), *Peer Gynt* (34), *Musik im Blut* (34), *Mazurka* (35), *Der Student von Prag* (36), *Mädchenjahre einer Königin* (36), *Jugend* (38), *Das Unsterbliche Herz* (39), *Le Corbeau* (43)—in collab. Andrejew, *Wozzeck* (47), *Morituri* (48), *Herz der Welt* (51), *Cuba Cubana* (52), *Hokuspokus* (53), *Königswalzer* (55), *Die Nackte und der Satan/The Head* (59), *Die Wahrheit über Rosemarie/Love Now, Pay Later* (59), *Die Botschafterin* (60)—in collab. Maurischat.

The Italian *Filmlexicon* considers W and Meerson the two greatest designers of European cinema; for Walter Kaul, W is "The Grand Old Man der Film Architektur." No designer holds a more impressive list of credits, and, unlike most of his expressionist colleagues, W's prolific work remained on a high level until well after WWII. See Eisner, *Haunted Screen*; Kaul, *Schöpferische Filmarchitektur*; Felix Bucher, *Screen Series: Germany* (NY, 1970), pp. 193–95; and Warm, "Meine Arbeit," *Filmkunst*, no. 43 (Vienna, 1965).

Welles, Orson b. 1915 Wisconsin. *Confidential Report/Mr. Arkadin* (55)—des. sets and costumes, dir., wrote script (based on his novel), and played title role.

Wells, Frank b. 1903. GB. Stud. Cambridge. A.d. British Instructional 1928, then with Gainsborough, London Films. After 1945 prod. of educational films and for Rank Screen Services. *Films dir. by Michael Powell. *The Rasp* (31), *C.O.D.* (32), *Star Reporter* (32), *His Lordship* (32), *Things to Come* (36; written by his father, H. G. Wells)—as asst. to Vincent Korda, *Under the Red Robe* (37), *Fire Over England* (37)—in collab. Meerson. Nearly all the best des. in British films in the 30s was by German-, Hungarian-, or Russian-born a.ds. *Under the Red Robe*, the beautiful last film dir. by Victor Seastrom, is an exception. Although the locale is 17th-century France, the somewhat Meersonian sets are gorgeously inspired by Vermeer.

Werndorff, Oscar Friedrich (Otto) b. 1887 Vienna. Stud. architecture. Entered cinema 1921. Dupont's *Varieté* was one of the great triumphs of the 20s—esp. in US where it had a considerable influence on Hollywood prods. During his German period, W also des. for Pabst, Oswald, Korda, and Wiene. In the 30s worked in England (for Gaumont British) where his films most likely to be remembered were those directed by *Hitchcock. *Der Pantoffelheld* (22), *Carlos und Elisabeth* (24), *Varieté* (25), *Eine Dubarry von Heute* (26), *Man Spielt Nicht mit der Liebe!* (26), *Venus im Frack* (27), *Die Grosse Abenteurin* (28), *The 39 Steps* (35), *First a Girl* (35), *Secret Agent* (36), *Rhodes of Africa* (36), *Sabotage* (36), *Keep Smiling* (38), *The Ware Case* (39). See Carrick, *Designing for Moving Pictures*, p. 34.

Weyl, Carl Jules 1890 Germany–1948 California. In 20s active architectural practice California. Started work at WB 1935, remaining there as unit a.d. for rest of career. *Films dir. by Michael Curtiz. *The Florentine Dagger* (35), *The Case of the Curious Bride* (35), *Personal Maid's Secret* (35), *The Payoff* (35), *We're in the Money* (35), *The Singing Kid* (36), *Bullets or Ballots* (36), *Kid Galahad* (37), *The Adventures of Robin Hood* (38), *The Amazing Dr. Clitterhouse* (38), *Confessions of a Nazi Spy* (39), *Dr. Ehrlich's Magic Bullet* (40), *All This and Heaven Too* (40), *Brother Orchid* (40), *The Letter* (40), *Out of the Fog* (41), *Desperate Journey* (42), *Yankee Doodle Dandy* (42), *King's Row* (42), *Casablanca* (42), *Mission to Moscow* (43), *The Constant Nymph* (43), *Passage to Marseille* (44), *The Corn Is Green* (45), *Saratoga Trunk* (45), *The Big Sleep* (46), *Escape Me Never* (47), *Cry Wolf* (47). See Higham, *Warner Brothers* (NY, 1975).

Wheeler, Lyle b. 1905 Massachusetts. Stud. Univ. Southern California. Industrial designer and magazine illustrator before entering films as a.d. for Selznick. With Selznick until early 40s; after a few years as unit a.d. MGM, went over to 20th–Fox 1945, where he succeeded Day as superv. a.d. Feb. 1947. Since early 60s has worked as prod. designer at Columbia, other studios. *Films dir. by Otto Preminger. *The Garden of Allah* (36), *A Star Is Born* (37), *Nothing Sacred* (37), *Prisoner of Zenda* (37), *The Adventures of Tom Sawyer* (38), *Gone with the Wind* (39)—in collab. Menzies, *Intermezzo* (39), *Rebecca* (40), *That Hamilton Woman* (41) —in collab. A. Korda, *Keeper of the Flame* (42), *Cairo* (42), *Dragon Seed* (44), *Anna and the King of Siam* (46), *My Darling Clementine* (46), *Forever Amber* (47), *The Art Director* (48) —an Academy project, made by 20th–Fox, *Whirlpool* (49), *The Robe* (53), *River of No Return* (54)—in collab. Addison Hehr, *The King and I* (56)—in collab. De Cuir, *The Diary of Anne Frank* (59)—in collab. George Davis, *Advise and Consent* (62), *The Cardinal* (63), *In Harm's Way* (65), *The Best Man* (64), *Where Angels Go, Trouble Follows* (68), *Marooned* (69), *Tell Me That You Love Me, Junie Moon* (70), *The Love Machine* (71), *Doctors' Wives* (71), *Posse* (75).

Wiley, Harrison   Late 20s, early 30s at Columbia where he des. films dir. by Christy Cabanne, Karl Brown, Erle C. Kenton, Roy William Neill, Alan Crosland, and *Frank Capra. *Driftwood* (28), *Nothing to Wear* (28), *The Power of the Press* (28), *Say It with Sables* (28), *The Scarlet Lady* (28), *The Sideshow* (28), *Submarine* (28), *Behind Closed Doors* (29), *The Donovan Affair* (29), *Flight* (29), *Wall Street* (29), *The Younger Generation* (29), *Ladies of Leisure* (30), *Prince of Diamonds* (30), *Rain or Shine* (30).

Wright, Joseph C.   Mid-30s at MGM; 40s, early 50s unit a.d. 20th–Fox where he worked on many garish Betty Grable musicals, and Busby Berkeley's *The Gang's All Here*, one of the wildest, most imaginatively des. musicals ever made. 1942 awarded 2 AAs. Since 1955 with other studios.
   The Woman of Bronze (23), *Daring Youth* (24), *The Unholy Three* (25), *The Exquisite Sinner* (26), *The Man Who Laughs* (28)—in collab. Charles D. Hall, *Golf Widows* (28), *The Sea Wolf* (30), *Delicious* (31), *Manhattan Melodrama* (34), *Rose Marie* (36), *Down Argentine Way* (40), *The Mark of Zorro* (40)—in collab. Day, *Lillian Russell* (40), *Blood and Sand* (41), *Swamp Water* (41), *Orchestra Wives* (42), *My Gal Sal* (42), *This Above All* (42), *The Gang's All Here* (43)—in collab. Basevi, *Coney Island* (43), *Sweet Rosie O'Grady* (43), *Irish Eyes Are Smiling* (44), *Billy Rose's Diamond Horseshoe* (45), *3 Little Girls in Blue* (46), *Mother Wore Tights* (47), *The Snake Pit* (48), *Unfaithfully Yours* (48), *Come to the Stable* (49), *Wabash Avenue* (50), *My Blue Heaven* (50), *On the Riviera* (51)—musical settings only, *Golden Girl* (51)—musical settings only, *Gentlemen Prefer Blondes* (53), *Man with the Golden Arm* (55), *Guys and Dolls* (55)—in collab. Oliver Smith, *Oklahoma!* (55), *The Strange One* (57), *Flower Drum Song* (61), *Days of Wine and Roses* (62), *The Wrecking Crew* (68).

Yakutovich, Georgi Vyacheslavovich   b. 1930. *Teni Zabytykh Predkov/Shadows of Our Forgotten Ancestors* (64), *Zakhar Berkut/Boyars Go Hunting* (70). One of the rare interesting talents to be found in the younger generation of Soviet designers. Fascinating sets for Sergei Paradjanov's wild, extraordinary *Shadows*, the only international triumph for the Kiev studios in several decades, a film in sharp contrast with the largely academic Moscow prods. of the 60s. See *Designers of the Soviet Cinema* for Y's sketches for *Shadows* and *Boyars*.

Ybarra, Alfred   In 40s unit a.d. RKO; later at WB, other studios. Specialist in westerns, esp. those with Mexican backgrounds. Des. films dir. by John Ford, Boetticher, Aldrich, Wellman, Hathaway, Walsh, Curtiz. *The Fugitive* (47), *Adventures of Casanova* (48), *Sofia* (48), *Borderline* (50), *One-Way Street* (50), *The Bullfighter and the Lady* (51), *Big Jim McClain* (52), *Blowing Wild* (53), *Hondo* (53), *The High and the Mighty* (54), *Track of the Cat* (54), *Run for the Sun* (56), *Legend of the Lost* (57), *Marines, Let's Go* (61), *The Comancheros* (61), *Major Dundee* (65), *Duel at Diablo* (66), *Hour of the Gun* (67).

Zazvorka, Jan   b. 1914 Czechoslovakia. Stud. architecture Prague. Since 1946 has taught cinema at the Prague Beaux Arts Academy. Often des. for Otakar Vávra and *Martin Fric. Several sci-fi films. *Vojnarka* (36), *Eva tropi Hlouposti/Eva Plays the Fool* (39), *Katakomby* (40), *Krakatit* (48), *Cisaruv Pekar/The Emperor and His Baker* (51), *Muz z Prvniho Stoleti/Man in Outer Space* (62), *Ikaria XB-1/Voyage to the End of the Universe* (63), *Dymky* (66), *Svata Hrisnice/The Holy Sinner* (71). For Z's fine work on *Ikaria* sets see Elliott Stein, "Science Fiction Festival at Trieste," *Sight and Sound* 32 (Autumn 1963).

Zehetbauer, Rolf   *Cabaret* (72)—in collab. Keibach, *Twilight's Last Gleaming* (76).

244

Two Letters from Wiard Ihnen

The following text is excerpted from a series of letters from Wiard Ihnen. I had written to this great art director asking several specific questions about his career, to clarify his filmography in this book. Although he is famed in the industry and was awarded two Oscars, his name is not as well known to the public—or to readers of film books—as it should be.—E.S.

.

February 11, 1976

This is a short history of my experiences in the Motion Picture Industry. I'll begin by telling you how Famous Players came to set up an Art Department staffed by real professionals from the field of Architecture and Decoration.

It—the story—starts when Jesse Lasky and George Fitzmaurice were making a picture during which they used a beautiful manor house at Convent Garden in New Jersey [ca. 1919].

Robert M. Haas and I made all of the drawings for this building while employed by Charles I. Berg Architect.

It still stands today as a fine example of Tudor–Elizabethan architecture. It was inspired by a great house in England called Compton–Wynyates.

While shooting there Fitzmaurice was talking to George Marshall Allen the owner. He bemoaned the fact that he would be unable to have Interior setting built at the studio that would be in keeping with the exterior.

Allen said why don't you hire the men who were responsible for this building?

This is how and why Bob Haas who was out of work—having just "got back from the war" so to speak—came to be engaged to set up the department.

At that time I was working for an architect by name of William H. Orchard. We were doing residences for the wealthy at a place called Pelham Manor in Westchester County.

Bob called me from time to time to tell me all about his work at the studio especially of the fine salaries being paid. I was not impressed since I enjoyed my work.

However one day I went out to visit a village they had built on Long Island. After looking it over the men decided we should have lunch at a speakeasy. Well—you can guess what happened—we all got a little drunk and I ended up agreeing that I would take a job at the studio. I was appointed as the number two man in the department.

Now to go back a bit it was while working for Orchard that I requested more help. While with Berg we had had an office boy by the name of Van Nest Polglase. I suggested that we hire him because I thought he was bright enough to come on as a draftsman!

So it followed that after a couple of months after I was working at the studio Van called me to say he would like very much to join us.

He did and stayed on for years. Bob Haas who was then the boss at the Long Island Studio quit and since I had left to join 2 other fellows to form our own company, Van succeeded to the job as head of the department. He remained so until he went over to RKO.

In the meanwhile my company called Tilford Studios had leased an old Opera House on 44th Street. We were financed by a traction company. The Opera House had been converted previously into a good studio we equipped with everything needed to make pictures. We engaged a good staff and started in the business of contracting for whatever the independent producer wanted. Sets, lights—the works.

We were very successful because the work and facilities were provided at a fixed fee.

Our first job was for a picture called *School Days* starring Wesley Barry and produced by Harry Rapf.

It was released by the Warner Bros. who had a small distribution and sales office on Broadway.

I worked my tail off. At times we had sets standing in four studios. One in Fort Lee, New Jersey, one in the old Pathé Studio in the Bronx, another in upper Manhattan. We got all the work we wanted but somehow didn't make much money.

245

The last and best contract we got was to produce four pictures to star Irene Castle. Her people supplied the star and the money.

We engaged Alan Crosland to direct. We found the stories, got the scripts prepared etc. It was when the boys went to Florida to make the last one that I left. I had had enough.

Previously we made two pictures for Mae Murray's independent company and others. I think one other was called *Dancing Daughters* in which one of the Bennett sisters starred and Hedda Hopper supported.

I obtained my license to practice architecture and spent several years as a struggling architect. That's when I took classes in painting and figure drawing at Art Students League.

I lived in Greenwich Village where I shared a small building with a sculptor named Oronzio Maldarelli. I rubbed elbows with illustrators, sculptors and painters.

At that time I met Barry Faulkner a successful muralist. He had been the teacher at the American Academy in Rome and received commissions from all the best architects. I went to work for him as an assistant for 1½ years.

Then I made the grand tour of Europe with Lawrence Laughlin—a young portraitist—in a model T Ford. When I came back I was stony broke and so after writing to friends for a job I received an offer from Van to come out as an art director at Paramount—that was in 1928. I stayed for 6 years. . . .

One more picture . . . was *Becky Sharp*, the first 3-color film by Technicolor. This is one of those where I did all the work but got no credit. I was in Taxco, Mexico on my sabbatical when I received a wire from Kenneth MacGowan to come up as "Technical Assistant" to Robert Edmund Jones. I thought it a good idea to get on the ground floor of the new process.

As it turned out Jones had been promised he would direct and produce the picture, but Lowell Sherman was made director and Kenneth MacGowan producer. "Jock" Whitney was the money bag since he was a big stockholder in Technicolor.

Jones turned the sets over to me. I made the sketches and built the sets in conference with Sherman. Jones was used to the theatre where the whole Modus Operandi was different. The technical aspects frightened him. His settings for the stage were rather 2-dimensional affairs and of course he had had no architectural experience.

He thought of himself as the artistic director and color coordinator. He began to feel that the whole project was over his head. He was a very sweet and proud man and a great artist in the theatre.

However Lowell Sherman died suddenly and everything stopped for a few weeks when Rouben Mamoulian was engaged. The sets had all, or mostly all, been built.

He approved the sets and filming was resumed. In the meantime Jones had been designing the clothes and having them built.

It ended rather sadly because Mamoulian would not let him on the sets! He had flats built around them and Jones had to content himself with a little portable office on the stage and busy himself with costumes.

A sad story for Jones. By the way, he took my sketches back to New York with him!

February 4, 1976

. . . . But on *Jane Eyre* I was astonished to learn that Bill Pereira got credit. He had some kind of contract with Selznick and Selznick owned the story. I was the sole and only designer on the production. It was entirely my concept and of course approved by Stevenson.*

When you say Everett Shinn got credit on *Fighting Blade* I am even more astonished. The picture was made in Fort Lee, New Jersey and we never saw hide nor hair of him. I worked night and day, frequently sleeping at the studio. Anyway he could not have helped me. He was an illustrator who drew pretty women.†

* Screen credits for *Jane Eyre* (20th Century–Fox, 1944; directed by Robert Stevenson) read: "Art Direction, James Basevi and Wiard Ihnen; Production Design, William Pereira."

† Screen credits for *The Fighting Blade* read: "Art Director, Everett Shinn; Technical Director, William B. Ihnen." During the 20s, the set designer was frequently titled "Technical Director"—which only added to miscomprehension of who did what. Ihnen is also known as William.

As to *Stagecoach*—I was engaged by Walter Wanger. We worked at the Goldwyn studio and I did not even know Toluboff and don't know how he got into it. The concept of the Indian architecture was entirely mine. I worked closely with Ford and was on the set with him most of the time. *

As to *Blue Bird* which merited an Oscar but . . . the picture was a box office bomb, I designed every detail, except of course the fire effects, and conferred with *no one* except Walter Lang and Darryl Zanuck. †

On *Blonde Venus* . . . I worked with Von Sternberg only. No one at the studio had anything to do with it. Strangely, V. S. would never look at the sets ahead of time. He approved of my sketches and only saw the set on the morning of the shooting. I guess he wanted to be surprised.

A side lite: One of the sets was a music hall in Paris. I designed a shot that brought Dietrich in from the street and followed her up stairs and into the box. This required the use of a boom. This piece of equipment was new at the studio. When Von S. saw it on the set he wanted to know who the hell had ordered it. I stepped forward and confessed to having done so, explaining how I had planned the shot and the set. It would have been impossible without it. He grumbled a lot but later in the day I visited the set and not only was he using it but he was actually sitting on it in the place of the camera operator!

After that he rode a boom almost constantly. We got along well and later I designed the very modern dressing room built for Dietrich.

Another picture I might mention was *The Robe*. I was engaged by Frank Ross to design the sets. The contract was written by RKO and the checks came from them. I was well paid. My drawings were completed. . . . I think it would have been a beautiful production. Then, I left town for a few days. When I returned, I was told by my secretary that Fox had come and taken everything—sketches, models and drawings. Ross had made a new deal with Fox. That was the end for me. I was heartbroken, but that's the way the ball bounced. . . .

I can tell you how Fegté got started. He came to my office at Tilford Studios one day carrying some sketches. I looked at them and admired them. But I had nothing for him, but called Van Polglase over at Long Island (Famous Players). He had me send him over and got a job.

About Bob Boyle. I was here in Hollywood working with V. P. at Paramount. I, being the senior man, always conferred with Van about things around the department. I suggested we engage a sketch artist. Previously we did our own sketches and drawings but sets were getting more elaborate so we were swamped. He said go ahead. I called U.S.C. dept. architecture. The dean said yes he had just the man for us.

The next day Boris Leven showed up. I said, oh you are Mr. Boyle! Well, Boris had heard about the job and hustled over. We engaged him and the next day engaged Bob as well.

As to *Jane Eyre*, I designed the sets entirely as I said, without collaboration with anyone at the studio except the director. But I have just turned up a review in the *Reporter* which credits James Basevi. Well, Jim was the "Supervising" Art Director and Dept. Head at the time but he never bothered me. We were good friends.‡

* Screen credits for *Stagecoach* read: "Art Direction, Alexander Toluboff" (supervising art director for Wanger) followed by "Associate, Wiard Ihnen." Books on the cinema, as much as anything else, merely add to the confusion about who did what. Credits for *Stagecoach* are incorrect in both of the two books on John Ford in print in English: "Set Decorator, Wiard Ihnen" (Peter Bogdanovich, *John Ford*, 1968), and "Art Director, Toluboff; Set Director [a meaningless term], Ihnen" (Joseph McBride and Michael Wilmington, *John Ford*, 1975). As another example, in the lengthy credits for *Rancho Notorious* in Peter Bogdanovich's *Fritz Lang in America* (1967) there is no mention of Ihnen, who designed the entire film and received screen credit for it; the art direction is credited to Robert Priestley, the film's set decorator.

† Although Ihnen "designed every detail," Richard Day received the main Art Direction credit for *The Blue Bird* (20th Century–Fox, 1940).

‡ The New York *Post* and other papers praised Basevi's work on *Jane Eyre*.

ACADEMY AWARDS FOR
ART DIRECTION AND SET DECORATION

From 1927 to 1940 the award was given in the category of Interior Decoration, from 1941 to 1946 in the categories of Interior Decoration and Set Decoration, and since 1947 in the categories of Art Direction and Set Decoration. In this list the names following the semicolons are the winners for set decoration. From 1940 to 1966, except 1957–58, the award was given for both black-and-white (bw) and color (c) films.

1927/28	*The Dove*	William Cameron Menzies
	The Tempest	William Cameron Menzies
1928/29	*The Bridge of San Luis Rey*	Cedric Gibbons
1929/30	*King of Jazz*	Herman Rosse
1930/31	*Cimarron*	Max Ree
1931/32	*Transatlantic*	Gordon Wiles
1932/33	*Cavalcade*	William S. Darling
1934	*The Merry Widow*	Cedric Gibbons, Frederic Hope
1935	*The Dark Angel*	Richard Day
1936	*Dodsworth*	Richard Day
1937	*Lost Horizon*	Stephen Goosson
1938	*The Adventures of Robin Hood*	Carl J. Weyl
1939	*Gone with the Wind*	Lyle Wheeler; honorary award to William Cameron Menzies for outstanding achievement in the use of color for the enhancement of dramatic mood in the production of *Gone with the Wind*
1940	*Pride and Prejudice* (bw)	Cedric Gibbons, Paul Groesse
	The Thief of Bagdad (c)	Vincent Korda
1941	*How Green Was My Valley* (bw)	Richard Day, Nathan Juran; Thomas Little
	Blossoms in the Dust (c)	Cedric Gibbons, Urie McCleary; Edwin B. Willis
1942	*This Above All* (bw)	Richard Day, Joseph Wright; Thomas Little
	My Gal Sal (c)	Richard Day, Joseph Wright; Thomas Little
1943	*The Song of Bernadette* (bw)	James Basevi, William S. Darling; Thomas Little
	Phantom of the Opera (c)	Alexander Golitzen, John B. Goodman; Russell A. Gausman, Ira S. Webb
1944	*Gaslight* (bw)	Cedric Gibbons, William Ferrari; Edwin B. Willis, Paul Huldschinsky
	Wilson (c)	Wiard Ihnen; Thomas Little
1945	*Blood on the Sun* (bw)	Wiard Ihnen; A. Roland Fields
	Frenchman's Creek (c)	Hans Dreier, Ernst Fegté; Sam Comer
1946	*Anna and the King of Siam* (bw)	Lyle Wheeler, William S. Darling; Thomas Little, Frank E. Hughes
	The Yearling (c)	Cedric Gibbons, Paul Groesse; Edwin B. Willis
1947	*Great Expectations* (bw)	John Bryan; Wilfred Shingleton
	Black Narcissus (c)	Alfred Junge; Alfred Junge
1948	*Hamlet* (bw)	Roger K. Furse; Carmen Dillon
	The Red Shoes (c)	Hein Heckroth; Arthur Lawson
1949	*The Heiress* (bw)	John Meehan, Harry Horner; Emile Kuri
	Little Women (c)	Cedric Gibbons, Paul Groesse; Edwin B. Willis, Jack D. Moore
1950	*Sunset Boulevard* (bw)	Hans Dreier, John Meehan; Sam Comer, Ray Moyer
	Samson and Delilah (c)	Hans Dreier, Walter Tyler; Sam Comer, Ray Moyer
1951	*A Streetcar Named Desire* (bw)	Richard Day; George James Hopkins
	An American In Paris (c)	Cedric Gibbons, Preston Ames; Edwin B. Willis, Keogh Gleason
1952	*The Bad and the Beautiful* (bw)	Cedric Gibbons, Edward Carfagno; Edwin B. Willis, Keogh Gleason
	Moulin Rouge (c)	Paul Sheriff; Marcel Vertès

1953	*Julius Caesar* (bw)	Cedric Gibbons, Edward Carfagno; Edwin B. Willis, Hugh Hunt
	The Robe (c)	Lyle Wheeler, George W. Davis; Walter M. Scott, Paul S. Fox
1954	*On the Waterfront* (bw)	Richard Day
	20,000 Leagues Under the Sea (c)	John Meehan; Emile Kuri
1955	*The Rose Tattoo* (bw)	Hal Pereira, Tambi Larsen; Sam Comer, Arthur Krams
	Picnic (c)	William Flannery, Jo Mielziner; Robert Priestley
1956	*Somebody Up There Likes Me* (bw)	Cedric Gibbons, Malcolm F. Brown; Edwin B. Willis, F. Keogh Gleason
	The King and I (c)	Lyle Wheeler, John De Cuir; Walter M. Scott, Paul S. Fox
1957	*Sayonara*	Ted Haworth; Robert Priestley
1958	*Gigi*	William A. Horning, Preston Ames; Henry Grace, Keogh Gleason
1959	*The Diary of Anne Frank* (bw)	Lyle Wheeler, George W. Davis; Walter M. Scott, Stuart A. Reiss
	Ben Hur (c)	William A. Horning, Edward Carfagno; Hugh Hunt
1960	*The Apartment* (bw)	Alexander Trauner; Edward G. Boyle
	Spartacus (c)	Alexander Golitzen, Eric Orbom; Russell A. Gausman, Julia Heron
1961	*The Hustler* (bw)	Harry Horner; Gene Callahan
	West Side Story (c)	Boris Leven; Victor A. Gangelin
1962	*To Kill a Mockingbird* (bw)	Alexander Golitzen, Henry Bumstead; Oliver Emert
	Lawrence of Arabia (c)	John Box, John Stoll; Dario Simoni
1963	*America America* (bw)	Gene Callahan
	Cleopatra (c)	John De Cuir, Jack Martin Smith, Hilyard Brown, Herman Blumenthal, Elven Webb, Maurice Pelling, Boris Juraga; Walter M. Scott, Paul S. Fox, Ray Moyer
1964	*Zorba the Greek* (bw)	Vassilis Fotopoulos
	My Fair Lady (c)	Gene Allen, Cecil Beaton; George James Hopkins
1965	*Ship of Fools* (bw)	Robert Clatworthy; Joseph Kish
	Doctor Zhivago (c)	John Box, Terence Marsh; Dario Simoni
1966	*Who's Afraid of Virginia Woolf?* (bw)	Richard Sylbert; George James Hopkins
	Fantastic Voyage (c)	Jack Martin Smith, Dale Hennesy; Walter M. Scott, Stuart A. Reiss
1967	*Camelot*	John Truscott, Edward Carrere; John W. Brown
1968	*Oliver!*	John Box, Terence Marsh; Vernon Dixon, Ken Muggleston
1969	*Hello, Dolly!*	John De Cuir, Jack Martin Smith, Herman Blumenthal; Walter M. Scott, George James Hopkins, Raphael Bretton
1970	*Patton*	Urie McCleary, Gil Parrondo; Antonio Mateos, Pierre-Louis Thévenet
1971	*Nicholas and Alexandra*	John Box, Ernest Archer, Jack Maxsted, Gil Parrondo; Vernon Dixon
1972	*Cabaret*	Jürgen Kiebach, Rolf Zehetbauer; Herbert Strabel
1973	*The Sting*	Henry Bumstead; James Payne
1974	*The Godfather, Part II*	Dean Tavoularis, Angelo Graham; George R. Nelson
1975	*Barry Lyndon*	Ken Adam, Roy Walker; Vernon Dixon

Top: The Road Back (Universal, 1937). Directed by James Whale. Art director: Charles D. Hall.

Bottom: Patton (20th Century–Fox, 1970). It won seven Oscars, including best picture, actor (George C. Scott in the title role), director (Franklin J. Schaffner), and art direction. Art directors: Gil Parrondo and Urie McCleary; set decorators: Antonio Mateos and Pierre-Louis Thévenet.

SELECTED BIBLIOGRAPHY

Works on Art Direction

American Cinematographer 55 (November 1974). The issue is devoted to *Earthquake*; articles
   include "The Production Design" and "The Special Mechanical Effects."
Barsacq, Léon. "Le Décor." In Marcel Defosse, ed., *Le Cinéma, par ceus qui le font*. Paris:
   A. Fayard, 1949.
———. "Les Décors de Lazare Meerson." In *Jacques Feyder ou le Cinéma concret*. Brussels,
   1949.
———. "Etudes sur le décor." *Arts* (Paris), no. 493 (1954).
Bessy, M., and Lo Duca. *Georges Méliès, Mage*. Paris, 1945.
Brosnan, John. *Movie Magic: The Story of Special Effects in the Cinema*. New York: St. Martin's
   Press, 1974.
Chase, Donald, for The American Film Institute. *Filmmaking: The Collaborative Art*. Boston:
   Little, Brown, 1975. "The Production Designer" (pp. 155–92) includes interviews with Harry
   Horner, Gene Allen, and Polly Platt.
Craig, Edward Anthony (Edward Carrick, pseud.). *Art and Design in the British Film: A Pictorial
   Directory of British Art Directors and Their Work*. London: Dennis Dobson, 1948.
———. *Designing for Moving Pictures*. London: Studio, 1941. Reissued as *Designing for Films* in
   1949.
Dreier, Hans. "Designing the Sets." In Nancy Naumburg, ed., *We Make the Movies*. New York:
   Norton, 1937, pp. 80–89.
Exposition Commémorative du Centenaire de Georges Méliès. Paris: Cinémathèque Française,
   1961. Catalogue of an exhibition at the Musée des Arts Décoratifs.
Fielding, Raymond. "Norman O. Dawn: Pioneer Worker in Special-Effects Cinematography."
   Journal of the Society of Motion Picture and Television Engineers 72 (January 1963).
Gibbons, Cedric. "The Art Director." In Stephen Watts, ed., *Behind the Screen: How Films Are
   Made*. London: Arthur Barker, 1938.
———. "Motion-Picture Sets." In *Encyclopaedia Britannica* 15 (1946): 858ff.; and in other
   editions.
Gillett, John. "Hans Dreier." In Roger Manvell and Lewis Jacobs, eds., *The International Film
   Encyclopedia*. New York: Crown, 1972.
Gough-Yates, Kevin. *Michael Powell*. London: National Film Theatre, 1971. Includes "Making
   Colour Talk" by Hein Heckroth and Michael Powell.
———. *Michael Powell*. Brussels: Belgian Film Museum, 1973.
Greene, Tom. "The Art of the Matte: Dissolving Albert Whitlock." *Filmmaker's Newsletter* 7
   (October 1974): 28–32. Whitlock is the head of Universal's matte department.
Hammond, Paul. *Marvellous Méliès*. New York: St. Martin's Press, 1975.
Hanson, Bernard. "D. W. Griffith—Some Sources." *Art Bulletin* 54 (December 1972): 493–515.

Hudson, Roger. "Three Designers." *Sight and Sound* 34 (Winter 1964–65). Ken Adam, Edward Marshall, and Richard MacDonald.

I.D.H.E.C. *L'Architecture–Décoration dans le film*. Paris, 1955.

Kaul, Walter. *Schöpferische Filmarchitektur*. Berlin: Deutsche Kinemathek, 1971.

Koenig, John. *Scenery for Cinema*. Exhibition catalogue, Baltimore Museum of Art (January 23–March 1, 1942).

Kuter, Leo K. "Art Direction Is an Important, and Little Understood, Component of a Movie." *Films in Review* 8 (June–July 1957): 248–58.

Laurent, Hugues. "L'Evolution du décor de cinéma en cinquante ans." *Bulletin de l'A.F.I.T.E.C.*, no. 16 (1957).

———. *La Technologie du décor de film*. Paris: I.D.H.E.C., n.d.

"The Look of a Picture: An Interview with Production Designer Richard Sylbert." *Film Heritage* 11 (1975), no. 1.

Mallet-Stevens, Robert. *L'Art cinématographique*. Paris: Félix Alcan, 1927.

———. *Le Décor moderne au cinéma*. Paris: Charles Massin, 1928.

Myerscough-Walker, R. *Stage and Film Decor*. London: Pitman, 1945.

Patterson, Barrie. "20 Leading Film Designers: An Index." In Peter Cowie, ed., *International Film Guide 1968*. London: Tantivy, and New York: A. S. Barnes, 1968.

Silanteva, T. A. (*Designers of the Soviet Cinema*). Moscow, 1972. Illustrates sketches and designs from Soviet films in black and white and color. Part of the text is in English. Distributed by Imported Publications, Inc., 320 West Ohio St., Chicago, Ill. 60610.

St. John Marner, Terence. *Film Design*. London: Tantivy, and New York: A. S. Barnes, 1974.

La Scenografia Cinematografica in Italia. Rome, 1955.

Sotheby–Parke Bernet, Los Angeles. *Catalogue of 20th Century–Fox Memorabilia*. Auction catalogue (February 25–28, 1971); published by McGraw-Hill. An amply illustrated, invaluable catalogue, published on behalf of a depressing event in the history of the American motion picture industry.

Stauffacher, Frank, ed. *Art in Cinema*. San Francisco, 1947.

Vallance, Tom. Review of *Lucky Lady* and filmography of John Barry, British production designer (*Phase IV*, *The Little Prince*, *Lucky Lady*). *Focus on Film*, no. 23 (Winter 1975–76).

Verdone, Mario, ed. *La Scenografia nel Film*. Rome: Ateneo, 1956.

West, Nathanael. *The Day of the Locust*. New York: New Directions, 1950, and later editions. The protagonist works in the art department of a movie studio.

General Works

Balshofer, Fred J., and Arthur C. Miller. *One Reel a Week*. Berkeley: University of California Press, 1967.

Baxter, John. *The Cinema of Josef von Sternberg*. New York: A. S. Barnes, 1971.

———. *Hollywood in the Thirties*. New York: Warner, 1970.

Bessy, Maurice. *Histoire en 1000 images du cinéma*. Paris: Port-Royal, 1962.

Brownlow, Kevin. *The Parade's Gone By*. New York: Alfred A. Knopf, 1969.

Capra, Frank. *The Name Above the Title*. New York: Macmillan, 1971. Includes observations on designing sets to suit stars (p. 263).

Chierichetti, David. *Hollywood Director: The Career of Mitchell Leisen*. New York: Curtis, 1973.

Clair, René. *Reflections on the Cinema*. Trans. by Vera Traill. London: William Kimber, 1953.

Coissac, G. M., et al. *Le Cinéma des origines a nos jours*. Paris: Editions du Cygne, 1932.

Butler, Ivan. *Cinema in Britain*. New York: A. S. Barnes, 1973.

Croce, Arlene. *The Fred Astaire and Ginger Rogers Book*. New York: E. P. Dutton, 1972.

Eisenstein, Sergei. *Notes of a Film Director*. New York: Dover, 1970.

Eisner, Lotte. *The Haunted Screen*. Berkeley: University of California Press, 1969.

———. *Murnau*. Berkeley: University of California Press, 1973.

Everson, William K. *Classics of the Horror Film*. Secaucus, N.J.: Citadel Press, 1974.

The Film Index: A Bibliography. Vol. 1: *The Film as Art*, ed. by Harold Leonard. New York: Museum of Modern Art and H. W. Wilson Co., 1941. Reprint edition, New York: Arno Press, 1966. Categories include "Production Effects" and "Set Design."

Filmlexicon degli Autori e delle Opere. Rome: Bianco e Nero, 1958. 5 vols. plus 2 supplement vols.

Fordin, Hugh. *The World of Entertainment! Hollywood's Greatest Musicals*. New York: Doubleday, 1975. Includes information about Jack Martin Smith, Horning, Pye, and other art directors on MGM musicals.

Higham, Charles. *Cecil B. De Mille*. New York: Charles Scribner's Sons, 1973.

————. *The Warner Brothers*. New York: Charles Scribner's Sons, 1975.

Higham, Charles, and Joel Greenburg. *The Celluloid Muse: Hollywood Directors Speak*. Chicago: Henry Regnery, 1969.

————. *Hollywood in the Forties*. New York: A. S. Barnes, 1968.

Hull, David Stewart. *Film in the Third Reich*. Berkeley: University of California Press, 1969.

Kulik, Karol. *Alexander Korda: The Man Who Could Work Miracles*. New Rochelle, N.Y., 1975.

Lapierre, Marcel. *Les cents Visages du cinéma*. Paris: Bernard Grasset, 1948.

Lasky, Jesse. *I Blow My Own Horn*. Garden City, N.Y.: Doubleday, 1957.

Leyda, Jay. *Kino: A History of the Russian and Soviet Film*. New York: Hilary House, 1960.

McCarthy, Todd, and Charles Flynn, eds. *Kings of the Bs: Working Within the Hollywood System*. New York: E. P. Dutton, 1975.

Minnelli, Vincente. *I Remember It Well*. New York: Doubleday, 1974.

Pearson, George. *Flashback: An Autobiography of a British Film Maker*. London: Allen and Unwin, 1957.

Robinson, David. *Hollywood in the Twenties*. New York: A. S. Barnes, 1968.

Sadoul, Georges. *Le Cinéma français (1890–1962)*. Paris: Flammarion, 1962.

————. *Dictionary of Films*. Trans. and ed. by Peter Morris. Berkeley: University of California Press, 1972.

————. *Dictionary of Film Makers*. Trans. and ed. by Peter Morris. Berkeley: University of California Press, 1972.

Siegel, Joel E. *Val Lewton: The Reality of Terror*. New York: Viking Press, 1973.

Steen, Mike. *Hollywood Speaks! An Oral History*. New York: G. P. Putnam's Sons, 1974. Includes an interview with MGM set decorator Arthur Krams.

Vidor, King. *King Vidor on Film Making*. New York: David McKay, 1972. Includes a chapter on the making of *Street Scene*.

Unpublished Resources

Austin, Texas. Humanities Research Center, University of Texas. A large collection of material by Junge—first sketches, finished designs, set photographs, stills, and correspondence.

East Berlin. Deutschen Kinemathek. Taped interviews by Gerhard Lamprecht with German art directors, including Gliese, Hasler, Kettelhut, Richter, and Warm.

Los Angeles. Special Collections, University of California. An extensive collection of drawings and designs by Grot for films of 1925–42.

New York. Columbia University. Large collection of Urban sketches.

New York. Film Study Center, Museum of Modern Art. Copy of a lecture on art direction by John Koenig, January 11, 1938, Columbia University–Museum of Modern Art Film Study University Extension Course.

Paris. Musée de Cinéma, Cinémathèque Française, Palais de Chaillot. A collection of designs and models for sets by Junge, Méliès, and others.

Washington, D.C. American Film Institute, Kennedy Center. Long taped interview with Ben Carré, in the AFI's oral history program.

Two shots from the credit sequence of Sleuth (20th Century–Fox, 1972). Directed by Joseph L. Mankiewicz. Production designer: Ken Adam; art director: Peter Lamont; set decorator: John Jarvis.

254

INDEX

Films

Numbers in *italics* refer to illustrations.

Film Makers and Artists

Numbers in *italics* refer to illustrations. Numbers in **bold face** refer to filmographies.